SUICIDE
AND
ATTEMPTED SUICIDE

•

SUICIDE
AND
ATTEMPTED SUICIDE

●

METHODS AND CONSEQUENCES

Geo Stone

Carroll & Graf Publishers, Inc.
New York

A NOTE TO THE READER:

There is some material you should be aware of that is not presented in this book: (1) Grisly photographs showing the results of suicide attempts; (2) detailed information about specific drugs: dosage, overdose, and toxic effects. Both of these will be available at my website (under construction), as are links to other suicide-related sites of all persuasions. There will also be an opportunity to make suggestions and corrections to the text there. Please do: all of us are smarter than any of us.

Attempting suicide is not a game or sport. This book was written to enlighten its readers on the general subject of suicide. Beyond the dissemination of general historical and statistical information, this book provides information that might save the lives of those who attempt suicide, as a means of seeking help, but who do not actually intend to end their lives. This book also provides information that might ease the physical pain of those who have made the decision to end their lives. This book is absolutely not intended to encourage anyone to attempt or to commit suicide.

First Carroll & Graf edition 1999

Carroll & Graf Publishers, Inc.
19 West 21st Street
New York, NY 10010-6805

Library of Congress Cataloging-in-Publication Data is available.
ISBN: 0-7867-0492-6

Manufactured in the United States of America

●

Leslie—gun; Laurie—drugs; Mike—drugs; Jessica—jump

Acknowledgments

"There is no new thing under the sun."—Ecclesiastes, I, 2; XII.

I owe large debts to the works of Margaret P. Battin, George Howe Colt, Herbert Hendin, and Cyril Polson. I am very grateful to them and others who have contributed to the mass of suicide literature.

I've also had assistance from Sarah Fallon, Peter Goodman, John Hofsess, Ted Miller, Sam Rosenfeld, the helpful reference librarians at the National Library of Medicine, George Washington University, and the Library of Congress, and, especially, Virgina Singer.

CONTENTS

●

SUICIDE
AND
ATTEMPTED SUICIDE

●

INTRODUCTION

●

> Razors pain you;
> Rivers are damp;
> Acids stain you;
> And drugs cause cramp;
> Guns aren't lawful;
> Nooses give;
> Gas smells awful;
> You might as well live.
> —Dorothy Parker, "Resume," 1926

This book describes, in sometimes-gory detail: (1) methods people use to commit suicide; (2) the medical consequences of suicide attempts; (3) how to carry out a safe suicidal gesture; (4) how to commit suicide as nontraumatically as possible.[a] You may find parts of it disturbing. But the consequences of ignorance are more disturbing: botched suicides, accidental deaths and maimed survivors, slow and painful deaths.

Every eighteen minutes someone in the United States kills himself.[b] A few are younger than ten years old; others over ninety. Between 7.5 and 16 percent take more than a day to die.[1] An estimated 300,000 to 600,000 survive suicide attempts, but suffer varying degrees of injury; 19,000 are permanently disabled each year.[2]

Only about one in ten or twenty suicide attempts is fatal. Given the easy availability of highly lethal methods, the conclusion must be that most people who attempt suicide don't want to die. Yet, many people who didn't intend to die succeed in killing themselves. Most lack knowledge of drugs and may unknowingly take a lethal overdose; some expect rescuers to save them. Others, who are really trying to die, live through their attempts. Many survive five-story jumps or head-in-the-oven gassing. Few have an accurate idea of how dangerous their chosen method is or of the consequences should their attempt fail.

Throughout this book, I try to provide evidence of the medical effects of each suicide method so that you can make more realistic decisions if you're thinking of suicide. For the same reason I also cite the sources of my information so that you can look at the original data unfiltered through my interpretations, biases, or errors.

Statistics, though informative, diminish the impact and reality of death. While this book is filled with figures and abstractions, behind each of these numbers is a real person, with a history, personality, and pain that is both particular to the individual and common to us all. These are not just numbers; these are our friends, and neighbors, and families, and selves. I include some of their words to give a sense of the quality of their lives, and the thinking that led to their choice of suicide. For example, listen to Karen, age sixteen, describe the situation that brought on her suicide attempt:

> I was really upset and depressed. My life just seemed to be in total chaos. My boyfriend just dumped me flat, and he said he loved the other girl and didn't love me at all. My parents and I also just got into another fight again about some really dumb things, so I just went into my room and closed the door. There was this bottle of sleeping pills my mother was using, and I had them with me. I sat and stared at it for a long time, weighing out the good and the bad things in my life. The bad things came out ahead. I poured some of the pills in my hand, and figured ten or fifteen ought to be enough to do it. Those pills . . . they all looked so innocent and peaceful, like they couldn't do much to hurt anyone. Well, I put them in my mouth and held them there for a long time, wondering if I should or shouldn't. I took a glass of water and swallowed. At first nothing

happened, and then they all hit me at once. The room started to blur and spin, small sounds were going on in my head. The last thing I remembered was trying to move and not being able to. I woke up in the hospital. They were pumping out my stomach—one of the worst things you can have done to you. My mother came into the room, and she apologized for the fight we had.[3]

The material here is intended both for those who want a quick and relatively painless death, and for those who want to carry out a suicidal gesture as safely and noninjuriously as possible. If it convinces some potential suicides to seek other solutions—suicide should be an absolutely last resort and mistakes may leave you crippled—so much the better. But the fact remains: there is no way to limit this knowledge to those whose aims we agree with.

To make my premises explicit: (1) Decisions concerning your death should be, ultimately, yours to make; (2) most—but not all—decisions to commit suicide are due to temporary problems and are therefore tragic mistakes.

My position comes from two principles: (1) self-determination and (2) mercy. The more fundamental, self-determination, says that each competent person may decide and act on (subject to noninterference with the rights of others) his or her own views of what constitutes a good life and death.

In practice, I think that temporary suicide intervention is appropriate when there is another reason to believe that someone's thinking is impaired (e.g., by depression), though both the nature (reversible) and timecourse (brief) of the intervention should be limited.

The principle of mercy holds that no one (or thing) should be made to suffer unnecessarily. This is necessarily the subordinate principle; one may choose to suffer for some perceived higher good. While mentioned in this book, these ethical and philosophical issues are treated in much greater detail elsewhere. (See suggested readings.)

For those who are religiously, philosophically, or ethically opposed to suicide under any circumstance, this publication will be of little comfort; those who believe that it is each person's right to decide, insofar as possible, when to die may find some answers to their questions and fears.

> Just as I shall select my ship when I am about to go on a voyage, or
> my house when I propose to take a residence, so I shall choose my
> death when I am about to depart from life.
> —Seneca, *Epistulae Morales*

I place suicide attempters in one of four groups: (1) Rational people facing an insoluble problem, generally a fatal or debilitating illness; (2) impulsive people, frequently young, truly but temporarily miserable, often drunk, who wouldn't even consider suicide six months later; (3) irrational people, often alcoholic, schizophrenic, or depressed; (4) desperate people, people trying to make a safe gesture as a "cry for help" or to get someone's attention.

The first group—and most of us will eventually be in it—has, in my view, the right to decide the time, place, and manner of their death. They ought to have medical help to die peacefully and without pain, but this, while sometimes surreptitiously done, cannot at present be relied on. Many of us have known people who have suffered long, agonizing deaths because they became too ill to kill themselves and their physicians were unwilling to act on their request. I will not mince words by calling it "euthanasia" or "self-deliverance": If you're terminally ill, I hope to provide you with information that will help you determine the best way to kill yourself—if that's your well-considered decision.

What about the young and impulsive, particularly teenagers? At the moment, they seem to have the worst of all worlds, where: (1) lethal and not-so-lethal suicide methods are readily available; (2) neither they, their parents, nor their teachers are likely to know how dangerous particular methods are; (3) personal ("Are you thinking about . . . ?") or practical ("How would you go about . . . ?") discussion of suicide is largely taboo.

While many schools now teach about AIDS and its transmission, more teenagers will attempt or commit suicide next year than will become HIV-infected. The ignorance, stigma, and fear about suicide would decrease if that topic were added to the curriculum and treated honestly.

A case will be made that people shouldn't commit suicide and that, therefore, a manual telling them how to go about it is pernicious.[c] This is like one of the arguments against sex education: "If they know how, they'll do it." Well, they do it anyway. Thirty thousand suicide deaths a year in the United

States should make this clear. In the absence of knowledge about suicide methods—and alternatives to suicide—people will continue to act in desperation and ignorance, as they have throughout recorded history, with gun, rope, blade, poison, and anything else available.[d] That is the reality. The methods people use, all too often leave them neither dead, nor fully recovered, but maimed and permanently injured: paralyzed from jumps, brain-damaged from gunshots, comatose from drugs.

But for *anyone* considering suicide (or even "safe" suicidal gestures; nothing is 100 percent reliable), I urge you to try every alternative first—and then try them again. These include a variety of antidepressant drug therapies, various flavors of psychotherapy, electroshock, and "reality therapy," which could be defined as helping people who are worse off than you. *Each of these will work for some; no single solution will work for everyone.* That's why it's vital not to give up if one or two or three different attempted "solutions" don't do much to decrease your pain. How do you know that suicide is the answer if you haven't tried everything else first? *You can always kill yourself later.*

> Every person's fight with death is lost before it begins. What makes the struggle worthwhile, therefore, cannot lie in the outcome. It lies in the dignity with which the fight is waged and the way it finds an end.
> —Joseph Fletcher

I've known several people who have killed themselves, and others who intended to, but waited too long. Three have been significant influences in writing this book.

One man had a series of small strokes and specified that if he had a major one he did not want so-called heroic measures used to save him. Soon afterward, he did suffer a massive stroke, which reduced him to a vegetative state, and he was kept alive contrary to his written instructions. His son, a physician himself, was appalled by the contravention of his father's instructions in a medically hopeless situation. Nevertheless, it took weeks of argument and delay before the hospital agreed to act in accordance with their wishes.

Another man, eighty years old, entered a hospital intending to kill himself (he said) if he didn't get better. After four months and a series of operations, he became too weak and disoriented to act on his intention. He "lived" another four months in the hospital, progressively deteriorating both physically and mentally.

A young woman took a drug overdose, expecting that her housemates would return soon. They were delayed. I would like to believe that, had she known about less lethal methods, she would be alive today.

NOTES

[a]The tone of some of the footnotes (and occasionally text) may strike readers as inappropriately flippant, given the nature of the subject. On the other hand, you might find it a therapeutic respite from page after page of unrelentingly earnest examination and preachy advice.

[b]I will use male pronouns for most suicides and female ones for most suicide attempts. This reflects the relative male/female numbers in each category, as well as the lack of grammatically "correct" sex-neutral pronouns in the English language.

[c]*Final Exit* recommended plastic-bag asphyxia or drug overdose for suicide. It was published in 1990 and became a best-seller. Comparing the number of suicides by those methods in 1990 and 1991, we find that plastic-bag asphyxias increased from 334 to 437, and intentional overdose deaths increased from 3,143 to 3,314. The total number of suicides decreased from 30,906 to 30,810. This is consistent with the idea that the book influenced the method used by a few people, but certainly did not unleash a wave of suicide, as some had predicted.

[d]To give you some idea, "Over the past two centuries people have committed suicide by jumping into volcanoes, vats of beer, crocks of vinegar, retorts of molten glass, white-hot coke ovens, or slaughterhouse tanks of blood; by throwing themselves upon buzz saws; by thrusting hot pokers down their throats; by suffocating in refrigerators or chimneys; by locking themselves into high-altitude test chambers; by crashing airplanes; by jumping from airplanes; by lying in front of steamrollers, by throwing themselves into the third [high voltage] rail; by touching high-tension wires; by placing their necks in vises and turning the handle; by hugging stoves; by freezing to death; by climbing into lions' cages; by blowing themselves up with cannons, hand grenades, or dynamite; by boring holes in their heads with power drills; by drinking hydrochloric acid or Drano; by walking in front of cars, trains, subways, and racehorses; by driving cars off cliffs or into trains; by swallowing poisonous spiders; by piercing their hearts with corkscrews or darning needles; by starving themselves; by swallowing firecrackers; by holding their heads in buckets of water; by beating their heads with hammers; by pounding nails or barbecue spits into their skulls; by strangling themselves with their hair; by walking into airplane propellers; by swimming over waterfalls; by hanging themselves with grapevines; by sawing tree limbs out from under themselves; by swallowing glass; by swallowing underwear; by stabbing themselves with spectacles sharpened to a point; by cutting their throats with handsaws, sheep shears, or barbed wire; by forcing teams of horses to tear their heads off; by decapitating themselves with home-made guillotines; by exposing themselves to swarms of bees; by injecting themselves with paraffin, cooking oil, peanut butter, mercury, deodorant, or mayonnaise; by crucifying themselves." [Colt, p235]; by swallowing coins; by swallowing crucifixes; by hanging themselves with tree roots from the branches of the same tree; by cutting their wrist with their teeth; by cutting off their arm with a kitchen knife; by stuffing rags into their mouth and pebbles up their nose; by exploding a stick of dynamite in their mouth; by sawing their skull with a band saw; by inhaling talcum powder; by injecting themselves with HIV-positive blood.

PART I
•
BACKGROUND

1
A BRIEF OVERVIEW OF SUICIDE

•

Most people, in committing a suicidal act, are just as muddled as when they do anything important under emotional stress. Carefully planned acts of suicide are as rare as carefully planned acts of homicide.

—Erwin Stengel[1]

Dying
is an art, like everything else.
I do it exceptionally well.

—Sylvia Plath, "Lady Lazarus"

It seemed like a good idea ... at the time.

—Anonymous

Throughout the world, about two thousand people kill themselves each day. That's about eighty per hour, three-quarters of a million people a year.[2] In the United States, there are more than eighty deaths from suicide every day, or about thirty thousand every year.[3] This is the equivalent of a fully loaded jumbo jet crash every fifth day. From another perspective, you are more likely to kill yourself than be killed by someone else.[a]

Another estimated 300,000 (or more) Americans a year survive a suicide attempt.[b] A majority sustain injuries minor enough to need no more than emergency room treatment. However, about 116,000 are hospitalized, of whom 110,000 are eventually discharged alive. Their average hospital stay is ten days; the average cost is $15,000.[4]

> Without knowledge of proper dosages and methods, suicide at-
> tempts are often bungled, leaving the victim worse off than before.
> Many intended suicides by gunshot leave the person alive but
> brain-damaged; drug overdoses that are not fatal may have the
> same effect. One eighty-three-year-old woman obtained an insuffi-
> cient number of pills and lost consciousness but did not die; her
> daughter ended up smothering her with a plastic bag.[5]

Seventeen percent, some 19,000, of these people are permanently disabled—restricted in their ability to work—each year, at a cost of $127,000 per person.[6] Such injury is tragic, whether the person was trying to commit suicide and failed, or, perhaps even sadder, if the suicide attempt was intended not to cause death, but to serve as a "cry for help."

About 1.4 percent of Americans end their lives by suicide,[7] making it the eighth leading cause of death in the United States. Suicide ranks fourth as a factor in years of lost life. The largest increase in the last thirty years has been among people between fifteen and twenty-four years of age, but the highest rates are still among the elderly. Men kill themselves at about four times the rate for women (19.8 in 100,000 for men versus 4.5 in 100,000 for women in 1994).[c] Around 3 percent of adults will make one or more suicide attempts.[8]

There are more suicides than the official numbers show,[d] but there is no general agreement as to how many more. Estimates of underreporting range from around 1 to 300 percent.[9] Reasons for underreporting include:

1. Families or family physicians may hide evidence due to the stigma of suicide. For example, "Physicians and surviving relatives have told me in confidence of many deaths which were suicides, but which had been certified as natural or accidental deaths by a physician, either through error, misinformation, or deliberate falsehood. . . . My own estimate is that there were an additional 10,000 deaths yearly [in the United

States] which would have been certified as suicides if there had been complete and impartial investigations."[10]

2. The determination of cause of death is judged by local standards, which vary widely. In one egregious instance, a coroner would cite suicide only in deaths where a suicide note was found—and suicide notes are only found in around one-quarter of known suicides.[11]

3. There are lots of ambiguous situations, some of which are suicides, but which almost always end up classified as "accidental" or "undetermined":[12] the single-car accident[e] with no skid marks; the fall off the night ferry; the stumble in front of the train; the inadvertent overdose; the gun-cleaning mishap.[f]

4. Compared to the "accidental" or "undetermined" motive categories, there is a much larger number of deaths officially classified as "ill-defined and unknown causes of mortality,"[g] where even the actual cause of death is uncertain, and some of which are undoubtedly suicides.

5. The frequency of physician-assisted suicide for the terminally ill is unknown, but, based on anecdotal evidence, is probably both substantial and increasing. More on this in the chapter, Assisted Suicide and Terminal Illness.

On the other side of the ledger, some doubtful cases are classified as suicides. These usually occur in institutions, such as prisons, hospitals, religious orders, and the military, which control their populations more or less completely. For such institutions a verdict of suicide is likely to be the least embarrassing (after "natural") cause of death: Homicides must be investigated and a murderer sought; accidents may be the basis of negligence lawsuits.[13h]

The number of suicide attempts is also subject to dispute. Based on a range of studies, there are probably between ten and twenty attempts for every successful suicide,[14] or roughly 300,000 to 600,000 attempts per year in the United States. Yet more than half of suicides kill themselves on their first try.[15] The overall 3- or 4-to-1 male-to-female suicide ratio in the United States is reversed for suicide attempts. Between 70 and 90 percent (studies differ) of suicide attempts are by medicine/drug overdoses, roughly 15 percent by wrist cuts.[16]

For adolescents, the attempt-to-fatality ratio may be 50:1,[17] but this average masks the fact that the death rate for boys is one hundred times higher than for girls: around 10 percent and 0.1 percent, respectively. About 11 percent of high school students have made at least one suicide attempt.[18] Ninety percent of adolescents' suicide attempts occur at home, and parents are home 70 percent of the time.[19]

What Is Suicide?

The numbers above refer to acts formally classified as suicides, but the more one thinks about it, the less clear the boundaries become. Should we include refusing medical treatment in a terminal illness? What about a suicidal gesture gone awry? How about martyrdom? And what of the "little suicides": the high-speed drag race, the drunk drive, the picking of a quarrel in a bar?[i] Among adolescents the combination of reckless (and inexperienced) driving with alcohol and/or drug use may be more dangerous than overt suicide attempts.[20]

In *Man Against Himself* Karl Menninger compiled some four hundred pages of self-destructive, or suicidal, behavior, ranging from making war to nail-biting. He divided these into three groups: "chronic" suicidal behavior includes alcoholism, martyrdom, psychiatric illness, and antisocial actions; "focal" suicide targets specific parts of the body, as in self-mutilation, or deliberate accidents; and "organic" suicide, where people supposedly lose their will to live and die of illness and disease that they would otherwise overcome. The items on his list, and subsequent additions to it, have been called "slow suicide" or "suicide on the installment plan."[21]

And there is the daily suicide of depression and apathy, as described here by James Carroll:

> A thousand people are "officially" dead of suicide every day, but they are not the only ones who are faced with the constant choice between life and death. We all are. . . . We might lack the nerve to commit the final act, and we might not recognize our "sinful" tendencies for what they are, but day in and day out we confront the problem of our innate attraction to self-destruction. We live in a world that encourages the small daily acts of negation that prepare

us for the great one. There are meanings of suicide that neither the courts nor the dictionaries admit, but that make it impossible for us to regard those thousand people a day who do themselves in as very different from us. They are not necessarily "sick" or "sinners," but simply our sisters and brothers. And who are we? We are the resigned housewives, the compulsive playboys, the despairing priests, the addicted teenagers, the reckless drivers, the bored bureaucrats, the lonely salesmen, the smiling stewardesses, the restless drifters, the walking wounded. . . . It may be nothing more than the steadfast commitment to sameness. The simplest form of suicide is the act of refusing the adventures and challenges that offer themselves to us every day. "No, thanks," we say. "I prefer not to," we murmur, like Melville's Bartleby, preferring to stare at the wall outside the window. Preferring, as I do on especially bad days, to stay in bed.[22]

If you play Russian roulette with a six-shooter, your odds of dying are one in six; if you climb Mt. Everest they're also about one in six.[23] The former is a generally condemned form of suicide; what, then, is the latter? Yet, Sigmund Freud wrote, "Life is impoverished, it loses in interest, when the highest stake in the game of living, life itself, may not be risked. It becomes as shallow and empty as, let us say, an American flirtation."[24]

NOTES

[a]The 1980-91 U.S. age-adjusted suicide rate averaged 12.5 per 100,000 population per year. During the same period the homicide rate was 10.2 per 100,000 per year (CDC web site, Morality database).

[b]There are many reasons these estimates vary widely. In addition to social and economic disincentives for people to seek help, medical data is both scanty and unreliable. For example, of 72 people who reported suicide attempts in an anonymous survey, only 18 (25 percent) sought medical care and 7 (10 percent) were hospitalized (Meehan, 1992). In addition, hospital records are notoriously unreliable (R. K. Lee, 1991; Birkhead, 1993; Blanc, 1993).

[c]While in most of the world about three males kill themselves for each female suicide, in China, India, and much of Southeast Asia a majority of suicides are female. The mid-1980s Chinese rates were 17.7 for males and 24.3 for females (per 100,000) population per year); the corresponding U.S. rates were 20.7 and 5.4 in 1986 (Li, 1991; Pritchard, 1996).

[d]Comparative international suicide data are particularly unreliable. Religiously devout so-

cieties that consider suicide a major sin have low official rates of suicide, but it is unclear how much of this is due to unwillingness to report suicides, especially at the local level. For example, the official suicide rate in Egypt is 0.0/100,000; yet the rate of suicide attempts in Cairo is 38.5/100,000, leading the researchers to state, "Official government records are misleading and do not represent the true rate" (Okasha, 1979). Similarly, the suicide rate in India (1972 data) was 7.8/100,000 but varied by state: from 0.70 in Muslim Jammu and Kashmir to 20.5 in Hindu Kerala (Headley, 216).

[e]A well-known fictional example is the suicide of Willy Loman, in Arthur Miller's *Death of a Salesman*, who killed himself in a car crash in order to provide life insurance money for his family.

[f]A probably apocryphal Irish coroner came up with a verdict of "accidental death" in a self-inflicted gunshot death: "Sure, he was only cleaning the muzzle of the gun with his tongue" (Alvarez, 82).

[g]This is the International Classification of Death (ICD) category 797-799. There were ten times as many of these deaths as there were "undetermined" (ICD 980-989) ones, 8.3 times as many as single motor vehicle deaths, and more than the total number of official suicides. Until recently, these "ill-defined" deaths were "systematically overlooked" in suicide studies, as were pedestrian deaths (D. P. Phillips, 1993).

[h]In prisons, some "suicides" are probably murders committed by guards (Smith, R, 1984); however, there are also misclassifications in the other direction. For example, in one study of Ohio prisons, L. M. Hayes found 46 suicides in 1981-82; prison records showed 22 (Hayes, 1989).

[i]Of several hundred homicides examined, more than 25 percent were overtly victim-provoked or "suicide by means of victim-precipitated homicide" (Wolfgang, 1959).

2
HISTORY OF SUICIDE

•

Death is before me today
Like the recovery of a sick man . . .
Like the longing of a man to see his home again
After many years of captivity . . . [1]
—"Man Disputing Over Suicide with His Soul," Egypt, ca. 2100 B.C.

The oldest known reference to suicide is Egyptian; a fragment is quoted above. There are seven suicides in the Old Testament;[a] none of them are criticized in that document. In the New Testament, the suicide of Judas seems to be implicitly condoned—it's mentioned without comment in Matthew 27:3—as a sign of his repentance; not until much later did the church claim that Judas's suicide was a greater sin than was his betrayal of Christ.

Early Christianity was strongly attracted toward suicide, perhaps because the act was often indistinguishable from martyrdom, and, "even the death of Jesus was regarded by Tertullian, one of the most fiery of the early Fathers, as a kind of suicide. He pointed out, and Origen[b] [another major early Christian theologian] agreed, that He voluntarily gave up the ghost, since it was unthinkable that the Godhead should be at the mercy of the flesh."[2]

While early Christianity accepted suicide, it condemned killing others through warfare, in self-defense, and by capital punishment. After all, Jesus had taught nonviolence: "Do not resist one who is evil. But if anyone strikes you on the right cheek, turn to him the other also. . . . I say to you, Love your enemies and pray for those who persecute you."[3] This was taken seriously by the early church fathers, for example, Tertullian, who asked, "Can it be lawful to handle the sword, when the Lord himself has declared that he who uses the sword shall perish by it?"[4]

However, as Christianity became the dominant religion in the Roman Empire, its views on suicide gradually changed, until suicide became a religious sin and a secular crime in the sixth century. In 533, Christian burial (a requirement for getting into heaven) was forbidden to suicides who killed themselves while accused of a crime. In 562 this was extended to all suicides, regardless of the reason or circumstances. In 693 even attempting suicide became an ecclesiastical crime punishable by excommunication, with civil consequences to follow.

St. Augustine, in his fifth-century book *The City of God*, was the first Christian to make a blanket condemnation of suicide. His only biblical justification for the change was a novel interpretation of the sixth commandment, "Thou shalt not kill"; his other reasons were, as Rousseau noted, taken from Plato's *Phaedra*.[5c]

Ironically, this well-intentioned and humanitarian opposition to suicide eventually degenerated into "legalized and sanctified atrocities, by which the body of the suicide was degraded, his memory defamed, his family persecuted."[6] Suicides were buried at crossroads with a stake through their bodies,[d] and their property was confiscated by the state. Perhaps the ultimate irony was the execution of people for the crime of attempting to commit suicide. A Russian exile in England, Nicholas Ogarev, wrote,

> A man was hanged who had cut his throat, but who had been brought back to life. They hanged him for suicide. The doctor had warned them that it was impossible to hang him as the throat would burst open and he would breathe through the aperture. They did not listen to his advice and hanged their man. The wound in the neck immediately opened and the man came back to life again although he was hanged. It took time to convoke the aldermen to decide the question of what was to be done. At length the aldermen assembled and bound up the neck below the wound

until he died. Oh my Mary, what a crazy society and what a stupid civilization.[7]

We have progressed far beyond such barbarism, and no longer condemn failed suicides. Now, for example, if a death-row criminal attempts suicide, every effort is made to save him (or, more rarely, her), so that a civilized, state-approved execution can be carried out.

Non-Christian societies have expressed a wide range of views about suicide. Buddhist, Confucian, and Shintoist ethics accept suicide and euthanasia in cases of incurable illness. The Vikings felt that Valhalla, with its perpetual Feast of Heroes and Gods, was reserved for warriors who died in battle. Suicides were second-best and might get to sit below the salt; people who died in bed could eat with the kitchen help and sleep in the barn.[e] The Scythians considered it an honor to commit suicide when they could no longer keep up their nomadic travels, while "death, passively awaited, is a dishonor to life."[8]

Various schools of Greek philosophical thought rejected (Pythagoreans, Aristotle), conditionally accepted (Plato, Epicureans), or approved of (Stoics, Zeno) suicide. The Romans followed the Greek lead in these matters, particularly that of the Stoics. "To the Romans of every class, death itself was unimportant. But the way of dying—decently, rationally, with dignity and at the right time—mattered intensely."[9]

The early Christians agreed that death was unimportant, but for entirely different reasons: They wanted to go to the glory of heaven and saw no good reason on earth to wait. Life was a gateway, filled with sins, snares, and temptations, all leading to eternal damnation. Thus they often invited persecution as a path to martyrdom, which automatically wiped the slate of any old sins, prevented new ones, and guaranteed a seat in paradise. This was carried to its logical conclusion by a sect known as the Donatists, of whom St. Augustine said, "to kill themselves out of respect for martyrdom is their daily sport."[10] They were noted for jumping from cliffs, and also burned themselves to death in large numbers. They are probably best known for their practice of stopping travelers and either paying them or threatening them with death to encourage them to kill the, presumably, heaven-bound martyr. The Donatists were eventually declared heretics and suppressed with notable lack of Christian charity.[f]

Much later, the thirteenth-century Albigensian (Catharist) heretics in southern France were slaughtered with incredible savagery, also, in part, because they sought martyrdom. This sin compounded their damnation for other theological errors—for example, they had the temerity to believe that religious orders should actually practice their vows of poverty. Not until the late Renaissance—one thousand years after Augustine—did people again dare, very cautiously, to argue the case for suicide in Christian Europe.

By the sixteenth century Roman and Greek philosophy had been rediscovered and the unconditional condemnation of suicide was being questioned. In Holland, Erasmus wrote *In Praise of Folly* (1509), in which he defended suicide which was committed to escape an unendurable life. Soon afterward Sir Thomas More, in his fictional *Utopia* (1516), proposed suicide for the purpose of euthanasia:

> They console the incurably ill by sitting and talking with them and by alleviating whatever pain they can. Should life become unbearable for these incurables the magistrates and priests do not hesitate to prescribe euthanasia. . . . When the sick have been persuaded of this, they end their lives willingly either by starvation or drugs, that dissolve their lives without any sensation of death. Still the Utopians do not do away with anyone without his permission, nor lessen any of their duties to him.[11]

Shakespeare (1564-1616), always theatrically pragmatic, portrayed fourteen suicides in his eight tragedies without condemning them, asking instead, "Then is it sin / To rush into the secret house of death / Ere death dare come to us?"[12] John Donne wrote the first English defense of suicide, *Biathanatos*, in 1608, but had second thoughts (as well as a job, Dean of St. Paul's, that required staying on good terms with the church) and found it expedient to wait until after his death to have it published, in 1644. Other justifications of suicide followed.

In the eighteenth century, the Age of Reason, traditional beliefs were reexamined from a rational, empirical, and skeptical perspective. Theological arguments against suicide were challenged, suicide was claimed to be a human right, and the subject became a secular matter as much as a religious one.

Of course, the traditional views had many defenders. For example, the renowned religious leader John Wesley (1703-1791) said, with dubious logic, that failed suicides should be hanged. Similarly, the eminent legal authority William Blackstone (1723-1780) asserted that suicide was a crime against both God and king. And the illustrious philosopher Immanuel Kant, whose writings remain unsurpassed in incomprehensibility, used suicide as an example of moral error that could be demonstrated with his logical rapier, the categorical imperative.[13]

During this time, the brutal treatment of suicidal people eased in some parts of Europe. For example, the laws against suicide were relaxed in France at the time of the French Revolution; and the Prussian penal code of 1794 (influenced earlier by the "liberal" monarch, Frederick the Great, and then by the French Revolution) did not punish attempted suicide. In England, however, trying to kill oneself remained a felony until 1961 (and was only decriminalized to encourage people to seek treatment), and anyone aiding, abetting, or counseling a suicide or attempted suicide is still subject to fourteen years imprisonment.[14]

The Romantics of the late eighteenth and early nineteenth centuries (Byron, Keats, and Shelley in England; Lermontov in Russia; Chateaubriand and Lamartine in France; Novalis and Goethe in Germany[g]) went further, and glorified suicide as the heroic last act of a free man.

Thus, from antiquity into the nineteenth century, suicide was mostly a philosophical, ethical, religious, and legal issue; the concern was under what circumstances might it be forbidden, acceptable, or even desirable? Starting in the early 1800s, it gradually became a sociological/statistical inquiry as well as a psychological one: *Who* killed themselves and *why* they did so.[h] The focus changed from philosophy and theology to the social conditions and personality traits associated with suicide.

More recently, with the advent of antipsychosis drugs, such as Thorazine in the 1950s, the concept of a biochemical basis for behavior has become increasingly persuasive. One of the effects of these changes has been to largely remove suicide from the category of moral crime. Instead, the fault has been shifted onto society, mental illness, or biochemical imbalance, things for which an individual can hardly be blamed.[i]

Thus, if suicide is involuntary and beyond an individual's control, rational or moral arguments against it will be useless. The only moral question, then, will be that of intervention, abstention, or assistance by concerned individuals or by society at large.

While today most people still consider suicide an abnormal, destructive behavior[j] that should be prevented (except, perhaps, in the case of the terminally ill), its failure is no longer punished—or should one say rewarded?—by death. And so we progress.[k]

NOTES

[a]Samson, Saul, Saul's armor-bearer, Abimelech, Zimri, Razis, and Achitophel. The precise number (three to eleven) and identity depend on the definition of suicide, whether the Apocrypha are included, and which version of a death one accepts (Barraclough, 1992).

[b]Origen's father was a martyr and he (Origen) reportedly wanted to carry on the family tradition. Dissuaded from this course of action by his mother, he did, however, perform a self-castration (G. Rosen, 1975). Her views on that are unknown.

[c]Augustine's justification of killing in war and capital punishment is based on the argument that such killing is either commanded directly by God (e. g., Abraham's sacrifice of Isaac), or by God's divinely constituted authority on Earth, that is, lawful government. At the same time, "private killing" of self (or in self-defense, it would seem) is forbidden. However, this argument can be turned around not only to **permit** suicide (e. g., Samson pulling down the pillars, presumably after an okay from God ["And when Samson destroyed himself, with his enemies, by the demolition of the building, this can only be excused on the ground that the Spirit, which performed miracles through him, secretly ordered him to do so." [Augustine, *City of God*]]), but to **require** suicide under some circumstances (e. g., Socrates drinking poison, as demanded by the Athenian court [" . . . one who accepts the prohibition against suicide may kill himself when commanded by one whose orders must not be slighted." [Augustine, ch 26]]). This of course makes hash out of the blanket Christian condemnation of suicide (Battin, 1994, pp210-11).

[d]The stake was to keep the restless ghost from escaping and going back to haunt its old neighborhood; the crossroads were to confuse any ghost—they apparently weren't very good at reading road signs—that escaped the stake, so that it couldn't find its way back home. Busy crossroads were preferred, because the traffic was supposed to discourage the evidently timid ghost from coming out (Alvarez, 44). In fact, the increase in vehicle traffic due to the automobile has decreased ghost sightings to an all-time low. The last recorded crossroads-cum-stake burial in England was in 1823, when a certain Mr. Griffiths was interred at the intersection of Eaton Street, Grosvenor Place, and King's Road in London (Stengel, 1974, 69).

[e]Odin, proprietor of Valhalla, was both the God of War and the God of the Hanged. (There was a sacred grove of Odin in Scandinavia where people went to hang themselves, and sev-

eral popular jump sites on cliffs.) He also had the Poetry and Wisdom portfolios. Valhalla (which apparently functioned like Hilbert's Hotel—always room for one more guest) had 540 doors, and every day its heroes would go out and do battle; every night they would feast and drink and listen to sagas. The Valkyries (Norse maidens who are invariably large blond sopranos in Wagner operas) would serve at the banquets, but also got to ride through the air and visit battles and suicide spots. With their spears, they would choose who would die and carry them back to Valhalla to take part in the festivities.

[f]The actual situation was, as always, much more complicated. It seems to have been precipitated by a dispute in Roman North Africa over whether a man who had evaded martyrdom by cooperating with the authorities should be a member of the commission that was choosing the local bishop. The faction later known as Donatists said no and installed their own candidate.

More generally, the Donatists were natives of North Africa (so was St. Augustine, who was a Libyan Berber, educated in Carthage) who were resisting Roman domination, and the religious aspect was one facet of the conflict. The modern-day Coptic Church in Egypt is a descendant of these early nativist Christians.

[g]Goethe's *Sorrows of Werther* (1774) was found so often with bodies of suicides that Goethe was accused of being a murderer, the book was banned in Leipzig, and the whole Italian edition printing was bought up (and, presumably, destroyed) by the Catholic Church in Milan (Clarke and Lester, 87).

[h]It should be noted that psychological views had appeared previously, as far back as Hippocrates (430-377 B.C.), who argued that people's mental state and character, among other attributes, were due to their predominant "humor" (choleric, melancholic, phlegmatic, or sanguine); but most notably Robert Burton's *Anatomy of Melancholy* in 1621. He wrote, "In other diseases there is some hope likely, but these unhappy men are born to misery, past all hope of recovery, incurably sick; the longer they live the worse they are, and death alone must ease them" (quoted in Alvarez, 161).

Burton was also the first Christian in many centuries known to advocate treating suicides with sympathy and charity: "What shall become of their souls, God alone can tell. . . . We ought not to be so rash and rigorous in our censures, as some are: charity will judge best: God be merciful unto us all!" (quoted in Alvarez, 162).

[i]Similar arguments have been made about criminal behavior, both in the United States and elsewhere. Thus in the Soviet Union, political dissidents were sometimes committed to psychiatric hospitals to be "cured" rather than jails to be "punished." This had the added benefits of allowing a wide range of "treatment" and indefinite incarceration. For a critique of psychiatric imprisonment, see Thomas Szasz, *The Manufacture of Madness*, 1977.

[j]It is ironic that killing other people (who, presumably, would prefer not to be killed) often generates less moral disapproval than killing oneself; indeed, some varieties of killing of others, such as war, are frequently considered heroic.

[k]Or perhaps not. In August 1995, Oklahoma prison officials found a death-row inmate unconscious from a drug overdose suicide attempt. Robert Brecheen was taken to a hospital where his stomach was pumped. After regaining consciousness, he was returned to the prison, where his scheduled execution was carried out, only two hours late.

3
THREE WAYS TO STUDY SUICIDE

•

Sociology, psychiatry, and biology[a] offer three different lenses currently used to study suicide as a pathology.

SOCIOLOGY

The sociological perspective looks at society's influence on its members; how do various social conditions (and their changes) affect suicide rates. Examples of such social variables are income, unemployment rate, birth order, gun ownership, divorce, and immigration. As its most eminent early proponent, Emile Durkheim, said, "social facts must be studied as things, as realities external to the individual."[1]

The sociological/statistical study of suicide actually began in the 1820s with research by Jean-Pierre Falret in France, and Johann Casper in Germany. Durkheim organized the earlier work and integrated it into a theoretical framework in the late 1800s. His groundbreaking book *Suicide: A Study in Sociology* was published in 1897.

Durkheim felt that the Industrial Revolution had massively disrupted Western communities. As a result, people who didn't have the structure of ties to family or religion became particularly susceptible to suicidal urges. He called suicide due to such social disintegration "anomic."

In other societies the individual is so highly integrated into the community that his life and behavior are tightly governed by the community's customs. In these circumstances, most suicide occurs because it is expected—almost required—rather than from personal sorrow or guilt.

Examples of such "altruistic" suicide include the Indian custom of *suttee* where widows (but not widowers) burn themselves to death; Japanese *seppuku* or *hara-kiri* where ritual disembowelment (sometimes followed by coup-de-grace decapitation) prevents, or atones for, dishonor. Among military officers in nineteenth-century Europe, suicide-by-pistol was the expected response to an inability to pay gambling debts. Suicide by groups seeing themselves as persecuted also falls into this category; the Branch Davidians (Waco, Texas, 1993) for example, or the members of the People's Temple at Jonestown (Guyana, 1978), who held suicide "rehearsals."[2]

Durkheim's third category, "egoistic" suicide, describes individuals who lack involvement with their reasonably stable societies. Such people are often misfits or criminals. A prototypic example might be an unemployed, isolated, man or woman living alone in a rooming house.

Sociology's forte is the statistics of suicide. Its self-acknowledged limitation is that it doesn't tell us anything about why one person kills himself while another person, in similar circumstances, doesn't. Nor does it offer any good explanation of cultural and national differences. For example, if, as frequently claimed, Catholic countries have lower suicide rates than Protestant ones because Catholicism is the more cohesive religion, why does Catholic Hungary usually have the highest suicide rate in Europe, and, often, in the world? The suicide rate in Hungary, for various age groups is anywhere between five and twenty-five times the corresponding rate in nearby Greece. And, the suicide rate of countries bordering Hungary is highest in the regions near Hungary and in those with large Hungarian populations.[b3]

Sometimes there are extraordinary or temporary circumstances that lead to a high suicide rate. In the mid to late 1990s Sri Lanka, in the midst of a protracted civil war, has had unusually high rates. However, Greenland (127 per 100,000 population in 1987) has the highest rate in the world.[4] This has been attributed to the cultural and social disintegration of the native Inuit population in the face of well-meaning Danish paternalism.

PSYCHOLOGY AND PSYCHIATRY

The psychological/psychiatric approach rose to prominence a bit later than the sociological one, at the end of the nineteenth and beginning of the twentieth centuries. It emphasizes and examines the individual, and the conflicts within a particular mind that may lead to self-destructive behavior.

> "When we learn that the most densely populated parts of the world have the highest incidence of suicide, and that suicides cluster in certain months of the year, do we thereby learn a single adequate, explanatory motive?" asked psychoanalyst Alfred Adler in 1910. "No, we learn only that the phenomenon of suicide is also subject to the laws of great numbers, and that it is related to other social phenomena. Suicide can be understood only individually, even if it has social preconditions and social consequences."[5]

While people with diagnoses of depression, schizophrenia, or psychosis have suicide rates five to fifteen times that of the general population, the vast majority of those who are so diagnosed do *not* attempt suicide. One limitation of the psychological strategy is the inability of experts to reliably predict who will carry out suicides and suicide attempts, even among the highest-risk groups.

> Robert Litman . . . believes that suicide-vulnerable individuals move in and out of periods of suicidal risk—sometimes for brief periods, sometimes for moderate or long periods—as their life circumstances fluctuate. But of all those people who enter that zone, very few actually kill themselves. "For every hundred people at high risk," he says, "only three or four will actually commit suicide over the next couple of years. . . . It's like a slot machine. . . . You can win a million dollars on a slot machine in Las Vegas, but to do that, six sevens have to line up on your machine. That happens only once in a million times. In a sense it's the same with suicide." Those spinning sevens represent all the biological, sociological, psychological, and existential variables that are associated with suicide—broken

family, locus of control, decreased serotonin [a chemical found in the brain], triggering event, and so on. "In order to commit suicide, a lot of things have to fall together at once, and a lot of other things have to *not* happen at once," says Litman. "There's a certain random element determining the specific time of any suicide and, often, whether it happens or not.... It's as if you need to have six strikes against you ... and we're all walking around with one or two or three strikes. Then you have a big crisis and you have four strikes. But to get all six really takes some bad luck."[6]

Hopelessness about the future seems to be a better predictor for suicide than is depression.[7] For example, in one group of 207 suicidal patients, 89 were ranked high on a widely used "hopelessness" scale. Thirteen of fourteen suicides within the next five years came from this subgroup, even though only half of them had a diagnosis of depression.[8] Nevertheless 76 of these 89 did *not* kill themselves, underscoring the difficulty in predicting suicidal behavior, even the highest-risk groups.

Indeed, in one study a computer program was better at identifying people who would attempt suicide than was a group of experienced clinicians. To add insult to injury, half of the patients preferred "talking" with the computer to talking with the human interviewers.[9]

Another issue is that there is dispute as to what extent, if any, various schools of psychological therapy are effective. For example, in one study psychotherapy was found to be *counterproductive* with those who had attempted suicide.[c10] Other studies have been equivocal. Current expert opinion seems to be that psychotherapy is about as effective as drug therapy for mild to moderate depression, but significantly less so for more severe cases.[11]

BIOLOGY

The biological view sees physical disorders, often a biochemical imbalance, as the cause of suicide and other psycho-pathological problems, like schizophrenia. This concept was articulated by Emil Kraepelin, a German contemporary of Freud's. The biological view didn't gain wide acceptance for a half century, largely because the biochemical tools for testing it were lacking.

In suicide, the biochemical problem often seems to be associated with a low level in the brain of the chemical nerve-impulse transmitter serotonin. Treatment consists of repairing or overcoming the original neurochemical imbalance. Some drugs increase serotonin levels and are used as antidepressants with moderate, but increasing, effectiveness.

Some evidence for, and limitations of, the biological model are:

1. Studies on twins provide the most persuasive evidence of a biological basis for suicide. In two investigations of suicide among twins, the identical twin of a suicide also killed himself in 19 percent of the cases (22 out of 118), while there were no instances (0 out of 254) where the fraternal (nonidentical) twin of a suicide had done so.[12]

2. Suicide tends to run in biological families. Adoption data show a significantly greater frequency of suicide among the biological relatives of suicides than among adoptive relatives. In a study of Danish adoptees diagnosed with depression, there were 15 suicides among 387 biologic relatives while only one suicide occurred in 180 adoptive relatives. Similarly, there were 12 suicides among 269 blood relatives of 57 adoptees who had killed themselves; there were no suicides among their 150 adoptive relatives.[13]

This is not to say that there is a suicide gene. But there are statistical associations between depression, aggression, and suicide, and depression clearly has a genetic component: For example, in 57 percent of identical twins studied, if one twin had major depression, so did the other.[14]

This evidence for a biological tendency to suicide is convincing. Yet even among identical twins, in more than four out of five instances the suicide of one twin was not followed by the suicide of the other. Tendency is not fate.

3. Studies on brain tissue and cerebro-spinal fluid (CSF) show that many people who kill themselves, especially those who use violent methods, have low levels of a brain tissue chemical neurotransmitter, serotonin, and its metabolic breakdown product, 5-hydroxyindoleacetic acid (5-HIAA). "Lower levels of 5-HIAA in CSF have been found to predict a 10-20 times higher mortality from suicide within 1 year after discharge from the hospital."[15] Especially interesting is the fact that whether the psychiatric diagnosis was depression, alcoholism, schizophrenia, or personality disorder, low

5-HIAA was associated with significantly more of the suicides and suicide attempts, as well as other violent or impulsive behavior. In this model, lower CNS serotonin levels make people more aggressive and impulsive, and thus increase the effects of stress, depression, and psychosis.

Moreover, the types of antidepressant drugs that increase serotonin levels are generally more effective in decreasing both suicidal thoughts and suicide attempts, than are other antidepressants that work by different mechanisms.[16]

There are also animal data that link aggression with low serotonin levels. For instance, blocking the formation of serotonin causes tame housecats to become ferocious, and nursing rats to bite their pups to death.[17]

The 5-HIAA hypothesis is not universally accepted. There are methodological criticisms.[18] Some studies have failed to find any connection between suicide and 5-HIAA, and most have found little or no correlation of 5-HIAA levels with nonviolent suicide. This murky picture should not be entirely surprising, since "suicide" lumps together groups as diverse as depressed teenagers, prisoners, alcoholic adults, political protesters, and the terminally ill. Most suicide is probably due to the interaction of multiple factors. Even if 5-HIAA is one of them, it may be overcome or augmented by others. Finally, it's not clear that even if there is a relationship between low 5-HIAA and suicide, violence, or impulsiveness, whether the low 5-HIAA level is a cause of the behaviors, an effect of the behaviors, or is the result of some other yet-undiscovered factor.

One supposed problem with the serotonin model is that there are a number of countries, like Denmark, Switzerland, and Japan, with low rates of outwardly directed violence (for example, homicide) but with high rates of suicide. A possible explanation for this is that there are cultural factors that influence whether violent impulses manifest themselves as suicide or homicide. An alternative view, that suicide is associated with prosperity, is discussed later.

A more significant weakness of the biological model as the prime mover in suicide is its difficulty in explaining the sometimes-large changes in suicide rates seen over short periods of time. For example, from 1958 to 1978 the suicide rate for Americans fifteen to twenty-four years old went from about 4 per 100,00 to about 14 per 100,000, an increase of roughly 250 percent. The suicide rate in Norway was an almost constant 7 per 100,000 from 1876, when central records were first collected, until about 1966.[19] It then increased 112 percent (from 7.3 to 15.5 per 100,00 between 1960-64 and 1990), while that of England decreased by 36 percent (11.7 to 7.5 per 100,000 between 1960-64 and 1991) and Ireland increased 170 percent (from 2.7 to 7.4 per 100,000 between 1971 and 1988). A convincing biological explanation has not been found.

An interestingly different perspective is provided by some evolutionary biologists, who note the persistence of suicide (about 1 percent of all deaths) across culture and time. While such behavior may seem counterproductive in a simple Darwinian sense—if you're dead, you probably won't be passing on too many more genes—they argue that this may represent (like altruism), a trait that has evolutionary benefits.

They suggest that suicide may be the sometimes-inappropriate expression of an instinct for self-sacrifice for the good of surviving relatives, who do pass on the deceased's genes. We see other forms of this in, say, parents perishing to save their children from danger, or old people killing themselves to leave more resources for their families. Consistent with this, psychiatrists have noted that many people who are considering suicide think of it in altruistic terms, as the best thing for their family and friends. "If you talk to people immediately after they [have] made a serious suicide attempt, they'll have a very altruistic explanation for what they did," says Dr. David C. Clark. "They believed it was the wise, clever and thoughtful thing to do."[20]

An alternate view is that the tendency for depression, rather than suicide, is the behavior selected for. In this picture, depression is useful because it forces people to contemplate and, presumably, learn from their mistakes. Suicide is, in this model, due to an excess of that process. Unfortunately (for the model), most patients with major depression never attempt suicide, and suicide rates for people with other diagnoses (for example, schizophrenia or substance abuse) are comparable to those with major depression.

Other researchers claim that traumatic or premature births are highly correlated with later suicide[21] and even with the suicide method employed.[22] There is both human and other animal evidence for each of these views, but they are no more convincing than other explanations.[23]

While it simplifies the picture, it may be counterproductive to limit one's understanding of suicide to biology, sociology, or psychiatry. There have been attempts to integrate some of these ideas under the label "suicidology." For example, Jack Douglas, in *The Social Meanings of Suicide,* argues that how the individual sees and interprets sociological situations determines their effects on her; a biologist might tack on a biochemically caused tendency toward impulsivity or violence. But, for the most part, we're still in the same position as the apocryphal blind men each describing a different part of an elephant: Each discipline tends to see suicide through its own filters and biases, and there is, as yet, no adequate synthesis.

NOTES

[a]We don't live in a philosophical age.

[b]As a curious aside, there are consistently high suicide rates in both Hungary and Finland, which share the same rare linguistic heritage, Finno-Ugric.

[c]Lest the antipsychiatry crowd get too smug, note that some antidepressant drugs (e.g., maprotiline) seem to *increase* suicidal behavior, as do some tranquilizers (e.g., alprazolam) (Rouillon, 1989; Gardner, 1985).

4
WHY PEOPLE ATTEMPT SUICIDE
●

Let them think what they liked, but I didn't mean to drown myself. I meant to swim till I sank—but that's not the same thing.

—Joseph Conrad

In a real dark night of the soul it is always three o'clock in the morning.

—F. Scott Fitzgerald

To be or not to be: that is the question.

—William Shakespeare

Thousands of books have attempted to answer the question of why people kill themselves. To summarize their findings in three words: to stop pain. Sometimes this pain is physical, as in chronic or terminal illness; more often it is emotional, caused by a myriad of problems. In any case, suicide is not a random or senseless act, but an effective, if extreme, solution.

A slightly more elaborate list of some reasons people commit or attempt suicide follows. The categories are arbitrary and overlap to some degree. However, this is just an outline, and there is no lack of books that discuss suicidal motivation in much more detail and from many different perspectives.

1. *Altruistic/heroic suicide.* This is where someone (more-or-less) voluntarily dies for the good of the group. Examples include the Greeks at Thermopolae; the Japanese kamikaze pilots[a] at the end of WWII; the Buddhist monks and others who, starting in 1963, burned themselves to death trying to stop the Vietnam War;[b] elderly Inuit (Eskimos) killing themselves to leave more food for their families; some Communists who confessed to invented (and often impossible) crimes during the Purge Trials of the late 1930s and early 1950s. Gandhi's tactic of hunger strikes, called *satyagraha* or "soul force," would have fallen into this category, had the British authorities failed to respond to his demands.[c]

2. *Philosophical suicide.* Various philosophical schools, such as stoics and existentialists, have advocated suicide under some circumstances.[1]

3. *Religious suicide.* There is a long history of religious suicide, usually in the form of martyrdom. This was widespread in the early years of Christianity and was also commonly seen in the various heresies uprooted before and during the Reformation, Counter-Reformation, and Inquisition. More recent examples may include members of the Solar Temple in Switzerland, France, and Canada; the San Diego Hale-Boppers in March 1997; the Branch Davidians in Waco, Texas; and some of the people at Jonestown, Guyana.

4. *Escape from an unbearable situation.* This may be persecution, a terminal illness, or chronic misery. There is no lack of historical examples: Epidemics of suicide were frequent among Jews in medieval Europe (sometimes they were given a choice between converting to Christianity and death).[d] Later, both Indian and black slaves in the New World committed mass suicide to escape brutal treatment. One slave owner supposedly stopped such desertion among his slaves by threatening to kill himself and follow them into the next world, and impose worse repression there.[2]

There were large numbers of suicides during times of pestilence in medieval Europe. More recently, AIDS has generated a similar response among many of its victims. There was also a wave of suicides among priests and their wives around 1075, after Pope Gregory VII imposed celibacy on the clergy, who had previously been allowed to marry.[3] Marriage had been only slightly more popular than damnation with the church

("It is better to marry than to burn"), but had been accepted for its first thousand years.

A significant number of killers commit suicide. Four percent of 621 consecutive murderers later killed themselves;[4] and about 1.5 percent of suicides follow murders.[5]

All of these situations can be readily seen as more or less unbearable. However, sometimes "unbearable" means failing an exam or missing a free throw in the big game. As George Colt notes,

> Most adolescent depression is caused by a reaction to an event—a poor grade, the loss of a relationship—rather than a biochemical imbalance. . . . Feeling blue after not getting into one's first-choice college is as appropriate as feeling happy after scoring a winning touchdown. But many adolescents who experience depression for the first time don't realize that it won't last forever.[6]

Or, as an anonymous teenager said, "It sounds crazy, but I think it's true—kids end up committing suicide to get out of taking their finals."[7]

5. *Excess alcohol and other drug use.* The observed high correspondence between alcohol and suicide[e8] can be explained in several ways, including: (a) Alcoholism can cause loss of friends, family, and job, leading to social isolation. However, this may be a chicken-and-egg question; it's equally plausible that family or job problems induce the excess alcohol use. In its later stages, the fact and consequences of alcoholism dominate the picture and are often blamed for everything; (b) alcohol and suicide may both be attempts to deal with depression and misery; (c) alcohol will increase the effects of other sedative drugs, frequently used in suicide attempts; (d) alcohol may increase impulsive actions.

The significance of the last two points is emphasized by findings that alcoholic suicide attempters who used highly lethal methods scored relatively low on suicidal-intent tests. The correlation between lethal intent and method was found only among nonalcoholics.[9]

Thus, to claim that alcoholism causes suicide is simplistic; while the association of alcohol abuse with suicide is clear, a causal relationship is not. Both alcoholism and suicide may be responses to the same pain. "A man may drown his sorrows in alcohol for years before he decides to drown himself."[10]

6. *Romantic suicide.* "My life is not worth living without him." This sentiment is most celebrated among the young, as in *Romeo and Juliet*, but is probably most frequent among people who have lived together for many years, when one of them dies.

Suicide pacts (dual suicide) constitute about 1 percent of suicides in Western Europe.[11] Most often, participants are more than fifty-one years old—except in Japan, where 75 percent of dual suicides are "lovers' pacts."[12]

7. *"Anniversary" suicide.* This is characterized by use of the same method or date as a dead loved one, usually a family member. "Imitative" suicide is similar to anniversary suicide in its focus on the dead, but uses a different date and method.

8. *"Contagion" suicide.*[13] This is where one suicide seems to be the trigger for others, and includes cluster and copycat suicides, most often among adolescents.[14] For example, on April 8, 1986, Yukiko Okada, eighteen, jumped to her death from the seventh floor of her recording studio. She had recently received an award as Japan's best new singer. Media attention was intense. Thirty-three young people, one nine years old, killed themselves over the next sixteen days, twenty-one of them by jumping from buildings.[15]

There are comparable examples from many parts of the world. The highly publicized suicide of a Hungarian beauty queen was followed by an epidemic of suicides by young women who used the same method.[16] Similarly, there was a spate of ethylene glycol (automobile antifreeze) intentional poisonings in Sweden following two accidental fatalities and "spectacular attention in the Swedish mass media."[17] In the United States there have been clusters of suicides, most often (or most often reported) among high school students, but not necessarily using identical methods.[18] Even fictional accounts may be enough, as in a claimed spurt of Russian roulette deaths shortly after the release of the film *The Deer Hunter*, with its powerful and nihilistic Russian roulette scene.[19]

On the other hand, other studies found no linkage between most newspaper reports and suicides.[20] Nor do copycat suicides occur consistently. For example, the 1994 death of Nirvana lead singer Kurt Cobain was not followed by a cluster of suicides.[21] In the seven weeks following his death there were twenty-four other suicides in the Seattle area, compared with thirty-one in the corresponding weeks of the previous year.

9. *An attempt to manipulate others.* "If you don't do what I want, I'll kill myself," is the basic theme here. However, the word "manipulative" does *not* "imply that a suicide attempt is not serious. . . . Fatal suicide attempts are often made by people who are hoping to influence or manipulate the feelings of other people even though they will not be around to witness the success or failure of their efforts."[22] Nevertheless, while people sometimes die or are maimed from their attempts, the intention in this case is to generate guilt in the other person, and the practitioner generally intends a nonfatal result.

10. *Seek help or send a distress signal.* This is similar to "manipulative" suicide except that there may be no specific thing being explicitly sought; it's the expression of an unbearable burden of pain and misery. This may occur at any age, but it is more frequent in the young. However, "Parents may minimize or deny the attempt. One study found that only 38 percent of treatment referrals after an adolescent attempt were acted on. Another found only 41 percent of families came for further therapy following an initial session. 'It's often difficult to get parents to acknowledge the problem because they *are* the problem,' says Peter Saltzman, a child psychiatrist."[23]

11. *"Magical thinking" and punishment.* This is associated with a feeling of power and complete control. It's a "You'll be sorry when I'm dead" fantasy. An illustration is the old Japanese custom of killing oneself on the doorstep of someone who has caused insult or humiliation. This is similar to "manipulative" suicide, but a fatal result is intended. It's sometimes called "aggressive" suicide. In a power struggle, if you can't win you can at least get in the last word by killing yourself.

12. *Cultural approval.* Japanese (like Roman) society has traditionally accepted or encouraged suicide where matters of honor were concerned. Thus, the president of a Japanese company whose food product had accidentally poisoned some people killed himself as an acknowledgment of responsibility for his company's mistake. It's almost unheard-of to find an American CEO who has voluntarily resigned on account of his company's misdeeds, let alone one who has committed suicide because of them. In Japan, 275 company directors killed themselves in a single year, 1986 (albeit for a variety of reasons).[24]

13. *Lack of an outside source to blame for one's misery.* Andrew Henry and James Short present evidence that when there is an external cause of one's unhappiness, the extreme response is rage and homicide; in the absence of an external source, the extreme response tends to be depression and suicide.[25] Thus, while marriage and children are associated with a lower suicide rate, they are also correlated with a higher homicide rate.

Henry and Short also suggest that, as economic quality-of-life improves, homicide should decrease and suicide increase. Longtime suicide researcher David Lester found such a correlation when comparing forty-three countries,[26] and also when comparing American states.[27]

However, national data are contradictory: It's easy to find countries with low suicide *and* low homicide rates (for example, Great Britain and Greece); or high rates of both (for example, Finland and Hungary). Furthermore, recent multinational increases in suicide rates are roughly matched by similar increases in homicide.

In addition, there are high rates of both suicide and homicide in prison. Most jail (short-term) and prison (longer-term) suicide rates have been reported between 50 and 200 per 100,000 per year, while the age-matched male rate in the general population was around 25. Jail suicide is more frequent than prison suicide.[28]

Still, Henry and Short's hypothesis can be used to explain some counterintuitive facts, such as the low suicide rate among Nazi concentration camp inmates,[f][29] among African Americans,[g] and during wartime; though, as Erwin Stengel observed, "It is a melancholy thought that marriage and the family should be such effective substitutes for conditions of war."[30]

14. *Other.* Most suicides have multiple causes.[31] Consider, for example, an existentialist with a serious illness who is devastated by a recent divorce and consequently suffering from "clinical major depression." He has a prescription for antidepressant medication which makes him feel well enough to go out of the house. He goes to a bar, gets drunk, comes back, and shoots himself with a loaded gun he kept in the bedroom. None of his neighbors responds to the noise and he bleeds to death. What "caused" his death: physical illness, philosophy, divorce, depression, medication, alcohol, availability of a gun, or social isolation? Or, perhaps, none of the above: From a

slightly different perspective, none of these factors *caused* the suicide; rather it is the pain associated with them (along with the unwillingness to bear it) that precipitates suicide.[32]

"Reasons" cited for suicide change with the times. Dr. Forbes Winslow wrote in 1840 that the increase in suicide was due to socialism, and particularly, Tom Paine's *Age of Reason*. Additional causes he cited were "atmospheric moisture" and masturbation, "a certain secret vice which, we are afraid, is practised to an enormous extent in our public schools." He recommended cold showers and laxatives.[33]

THE QUESTION OF INTENT IN SUICIDE ATTEMPTS

The survivor of a suicide attempt act is regarded by the public as either having bungled his suicide or not being sincere in his suicide attempt intention. He is looked upon with sympathy mixed with slight contempt, as unsuccessful in an heroic undertaking. It is taken for granted that the sole aim of the genuine attempt is self-destruction, and therefore the dead are successful and the survivors unsuccessful.

—Erwin Stengel[34]

People who carry out acts lumped together as "suicide attempts" actually have a variety of motives, and combining various intents masks important differences. According to Louis Dublin, a respected statistician, almost a third fully intend to kill themselves; fewer than half of these succeed. Those who fail generally do so because of unexpected rescue, or, more often, mistakes in planning or knowledge. These people tend to use generally lethal methods (guns, hanging, drowning, jumping) and are disproportionately older and male.[35]

Another third clearly do not want to die. Their suicide attempt, more aptly called a "suicidal gesture," is a cry for help or attention. They're trying to change their circumstances or to influence important people in their lives, usually parents or a spouse or lover. They make every effort to be saved, often scheduling the attempt to coincide with the expected return of a designated rescuer.

Of course, rescuers are sometimes delayed—or uninterested. Forensic texts provide some charming examples. In one case a woman took an overdose of barbiturates and pinned a note to herself saying, "If you love me, wake me up." Her husband came home around 10 P.M., saw the note, tossed it into the trash, and went out to a bar. When he returned early next morning, she was dead. The official cause of death was suicide. Criminal charges of homicide were considered, but not filed.[36]

These suicide "attempters" are more likely to be younger and female, and use less lethal means than the first group, most frequently drug overdoses and wrist cutting. Note that a "failed" suicide attempt in this group is one in which the person dies, which is the opposite of failure in the previous group.

The last third are people tossing the dice. They are in such emotional pain, rage, or frustration that they don't much care if they live or die, as long as the pain stops. They tend to be impulsive, not plan carefully (if at all), and leave their survival to chance.[37] In another study, of 500 suicide attempts, only 4 percent were described as "well-planned," but only 7 percent turned out to be more or less harmless.[38]

The relationship between the seriousness of someone's intent to kill herself and the lethality of the attempt is controversial. While it would seem intuitively plausible that the more seriously one intended to die the more lethal the resulting suicide attempt would be, numerous studies have reached contradictory conclusions: Some have found an association, others have not.[39]

The debate is more than academic. If the connection between serious intent and lethality of attempt is real, it implies that suicide prevention strategies that focus on decreasing the availability of lethal methods (for example, gun-control laws) will fail, because people wanting to die will simply switch to other, similarly lethal methods, such as hanging.

If, on the other hand, there is no good correlation between intent and lethality, then a decrease in the availability of lethal methods will be effective in decreasing suicides, because serious (but not fully rational) attempters will tend to switch to methods of lesser lethality.

Other evidence suggests a third possibility, that impulsivity or depression might have the best correlation with use of lethal methods; and that these in turn, are associated with neurochemical imbalance.[40]

And we find ourselves back to the biological issues raised in chapter 3.

NOTES

[a]The difference between committing suicide by ramming one's plane into an enemy ship and other hazardous military missions (say, flying in an American bomber over Germany in 1942 or being part of a U-boat crew) may be more one of intent than of result. Only one out of seven German submariners survived the war.

[b]The Buddhists were also protesting what they considered the anti-Buddhist laws and policies of the (Catholic) Diem regime. The first self-immolation was sparked by the Diem government's revocation of draft deferments for Buddhist seminary students.

[c]More recently, stubborn British authorities have allowed several equally pigheaded IRA (Irish Republican Army) prisoners to starve themselves to death over such critical issues as what kind of clothing they should wear in jail. The British wanted them to wear standard prison garb; the prisoners wanted uniforms consistent with their claimed status as prisoners of war.

[d]"The Jews are a frightened people. Nineteen centuries of Christian love have broken their nerves" Israel Zangwill (1864-1926).

[e]Data from Australia show that 103 of 509 suicides (20.2 percent) had blood alcohol levels of at least 0.08 mg/100 ml blood, the "legally impaired" level.

At autopsy there were usually higher alcohol levels in urine than in blood (1.3 to 1 ratio), implying "that in the great majority of cases alcohol had been consumed some hours before, and that in only four instances [out of the twenty-nine studied] was the alcohol most likely to have been taken just prior to death ... the act had been committed either during, or in the early hours of the morning following a period of alcohol consumption" (James, 1966).

[f]An alternative explanation for the low suicide rate in concentration camps is that a prisoner who wanted to die would not have to do anything—just stop eating or draw the attention of the guards.

[g]This is also the situation in South Africa, where blacks have higher homicide rates and whites higher suicide rates (D. Lester, 1989).

5
YOUTH SUICIDE

•

I want to kill myself, but I don't want to be dead.

—a fifteen-year-old

Most things, except agriculture, can wait.

—Jawaharlal Nehru

Teenagers attempt suicide roughly ten times more frequently than adults, although their fatality rate of 11.1 per 100,000 people is about the same as adults'. Suicide is the third leading cause of death among fifteen- to nineteen-year-olds. For this age group, there were 5,174 motor-vehicle deaths in 1994, compared to 1,948 suicides.

According to U.S. national data released in September 1991, about 1 million teens (out of about 25 million) attempt suicide each year, of which an estimated 276,000 sustain injuries serious enough to require medical treatment.[1]

Some other estimates (these are total, not per-year) are considerably higher: 3 percent of elementary school, 11 percent of high school, and 17 percent of college students. However, "most were low-lethality attempts for which medical or other attention was not sought. Accordingly, the vast majority of [these] suicide attempts will not be uncovered by investigations dealing solely with clinical or medically identified populations."[2] Thus, estimates or calculations of teenage suicide-attempt rates are particularly unreliable.

About four times more girls than boys make suicide attempts, but boys are much more likely to die: About 11 percent of (reported) males' attempts were fatal, compared to 0.1 percent of females', a ratio of more than 100:1.[3] This also yields a ballpark average of about fifty attempts for every fatality in this age group.

This low fatality rate might be taken to mean that most of these adolescents don't want to kill themselves (true) and that there is generally one or more "warning" attempt before a lethal one (not true). In a study from Finland, only 30 percent of male, and 68 percent of female suicides thirteen to twenty-two years old had made a previous (known) suicide bid.[4] This suggests that many of these lethal first-attempters intended to die.

Compared to those of older people, adolescents' suicide-attempt statistics show two significant differences. First, the fatality rate for boys is a hundred times that of girls, a much greater gender difference than with any other age group. The immediate reason is clear enough: Most teenage girls use relatively low-lethality methods like drugs and wrist cuts, while a substantial number of boys use guns and hanging. The reasons behind these choices are not known.

Second, the fatality rate among adolescents, less than 2 percent, is much lower than that among the elderly, variously reported to be between 25 and 50 percent. This may be because the young, however miserable, usually have more reason for optimism about the future than do the old, who are too often without friends, family, job, and health.

Nevertheless, the adolescent suicide rate is increasing and approaching the national average. U.S. suicide rates for fifteen- to nineteen-year-olds and those over sixty-five are shown in Table 5.1.

Table 5.1: U.S. suicide rate for selected age groups			Rate per 100,000 population, not age-adjusted
Year	U.S. Rate	15-19 year old rate	over 65 year old rate
1970	11.6	5.9	20.8
1980	11.8	8.5	17.6
1981	12.0	8.6	17.0
1982	12.2	8.7	18.3

Year	U.S. Rate	15-19 year old rate	over 65 year old rate
1983	12.1	8.6	19.2
1984	12.3	8.9	20.0
1985	12.5	9.9	21.0
1986	12.8	10.1	21.6
1987	12.7	10.2	21.7
1988	12.4	11.1	20.9
1989	12.2	11.1	20.1
1990	12.4	11.1	20.6
1991	12.2	11.0	19.7
1992	12.0	10.8	19.0
1993	12.1	10.9	19.0
1994	12.0	11.0	18.2

This corresponds to about two thousand suicides among fifteen- to nineteen-year-olds per year. While it's true that the suicide rate is substantially higher among old people, suicide is a relatively more frequent cause of death in the young, who have few deaths from illness. That's why it's the third leading cause of death among fifteen- to twenty-four year-olds, but ranks ninth or tenth for those fifty-five to seventy-four.[5]

These numbers show that overall U.S. suicide rates have been essentially unchanged between 1980-94. The rates for fifteen- to nineteen-year-olds have risen significantly while elderly rates held steady.

Among children between the ages of ten and fourteen, the suicide rate increased 110 percent (from 0.8 per 100,000 to 1.7 per 100,000) between 1980 and 1994.[6] There are also claims of an epidemic of youth suicide, with increases on the order of 300 percent between the early 1950s and late 1980s.[7] In 1950 the official rate for adolescent suicides was 2.7 per 100,000; by 1980 it had increased to 8.5 per 100,000. However, there is dispute about the magnitude of this "epidemic" in part because (1) the base rate chosen was the lowest in this century; (2) there is a greater willingness to admit to teen suicides now than in the 1950s.[8]

The reasons for this rise are also in dispute. Along with the usual social rationales (for example, higher divorce rates), "some statistics indicate that suicide attempts among younger persons have not increased, but the methods and means they are using are more lethal, making the attempts more successful," says the Centers for Disease Control's Dr. Alexander E. Crosby.[9]

According to Crosby, in 1992 firearm-related deaths accounted for 64.9 percent of suicides among people under twenty-five. Among those aged fifteen through nineteen, firearm-related suicides accounted for 81 percent of the increase in the overall rate from 1980 to 1992.

INTERNATIONAL DATA

Data from around the world show no consistent suicide pattern.[a] Twenty of twenty-seven national rates rose between 1970 and 1980; so did twenty-two of twenty-seven youth rates. The male youth-suicide rate generally increased more than the female rate. In most countries, the youth suicide rate is around one half of the adult rate, but in Chile, Venezuela, and Thailand, the youth rate is somewhat higher than the overall adult rates. The reasons are uncertain; and youth suicide rates show fewer correlations with social variables, such as income or national birth rate, than do adult rates.[10]

In terms of methods, a sixteen-country survey found rates from 1960 to 1980 increased for suicide by motor-vehicle exhaust (carbon monoxide), guns, and hanging; decreased for domestic gas; and were stable for solid and liquid poisons, drowning, and cuts/stabs.[11]

ADOLESCENT MISERY

Suicidal adolescents are so caught up in their own misery, that they can't see they have choices. Most have had little experience dealing with problems. They often can't or won't talk with their parents and may have no other trusted adults in their lives. Frequently they have withdrawn from their friends. This isolation further decreases their contact with other ideas and views.

Death may seem like the only solution to teenagers grieving over a major loss in their lives. In the bleak words of one fourteen-year-old girl, "If I died, I wouldn't hurt as much as I do now."

"But if you could say to them, 'Don't commit suicide because I can get you away from the pain without dying,'" says psychiatrist Michael Peck, "they'd likely be ready to do it."[12]

One counselor's description of a session with a suicidal college student follows: The student was highly religious, single, and pregnant. Overcome by guilt, she wanted to kill herself. The counselor tried to show her that there were other possible solutions:

> I did several things. For one, I took out a single sheet of paper and began to "widen her blinders." Our conversation went something on these general lines: "Now, let's see: You could have an abortion here locally." ("I couldn't do that.")....."You could go away and have an abortion." ("I couldn't do that.") "You could bring the baby to term and keep the baby." ("I couldn't do that.") "You could have the baby and adopt it out." ("I couldn't do that.") "We could get in touch with the young man involved." ("I couldn't do that.") "We could involve the help of your parents." ("I couldn't do that.") "You can always commit suicide, but there is obviously no need to do that today." (No response.) "Now, let's look at this list and rank them in order of your preference, keeping in mind that none of them is perfect."
>
> The very making of this list, my nonhortatory and nonjudgmental approach, had already had a calming influence on her. Within a few minutes her lethality had begun to de-escalate. She actually ranked the list, commenting negatively on each item. What was of critical importance was that suicide was now no longer first or second. We were then simply "haggling" about life—a perfectly viable solution.[13]

Sometimes the triggering event is astonishingly trivial: George Colt mentions,

> the fourteen-year-old boy who, according to his parents, shot himself because he was upset about getting braces for his teeth that afternoon; the girl who killed herself moments after her father refused to let her watch "Camelot" on television.... Such incidents are often misinterpreted as the "reason" for a suicide, but they are usually the culmination of a long series of difficulties.[14]

Even so, there may be qualitative differences between suicidal adolescents and older people. "When young people are suicidal, they're not necessarily thinking about death being preferable, they're thinking about life being intolerable," says Sally Casper, former director of a suicide prevention agency in Lawrence, Massachusetts. "They're not thinking of where they're going, they're thinking of what they're escaping from. Recently, a fifteen-year-old girl came in here. In one pocket she had a bottle of sleeping pills, and in the other pocket she had a bottle of ipecac, a liquid that makes you vomit. She said, 'I want to kill myself, but I don't want to be dead. I mean, I want to be dead, but I don't want to be dead forever, I only want to be dead until my eighteenth birthday.'"[15]

The fact that more than 95 percent of adolescents who live through their suicide attempt do not go on to kill themselves suggests that their problems are not as permanent or serious as their attempted solution. Feeling miserable and hopeless, these adolescents choose an irrevocable solution to temporary problems and, "reject not just a last few bitter moments, but life, all of it and at once, with all its myriad possibilities."[16] This is what make youth suicide especially heartbreaking.

NOTES

[a]To put it mildly. I quote from the abstract of a journal article:

"Suicide rates between 1960 and 1989 were explored for eight predominantly English speaking countries with similar national characteristics. New World countries showed significant similarities but differed from Old World countries. The two North American (NA) New World countries showed more similarity to each other than the two Australasian New World countries. The NA countries showed a unique plateau in the 1980s for males aged 15-29 years. Old World males of all ages showed common rises, suggesting a partial sex-specific influence in the young. However, trends among the 15- to 19-year-olds were significantly different to trends among the 20- to 29-year-olds in both sexes, suggesting a substantial youth-related contribution to the rises. Rates among 15- to 19-year-old females rose in the early 1960s, ahead of males but in parallel with rises among older females, suggesting part of the rise was sex- as opposed to age-related. Although rates among the 15- to 19-year-old females showed little change since 1970, this may be partly a function of sex-related improvements observable in older females disguising unfavourable youth-related influences. Possible aetiological factors are suggested but remain speculative" (Cantor, 1996).

6
SUICIDE IN THE ELDERLY
AND OTHER GROUPS

•

Lord save us all from old age and broken health and a hope tree that
has lost the faculty of putting out blossoms.
                                                    —Mark Twain

When an old person attempts suicide he almost fully intends to die.[1]
                                        —American Psychiatric Association

STATISTICS

The elderly (defined as those over sixty-five years old) have, historically
and currently, the highest suicide rates in most—but certainly not all—
countries of the world.

The death rate in adolescent suicide attempts is roughly 2 percent; among
men over 45 years old, R. W. Maris found 88 percent of first-time attempts
are fatal.[2] Other estimates are lower, but still on the order of 25 to 50 percent,[3] though psychiatrist Herbert Hendin, questioning these numbers,
points out that there seem to be many more elderly survivors of suicide attempts than there are suicide deaths in this age group.

Despite recent decreases in old-age suicide frequency and increases in
youth suicide, the suicide rate for the elderly in the United States is still
more than 50 percent higher than that of fifteen- to twenty-four-year-olds.

Twenty-six percent of the population is over fifty years old; 39 percent of suicides are from this group, a rate 1.5 times the national average. White males over fifty years old are about 10 percent of the population, but account for 33 percent of the suicides in the United States.[4] Elderly white males have a suicide rate five times the national average.[5]

Among people over sixty-five years old (12 percent of the population), the suicide rate was about 22 per 100,000 (21 percent of suicides) in 1986, or almost twice the national average.[6] The actual rate for the elderly is probably a good deal higher, since, "many deaths from suicide are never investigated and are reported mistakenly as accidents or deaths from natural causes, particularly when the victim was old."[7]

The annual suicide rate for elderly women (6.7 in 100,000) is lower than that for middle-aged women (7.9 in 100,000), and about one-sixth that of elderly men (around 40 in 100,000); however, the rate for women is relatively underreported, since they tend to use methods (for example, overdose) that leave room for other verdicts.[8] Since American men most often use guns, these deaths are harder to attribute to "natural" or other causes.

Nevertheless, the fact that American male suicide rates peak in old age while female rates are at their maximum during middle age is difficult to explain. The unpleasant realities of old age—increasingly poor health, death of a husband or wife, relegation to a nursing home—fall more frequently on women than men, due to the former's greater longevity. On the other hand, women are generally better than men at maintaining social and family contacts. And men, due to the traditionally higher status and more competitive nature of their activities (for example, business, sports, war) lose more social standing to the infirmities of old age than do women, who have generally lower rank and thus less distance to fall.

Reasons for these high rates seem to include:

1. Social isolation and loneliness, especially among widowers.
2. Physical isolation: Because many old people live alone, a suicide attempt may not be discovered soon enough to survive it.
3. The accumulation of losses, such as of friends, physical and mental abilities, social status, and health.
4. The elderly use more lethal methods than do younger people.[a]

5. Old people are less likely to survive any given level of injury than are younger, healthier, ones.

Some specific reasons were identified among elderly suicides from the Miami area. The single most-cited cause was "physical health concerns," which were more frequent than the next two reasons ("depression" and "unknown") combined.

Such health concerns are not necessarily accurate. In one study of 248 suicides, more people (eight) killed themselves in the mistaken belief that they had cancer than the number of suicides who, in fact, had terminal cancer.[9]

The real rates are probably a good deal higher than the official ones. This is because many drug overdoses have no witnesses, no wounds, and look like a natural death. Since serious preexisting illness is common in the elderly, such deaths are particularly likely to be misdiagnosed as "natural." In one study, 15,000 autopsies in apparently natural deaths were reviewed: 764 (5.1 percent) of the bodies contained enough poison to account for death.[10]

About half of the elderly who commit suicide are "depressed," but depression is common among old people. Both psychiatric and physical illness are more common in elderly suicides than in younger ones, whose deaths are more often precipitated by relationship, school, job, or jail problems.[11] Between 60 and 85 percent of elderly suicides had significant health problems and in four out of every five cases this was a contributing factor to their decision.[12] On the other hand, nonsuicidal elderly had rates of physical illness similar to the suicidal.[13]

Does depression affect willingness to accept treatment for other medical problems? In one study, depressed patients were less inclined than nondepressed ones to want medical treatment when the likelihood for improvement in some physical disease was good, but there was no difference between the two groups when the prognosis was poor. It seems that both groups were equally realistic about a poor prognosis, but that the lower quality-of-life and hopes-for-the-future expectations among depressed patients decreased their willingness to seek or accept help even when the probability of improvement was good.[14]

This is consistent with other data. For example, a survey of elderly (sixty to one hundred years old) visitors to senior centers in Indiana found that depression, low self-esteem, and loneliness were not associated with a decision to end their lives if faced with terminal, or debilitating chronic, illness.[15] Again, both the depressed and nondepressed elderly were similarly pragmatic about their options under these circumstances.

However, when the severity of the depression is taken into account, differences appear. Elderly patients who were hospitalized for major depression were asked, before and after antidepressant medication, whether they wanted life-sustaining treatment for their current physical health problems and for two hypothetical physical illnesses. In the relatively mild to moderate cases, remission of their depression did not increase their willingness to accept medical intervention; however, in the most severely depressed people, it did. This suggests that people in the midst of severe depression should probably not make life-and-death decisions, because their views are likely to change after antidepressant treatment.[16]

Poverty is not a good suicide predictor. Sweden and Denmark both have high per-capita income as well as comprehensive social welfare for the aged. They also both have high suicide rates among the elderly, as well as in the general population. Greece and Mexico, which have a far lower (economic) standard of living than Sweden and Denmark, have particularly low rates, though even these rates are higher in the elderly than in the general population. Interestingly, in the United States, during times of economic prosperity, the elderly suicide rate goes down while the suicide rate of younger adults goes up.[17]

A final observation: Suicide notes left by the elderly tend to show a desire to end their suffering, rather than dwelling on interpersonal relationships, introspection, or punishing themselves or others, which are common themes in younger suicides.[18]

SUICIDE RATES AMONG VARIOUS GROUPS

Native Americans have the highest "racial" rate: 16.2 in 100,000 (1991-93, age-adjusted); while the rate for white Americans was 11.1 in 100,000 (1992, age-adjusted). Among Native Americans, the pattern of suicide resembles that of African Americans: a male peak in the early twenties and decreasing thereafter. This pattern differs from that of white Americans, where elderly white males have the highest rates.[19]

Black Americans have reported suicide rates substantially lower than those of whites—except among males twenty-four to thirty-five years old, whose rates are similar. The overall rate for African Americans (6.2 in 100,000 in 1980; 7.0 in 100,000 in 1994) is roughly half that of whites, a ratio which has been consistent over many years. There is, however, some evidence that a small part of the difference is due to African American suicides being more underreported than white suicides.[20]

The best single socioeconomic predictor appears to be religious affiliation. Suicide is infrequent in Moslem populations, typically reported as less than 1 in 100,000 per year. It also is uncommon in many Catholic countries, with rates of 2 to 8 per 100,000 per year. On the other hand, Catholic Austria and Hungary have rates of 23 and 39 per 100,000 per year, respectively. Protestant, Hindu, and Buddhist regions have, with a few exceptions, higher reported suicide rates than Moslem or Catholic ones.

However, there is substantial skepticism about the accuracy of suicide statistics, particularly from societies in which suicide is most condemned. Psychiatrist Erwin Stengel observes, "In Roman Catholic and Moslem countries a verdict of suicide is such a disgrace for the deceased and his family that it is to be avoided wherever possible."[21]

The suicide rate is not reliably correlated with such factors as income, education, and health-care availability. The effect of unemployment is in dispute. For example, while some studies have found an association between unemployment and suicide, in England there was a 35 percent decrease in the suicide rate between 1963 and 1975, the same period that showed a 50 percent increase in unemployment.[22]

While there is no good correlation with wealth or poverty and suicide, certain professions have especially high rates: psychiatrists, physicians, lawyers, and retired military officers.

However, (to list a few risk factors for suicide) the highest suicide likelihood would probably be found in depressed, ill, elderly white Protestant male immigrants, who are widowed, divorced or unmarried, who sleep more than nine hours a day, have more than three drinks a day, smoke, and keep a gun in the house.

NOTES

[a]However, the use of guns, the most lethal method, is fairly constant in different age groups in the United States: (Source: CDC, years 1979-1995)

Age	Percentage of suicides by gunshot
10-14	56
15-19	64
20-24	62
25-34	55
35-44	53
45-54	57
55-64	62
65-74	67
75-84	67
85 +	58

7

SOME FREQUENTLY ASKED QUESTIONS ABOUT SUICIDE

•

ARE SUICIDAL PEOPLE CRAZY?[a]

Yes, no, not necessarily, and so what. Certainly, people with a diagnosis of schizophrenia have a high lifetime risk of suicide (10 percent)[1] as do people with severe depression (15 percent)[2] and/or alcoholism (2 to 11 percent).[3] But so do people with medical illness: 18 to 85 percent—studies are all over the map—of suicides had a physical illness; for 11 to 69 percent this was an "important contributing cause"; however, only around 5 percent were terminally ill.[4]

In addition, the association of suicide with mental illness or alcoholism does not mean that suicide cannot be rational: chronically depressed, alcoholic, or schizophrenic persons may decide that it is better to be dead than to continue living as they are.

And to insist that suicide is irrational and attribute it to depression or mental illness "is absurd and infuriating to those who have spent time at the bedside of dying patients who are suffering severely with no good choices."[5] Besides, "who wouldn't be depressed with such severe limitations to a meaningful life as incontinence, inability to speak, heavy curtailment of the ability to move, and loss of dignity?"[6]

Moreover, one doesn't need to be terminally ill to decide that one's physical, mental, or emotional limitations have become unacceptable, and that it's pointless to go on living. As an eighty-four-year-old woman said to her son, a professor of health policy:

> Let me put this in terms you should understand, David. My "quality of life"—isn't that what you call it?—has dropped below zero. I know there is nothing fatally wrong with me and that I could live on for many years. With a colostomy and some luck, I might even be able to recover a bit of my former lifestyle, for a while. But do we have to do that just because it is possible? Is the meaning of life defined by its duration? Or does life have a purpose so large that it doesn't have to be prolonged at any cost to preserve its meaning?
>
> I've lived a wonderful life, but it has to end sometime and this is the right time for me. My decision is not about whether I'm going to die—we will all die sooner or later. My decision is about when and how. I don't want to spoil the wonder of my life by dragging it out in years of decay. I want to go now, while the good memories are still fresh. Help me find a way.[7]

Studies have claimed to find among suicides about three times the rate of mental disorders as among people with nonsuicidal natural deaths (77 percent versus 25 percent).[8] Other studies have found similar,[9] higher,[10] and lower[11] rates. However, some of these investigations have had the benefit of hindsight:[12] "the highest estimate of mental illness when a sample had been diagnosed *before* suicide was 22 percent. Afterward the highest estimate was 90 percent."[13]

After-the-fact diagnosis is rightly criticized[14] for lack of objectivity: When a psychiatrist knows that someone died a suicide, his conclusion will be influenced by that knowledge, particularly if the psychiatrist believes that people who kill themselves must be crazy:[b]

> The diagnosis of mental illness is especially suspect when it comes to self-destruction. The argument connecting suicide and mental illness is tautologically based upon our cultural bias against suicide. . . . We say, in essence, "All people who attempt suicide are mentally ill." If someone asks, "How do you know they are mentally

ill?" the implied answer is, "Because only mentally ill persons would try to commit suicide."[15]

But there is a wide range of opinion, even within the psychiatric community:

> Is every suicide mentally ill and in need of hospitalization as [interventionist] Eli Robins believes?[16] ... Or is he simply called mentally ill for the purpose of controlling his behavior, as [radical Thomas] Szasz believes?[17] Or does he have the right to kill himself whether or not he is mentally ill as [libertarian Eliot] Slater advocates?[18] These views reflect the diversity of psychiatric thought with regard to suicide. My own view is that each of these positions contains some truth and that no one of them is an adequate guide for social policy. Most suicide can be diagnosed under present clinical standards as mentally ill; many diagnoses are influenced by the concern with suicide and the desire to prevent it through hospitalization; and the diagnosis of mental illness is not only insufficient to explain suicide but does not by itself justify taking away an individual's rights. . . . [But] Surely confinement for a limited period for the purpose of evaluation with a view to providing help is indicated.[19]

I would agree that it is better to err on the side of temporary intervention. People sometimes regret things they do; suicide is hard to regret. You can usually kill yourself later, but you can't bring yourself back to life. On the other hand, it remains all too possible to turn "temporary" into permanent; to subject people to conditions that worsen their state; to drug them into submission or to lock them up indefinitely. There need to be clear limits to both the duration and nature of any intervention; and if someone is persistent in wanting to end their life, that, however distressing, must—and ultimately will—be their decision to make.

> You don't have to be "crazy" to commit suicide. You just have to be desperate, and in need of attention and care.
>
> —Emilinda, age fifteen[20]

The notion that suicidal people are crazy also tends to isolate those who are feeling suicidal. Because of the stigma associated with mental illness, they may not be willing to seek help, even in a crisis.

Thus, one of the ironies of suicide is that a suicide attempt—if survived—is probably the most dramatic and convincing way to draw attention to a problem and get help. Often family, psychiatric, and social service resources become suddenly available. A survey of Swiss survivors found that a majority felt that their actions had positive consequences for them.[21] In Erwin Stengel's words, "The suicidal attempt is a highly effective though hazardous way of influencing others and its effects are as a rule . . . lasting."[22]

Optimists may derive comfort from the fact that only about 1 percent of suicide survivors kill themselves within one year;[23] of 886 suicide survivors in another study, only 3.84 percent killed themselves within five years.[24] A Swedish study with a thirty-five-year follow-up found 10.9 percent of its subjects ultimately died by suicide.[25]

A pessimist might note that about half of the people who make a suicide attempt will make another one;[26] the one-year suicide rate of 1 percent is 50 times the rate of nonattempters; and 10 to 15 percent will eventually kill themselves, a rate 10 to 15 times that of the general population.[27]

HOW WOULD I KNOW IF SOMEONE CLOSE TO ME WAS CONSIDERING SUICIDE?

There are two general areas, which overlap to some degree, to look at: (1) sociological or biological risk factors and (2) individual signals. Risk factors are discussed in chapter 3 and elsewhere. The most familiar method of finding out if someone is contemplating suicide consists of being sensitive to various verbal and behavioral signs; but the fact is, while many people consider, mention, or threaten suicide, far fewer make a suicide attempt. Probably the closest we can get to knowing is to ask—usually not a comfortable question to think about, let alone ask.

The most important suicide warning signs are:

1. A previous suicide attempt. Between 20 to 80 percent of suicides (studies vary wildly) have made one or more prior attempts.[28]

Whatever the actual number, this is the single most significant flag.

2. A major change in behavior or personality. A normally cheerful person may become quiet and withdrawn, and stop formerly pleasurable activities. Insomnia, or more often an excess of sleep, may be seen. Giving away prized possessions is sometimes a sign that a decision for suicide has been made. However, in all of these and other changes, alternative reasons for the behavior are entirely possible.

3. Reckless behavior. "I don't care" or "leave it to chance" actions are close to out-and-out suicidal behavior. An example of this is "Russian roulette."

4. Severe depression. Some of the components of depression are hopelessness, inability to concentrate, sleep disturbances, feelings of worthlessness, loneliness, and sadness. Such a person might say things like, "You would be better off without me," or "Everything I touch turns into ashes." However, some people are so depressed that they don't have the energy to kill themselves. These folks are actually at higher risk when they're just starting to feel a little better.

As one suicidal woman noted,

> It takes a tremendous amount of energy to figure out how you're going to kill yourself. . . . I wanted something that was final and wasn't going to be messy. I didn't want to jump off the roof; I might end up only half dead, and I wouldn't like that. I didn't want to blow my head off—I didn't happen to feel that physical disembodiment would be a particularly pleasant thing for everybody. . . . I kept thinking about what would be easiest for everyone else. Of course the easiest thing would have been if I'd lived.[29]

Since thought disturbances and hopelessness are generally associated with depression, severely depressed people may not recognize the serious nature of their problem, or, if they do, they may lack the will to try to get help: "Their thought processes often seem tailored to narrow possibilities, for their rigidity often makes them unable to see al-

ternative solutions, while depression alters their judgment about possibilities for the future."[30]

> When I was nineteen, I had my first deep depression. I was
> terrified. Everything—the way I walked, the way I talked—
> slowed to a crawl. I felt empty, like everything inside me had
> been cut up and pulled out. It was as if something had died in-
> side me and was disintegrating. I couldn't concentrate. Reading
> a book, I'd find myself skimming the same passage over and over
> until I'd realize I had read the same paragraph sixteen times.
> After eight months I began to wonder whether my depression
> would ever lift. I envisioned spending my whole life like that. The
> feeling that it was never going to end is what made me think of
> suicide.[31]

The author of this passage, Anne-Grace Scheinin, made six suicide attempts in the two years before being diagnosed as manic-depressive
and being treated with lithium. There were no suicide attempts in the
following ten years.[32]

5. Talking, or dropping clues, about committing suicide. This is usually
an indirect, but unmistakable, plea for help, and shouldn't be ignored.
Adolescents, in particular, generally place high value on indepen-
dence, privacy, and self-reliance. If they're asking for help, they're
probably in serious pain.

The idea that people who talk about suicide won't carry it out is
dead wrong. Erwin Stengel estimates that three-fourths of the people who either commit suicide or make an attempt give clear warning of their intent; perhaps some act *because* they were not taken
seriously.

On the other hand, depression is often hidden (remember
Thoreau's caveat, "The mass of men lead lives of quiet desperation")
or unnoticed. Thus, as discussed later, physicians often don't recognize depression in their patients.

RISK FACTORS FOR SUICIDE

One identification strategy takes a statistical look at the social, biological, and psychiatric components associated with suicide: Are there characteristics that suicidal people tend to share? One small study looked at a few such risk factors among New York teenagers:[33]

In Table 7.1, below, column 2, the "odds ratio," shows the relative likelihood of someone with a particular risk factor killing themselves, compared to similar persons without that trait. In this study, the greatest risk factor was a prior attempt, 22.5 times the general population rate.

Table 7.1	Risk factors for male teenage suicide (New York)
Risk Factor	**odds ratio**
Prior attempt	22.5
Major depression	8.6
Substance abuse	7.2
Antisocial behavior	4.4
Family history of suicide	3
(Source: Shaffer, 1988)	

In another study, J. A. Motto looked at risk factors in 2,753 people hospitalized for depression or a suicide attempt.[34] Out of 101 factors he examined, which ranged from "age-difference of siblings" and "value of church as resource" to "preparation of attempt" and "seriousness of present suicide attempt injury," fifteen were found to be most predictive of suicide within two years, for this population. In order of importance, they were:

Factor	*High-risk category*
Presence of suicide impulses	Yes
Seriousness of present suicide attempt, based on intent	Unambivalent or ambivalent but weighted toward suicide
Sexual orientation	Bisexual, active; or homosexual, inactive
Special stress (unique individual problem)	Severe
Threatened financial loss	Yes
Weight change (in present loss episode)	Gain; or 1 to 9 percent
Ideas of persecution	Yes
Result of previous efforts to obtain help	Negative or variable
Occupation	Executive, business owner, administrator, professional, semi-skilled worker
Emotional disorder in family	Depression, alcoholism
Interviewer's reaction to subject	Risk increases with negative reaction
Sleep (hours per night)	Risk increases with more sleep
Financial resources	Risk increases with resources
Age	Risk increases with age
Previous psychiatric hospital admissions	Risk increases with number of admissions

Among the lowest-risk group, there were no suicides within two years; in the highest-risk group there were 57 (20.7 percent). Nevertheless, even in the highest-risk set of a high-risk population, four out of five did not kill themselves.

The fact that the U.S. suicide rate has been fairly stable over several decades suggests that our ability to identify and treat the suicide-prone has not improved much, though it's certainly possible that the rate would be higher without such improvements as have occurred.

In other words, our ability to anticipate—using any or all sociological, psychological, or biological measurements now available—whether a particular individual will or will not commit suicide, remains negligible. In the words of psychiatrist Alex Pokorny,

Although we may reconstruct causal chains and motives after the fact, we do not possess the tools to predict particular suicides before the fact. . . . The conclusion is inescapable that we do not possess any item of information or any combination of items that permit us to identify to a useful degree[c] the particular persons who will commit suicide. . . . Even for someone in a high-risk category the chances of suicide within a year are much less than the chance that he will *not* have committed suicide within that time. In twenty-five years I can remember perhaps three cases where I felt the chance of a certain person committing suicide within the next year was more than 10 percent.[35]

Pokorny makes a distinction between long-term prediction, about which he is pessimistic, and short-term crises (minutes, hours, or days) which, he argues, require identifying a crisis that is already here, and which, he feels, psychiatrists do reasonably well.

However, clinical judgment seems unreliable for predicting suicide attempts: A computer program was superior to experienced clinicians in identifying patients who would attempt suicide.[36]

The current situation still seems to be,

No one knows why people kill themselves. Trying to find the answer is like trying to pinpoint what causes us to fall in love or what causes war. There is no single answer. Suicide is not a disease like cancer or polio. It is a symptom. "The problem of suicide cuts across all diagnoses," says John Mack, a psychiatrist and coauthor of *Vivienne*, the story of a fourteen-year-old girl who hanged herself.[37] "Some are mentally ill, most are not. Some are psychotic, most are not. Some are impulsive, most are not." Says psychologist Pamela Cantor, "People commit suicide for many reasons. Some people who are depressed will commit suicide, and some people who are schizophrenic will commit suicide, and some people who are fine but impulsive will commit suicide. We can't lump them all together." And just as there is no one explanation for the five thousand adolescent suicides each year, there is no one explanation for any one suicide.[38]

Does bringing up the subject of suicide with a depressed person put the idea into her head?

No, you can be sure that the idea was already there. However, "If they are feeling suicidal, it can come as a great relief to see that someone else has some insight into how they feel."[39]

WHAT DO SUICIDE-ATTEMPT SURVIVORS THINK OF SUICIDE?

Many people have speculated that if you could talk to someone who was in midair after jumping from a tall tower, you might find out that he no longer was so sure he wanted to die. Over the past thirty years I have seen four people who survived six-story suicide jumps.

Two wished to survive as soon as they jumped, two said they did not, but one of the latter two who professed to be furious at having survived made no subsequent suicide attempt.[40]

Similarly, of 515 people who had been prevented from jumping off the Golden Gate bridge, only 25 (5 percent) went on to kill themselves later.[41] Of eight known survivors in 1975, one subsequently killed himself.[42]

According to another source, only 2 percent of survivors of suicide attempts objected to having been saved, while 70 percent said their suicide attempt was "stupid."[43] The same author, Jaques Choron, cites Japanese data that claim 90 percent of survivors studied were happy to be saved. Similar studies from Norway found that 57 to 75 percent of suicide survivors said they were glad that their attempt had failed.[44]

It seems also to be the case that surviving a serious suicide attempt sometimes ends depressions[45]—even if there is permanent injury. Hendin suggests that sometimes a self-inflicted permanent injury is "therapeutic" in the sense that it satisfies a need for self-punishment.[46] On the other hand, our inability to interview dead people—generally the most serious and thorough of attempters—limits our knowledge of their interest in being saved.

How do Clinicians Treat Suicidal People?

The immediate goal of a therapist, counselor, or anyone else dealing with highly suicidal people should be to reduce the pain in every way possible.... Help them by intervening with whoever or whatever is causing their distress—lovers, parents, college deans, employers, or social service agencies. I have found that if you reduce these pressures and lower the level of suffering, even just a little, suicidal people will choose to live.[47]

This is not always as gratifying as it sounds: Some suicidal people are "extremely difficult: provocative, ambivalent, openly hostile, or passive-aggressive and vengeful."[48] Thus,

The clinician's first job is to manage his or her own feelings generated by the crisis situation and not be driven by discomfort. The clinician can act out in a variety of ways, from failing to inquire about suicidality with an obviously upset or depressed person ("It sounds bad, but surely you're not *suicidal*"); by fleeing from the subject when the patient brings it up ("Uh-huh. And how's your appetite?"); by actively colluding with the patient's wish to commit suicide ("Sounds like there isn't any reason for you to live"); or by openly or covertly directing the patient to die ("Why don't you do it *right* the next time!") [49]

Can Treatment Prevent Suicide Attempts?

Though often useful, professional help is no guarantee against suicide. Two-thirds of the suicides in one study had consulted their family doctor within a week of their death.[50] In another study, over 90 percent of suicides had been seen by a psychiatrist or a family doctor within a year of death; 48 percent within a week.[51] However 48 percent of physicians were "very surprised" by the suicide of their patient.[52]

In fairness to the physicians, most of these people came in with somatic complaints: headache, insomnia, tiredness, backache, and so forth. In addition, patients are often on their best behavior at the doctor's and tend to minimize their psychiatric problems. It's also the case that a substantial number of these suicides saw the physician specifically to get enough drugs to kill themselves. In one study, this motivation was found in 43 percent of drug-overdose deaths immediately (within twenty-four hours) following physician visits.[53] All of this does not imply that therapy is useless or counterproductive—any more than the fact that many people who see heart specialists end up dying from heart disease—only that it is far from universally effective.

On the other hand, current antidepressant drugs[d] are fairly good at making people feel better—about 75 percent of users seem to be helped[54]—and should certainly be tried by just about anyone considering suicide. However, they don't work instantly and might take as long as six weeks to show an effect, and the dose may need to be adjusted for an optimal response. Drug treatment should be generally continued for several months; less than 4.5 months of antidepressant use is associated with an increased rate of treatment failure.[55] In addition, most of these drugs work for some people but not for others, possibly requiring trials with more than one antidepressant.[56]

In a study of people in New York City who killed themselves between 1990-92, 16.4 percent (268 in 1,635) had been taking antidepressants.[57] This is similar to data from Sweden where 15.9 percent (542 in 3,400) of suicides had been using antidepressants.[58] It is not clear if this is good news (a lot of suicides might not have killed themselves had they been using medication) or bad news (a lot of people taking antidepressants kill themselves anyway).

In fact, while most antidepressants are reasonably good at making people feel better, they are less effective in decreasing suicidal thoughts and behavior.[e] This is particularly true of the older tricyclics (TCAs) such as amitriptyline (for example, Elavil) and imipramine (for example, Tofranil). In fact one, maprotiline (Ludiomil), significantly *increased* suicidal behavior—14 suicide attempts among 777 patients compared to 1 attempt among the 374 patients taking no medication. Particularly interesting is that a low dose was just as suicide-provoking as a higher dose, while less effective in decreasing depression. The implication is that lower doses of such drugs, sometimes chosen for "safety," may be equally dangerous and less therapeutic than higher doses.[59] Curiously, none of the five completed suicides was by maprotiline overdose, even though it is a fairly toxic drug.

More recent antidepressants of a type called "serotonin-specific reuptake in-hibitors" (SSRIs), like Prozac (fluoxetine), Welbutrin (bupropion) and Effexor (venlafaxine), seem to be safer, somewhat more effective, and faster acting than either TCAs or MAOIs, especially in severe depression or where there is a large anxiety component of the depression. However, there is some evidence suggesting that fluoxetine itself can cause suicidal thoughts and/or behavior.[60]

But, even effective antidepressants can be a two-edged sword: Sometimes they make people feel just enough better to have the energy to kill them-selves, as well as providing them the means to do so.

Especially in adolescents and in people experiencing severe depression for the first time, it's important to remember the probability that, as Leigh Orf says, "in six short months someone who was threatening suicide daily will change their tune to 'Gee, am I glad I didn't off myself' because of some rather insignificant event, in the Grand Scheme of Things, like finding a new friend, S[ignificant] O[ther], or hobby."

How Do Telephone Hotlines Work?

Hotlines provide an anonymous way for people to speak to a counselor about a problem. Some callers feel that they have no one they can talk to. For others, the telephone is simply less threatening than a face-to-face meeting would be. Assistance is available whether you're having a crisis yourself, are concerned about someone else, or just need someone to talk with. They generally do not provide "treatment," but usually have informa-tion about other available services that you may not have thought of.

Hotlines are often staffed by volunteers—about one-third have no paid staff—and operate on shoestring budgets. As a result, they may be closed, or busy with other clients when you call. However, there is frequently more than one hotline locally available. Suicide hotline phone numbers may be found under "Crisis," "Suicide," or "Hotline" in the telephone book or in the Local Government listings. If you can't find one, you can call the American Association of Suicidology (202) 237-2280 for the nearest agency.

Be aware that some suicide hotlines will call the police to trace a call if they think the caller is about to kill herself; others will not. If this is relevant to you, ask first.

Surprisingly, there is little or no difference in the suicide rate in comparable communities that have hotlines and those that don't. This was found to be the case both in the United States and in England. A likely reason is that the most seriously suicidal people are the least apt to use such a service. Most of the legitimate calls (about half are cranks) are from unhappy people needing someone to talk with, but only a small fraction of them are suicidal. Only about 5 percent of suicides had been in contact with a hotline.[61]

WHAT SUICIDE-RELATED RESOURCES EXIST ON THE INTERNET?

There is a lot out there, but there's no quality control on the Internet: *caveat emptor.*

The Samaritans is probably the oldest organization offering suicide prevention counseling on the Internet. They are based in England and have been providing hotline and hands-on help for more than forty years. E-mail is read and answered 365 days a year. Note that the Samaritans will not break a caller's confidentiality on any matter pertaining to suicide. To reach them, send e-mail to: *jo@samaritans.org*, or visit their web site: *http://www.samaritans.org.uk.*

Nothing is 100 percent snoop-proof, but there are a number of "anonymous re-mailers" who will forward your e-mail while removing your identification. For more information about, and links to, these sites, try: *www.anonymizer.com.* However, be aware that using a re-mailer is often much slower (hours, rather than minutes or seconds) than direct e-mail.

There are several discussion Usenet newsgroups under the alt.support hierarchy: *alt.support.depression* has been recommended by Graham Stoney as having a detailed and excellent Frequently Asked Questions posting covering many facets of depression. Other alt.support groups include: *alt.suicide.holiday,* or ASH, and a newer group, *alt.suicide.exams* which is most active around student-exam times.

Note that (1) the Internet changes rapidly; (2) not all Internet service providers carry any or all alt groups.

The *IRC Suicide Chatline* "continues to remain [sic] a place for people to drop by and chat about themselves, their problems, depression, and life in general. . . . Keep in mind that this is not a suicide hotline and that there are no professionals who frequent the channel: you are on your own." You can reach the chatline at: *http://www.yahoo.com/Computers;_and_Internet/Internet/Chatting/IRC/.*

The address of John Grohol's mental health page is *http://www.coil.com/~grohol/.* It offers support, questions, and answers.

Suicide Awareness\Voices of Education (SA\VE) is "a page devoted to suicide support, questions, and answers. It's at: *http://www.save.org/.*

"The suicide-support mailing list provides an electronic support group. Membership to the list is open to anyone seeking emotional support regarding potentially self-destructive situations [or to anyone who has had a family member, close friend, or loved one complete suicide], and to people willing to offer support in a nonjudgmental manner. List members who offer support do so in their spare time on an ad-hoc basis, and come from a diverse variety of backgrounds and experiences. To subscribe, send mail to *listserv@research.canon.oz.au* containing 'subscribe suicide-support your name' in the body of the message."

Some other resources:

AFTERWORDS is a letter about suicide and suicide grief published quarterly by Adina Wrobleski, parent of a teen who killed herself. She also travels and speaks on suicide and has pamphlets and tapes. 5124 Grove St., Minneapolis, Minnesota, 55436-2481; 612-929-6448.

AMERICAN ASSOCIATION OF SUICIDOLOGY, 4201 Connecticut Ave. N.W., Suite 310, Washington, D.C. 20008; 202-237-2280, is a national clearinghouse for suicide information. It has, among other things, phone numbers for local hotlines. *http://www.cyberpsych.org/aas.htm*

BOYS TOWN SUICIDE HOTLINE offers short-term intervention and counseling, local referrals, counseling. 800-448-3000; TDD: 800-448-1833.

COMPASSION IN DYING, P.O. Box 75295, Seattle, WA 98125, helps terminally ill people "who choose rational suicide after reaching the limits of benefit from medical therapy." *http://www.compassionindying.org/cidpatnt.htm*

EUTHANASIA AND PHYSICIAN-ASSISTED SUICIDE: All Sides is at *http://www.religioustolerance.org/euthanas.htm*

EUTHANASIA WORLD DIRECTORY includes a list of right-to-die groups, and how to contact Dr. Jack Kevorkian. *http://www.efn.org/~ergo/*

HEMLOCK SOCIETY supports the right of the terminally ill to commit suicide. P.O. Box 10810, Denver, CO 80250 (1-800-247-7421). *http://www.hemlock.org*

HOSPICE CARE provides a reasonable alternative for dying patients who choose to give up some length of life for improved quality of life in their last months. Hospice programs in the United States only started in the mid-1960s, but thirty years later there are more than two thousand. They provide "comfort care" for the dying, often at home. There are many hospice web pages on the Internet. The National Hospice Organization address is 1901 N. Moore St., Suite 901, Arlington, VA 22209; 1-800-658-8898.

INTERNATIONAL ANTI-EUTHANASIA TASK FORCE is just what it says. It's a good source for anti-euthanasia arguments and evidence. *http://www.aeitf.org/*

LAST RIGHTS INFORMATION CENTRE "provides the latest information available on a wide range of concerns associated with the dying process: news about 'living wills'; palliative care; legislation concerning voluntary euthanasia and assisted suicide; support groups for those afflicted with life-threatening illness; and access to public forums (newsgroups and mailing lists) exploring the medical, legal, political and ethical issues associated with death and dying." P.O. Box 39018, Victoria BC V8V 4X8; fax 604-386-3800. The center can also be reached on DeathNET on the Internet: *http://www.islandnet.com/~deathnet*

MENTAL HEALTH NET is at: *http://www.cmhc.com*

RAY OF HOPE INC, of Iowa City, is a national nonprofit with information and training on setting up support groups, telephone counseling: 319-337-9890.

SURVIVORS OF SUICIDE is a national network of support groups: Call 414-442-4638 or write Sharry Schaefer, 3251 N. 78th St., Milwaukee, WI 53222 and enclose self-addressed stamped envelope. *http://www.main.org/sos/*

This is just a sampling of what's out there.

HOW DOES SUICIDE AFFECT FRIENDS AND FAMILY?

The family is left to pick up the pieces, figuratively and sometimes literally.[f]

Such deaths often leave scars on family and friends: guilt, sorrow, anger, abandonment, silence. Even young children instinctively know this when they scream (or fantasize) to their parents, "I'll die and then you'll be sorry!" Mark Twain describes this situation in Tom Sawyer's elaborate death ruse—he is supposed to have drowned, but is actually hiding under the bed listening while his Aunt Polly and her friend, Mrs. Harper, sorrowfully express their belated love and guilt at his untimely demise.

In one study, all family members said they were shocked by finding the body or being informed of the suicide; 89 percent said they were later angry, and 57 percent reported depression. Some described persistent memories of the smell of gunpowder and finding bone and tissue parts.[62]

On the other hand, depending on attitudes and circumstances, sometimes the death is also a relief, particularly in cases of terminal illness or chronic suicidality. One 57-year-old woman said of her husband, "It was at the back of my mind that it was going to happen. And when it did, it was a shock, but I felt, 'Okay, he's finally at rest. . . . ' I felt relieved that he was finally at peace, because I had done all I could."[63]

NOTES

[a]Perhaps it would be more useful to turn the question around and ask, under what circumstances is suicide rational. G. C. Graber argues that suicide is rationally justified "if a reasonable appraisal of the situation reveals that one is really better off dead" (Graber, 65).

[b]One historical impetus for this view is that both European (and European-colonized) states and the Catholic Church inflicted severe penalties for suicide (confiscation of property and unconsecrated burial, respectively) unless the deceased was insane. Thus, there was a tendency for sympathetic coroners (and later, psychiatrists) to find that, in English common-law language, the individual killed himself "while the balance of his mind was disturbed."

And while suicide is associated with mental illness in the West, "In numerous other . . . non-Western cultures the association of suicide with mental illness seems to be much less strong, and in some cultures is quite low" (Battin, *Issues*, 6). These are societies where philosophic or institutional suicide is common, e.g., Japan, or India (Farberow, 1975).

It is also cautionary to remember that until 1973 homosexuality was classified as a psychiatric pathology—a mental disease in need of treatment—by the American Psychiatric Association.

[c]One major problem with identifying potential suicides is that any current screening test or combination of tests that picks up a significant number of people intending suicide generates too many "false positives." This is a general problem in the use of screening tests for uncommon occurrences (Rosen, 1954). Thus, any currently available screen that will detect, say, 80 out of 100 future suicides will also (besides missing 20 suicides) wrongly identify many nonsuicidal people as suicidal for each correct identification.

The problem is one of designing tests with both high selectivity and high sensitivity. A highly selective screen is one that distinguishes people intending suicide from all others. An example of a selective screen population might be the set of all people standing on the edge of a cliff, holding a gun to their head. A large fraction of such people are probably suicidal; there will be few false positives. The difficulty with such a selective screen is that it is not very sensitive—it might only pick up one suicide in a thousand since few meet the screen's criteria.

On the other hand, a highly sensitive filter, for example, one that picks out all people who are one or more of the following—schizophrenic, depressed, alcoholic, lonely, hopeless, elderly, a psychiatrist or female physician, have made a previous attempt, or have a family history of suicide—might pick up 90 percent of suicides, but also scores of nonsuicidal people for each genuinely suicidal one. Such a sensitive test is too unselective to be very useful.

[d]Older antidepressants—TCAs (tricyclic antidepressants) and MAOIs (mono amine oxidase inhibitors)—are both more toxic and have significant unpleasant side effects; thus patients tend to take them in subtherapeutic doses. As a result, such people are more likely to remain depressed *and* have a highly lethal drug available for a suicidal overdose.

More recent SSRI (serotonin-specific re-uptake inhibitor) drugs are not much more effective than TCAs, but are safer and have fewer side effects (Montgomery, 1995). In late 1998 a new class of drug began clinical testing. These drugs block a poorly understood brain chemical called "substance P" that seems to be associated with emotion.

[e]Despite its checkered history, ECT (electro-convulsive threapy; electric shock) is the single most effective treatment for major depression. It's not the first thing to do, but is certainly worth trying for people for whom other methods have failed to help (*SAM*, 9).

[f]Most use a professional cleaning service, but find that they need to scrub the area again (Van-Dongen, 1991).

8
IS SUICIDE APPROPRIATE?
IS INTERVENTION APPROPRIATE?
WHO DECIDES?

●

It is not a thing to do while one is not in one's best mind. Never kill
yourself while you are suicidal.

—Edwin Shneidman[1]

Never do today what you can put off till tomorrow. Delay may give
clearer light as to what is best to be done.

—Aaron Burr

WHEN IS SUICIDE JUSTIFIED?

People have been arguing this question for millennia. There are about one
thousand books in print on suicide in the United States. Sherwin Nuland,
physician and author of *How We Die*, puts it well when he says, "The importance of airing different viewpoints rests not in the probability that a stable consensus will ever be reached, but in the recognition that it will not. It
is by studying the shades of opinion expressed in such discussions that we
become aware of considerations in decision-making that may never have
weighed in our soul-searching."[2]

Some people think suicide is never justified. A minority argue the merits
of suicide: It allows one to choose (as much as one can choose these things)
the time, place, manner, cause, purpose, and painfulness of death,[3] and pro-

ponents maintain that it is a decision each individual must make.[4] Most of us would understand why someone might prefer suicide as opposed to unceasing and unbearable pain.[a] Many would, I think, agree with Nuland when he says, "Taking one's own life is almost always the wrong thing to do. There are two circumstances, however, in which that may not be so. Those two are the unendurable infirmities of a crippling old age and the final devastations of a terminal disease."[5]

As philosopher Richard W. Momeyer puts it,

> Suicide is an act that does not occur in a vacuum, and it is ordinarily not without very serious and often devastating consequences for others. Even if it can be claimed as a right, it is not inappropriate that one be very careful to assure that exercising that right is the right thing to do. Having a right to do something provides us some entitlement to do it; it does not assure that doing it is right. It is appropriate to set very high standards of justification for exercising a right to suicide, given how often it is undertaken in an ill-considered manner, how frequently suiciders suffer diminished competence from mental illness, and how widespread and serious are the consequences for others.[6]

INTERVENTION IN SUICIDE

There seem to be two central questions about intervention to stop suicide: (1) Under what (if any) circumstances, and (2) by what means, is it appropriate?

Most people would argue that suicide intervention is justified in the absence of terminal illness. This is especially true if the potential suicide is young; their thinking is impaired[b] by depression, alcohol, or other drugs; they are ambivalent; or there's likelihood of "improvement," that is, a change of mind or condition. On the other hand, about two-thirds of Americans feel that suicide or euthanasia is sometimes proper for people who are dying.[7]

However, the issue becomes less clear when one asks, "For how long, and by what methods, may the exercise of the right to suicide be limited?" For example, should someone be locked up or drugged[c] solely because they may commit suicide? If so, for how long? In the United States,

> … suicidal persons are the only people who may be held against their will for weeks, months, or even years on the sole basis of what they "might" do in the future rather than what they have done in the past—and not to others but to themselves. One Arizona woman spent fifty-eight years without comprehensive review in a state mental hospital after a suicide attempt. "If a sociologist predicted that a person was 80 percent likely to commit a felonious act, no law would permit his confinement," comment the authors of an article on "Civil Commitment of the Mentally Ill: Theories and Procedures" in the *Harvard Law Review*. "On the other hand, if a psychiatrist testified that a person was mentally ill and 80 percent likely to commit a dangerous act, the patient would be committed."[8]

The Supreme Court, in its wisdom, has seen fit to provide weaker safeguards of due process and standards of proof in civil commitment cases than in criminal cases. In criminal cases the standard of proof for guilt is "beyond a reasonable doubt" and the belief is that it's better for a guilty person to go free than for an innocent one to be unjustly imprisoned. In spite of this principle, the Supreme Court does not "appear to believe, as it does in criminal cases, that it is better for a mentally ill person to go free than for a normal individual to be committed."[9]

Whether someone is involuntarily hospitalized depends, to a substantial extent, on social factors: age, sex, status—older, female, and lower socioeconomic-class people are more likely to be involuntarily committed[10]—and whether the patient has a lawyer at the commitment proceedings.[11]

In addition, psychiatrists consistently overestimate the danger to and by the patient in commitment hearings. This is not surprising, since (1) psychiatrists' ability to accurately predict who will commit suicide is small, and (2) the consequences to the psychiatrist, and (perhaps) to the patient, are much more severe if a released patient commits suicide than if the psychiatrist mistakenly hospitalizes someone.[12] And, if the patient kills himself while hospitalized, this can be cited as evidence of the need for the hospitalization, however regrettable the outcome.

Is ambivalence about suicide—for example, seeking help, calling a hotline, or standing on a ledge—sufficient grounds for intervention? Ambivalence means wanting, or being undecided between, two mutually exclusive things, in this case, life and death. The problem with suicide is that we can go from life to death, but not from death to life; a hundred decisions for life are overcome by a single one for death. One can argue that what suicides want is not death but the end to their pain, however it be achieved, and that if life equals pain then death equals end-of-pain. The results, however, are the same.

> Ambivalence toward suicide is indicated by the fact that three-fourths of all suicides communicate their intentions, often with the hope that something will be done to make their suicide unnecessary. In a high proportion of cases, such communications are varied, repeated, and expressed to more than one individual. Studies of those who have survived a serious suicide attempt have revealed that a fantasy of being rescued is frequently present.[13]

But even if we can agree that intervention is sometimes appropriate, what are we to do with the suicidal people who do *not* agree? May we force them to take mind-altering drugs? For how long? Electroshock? How many times? Lock them up? For how many days, months, years? By what right may we continue to intervene in the face of someone's persistent demand to make the decision as to the time and manner of their death? Ultimately the question cannot be evaded: Whose life is it? As Frederick Ellis eloquently puts it, "[Death] is my final civil liberty, and I do not choose to surrender it to the state, a church or a physician."[14]

Does Hospitalization Help?

In the heat of this argument, an important question is often overlooked: Does hospitalization help? The answer is far from clear. Suicide rates in psychiatric hospitals are roughly five times higher than they are on the outside,[15] and there have been suicide epidemics inside such institutions.[16] Some of the antisuicide regimens, such as twenty-four-hour-a-day watch or isolation, may be terrifying or enraging to the patient/prisoner, and may be imposed because of the staff's fear of being accused of not having done everything possible to prevent a potential suicide.

Some evidence that has been uncritically used to support hospitalization is subject to other interpretations. For example, one study found that a significant number of hospitalized mental patients killed themselves while temporarily at home on leave. This was taken to mean that it was the return to the scene and situation at home that triggered the suicide.[17] The notion that an unwillingness to go back to the hospital might have been the catalyst was never examined.

Similarly, the fact that 7 percent of a group of recently released psychiatric patients killed themselves was used to make a case for hospitalization.[18] But, as psychiatrist Herbert Hendin notes,

> There is as much justification for concluding that … the experience of hospitalization contributed to the suicide as there is for maintaining that hospitalization would have prevented it. … For some acutely suicidal patients it may be life saving. … Other suicidal patients are made more upset by their confinement. The decision for hospitalization is too often made, not on the basis of a realistic evaluation of whether it will help a particular patient, but because therapists want to shift the responsibility for a possible suicide onto an institution.[19]

DISCOMFORT WITH SUICIDE

We're all going to die eventually; the only uncertainties are when and how. Why, then, does suicide bother us in a way and to a degree that numerically greater—and easier to prevent—causes of death, like automobile wrecks (40,000 to 50,000 per year) or cigarette smoking (400,000 per year) don't? Writer Jacques Choron speculates,

> It has been suggested that suicide "troubles and appalls us because it so intransigently rejects our deeply held conviction that life must be worth living."[20]

While there is undoubtedly some truth in this, in more cases than one would like to admit the reason for the shock may not be the challenges to the belief that life is good, but the fact that one is not really quite sure that it is. As . . . [Spanish philosopher] Jose Ortega y Gasset noted, for most people at all times "life" meant limitation, obligation, dependence, and oppression. They go on living simply because they happen to have been born, sustained by the force of habit, sometimes out of curiosity or vague hopes for a better future, and because they are afraid of the alternative—death.[21] But the suicide seems to have conquered this fear. Thus he confirms not only the suspicion that life may not be the highest good but the one that death may not be the greatest evil.[22]

Choron goes on to ask,

Should not the multitudes who die painfully and miserably each year be allowed to decide for themselves what is best for them? Moreover, it would be interesting to ascertain how many among physicians, whose suicide rate is many times that of the average population, are actually euthanasic suicides, due to the discovery of their own terminal illness, their knowledge of how prolonged and painful dying can be, and the easy accessibility of quick-acting lethal drugs.[23]

Good question. Consider these statistics: about 3 percent of male and 6.5 percent of female U.S. physicians' deaths in 1986 were suicides;[24] 35 percent of premature deaths among physicians were due to suicide;[25] suicide is the leading cause of death for physicians under 40 years old;[26] and the suicide rate for psychiatrists is almost twice that for other doctors.[27]

Data from Australia also show moderately elevated suicide rates for male physicians, and substantially higher rates for female doctors.[28] And in Switzerland, the problem is so severe that the life expectancy of female physicians is ten years less than that of the general female population.[29]

NOTES

[a]Physical pain should almost never be severe enough that suicide is chosen—but it often is. While some dying patients kill themselves in order to achieve a sense of dignity, self-determination, and control over their lives, even in terminal illness "persistent and intense suicide thinking is rare in the absence of depression or of uncontrolled physical symptoms such as pain" (Breitbart, 1990a). Despite the availability of effective drugs, a majority of medical patients who committed suicide had inadequately controlled severe pain (Bolund, 1985).

The unwillingness of too many physicians to provide adequate pain medication, even to dying people, is well documented—and inexcusable: "The most common reason for unrelieved pain in U.S. hospitals is the failure of staff to routinely assess pain and pain relief" (American Pain Society, 1992). Seventy-six percent of cancer specialists expressed similar views (Von Roenn, 1993).

There have been attempts to teach physicians better pain management, but this has not been a generally high priority. In my opinion, this problem will not go away as long as pain-medication decisions remain in the hands of the physician rather than the patient.

[b]However, this "limited-paternalist" argument—that someone else can decide what is in a person's best interests when the latter's thinking is impaired—can be turned around to *require* euthanasia when death is seen to be in the person's interest.

[c]And nothing has only one effect. For example, haloperidol (Haldol) is a drug widely used with schizophrenic or psychotic patients. Because of its sedative effects, it's often the drug of choice to control aggressive or agitated behavior. However, following large doses, serious side effects (i.e., not the effects one wants) are common: "Herein is an example of a medication administered as a modality of psychiatric therapy that has possible side reactions that sound like a symptomatic litany of a major disease" (Tedeschi, 1206-07).

9
ASSISTED SUICIDE AND TERMINAL ILLNESS

•

Whereas a prolonged life is not necessarily better, a prolonged death is necessarily worse.

—Seneca

I believe often that death is good medical treatment because it can achieve what all the medical advances and technology cannot achieve today, and that is stop the suffering of the patient.

—Christiaan Barnard[1]

PROLONGED DYING

Dying has changed drastically over the last century. In 1900 the life expectancy in the United States was forty-seven years; by the mid-1990s it had risen to seventy-seven. Whereas, in earlier times, people typically died quickly from infectious disease or infections following injury, now most Americans are living long enough to develop degenerative diseases: heart disease, diabetes, stroke, cancer. Now, 70 to 80 percent of us will die of something we have for months or even years.[2]

Four out of five Americans now die in an institution: hospital, nursing home, or other extended-care facility in which, typically, patients forfeit control over what to wear, when to eat, and when to take medicines, for example. Furthermore, they almost inevitably lose substantial privacy—intimate body parts are examined, highly personal facts are written down, and someone they have never seen before may occupy the next bed. Finally, trust must be placed in strangers selected by the institution: Care is given by professional experts who might well be, and who frequently are, substituted freely for one another to accommodate work schedules and institutional needs. All of these factors serve to isolate patients, rob them of their individuality, foster dependence, and diminish self-respect and self confidence, even when illness, medication, and surgery have not already had these effects.[3]

In addition, the infrequency of home deaths has drawn a curtain of ignorance around dying, which make it easier to misunderstand and—up to the point of personal involvement—neglect the process.

Medical ability to maintain hopeless life has increased tremendously. Social critic Ivan Illich calls this "managed maintenance of life on high levels of sublethal illness" the "ultimate evil" of medical progress.[4] We're still sorting out the individual, social, and medical consequences of the widespread shift from acute to chronic disease, from dying at home to dying in a hospital,[5] from dying quickly to dying slowly. Illness-driven suicide and euthanasia are two of these consequences.

Between 1920 and 1993, 519 cases of mercy killing were recorded in the United States. Ninety-two percent of these have occurred since 1973,[6] suggesting one response to prolonged, high-tech dying—or to the fear of it.

The frequency of suicide among the terminally ill is in dispute. Studies of cancer patients have found suicide rates ranging from the same as to ten times that of the rate among the general population.[7] The reported rates are probably substantial underestimates, however, since families are relatively unlikely to confess to a suicide and physicians or medical examiners unlikely to investigate deaths under these circumstances. In addition, dying patients may be unwilling to admit to suicidal thoughts or plans for fear of being classified as "depressed" and being deprived of pain-relieving drugs.[8]

ASSISTED SUICIDE AND EUTHANASIA

Much has been written on the topic of assisted suicide and euthanasia, and I will add only a few passing observations.

First, there is a good deal of confusion about language, particularly concerning the terms "assisted suicide" and "euthanasia." Though they are often used interchangeably, in this book the distinction is that in assisted suicide, while someone else provides the lethal agent, the person who is dying administers it; in euthanasia, someone else does the administration.

Assisted suicide is probably easier on the assistant's conscience than euthanasia and does decrease the possibility of misunderstanding or abuses; however, it also substantially increases the chance of other errors, such as the patient falling asleep before swallowing a lethal dose or vomiting it up. On the other hand, where a dying patient has made the request for such help clear, but has lapsed into physical or mental inability to act, assisted suicide would no longer be an option.

Euthanasia may be voluntary, where the person dying has made a request for it. It may be nonvoluntary, where a person who has not made her wishes on this matter known is put to death; such people are often in a coma. "Involuntary euthanasia" might be the oxymoronic term if the person dying had expressed opposition to such a procedure. The more common word for this is murder.

Assistance may be active, for example, administering a lethal injection; or passive, such as disconnecting someone from life-support apparatus. Thus, Dr. Jack Kevorkian has carried out, so far, passive-assisted suicides. He has, in most cases, set up a carbon monoxide apparatus that requires the patient to open a valve to start the gas flow. (His first three assisted suicides were accomplished by means of intravenous potassium as the lethal agent. However, starting an IV line is not always easy, which may be why Kevorkian subsequently switched to carbon monoxide.)

Some people believe there is an ethical or moral difference between active and passive euthanasia.[9] However, as Lonny Shavelson notes, "the major difference today between passive and active euthanasia is that people who believe in passive euthanasia are allowed to have it; for those who would choose active euthanasia, it is forbidden."[10] Or, in the words of Dr. Pieter

Admiraal, "the only thing passive about passive euthanasia, is the physician."[11]

While there is an obvious difference between "killing" and "allowing to die," those who feel that there is a clear moral distinction between the two seem to be saying that we may allow an evil—choosing to die—by acts of omission, but may not commit the identical evil by acts of commission. Would it then be morally acceptable to stay aboard a sinking ship to make room for someone else in a lifeboat, but not to jump out of a lifeboat for the same purpose? Why is it legal and ethical to act on a terminally ill patient's request to turn off her ventilator, but illegal and unethical to carry out the same patient's request for an overdose of morphine? Is it not as much a choice to die from asphyxia or cancer as from an overdose? In the ethical triad of intent, method, and result, when the intent and result of passive (for example, removing life support) and active (for example, administering a lethal overdose) euthanasia are the same, it seems obtuse to ignore those similarities and focus on differences of method.

I would suggest that to turn off life-support and let the patient die "naturally" hours or days later is often the immoral act. If a dying person's condition is so hopeless or painful that withdrawal of life-support is appropriate, then the most merciful action is that which brings this life to an immediate end. In Margaret Battin's words, "To impose 'mercy' on someone who insists that despite his or her suffering life is still valuable to him or her would hardly be mercy; to withhold mercy from someone who pleads for it, on the basis that his or her life could still be worthwhile for him or her, is insensitive and cruel."[12]

"ACTIVE" VERSUS "PASSIVE" METHODS OF DYING

While the ethical arguments when someone in a coma has not made their desire for (or disapproval of) an expedited death known are more complex than in assisted suicide, the distinctions between "active" and "passive" are solely differences of method rather than intent, result, or consent, and of little independent ethical interest.

Except that method matters. When a physician removes food and water IVs from a terminal patient, fully expecting and intending that the patient will die within a few hours or days as a result of this action, why does he or she not administer a lethal drug and put an end to the suffering? What is the lofty ethical principle being preserved here? Keeping one's hands clean? The dog pound treats injured strays better.

In fairness to physicians, a major reason for their aversion to "actively" hasten death is, I think, that it remains illegal to do so. As a result, a tormented patient is at the mercy of the doctor's willingness to take risks, put his or her own career on the line, and perhaps go to jail. In 1991 Dr. Timothy Quill, professor of medicine and psychiatry at the University of Rochester Medical School, gave a dying patient a prescription for a lethal quantity of barbiturates knowing that she intended to kill herself with them. After Quill bravely (or foolishly) wrote about it in a letter to the *New England Journal of Medicine*,[13]: Rochester, New York, prosecutor Howard Relin ("the People") tried to get a grand jury indictment on a charge of assisting a suicide, which carries a five- to fifteen-year prison sentence. The grand jury (the People) refused.

Eleven physicians since 1935 have been charged with murder in mercy-killings (eight of these since 1980); most were acquitted, one committed suicide, none served prison time.[14] Still, such legal sanctions discourage physicians from both assisted suicide and euthanasia even when all parties involved agree that it would be the right, as well as the best, thing to do.

And while individual doctors may carry out assisted suicide or euthanasia, as Anthony Flew notes, "it is entirely wrong to expect the members of one profession as a regular matter of course to jeopardize their whole careers by breaking the criminal law in order to save the rest of us the labour . . . of changing that law."[15]

Flew makes a valid point. Nevertheless, I find the withdrawal of food and water inexcusably cruel: It is the socially acceptable torture of the helpless due to the moral cowardice of legislators, physicians, and the public.

RIGHT TO REFUSE MEDICAL TREATMENT

Oddly, in the midst of the heated assisted-suicide debate, there is little discussion of the generally accepted, and legally undisputed, right to refuse medical treatment, even when the refusal will directly lead to death.[a]

For example, the death of about one in five kidney dialysis ("artificial kidney") patients is due to quitting dialysis[16]—knowing that they will die within two weeks as a result of their decision.[b] The average survival time is a little over a week.[17]

There are also large numbers who refuse blood transfusions, chemotherapy, or surgery for a variety of personal or religious reasons. The ethical distinction between refusing treatment in order to die and suicide (assisted or not) for the same purpose is not apparent.

Nevertheless, treatment refusal often does not lead to a "good" death: one that is painless, dignified, conscious, and leaves time to review one's life and say good-byes. Moreover, the definition of a "good" death varies from one person to the next. For some people it is the least painful, for some it is the fastest, for some it is the most delayed, for some it is the least disfiguring, for some it is that which best allows final conscious time with family and friends. These preferences provide all the more reason to respect the autonomy and choices of each individual.

In the United States treatment refusal is the only legally protected method for choosing death. It is available to (legally) competent and (indirectly, through proxy) noncompetent individuals. This right was asserted by courts at least as early as 1914: "Every human being of adult years and sound mind has a right to determine what shall be done with his own body."[18] More recently, in *Griswold v. Connecticut* and *Roe v. Wade*, the U.S. Supreme Court reached similar conclusions, based on a constitutional right to privacy.

The Ninth Circuit Court of Appeals used this as the basis for overturning the Washington State ban on assisted suicide. A month later, in April 1996, the Second Circuit Court of Appeals overturned New York's ban on assisted suicide, but used the "equal protection" clause of the Fourteenth Amendment as the rationale, noting that terminally ill people who were on life-support could legally "pull the plug," while those not on life-support had no similar option. In June 1997, the Supreme Court reversed the two Appeals Court decisions and ruled that there is no constitutional right to physician-assisted suicide. They seem to have been unpersuaded by the part of the (New Jersey Supreme Court) *Quinlan* (1976) decision that stated:

> Constitutional protection from criminal prosecution where death is accelerated by termination of medical treatment pursuant to right of privacy extends to third parties whose action is necessary to effectuate the exercise of that right where the patients themselves would not be subject to prosecution or the third parties are charged as accessories to an act which could not be a crime.[19]

Thus it remains legal to pull the plug on a respirator and let a permanently comatose patient suffocate, but a crime—murder—to end that same life by a deliberate overdose of painkiller.

"NATURAL" PROCESS VERSUS "ARTIFICIAL" INTERVENTION

The assertion has been made that there is a crucial difference between "pulling the plug" and deliberate overdose: One consists of letting a "natural" process continue while the other is an "artificial" interference with that process. This claim is absurd. Why is it only ethical to die "naturally," after a long illness filled with highly unnatural life-extending medical procedures? Why is it unethical to choose to die swiftly and painlessly?

Scottish philosopher David Hume addressed the theological form of this argument around 1750:

> Were the disposal of human life so much reserved as the peculiar province of the Almighty that it were an encroachment on his right, for men to dispose of their own lives; it would be equally criminal to act for the preservation of life as for its destruction. If I turn aside a stone which is falling upon my head, I disturb the course of nature, and I invade the peculiar province of the Almighty by lengthening out my life beyond the period which by the general laws of matter and motion He had assigned it.[20c]

Thus the argument by "natural physical law" fails: If one may intervene in *some* natural laws, one may intervene in others; and suicide cannot be opposed on these grounds. That is, one must also show that some laws of nature, but not others, should be left alone.

In any case, the natural law argument is fundamentally flawed, since it claims the existence of a natural physical law (in this case, that suicide is contrary to the "law of self-preservation") as the justification to enforce obedience to that same law. However, to the extent that what is called a natural law really is one, it doesn't need legislative or moral reinforcement: The law of gravity seems to work equally well with or without human approval.

Consequences of Legalizing Assisted Suicide

There are numerous cases of desperate, hospitalized people carrying out desperate suicides. In one instance, a man dying of cancer, immobilized in a frame and partly paralyzed, poured lighter fluid on his chest and ignited it. In another case, "one terminally ill seventy-eight-year-old, who was intubated and connected to life-support systems despite repeated requests to be left alone to die, switched off his own ventilator during the night and suffocated. He left a final message for his attending physician: 'Death is not the enemy, doctor. Inhumanity is.'"[21]

In Richard Momeyer's words,

> A decent society finds ways of caring for those even in the most extreme distress; rarely is it the case that such caring is best done by encouraging death, either through suicide or euthanasia. Rarely, I said, but not never. For neither is it the case that in a decent society we would burden those for whom death is in their best interest with the sole responsibility for ending their lives, any more than we burden everyone with sole responsibility for sustaining their lives when this is best.[22]

One of the ironic and presumably unintended results of making assisted suicide illegal is the pressure it puts on the old, infirm, and ill to kill themselves while they are still able to do so, and sooner than they would if they could count on help. Part of author Arthur Koestler's[d] suicide letter addresses this issue: "After a more or less steady physical decline over the last years, the process has now reached an acute state with added complications which make it advisable to seek self-deliverance now, before I become incapable of making the necessary arrangements."[23] Nobel physicist Percy Bridgman, dying from cancer, shot himself after his physician refused to help him die. He left the following note: "It isn't decent for society to make a man do this thing himself. Probably this is the last day I will be able to do it myself."[24]

Koestler's and Bridgman's concern was not without foundation: Sometimes people wait too long. AIDS patients are particularly prone to suicide, but doctors who have many AIDS patients say that they have often seen these people prepare to kill themselves, but then become demented from their disease and thus unable to carry out their plans.[25]

What should physicians do under these circumstances? Margaret Battin, a medical ethicist, argues:

> The physician's obligation is not only to respect the patient's choices, but also to make it possible for the patient to act upon those choices. This means supplying the knowledge and equipment to enable the person to stay alive, if he or she so chooses. . . . But it may also mean providing the knowledge, equipment, and help to enable the patient to die, if that is his or her choice. . . . [26] To restrict the right to die to the mere right to refuse unwanted medical treatment and so be "allowed" to die . . . is an indefensible truncation of the more basic right to choose one's death in accordance with one's own values.[27]

On the other hand, the capability of committing suicide sometimes decreases the perceived need to do so prematurely. In 1994, George Kingsley was a forty-eight-year-old man with AIDS. He collected the pills he intended to use and gave away many of his possessions: "[Having the means to kill myself] has made my every day better, much much better," he said. "It has diminished my horror, as though I was facing an enemy on a battlefield stark naked and now I have armor."[28]

Data from the Netherlands are consistent with this idea. Twenty-two percent (29 out of 131) of a group of AIDS patients died by physician-assisted suicide (PAS) or euthanasia, compared to about 2 percent of all deaths. Based on an examination of each case, "[There was not] any substantial shortening of life by euthanasia/PAS . . . most of these patients would have died naturally within one month."[29]

When physicians singlemindedly fight against death, it is, too often, at the expense of their equally important obligation to ease suffering. It is a medical atavism based on an acute-illness model that doesn't apply: "If we can pull them through this crisis, they'll recover sufficiently to have a worthwhile remaining life." In many situations, they won't. The use of so-called "heroic" measures to maintain and resuscitate a terminally ill person who wants to die can better be described as "killing slowly and without mercy."

PHYSICIANS' AND NURSES' VIEWS

From Australia comes an eloquent Open Letter to the State Premier (Governor) of Victoria:

> Each of us who has signed this letter has personal experience of treating terminally ill patients whose condition has moved them to ask for assistance in suicide and each of us has, on occasion, after deep thought and lengthy discussion, helped such a patient to die. . . . We have assisted patients to end their lives and we know others who have. We believe that we have acted in the best tradition of medical ethics, offering our patients relief from pain and suffering in circumstances where it would have been an act of cruelty to deny them. We respect life. All of our professional training and work deepens that respect. However, the reality is that there are some patients who are beset by physical and mental suffering which is beyond the reach of even our most sophisticated efforts at control. When such patients clearly and repeatedly express a rational plea for help, it is out of respect for them that we have felt compelled to act. However, as long as the law maintains that our behaviour is criminal, there will be numerous patients who will die in unnecessary misery. There are many who cry out for help and who are denied it by doctors who may sympathise with their plight but who are unwilling to break the law. There are some who attempt to end their lives unaided and who botch the attempt and survive

with their misery redoubled. There are others who may be helped by a doctor but who, for fear of incriminating their friends and family, must choose to die alone without the chance to say farewell.

Increasing numbers of doctors and nurses throughout the world have reached similar conclusions. The *Medical Journal of Australia* published a 1988 survey that found 60 percent of physicians in Victoria wanted the law changed to decriminalize assisted suicide under some circumstances; 78 percent of nurses in Victoria agreed. Of those Australian doctors who treated incurably ill adult patients, 29 percent had "actively" hastened the death of some who had asked to die; 80 percent had done this more than once.[30]

In another state, New South Wales and the Australian Capital Territory, almost half of 2,000 surveyed physicians had been asked to carry out euthanasia; 28 percent had done so.[31]

A survey of California physicians arrived at generally similar numbers, with 23 percent of doctors having quickened a patient's death.[32] Among San Francisco Bay area doctors with substantial AIDS practices, it was 53 percent.[33] A more recent national sampling found 7 percent of U.S. physicians had written lethal prescriptions or given lethal injections. Most had done so infrequently, but one reported assisting 175 deaths.[34]

Nurses act in much the same way. Seventeen percent (141 in 852) of American critical-care nurses surveyed had been asked by patients and/or patients' families to carry out euthanasia (which included high doses of pain medication that results in both pain control and life shortening, but excluded withdrawal of life-support equipment); 16 percent (129) had done so, and an additional 4 percent (39) said they had hastened patients' deaths by withholding life-sustaining treatment ordered by a physician. Most said they had done these three or fewer times; however 5 percent said they had done so twenty or more times.[35]

In Canada, 44 percent of surveyed physicians said that physician-administered euthanasia was sometimes justified; 51 percent said that the law should be changed to permit patient-requested active euthanasia.[36]

In the Netherlands, where both euthanasia and assisted suicide have been more or less openly practiced since 1973, physician approval is around 80 to 90 percent.[37]

In the United States, medical opinion is closely divided. A 1993 survey of 938 doctors in Washington State[38] found that half supported physician-assisted suicide in some cases, while 39 percent said it was never justified. Forty-two percent felt that it was acceptable for the physician, rather than the patient, to administer the lethal overdose, while 48 percent said it was not.[e] Interestingly, psychiatrists were most likely to support physician-assisted suicide; cancer specialists least likely. Female doctors were significantly more favorable toward assisted suicide than were their male colleagues. One wonders if psychiatrists and female physicians might also be higher in measures of empathy and compassion.[39] A more recent study, published in 1996,[40] found increased physician support. Sixty percent of the Oregon doctors most likely to work with terminally ill patients (out of 2,761 responses) favored physician-assisted suicide under some circumstances. Older doctors were more approving than younger ones; perhaps they are more realistic about the limits of medicine. Catholics, nondenominational Christians, and Mormons were less likely to approve than were other religious affiliations. Twenty-one percent of these doctors had been asked to write a prescription for a lethal drug dose in the previous year; 7 percent had done so.

Meanwhile in Michigan, 77 percent of doctors felt that physician-assisted suicide should either be explicitly legalized (40 percent) or that there should be no law at all concerning it (37 percent); only 17 percent said it should be illegal. Thirty-five percent said that they might carry out such assistance, if legal.[41] Among Michigan cancer specialists, 18 percent admitted to assisting in suicide(s) and 4 percent to carrying out euthanasia.[42]

The American Medical Association's governing body recently reaffirmed its longstanding opposition to physician-assisted suicide[43]—while simultaneously respecting a dying patient's wishes concerning treatment *and* maintaining the position that a doctor may withdraw all life-support treatment, including food and water, from a patient who is in an irreversible coma.[44] To hold these views simultaneously is an impressive intellectual feat. However, there has been increasing protest: One delegate argued that the official AMA position "fails to respond to the crying need of our patients in prolonged agony." Another said he was amazed by the number of fellow doctors he had polled who had admitted assisting suicides.[45]

Significantly, a large majority—almost 90 percent—of doctors and nurses surveyed said that *they* would not want treatment if they had severe dementia or were in an irreversible coma. In the case of a possibly reversible coma, 70 percent of the nurses and half of the physicians said that they would not want treatment. In the words of the study's authors, "physicians and nurses, who have extensive exposure to hospitals and sick patients, are unlikely to wish aggressive treatment if they become terminally ill, demented, or are in a persistent vegetative state. Many would also decline aggressive care on the basis of age alone."[46]

Yet they are willing to inflict treatment on patients in comparable circumstances. In the hypothetical case of a demented elderly patient with life-threatening gastro-intestinal bleeding, physicians were more than twice as likely to want only palliative (comfort) care if *they* were the patient than if the patient were a stranger.[47]

This attitude is also seen in "active life termination" issues. In interviews with 155 cancer patients, 193 members of the public, and 355 oncologists (cancer doctors), about two-thirds of the patients and public thought doctor-assisted suicide or euthanasia were acceptable for patients in uncontrollable pain. Less than half of the physicians agreed; however, almost one in seven had carried out such acts.[48]

PUBLIC OPINION

Nonmedical opinion has also moved in the direction of increased acceptance of life termination. Barbara Logue has collected a series of public opinion surveys published between 1937 and 1991.[49] They all show a gradual, but remarkably steady, shift from about two to one opposed to euthanasia-assisted suicide to two to one in favor.

What is most striking about these data is that every multiyear poll shows increasing approval for every time interval. This was true irrespective of who (Gallup, Harris, Roper, General Social Surveys) carried out the survey or how the questions were worded. A typical survey question, from Harris polls between 1973 and 1985 is: "Do you think the patient who is terminally ill, with no cure in sight, ought to have the right to tell his doctor to put him out of his misery, or do you think this is wrong?" The response to this particular question went from 37 percent right and 53 percent wrong to 61 percent right and 36 percent wrong over those twelve years.[50] When these questions were asked only to the elderly, whose interest in such matters is least likely to be abstract or hypothetical, a similar pattern of increasing approval was also seen.[51]

The impetus for this shift has not come from the medical, legal, or political establishment, which has, in typical conservative fashion, generally resisted change. Rather, the pressure for change has been the result of the experiences of millions of the slowly dying, their families, and increasing numbers of their physicians.

NOTES

[a]There is debate about the boundaries, as when an adolescent refuses anti-cancer chemotherapy. "It is now the case that a child patient whose competence is in doubt will be found rational if he or she accepts the proposal to treat, but may be found incompetent if he or she disagrees" (Devereux, 1993).

[b]Since potassium buildup is one of the dangerous consequences of kidney failure, a dialysis-withdrawal patient could speed up his or her death by eating potassium-containing salt-substitutes (see the chapter on drugs) or high-potassium foods, like avocados.

About 23,000 Americans started long-term dialysis in 1983; only 6,000 received a kidney transplant, due to a lack of kidney donors. If you plan to kill yourself, it would be a thoughtful gesture to fill out an organ donor card beforehand.

[c]The essay from which this is quoted was not published until 1777, after Hume's death, and was promptly suppressed.

[d]Koestler's 1940 novel, Darkness at Noon, is, I think, the finest book about the Soviet Purge Trials of the 1930s. The main character's confession was quoted from memory in the Czech trials of the early 1950s by a doomed defendant who used it to simultaneously "confess" to imaginary crimes and to mock the proceedings.

[e]After considerable thought, I still fail to see any ethical basis for this distinction. If committing suicide is ever appropriate, then assistance (in such a case) would also seem appropriate. But then, I'm not administering the lethal dose.

10
THE MEDICAL SYSTEM IN TERMINAL ILLNESS

•

Life must go on.
I forget just why.

—Edna St. Vincent Millay

The driving force behind assisted suicide is, in large part, the failure of the medical system and some of its practitioners to deal caringly and compassionately with the dying. "Kevorkian is a symptom of a medical care system gone seriously wrong at the end of life," wrote George J. Annas, professor of health law at Boston University, recently in the *New England Journal of Medicine*.[1]

> "What's going on here is not that everyone in the U.S. wants to commit suicide," agrees Christine K. Cassel, chief of Internal Medicine at the University of Chicago Medical Center [and president of the American College of Physicians]. "What's going on is that people don't trust us anymore to take care of them when they're dying."[2]

With good reason. Sometimes treatment is worse than its absence, and patients become trapped in medical hell. Susan Cahill, a former ICU nurse, looking back, now says,

> In the name of life support, I did things that were much worse [than euthanasia], things I can't forget and for which I still can't for-

give myself. I wonder at the irony of it all: that they arrested Kervorkian for helping his patients find relief in death but not me for tormenting my patients as they declined and died. . . . Most of the time, these patients were too far gone to communicate, but one woman managed to write "Let me die" on a piece of paper. I didn't let her; I wasn't allowed to. . . . I used . . . high-tech tools on people who everyone knew couldn't be helped by them and who didn't want them used and asked to have them stopped. But I didn't stop. I helped prolong the agony of these patients' deaths. . . . I knew that that was what I was doing. I did this often, sometimes every day, and I did it with the blessing of the medical community and the law. . . . The continuing debate over Kevorkian seems ludicrous. The people who sought him out were fully informed about the consequence of their "treatment," unlike many of the people who became entrapped in the high-tech world of life support gone wrong. Too often I worked with patients who never had explained to them what the real repercussions of their treatments might be, even when such discussions weren't precluded by urgency. Why didn't someone arrest the health care professionals whose patients ended up strapped down and pierced with needles and tubes they didn't want?[3]

Let's look at one case, one man, one family.[4]

Earl Blaisdell, fifty-seven, had multiple sclerosis for eleven years. MS is a degenerative disease with no known cause or cure. It produces "multiple" lesions in the myelin sheath surrounding nerves, which interferes with the normal transmission of nerve impulses. Depending on the severity and location of the damage, symptoms may include: muscle weakness, spasm, or paralysis; pain; visual impairment; loss of bladder, bowel, and sexual function.

Some cases are mild. His was not.

"He was in absolute agony from this," said John Richert, director of the Multiple Sclerosis Center at Georgetown University Medical Center. "We were grasping at straws."[a]

After losing bladder control, a catheter was inserted, leaving him prey to recurrent infection. A few months later his large intestine was removed; waste products exited through a tube in his abdomen into a bag. Eventually, all he could move were his face, neck, and, to some degree, left hand. His muscles were so inflexible that it took one person to straighten and hold his legs while another person washed him.

He brought up the topic of killing himself and said to his wife of twenty-three years, Carmi, "If I could lay my hands on a gun, this would be all over." She was horrified and lied that his life insurance policy had a suicide exclusion.

He asked at least three people in one week to bring him a bottle of aspirin. They refused and told Carmi. As a result, his medicines were kept in another room and doled out to him; he was not permitted glassware, or use of non-battery-powered electrical appliances. He tried to reach Dr. Jack Kevorkian by telephone, but was unsuccessful. He asked for suicide help from his physician, Dr. William Benjamin III, who declined on "ethical" grounds, saying later, "I personally could not do it."

On May 21, 1994, Earl Blaisdell told Carmi, "I want you to know that I've just eaten my last meal." He had decided to starve himself to death. She tried to talk, cajole, and threaten him out of it. He was adamant. She cooked his favorite foods; he wouldn't touch them. Other family and friends tried as well, with similar results. "The dog ate very well," their daughter recalled.

Blaisdell thought he would die in a week. He received last rites on day twelve, but his pain-racked body kept going. Finally, he died. It took forty days.

He left a tape recording that he had secretly made two months before his death. In it he said, "I know you folks are trying to convince me that I should stay alive. But if you were layin' in this bed like this, you wouldn't do it either. . . . If I can find a way to get out of here, I'm going to try to find it. . . . Don't feel bad about me being gone. I'm plain better off." A year and a half later, his family still had mixed and contradictory feelings about his death.

"I miss him," says his thirty-five-year-old stepson, Michael. "I respected his choice, but I don't respect the way he died . . . he did it with strength, and a lot of will, but he took the coward's way out. . . . [I'm left with] the guilt—that somehow [I] could have done something to make life more meaningful to him so he wouldn't have felt he had to do what he did."

A few months later the family's old dog was "put to sleep." "We had him fifteen years," Carmi mused. "I said to myself: It took Brandy forty-five seconds to die. It took Earl forty days of starvation."

NOTES

[a]One of the straws he didn't grasp is made from hemp. Marijuana (cannabis) has been used with some success to treat the severe muscle spasms of MS. In the boundless wisdom of our political leaders, cannabis has been denied to MS victims, and also to people with glaucoma (it lowers intra-ocular pressure) and cancer patients (it decreases the nausea from anti-cancer drugs). It is even illegal to use this fearsome drug in clinical medical research, though it is one of the least toxic medicines in existence and there is no known case of a lethal overdose (Pettinger, 1988).

A 1990 survey found that 44 percent of oncologists had recommended smoking marijuana to their patients (Dolbin, 1991). This is the same drug that the DEA (Drug Enforcement Administration), overruling its own Chief Administrative Law judge, says has a high potential for abuse, lacks any accepted medical use, and is unsafe to use under medical supervision. Are all these physicians guilty of malpractice?

Some opponents of cannabis use argue that marijuana's therapeutic properties have been exaggerated and have not been proved by rigorous studies. Such studies are, of course, difficult to do when they have been made illegal.

11
PAIN CONTROL AND HOSPICE CARE

•

A long illness seems to be placed between life and death, in order
to make death a comfort both to those who die and to those who
remain.

—Jean de La Bruyere (1645-1696)

Death is a punishment to some, to others a gift, and to many a favor.

—Seneca

PAIN CONTROL

Opponents of assisted suicide assert that almost all dying patients can be
kept pain-free. Some hospice physicians go further, arguing that *any* failure in pain control is due to lack of knowledge on the part of the physician. Hospice physician David Cundiff says, "We have the knowledge and
the means to assure that no terminally ill person need beg for death to end
his or her suffering. Those patients who have asked me for assisted suicide
or euthanasia have changed their minds once I took care of their symptoms."[1]

Proponents of this view are certainly partly right. Pain control is inadequately and incompetently handled by many American physicians: Almost
half of cancer patients receive inadequate pain medication,[2] while 81 percent

of nurses surveyed agreed that "the most common form of narcotic abuse in caring for dying patients is undertreatment of pain."[3]

The problem is similar elsewhere. From Germany: "The majority of cancer patients . . . are not treated for pain at all, and that those patients who receive treatment are treated inadequately."[4] From France: "In the light of the high prevalence and the severity of pain among patients with cancer, the assessment and treatment of cancer pain in France remain inadequate, emphasizing the need for changes in patient care."[5] From Australia: "One-third of patients with terminal cancer in a general teaching hospital received inadequate pain relief; the reasons for this included lack of medical expertise in the use of analgesics for chronic cancer pain."[6] From Sweden: "About 30 percent of physicians believe that all patients have moderate to severe pain at the time of their death. Up to 78 percent of physicians and nurses believe that periodic severe pain is common in terminal cancer patients. . . . More than 50 percent of physicians and nurses admit that they have inadequate knowledge about pain evaluation techniques, newer analgesics and newer drug delivery systems."[7]

A large American study recently found that 42 percent of cancer patients were given inadequate pain medication.[8] Women, minorities, and people over seventy fared worst. The reasons for this are complex and debatable. In my opinion, they center on power, fear, and ignorance. First, physicians have the power to dispense or withhold pain medications and they are loath to surrender it, particularly to the least powerful of their patients. Second, they are on far safer legal ground if they undermedicate rather than overmedicate a patient. If a patient dies in agony there will be no consequences to the doctor, but if the patient uses prescribed pain medication to commit suicide, there may be legal or professional repercussions.[a] Third, most physicians' knowledge of pain control is inadequate.[9] In a study of medical texts on the care of cancer patients, only twenty out of five-thousand pages mentioned pain control, and until 1995, there were no questions on pain control on cancer-treatment specialty certification board exams.[10] And just five out of 126 American medical schools offer a course in care of the dying.[11] Fourth, ambiguous and sometimes contradictory state and federal prescribing regulations adversely affect treatment decisions. For example, the Medical Disciplinary Board of Washington State made the following policy statement in 1985: "The Board does not recognize repeated prescribing of controlled substances as appropriate therapy for chronic pain."[12] One might reasonably ask just what they would recommend instead. The board subsequently modified its position, but not before adding to the difficulties and uncertainties for physicians, who become understandably hesitant to prescribe narcotics in higher-than-normal dosage even when it's the only way to relieve severe pain.[13]: Finally, the exaggerated fear of narcotic addiction, despite evidence to the contrary,[14] is nowhere more irrational than with dying patients. Yet it continues to play a large part in pain medication decisions in the minds of legislators, physicians, and patients.

In the words of one cancer specialist, C. S. Hill, "Despite . . . the availability of appropriate opioid analgesics, inadequate pain management of cancer patients remains pervasive."[15]

> The methods used by boards/agencies to determine standards of practice for opioid use result in interpreting the language in these regulations based on myths, prejudices, and misinformation about opioids, and the unexamined belief that mere exposure of patients to these drugs causes psychological dependence (addiction) on them to all patients in all instances. Interpretation is also strongly influenced by a failure of regulatory and enforcement bodies to recognize their coequal obligation of making opioids readily available to those who need them for legitimate medical purposes, while simultaneously policing their diversion to illegitimate uses.[16]

While this problem is worldwide, there has been some progress. For example, in Norway administration of morphine to cancer patients increased *twelvefold* (per patient) between 1983 and 1990. Even so, examiners found that "several Norwegian hospitals still lag behind in this respect. Consequently much pain remains unrelieved."[17]

This is a truly bizarre situation: *every* study I've seen finds pain seriously undertreated; *every* expert recommends more use of pain medications. Yet the problem persists. Thus, Dr. Cundiff believes, with considerable justification, "We don't need a law to legalize assisted suicide, we need a law to teach doctors how to treat pain."[18]

HOSPICE AND SUICIDE

Partially as a result of this belief, hospice organizations are adamantly opposed to assisted suicide and euthanasia. In 1991 the National Hospice Organization stated that it

> " ... rejects the practice of voluntary euthanasia and assisted suicide in the care of the terminally ill ... [while] ... champion[ing] the ideals of relief of suffering, freedom of choice,"—as long as one of the choices is not suicide, assisted suicide, or euthanasia—"and death with dignity."[19]

But one of the results of this attitude is that a patient considering suicide may be unwilling to talk about it with hospice workers—the very people who might be in the best position to tell the patient about better alternatives.

Lonny Shavelson quotes a hospice nurse:

> We are instructed that if a hospice patient has a firm plan for suicide, we absolutely must intervene. This results at least in taking away medicines that he might use for an overdose, or hospitalizing the patient against his wishes and getting him psychiatric help. . . . Now let's face reality. Not everybody can have the death that we read about in a hospice textbook. . . . We are great at helping almost everybody along, both physically and emotionally, but we just can't fix everybody.[20]

And, whose decision should it be? Is there only one morally correct way to die? One dying patient's acerbic response to this hospice policy went to the heart of the matter: "If they don't approve of suicide, they don't have to kill themselves."[21]

Nor do all hospice doctors agree. Dr. Timothy Quill observes,

> Those who have witnessed difficult deaths of patients on hospice programs are not reassured by the glib assertion that we al-

ways know how to make death tolerable.[22] . . . The simplistic ethical rule that a doctor may not intentionally aid a patient's death falls apart in real clinical situations; it may inhibit prescribing sufficient pain-relieving medicine when a patient is near death, even if the patient is in agony.[23]

Reacting to the public debate following a recent assisted suicide carried out by Dr. Quill, a New York State Task Force on "Life and the Law" recommended "comfort care," which emphasizes relieving symptoms and enhancing the patient's quality of life, as the appropriate treatment for terminal patients.[24]

Dr. Quill agrees, up to a point:

Comfort care is a far cry from "not doing anything." It is completely analogous to intensive medical care, only in this circumstance the care is directed toward the person and his or her suffering, not the disease. Dying patients need our commitment to creatively problem-solve and support them no matter where their illness may go[25]. . . . [but] to think that people do not suffer in the process of dying is an illusion. . . . I am deeply troubled by our profession's unwillingness to openly acknowledge its limitations.[26]

Ira Byock, another member of the Academy of Hospice Physicians, offers a different perspective:

Dying is not simply suffering to be avoided. Once pain is skillfully controlled, most of our patients experience a surprisingly high degree of quality of life and see this time as a very precious time for them and their families. That is something I hear daily.[27]

He concedes that pain control fails with some patients, but suggests placing such people under general anesthesia until they die. It's not entirely clear what the point is. The permanently unconscious patient derives no benefit from being "alive." Indeed, it is ironic that, with permanent anesthesia, Byock is advocating the functional equivalent (to the patient) of euthanasia.

Under these circumstances, when death is imminent and inevitable, why must life be prolonged?

Dr. Byock feels that the family should help care for their comatose relative:

> [I]n the turning and washing . . . family members are called to honor the person departing . . . this type of continuing care is a mature, balanced expression for the inner turmoil—the grief—that we may feel.[28]

But, as one hospice nurse observes, ". . . harsh as it sounds, some families simply do not want to be caregivers. They do not relish the thought of weeks/months of bedbaths, pureed foods, and incontinence care. 'If I had wanted to be a nurse, I would have become one,' they tell me, and they mean it."[29]

A 1990 National Hospice Organization resolution says,

> Family members can often use this final period of peaceful pharmacologically-induced sleep to begin to separate from their loved one in preparation for the time of actual death. . . . [this] is less of a burden to the family and the caregivers than having to directly cause death as the only way to relieve the patient's suffering.[30]

While this may be true for some, it seems equally plausible that a chosen time of death provides the best opportunity for reconciliation, last words, and good-byes.

I would not presume to decide this for you.

ADDITIONAL PROBLEMS IN HOSPICE CARE

One of the problems with hospice care is that many people start it too late to get much benefit from it. Even though Medicare and most health insurance plans cover some form of hospice care for up to six months, the average survival time was less than one-fifth of that, 36 days; and one-sixth of the patients died within a week.[31] Part of this simply reflects the uncertainties of prognosis: 15 percent lived longer than 6 months, 8 percent longer than a year; but some of the lateness of hospice care is probably because neither patients nor doctors want to concede that a case is really terminal.

There are also legal problems due to the way many health insurance plans define "acute care": they will only pay for treatment intended to "cure." As a result, most (U.S.) hospice patients are treated at home—which requires someone else to live there and act as the primary caregiver. For similar legalistic reasons, people in hospital-based hospice are much more likely to receive unwanted "care" and resuscitation than those in home-hospice. For example, hospital-hospice will routinely treat pneumonia—including by traumatic intubation—and thus allow terminal patients to die of their underlying illness, say metastatic cancer.

LIMITS OF PAIN MANAGEMENT

Few people, on either side of this issue, would disagree with the principle or desirability of hospice or comfort care, but it is naive to imagine that all patients can be made comfortable through better pain management.

Some medical conditions generate pain that has proven to be resistant to control (short of sedation-to-unconsciousness). These include cancers that have invaded bone tissue, and elevated intracranial pressure.[32]

Side effects of high-dosage pain medication may include severe nausea, vomiting, inability to concentrate, nightmares, dizziness, or constipation. Nor is the relief of pain the same as the relief of suffering. Loss of physical or mental abilities, loss of friends, loss of a spouse, loss of interest in living, are all forms of suffering that pain medication won't help. What should be done when comfort care no longer works, suffering becomes unbearable, and a longed-for death is the only escape?

In Dr. Quill's words,

> None of these [dying patients] would want to die under other circumstances. But some reach the point where they would rather die than continue to live under the conditions imposed by their illness. We currently acknowledge this choice under some circumstances, for example when the patient rationally decides to stop a life-sustaining treatment like renal dialysis because of the burdens

of the illness and its treatments. Yet if there are no such treatments to stop, we do not allow other patients the same choice, even in the face of overwhelming and irreversible suffering.[33]

Even with satisfactory pain management, some dying patients choose suicide. But there are pitfalls, as we see in data from *Compassion in Dying*, a Washington State-based organization that counsels and aids terminal patients.

In their first 13 months, *Compassion* was contacted by 300 people who wanted help in dying. Forty-six met *Compassion*'s rather restrictive criteria (and died during this time). Twenty-two had cancer, 16 AIDS, 5 neurological diseases (MS [multiple sclerosis], ALS [amyotrophic lateral sclerosis]), and 3 lung diseases. Each of these people was terminally ill and confined to bed or chair. Pain was adequately controlled in all cases, and was not the primary reason for suicide in any patient.

Nine were in institutions (hospital, hospice, or nursing home) and unable to acquire drugs for suicide. Four of these people starved themselves to death.

The other 37 died at home. In 8 cases their physician would not prescribe a lethal drug. Three of these people killed themselves, two by starvation, one by gunshot; the other five died of their illness.

Of the 29 cases where their doctor did write a prescription for a lethal drug, five people died without using their prescription; the other 24 died from deliberate drug overdose. These drugs were barbiturates, narcotics, and/or benzodiazepines. Time-to-death averaged three hours and ranged from 25 minutes to 10 hours (a later patient survived 24.5 hours).

Thus, for those people confined to an institution or with a physician unwilling to prescribe a lethal quantity of drugs, the fraction achieving a chosen and relatively untraumatic death was low. Of those at home and having a cooperative doctor, none died of starvation—which took between 10 and 24 days in the people who used this means—or violent methods.

NOTES

[a]"Defensive medicine," also known as covering your ass, plays a large and increasing role in American medical (and nonmedical) decisions. There are, literally, thousands of examples. To pick just one at random, a recent study of emergency room physicians found that 55 percent of them attempted to resuscitate heart attack victims who they thought had no realistic expectation of meaningful recovery. And 98 percent said that they had attempted to revive patients who were in such condition that they (the physician) would not want to be treated. Why? Sixty-two percent cited fear of lawsuits or criticism by colleagues (Marco, 1997).

12
ADVANCE DIRECTIVES: LIVING WILL, POWER OF ATTORNEY FOR MEDICAL DECISIONS, AND DO NOT RESUSCITATE ORDERS

●

"If I ever get that way, shoot me," my uncle said after my father died in the hospital, hooked up to tubes and a respirator, pumped full of drugs, even though his brain was destroyed. The father we loved was gone, felled by a sudden heart attack. Yet he lingered a week in intensive care, a human vegetable covered by Medicare. In the end, all of us in the family were victims of the American Way of Dying.

—Abigail Trafford

LEGAL ASPECTS—OVERVIEW

Many people have heard of living wills, powers-of-attorney, and Do Not Resuscitate orders (collectively called "advance directives"), but most folks are unclear about their features and differences.

Living will or "Natural Death Act Declaration": a document that allows you to specify, in advance and in writing, what medical procedures you want and don't want, should you become unable to make those decisions. A living will is valid only *if* you are terminally ill[a] *and* incapable of making decisions.

Power-of-attorney: a document giving to someone you choose the authority to make medical decisions for you—treatment, no treatment, or what treatment—valid only *if* you are unable to make such decisions. You do not have to be terminally ill for this to take effect.

Emergency Medical System (EMS) Do Not Resuscitate (DNR) order: a document, valid in about half the states, that prohibits emergency medical technicians from attempting to resuscitate you if your heart stops or you stop breathing. This is usually, but not always, limited to terminal patients. There are also in-hospital DNRs, valid in every state, that direct the medical staff to not try resuscitation in case your heart or breathing stops.

There seem to be two driving forces behind the increasing public interest in, and use of, advance directives. First, I think, is fear of powerlessness in end-of-life situations, which might result in days or weeks or even years of hopeless "treatment." Second, is the concept of "responsible dying":[1] that we owe it to ourselves, our families, and our society to accept responsibility for making end-of-life decisions.

While most people are in favor of advance directives, only about 20 percent actually have them;[2] most of us prefer putting off unpleasant decisions.

> When the subject comes up, the language is vague ... what [Dr. Joanne] Lynn calls the "I don't want to end up like Aunt Esther" remark. Everyone nods in agreement, but the details of what happened to Aunt Esther, and why, get buried, as the cultural mechanism of denial kicks in and the family moves on to more pleasant subjects.[3]

Be aware that if you don't specify otherwise, hospital physicians will use the full arsenal of life-sustaining equipment and procedures. And, once you start down this road, it is difficult to stop (another version of the slippery-slope argument) because procedures tend to require more procedures to limit and correct the initial ones. In addition, you will probably not be in the best condition to make good decisions: severely ill and either sedated or in pain.

However, doing nothing is also a choice and has consequences. If you don't make these decisions—and too often if you do—someone else, often a family member but perhaps a stranger, will make them for you. "The toughest cases are when someone rolls into the intensive care unit, and we have no idea what they want," said Thomas Rainey, director of critical care medicine at Fairfax (Virginia) Hospital. "We will always err on the side of saving life, but those efforts are often brutal."[4]

Awareness of the limitations of advance directives is critical. First, it's important to understand that these documents are in effect only while you are incapacitated. If, and as long as, you are alert and coherent a living will and power-of-attorney are not in force; it doesn't matter what they say or don't say. Your physician is, in fact, forbidden to act on them. Decisions are (supposed to be) made by you, preferably in consultation with doctor, family, and friends. You don't need to be able to speak as long as you can communicate your coherence and intent.

Second, advance directives cannot be used to request or receive "active" help in dying. They merely *allow* you to die without further medical intervention. Thus they will not be useful in ending a terminal illness; at best they will just prevent the process from being artificially extended.

This sounds quite straightforward, but in the real world, many hospital patients are somewhere between mentally competent and incapacitated. In addition, the physician usually has the monopoly on medical knowledge and here, as elsewhere, knowledge is power.

Looking at things from the other side, while "patient empowerment" through advance directives and "informed consent" may be ethically necessary, it also leaves life-and-death decisions in the hands of people who are, often, both debilitated and medically ignorant. A conscientious physician will thus spend much time explaining the medical situation.

LIVING WILL—DETAILS

A living will is a limited document and has serious shortcomings. It specifies what medical treatment you want if you become unable to convey your wishes; for example, whether or not you want attempts made to extend your life by procedures such as CPR. Again, in most states, *a living will only applies if you are terminally ill and unable to make decisions.* Thus, it would not apply in many circumstances, such as if someone were brought into the ICU after a stroke. This is probably a reasonable restriction on living wills since there are so many variables and uncertainties in emergency medical deci-sions that can't be predicted in advance; but it also means that someone who has specified that he does not want intervention will, under many circum-stances, likely receive it anyway.

There are two styles of living wills. One describes a person's treatment goals and philosophy; the other is a checklist of medical conditions. An ex-ample of the first style, if you don't want heroic, or life-extending procedures (if you do, you should make *that* preference clear) might be something like,

> If I'm terminally ill, in a persistent coma, or permanently de-mented, I want to die as quickly and comfortably as possible. In such circumstances, I hereby decline any and all life-extending mea-sures, including artificial nutrition and/or hydration, and accept only such treatment as is intended to make me comfortable . . .

The checklist version attempts to designate the desired level of treatment for a wide range of medical conditions: (1) do everything possible; (2) do con-servative care (for example, antibiotics) but no extraordinary measures (for example, CPR); (3) do comfort care only. The advantage of this approach is that it specifies what you would want done in a particular described situa-tion; the disadvantage is that there are many more circumstances than one can possibly anticipate. In addition, it requires an unrealistically high level of knowledge of diseases, treatments, and consequences.

Timothy Quill suggests that "patients . . . specify their treatment goals and objectives under circumstances commonly associated with incompetence, including, but not necessarily restricted to, irreversible dementia, terminal illness, and persistent vegetative state," as opposed to using the checklist form.[5]

This approach avoids Scilla, but often runs into Charybdis: A sufficiently general document may be too vague to guide a doctor, particularly one who is unfamiliar with the patient, as is frequently the case in big-city and teach-ing hospitals. It will almost always help to have a personal physician, with whom you have discussed these issues.

While there have been lawsuits by families wanting to let a dying relative expire, the courts have generally allowed this only when the individual has made such a living will. There have been some exceptions (see discussion of *Quinlan* and *Cruzan*, below), but only in extraordinary circumstances.

LEGAL ASPECTS—CASE LAW

Karen Quinlan suffered extensive brain damage in 1975. Eventually her parents, acting to exercise her right to refuse treatment, decided that life-support should be ended. Her doctors, though stating that her condition was permanent, refused and a court case ensued. The New Jersey Supreme Court sided with the parents and Karen Quinlan's respirator was removed. However, the nuns at her hospital, anticipating and disagreeing with the decision, had weaned her off the respirator, and she continued breathing on her own, surviving until 1985. During most of those ten years she was "a comatose eighty-pound figure, curled in a fetal position and kept alive by intravenous feeding . . . completely unaware of the outside world."[6] Her parents did not, apparently, try to have the IV food and water ended.

The legal significance of the case is that it is the first time the courts found a constitutional right to privacy to be the basis on which an individual could make medical care decisions, including withdrawal of treatment.[7] This was extended to withdrawal of treatment by a conscious, competent individual—with a quickly fatal illness—in *Satz v. Perlmutter* (Florida, 1978).

The first of these cases to reach the U.S. Supreme Court started in 1983. In that year twenty-five-year-old Nancy Cruzan suffered severe and irreversible brain damage as a result of a car wreck. She lost control of her car on a country road, was thrown out, and landed facedown in a water-filled ditch. By the time she was pulled out, she had, essentially, drowned. Enough of her brain stem remained functional to allow her to breathe without a respirator, but she was in a coma, had no swallowing reflex, and had to be fed and watered through a surgically implanted feeding tube in her stomach. When Nancy showed no signs of improvement after four years, her parents accepted that she would not recover, and asked that the feeding tube be removed.

In *Cruzan v. Director, Missouri Department of Health*, 497 U.S. 261 (1990), the court ruled that while refusing treatment was each competent individual's right, a state could restrict the right of surrogates, in this case Nancy

Cruzan's parents, to make such decisions for an incompetent person and that the burden was on the Cruzans "to prove unequivocally that she would not want to be treated."[8] This burden of proof is a strong argument in favor of having a living will and a power-of-attorney for health care document, because, if you don't specify otherwise, the state will insist on continuing treatment, however hopeless.

Conveniently, some of Nancy Cruzan's friends remembered that she had told them that she would not want to be kept alive under such circumstances. This tipped the scales of proof and, in 1990, after almost eight years of vegetative maintenance (at around $130,000 per year)[9] a Missouri court agreed to the feeding tube removal; this was done on December 14, 1990, but opponents invaded the hospital in order to reattach the apparatus and threatened to kidnap Cruzan. These attempts failed, but Nancy Cruzan survived for another twelve days, dying slowly of dehydration. "Nancy's lips dried and blistered. Her tongue grew sticky and swollen, and her eyelids dried and began to stick shut."[10] Of course, if someone, perhaps outraged by this totally senseless suffering, had done anything to end it—say, injecting a lethal drug—this would have been murder under the laws of every state.

On her tombstone is written:

Nancy Beth Cruzan
Most Loved
Daughter—Sister—Aunt
Born July 20, 1957 Departed Jan. 11, 1983
At Peace Dec. 26, 1990

The significance of these cases (and the more recent *Quill v. Vacco* and *Compassion in Dying v. State of Washington* (1997) is that (1) the current conservative U.S. Supreme Court, while reluctantly recognizing a right to privacy, is unwilling to extend it any further than precedent requires, if that far; (2) state court decisions are all over the map: the Missouri Supreme Court (*Cruzan*) found a compelling state interest and required "clear and convincing proof" that withdrawal of life-support was what the permanently comatose patient wanted. Meanwhile, the New Jersey Supreme Court (*Quinlan*) reached the opposite conclusion, stating, "We have no hesitancy in deciding . . . that no external compelling interest of the State could compel Karen [Quinlan] to endure the unendurable, only to vegetate a few measurable months with no realistic possibility of returning to any semblance of cognitive or sapient life" (*In re Quinlan*, 1976, 39).

In Great Britain, a less individualistic society with socialized medical care, a different standard is used. Under comparable circumstances to *Cruzan* or *Quinlan*, British judges have come to ask: "What is in the best interests of the patient?" rather than "What did the patient want?" Thus an appeals court judge said, "Looking at the matter as objectively as I can, and doing my best to look at the matter through Mr. Bland's [a permanently vegetative patient who had been crushed in a crowd during a soccer match] eyes and not my own, I cannot conceive what benefit his continued existence could be thought to give him."[11]

The British judges also seem to be a good deal more honest about what they're doing. In the same case, another judge said, "The whole purpose of stopping artificial feeding is to bring about the death of Anthony Bland."[12] The initial ruling, the appeal, and the final appeal to the House of Lords were all unanimous decisions in favor of ceasing maintenance for Mr. Bland.

The British courts are not yet willing to permit active euthanasia, but they are becoming increasingly uncomfortable with the contradictions in their position. In the words of another of the House of Lords judges,

> Finally, the conclusion I have reached will appear to some to be almost irrational. How can it be lawful to allow a patient to die slowly, though painlessly [perhaps true in the Bland case, but often not], over a period of weeks from lack of food but unlawful to produce his immediate death by a lethal injection, thereby saving his family from yet another ordeal to add to the tragedy that has already struck them? I find it difficult to find a moral answer to that question. But it is undoubtedly the law and nothing I have said casts doubt on the proposition that the doing of a positive act with the intention of ending life is and remains murder.[13]

It is an interesting distinction that turning off a respirator or removing a feeding tube is not a "positive act," while administering an injection is. I find these actions morally equal; and if the first is justified, so is the second.[14]

Often, the opposite situation arises: The family insists on futile treatments, despite the wishes of the medical staff. In one case an eighty-seven-year-old woman in an irreversible coma was kept on a respirator for a year-and-a-half (at a cost of almost a million dollars). Her physicians went to court for permission to disconnect her life-support.[15]

This case gets more complex when you try to balance several sometimes-competing interests and issues: (1) What is in the best interests of the patient? (2) What did the patient want? (3) What does the family want? (4) Is there an unlimited right to medical treatment?

In this instance, the medical staff determined that Helga Wanglie was in a persistent vegetative state[b] and that to continue artificial respiration was both futile and not in her interest. However, the patient, according to her family, did not want her life "snuffed out."

The Minnesota court ruled that the patient's alleged desire for treatment had priority over the medical judgment that it was useless. I don't know if they (or other courts) have addressed where the limits to the implementation of those desires lie.

While I support the right of a person to refuse treatment, does this compel my similar support of a right to *require* treatment? I think not; certainly not without bounds and not under every circumstance. In the real world of limited medical resources, I find it insane to spend a million dollars to maintain the body of a brain-dead eighty-seven-year-old.

These are often, however, not easy decisions to make:

> Withdrawing treatment from someone who might recover fully is excruciating every time. Watching the prolonged suffering of someone who has very little chance of "making it" is similarly excruciating . . . [but sometimes] the situation forces a choice between these two options and we temporize briefly hoping for more clarity.[16]

POWER OF ATTORNEY—DETAILS

A more flexible and less restrictive document is the power-of-attorney for health care, or health-care proxy. Like a living will, this only comes into effect if and while you are incapacitated, but is not limited to terminal conditions. Rather than specifying the response to an unknown future medical crisis, it gives, to someone you choose, the power to make health-care decisions on your behalf. This includes the decision to accept or withhold treatment, so it is absolutely necessary to have someone who understands what you want—and don't want—preferably agrees with it, and who is tough enough to insist that your wishes be carried out.

The primary reason such a power-of-attorney is useful is that it is impossible to anticipate all possible medical circumstances in a living will, no matter how detailed. A health-care proxy provides the flexibility to make decisions, consistent with what you want, in unexpected situations. It is important to have *both* a living will and a power-of-attorney document, since some states will not permit actions, such as removal of feeding tubes, based on the proxy's understanding of what the patient would have wanted. They require corroborating evidence. Thus, language stating your refusal to accept artificial feeding and water (if that's what you want) should be included in both documents.

This is a new and fuzzy area of law. For example, what happens if there is a conflict between a living will and the health-care proxy's decision? The more detail you specify about what you want and don't want in a living will, the less basis the courts have to interfere, but the less flexibility a health-care proxy will have as well. In light of this, Timothy Quill recommends writing the living will as a general description of goals, as described a few paragraphs ago, and giving the health-care proxy—if it's someone you can rely on—room to respond to the situation at hand, within those guidelines.

Even so, it may not be enough. In one case, poet and editor Brenda Hewitt had a living will and a health-care proxy she trusted. "The proxy arrived at the hospital with her. But he was ignored, pushed aside, and threatened by staff members as he tried repeatedly to act according to the patient's instructions and prevent the aggressive medical interventions she had feared all along."[17] And, according to health law professor George Annas, the treatment received by Brenda Hewitt and her proxy is "a cruelly common occurrence."[18]

In another instance a dying hospital patient, a surgeon, told his son, who was his health-care proxy and also a physician, "Norman, I have been a surgeon for almost fifty years. In that time I have seen physicians torture dying patients in vain attempts to prolong life. I have taken care of you most of your life. Now I must ask for your help. Don't let them abuse me. No surgery, no chemotherapy." These instructions were ignored; the father was subjected to a series of useless, unnecessary—and billable—procedures and operations despite his express instructions and those of his son. The intervention of another son, a lawyer, was equally unsuccessful in stopping the events. The tab came to $150,000 for a man who "needed only a bed and some morphine."[19]

Afterward, the younger Dr. Paradis wrote, "If a doctor and a lawyer could not get decent care for a doctor, what chance does the public have?"[20]

Do Not Resuscitate (DNR) Order—Details

Yet a third document is needed to keep the rescue squad medics from doing CPR and otherwise trying to revive you even if you are terminally ill, incapacitated, *and* have a living will that says that you do not want such treatment. This one is called an Emergency Medical System (EMS) do not resuscitate (DNR) order. Twenty-four states have implemented these (as of December 1994) in response to the usual horror stories.

In one typical case, a seventy-seven-year-old Washington, D.C., man died at home with his family at his side as he had wanted. When he stopped breathing, the family called the police nonemergency number to inform city officials of his death. A few minutes later a firefighting team— remember, this is Washington—showed up, entered, and began trying to resuscitate him. "I heard my mother screaming at the top of her lungs, 'What are you doing? What are you doing?'" said the man's son, who said firefighters ignored a living will the family showed them. "It was a nightmare."[21]

EMS DNRs can be issued, by their doctors, to terminal patients whose death is impending and who want to die at home, or at a nursing home or hospice, rather than in a hospital. Some states do not require the death to be imminent; a few states do not require terminal illness at all. Since in most emergencies there is little time to look for DNR documents, a few states (and counties) permit DNR bracelets.

Where there is an EMS do not resuscitate order, emergency personnel are not supposed to perform CPR if the patient's heart or breathing has stopped. But they will treat other problems they find. Thus if a DNR patient falls and hits her head, she will be treated for that.

"We've had very positive experience with this," said Nancy Taylor, director of a hospice organization in the Washington, D.C., area. "It comes as a relief to most people to have this option." All fifty states and the District of Columbia have some form of advance directives, but the state laws differ in crucial details and don't honor one another's documents; so check in your jurisdiction—and don't get sick while traveling. *Choice in Dying*, a New York–based organization that promotes patients' rights, will provide you with the appropriate state forms. You can get a copy (via the Internet: http://www.choices.org; or $3.50 by mail), or get more information by calling them at 1-800-989-WILL. A lawyer is not needed to write an advance directive.

EMS do not resuscitate orders of one sort or another are (as of May 1994) legal in Arizona, Colorado, Florida, Georgia, Illinois, Maryland, Montana, New Mexico, New York, Pennsylvania, Rhode Island, Tennessee, Utah, Virginia, Washington, West Virginia, and Wyoming, according to *Choice in Dying*.

Any of these documents can be revoked or changed at any time by a legally competent patient. A do not resuscitate order can also be canceled by the holder of the power-of-attorney. That's the good news about advance directives. The bad news is that often a living will and power-of-attorney are useless.

LIMITATIONS AND FAILURES OF ADVANCE DIRECTIVES

A lack of advanced directives in the face of lost [mental] capacity is the most frequent cause of inhumane overtreatment. . . . The apparent reluctance of physicians to discuss such

issues with their patients before capacity is lost is a cause of
much unnecessary suffering.[22]

—S. J. Regan, hospital attorney

What we have here, is failure to communicate.

—from *Cool Hand Luke*

The evidence is clear that physicians and hospitals cannot be relied on to ask
about the existence of, let alone honor, a living will and a power-of-attorney
for health care. Still, these documents are better than nothing: A doctor who
ignores a valid living will "may be held civilly liable for breach of contract,
battery, and intentional infliction of emotional distress."[23]

It must be noted that patients and their families share responsibility for
the failure of these well-intentioned directives. They may be ambivalent.
Their expectations may be unrealistic. They frequently wait until a medical
emergency before trying to make these decisions. And most people do not
make their best decisions under stress. In addition, there are all the pushes
and pulls of family dynamics: Who wants to live with the guilt of ordering
their parent's respirator turned off? There are many times when it is the
family that insists on carrying on, past the point where the physician would
have stopped treatment that was hopeless.

Sometimes a living will that specifies "no heroic measures" is ignored by
the physician because he thinks he knows better—and sometimes he does.
But more often, a doctor will carry out a family's demand to "do everything"
possible despite living will instructions to the contrary. Why? Because
they're a lot more likely to be sued for malpractice by a living family member than by a dead patient, even though forty-seven states (up to 1993) have
passed legislation protecting doctors from lawsuits for failing to treat when
the patient has executed a living will specifying withdrawal of treatment.[24]
And then there's the money. In the words of Dr. Sam Brody, the physician's
thinking goes:

> We've got to cover our asses or they will sue us or worse. The
> family wants anything done.... [Doctors] repeat this mantra of self-
> serving paranoia as we put our patients through paces that fre-

quently serve only our own interests.... I realize that if DNR meant "Do Not Reimburse" instead of "Do Not Resuscitate," far fewer of the terminally and hopelessly ill would receive pointless treatment.[25]

On the other hand, what we hear about are the horror stories, the cases where patient and family want treatment to stop and are ignored, pressured, or intimidated by the physician. We don't hear about cases where the patient, doctor, and family agree, and act accordingly.

Nevertheless, the bottom line on advance directives is that they don't seem to have worked very well. As Daniel Callahan, a specialist in medical ethics, noted, "It looked so easy . . . yet here we are, some twenty-five years at least after the introduction of the advance directive movement—the principal vehicle for implementing patient preferences . . . [still] trying to get straight about the last weeks and days of dying life."[26]

WHY HAVE ADVANCE DIRECTIVES NOT WORKED BETTER?

"I am eighty-two years old, and I don't want this done," the still-competent patient told the medical team. Like her voice, Harriet Shulan's living will, filed in another state, was useless when she was hospitalized in Arizona. So the "life-sustaining tubes were inserted up her nose and down her throat and into her arms." While she was too weak to refuse consent, major surgery was performed; her condition worsened and she was placed on a respirator, while her continuing requests ("Please let me die") were disregarded because the hospital feared a lawsuit. When she tried to remove the tubes herself, her hands were strapped to the bed.[27]

The federal Patient Self-Determination Act, which took effect in 1991, requires, among other things, that a hospital inform patients of their right to refuse or accept treatment, and ask if an advance directive exists and note yes or no in the chart.

This is not reliably done. In one study, published in August 1995,[28] of 114 cases where patients had written living wills and chosen another person to make medical decisions for them by means of power-of-attorney, only 26 percent were noted in the patient's chart during their hospitalization. In the rest there was no indication that the medical staff had consulted either the living will or the designated health-care proxy before (or after) making medical decisions.

There were no lack of reasons: Nursing homes failed to transfer the documents, patients did not volunteer the information, the chosen health-care proxies failed to be assertive, and the hospital staff failed to ask about advance directives or ensure that they were part of the patients' charts. Whatever the cause, the result was the same: Only in one of four cases of patients with advance directives was the physician even aware of the existence of such a document.

Another study looked at the widely held notion that, despite shortcomings, advance directives encourage patients and doctors to discuss end-of-life issues. The findings, published in 1994, suggest otherwise. Two out of three patients who had advance directives never talked about these topics with their doctors. In this group of patients who had a living will or a power-of-attorney, 76 percent of their physicians thought they didn't or said they didn't know. In the authors' words, "We are struck by how infrequently these discussions are reported to have taken place, and it appears that physicians are for the most part unaware whether their patient has executed an advance directive."[29]

What about people who were terminally ill? In one study, 2,600 dying patients, with life expectancies of less than six months, were asked if they wanted attempts made to resuscitate them if their hearts stopped. In only half the cases did the physician know what the patient wanted.[30] In almost one-third of the cases, a patient's desire not to have CPR attempted was at odds with their doctor's perception of what the patient wanted. When the patient didn't want CPR, the doctor was right 47 percent of the time, wrong 30 percent, and unsure 23 percent; when the patient wanted CPR, the physician was right 57 percent of the time, wrong 17 and unsure 26. And this massive failure in communication doesn't even begin to address the issues that arise when the physician does understand what the patient wants, but disagrees with it.

Wait—it gets worse. From a large, multiyear study of nine thousand severely ill patients in five hospitals,[31] *despite written and oral instructions to the contrary*, many of these people suffered long and painful deaths because their doctors ignored or were unaware of their wishes, including those written into living wills.

A Support study deserves further attention: Particularly since the Quinlan case, there has been a growing belief among physicians and medical ethicists that the best and most effective way to change the way we die is to arrange for better communication between doctors and patients. If both doctor and patient knew the prognosis, and understood the options, and if the doctor knew what the patient wanted—and didn't want—this would lead to better hospital care for the dying and fewer inappropriate "heroic" measures that merely prolong death.[c]

The evidence shows otherwise. Not only was there amazingly poor communication between physicians, terminally ill patients and their families, but the measures specifically designed to improve communication had no effect. As Dr. Joanne Lynn, a codirector of the project said, "We did what everyone thought would work and it didn't work at all."

In one part of the study, patients were randomly divided into two groups. One received standard care, while the other got extra help. This assistance included providing their physicians with a daily computer-generated prognosis of survival time, probability of disability within two months, and the patient's wishes concerning treatment. Each patient was also assigned a specially trained nurse to be the patient's advocate and go-between, in order to facilitate communication between doctor and patient, to find out patient preferences, improve patient understanding of medical procedures and outcomes, and assist with pain-control problems.

None of these steps had the slightest effect on four variables: (1) the time spent in a coma or hooked up to "assisted breathing" apparatus; (2) pain; (3) hospital costs; and (4) treatment decisions, such as do not resuscitate orders.

"These data are astonishing," said Dr. Lynn. "No study comes up with findings this flat. . . . There's not even a wrinkle."

The specific findings are grim. Of the dying patients:

- 38 percent spent ten or more days in ICU in coma and/or on mechanical breathing apparatus before expiring.

- 50 percent suffered moderate or severe pain during most of their last three days.
- 31 percent of families lost most or all of their savings.
- 70 percent of physicians did not discuss CPR with patient.
- 50 percent of physicians did not write a do not resuscitate (DNR) order when patients wanted CPR withheld.

The unequivocal failure of the additional measures to make any difference shocked the researchers.

> If I become old and develop a chronic illness—prostate cancer, say, or lung disease—I'm going to make sure I'm not whisked off to the hospital and put into the ICU and attached to technology. . . . I do not want to die in an ICU. I've seen too many cases where the patient is surrounded by so much technology and so many machines that the family can't even get in and hold their hand. . . . Dying is important. It's the last memory we leave with those we love.

These are not the words of Jack Kevorkian; they are from the lead author of the *JAMA* study, William Knaus, who has spent most of his medical career working in and studying ICUs.[32]

Where does that leave the rest of us?

NOTES

[a]"Terminally ill" is often defined as having a life expectancy of less than six months. By this definition someone with Alzheimer's, or in a permanent coma, would not have an operative LW because their "life" expectancy was too great. As a result of this problem, some states have modified their law, either by statute or by case law (Kamisar, 1993).

In addition, the ability to accurately predict life expectancy is not very good. "Many patients died within a few days of having a prognosis that still allowed hope for some recovery," notes the lead author of a study on five thousand severely ill hospital patients. One week before death, *half* the patients had received a 50 percent prediction of surviving two months (Lynn, 1997, 56-61).

[b]Minnesota.

[c]I am aware that agreements in principle about "heroic" measures can easily break down

under the stress of life-and-death decisions made at the bedside of a family member. And, as Marilyn Follen, a nurse at one of the *JAMA*-study hospitals said, even when it's clear that the chance of recovery is nil, "there's still this gap between the head and the heart" (*Washington Post,* December 5, 1995).

13
SOME PRACTICAL ISSUES IN ASSISTED SUICIDE

•

There is only one prospect worse than being chained to an intolerable existence: The nightmare of a botched attempt to end it.
—Arthur Koestler[1]

Facts do not cease to exist because they are ignored.
—Aldous Huxley

Friends help you move. *Real* friends help you move bodies.
—Anonymous

There are two related practical problems with assisted suicide: (1) In most places it's illegal; (2) in many cases the job is bungled. As a result, end-of-life discussion between patient and doctor is often inhibited: physicians fear prosecution; patients fear involuntary commitment and deprivation of pain medication. The result is, all too often, ill-informed decisions badly carried out.

LEGAL SITUATION AND CASES

The legal situation is both murky and quirky: While committing or attempting to commit suicide is not illegal,[a] helping someone else to do so is. Quite bizarre, when you think about it. Philosopher James Rachels makes a logical argument for legalization of assisted suicide: "If it is permissible for a person (or if a person has the right) to do a certain action, or bring about a certain situation, then it is permissible for that person (he or she has the right) to enlist the freely given aid of someone else in doing the act or bringing about the situation, provided that this does not violate the rights of any third parties."[2]

Nevertheless, assisting a suicide is illegal in most U.S. states[3] and foreign countries, but is not necessarily a crime in Switzerland, Germany,[b] Norway, Uruguay, the Netherlands, and Colombia.[4] Some state laws have been challenged in court, generally without success, but only a small fraction of cases are ever prosecuted.

One that was comes from Connecticut. In 1991 William Meyer, Jr., eighty-eight, died from asphyxia induced by securing a plastic bag over his head. He had colon cancer that had spread to his lungs. He had written, in letters to eighty people to be mailed upon his death, "I happily decided that it was more kind and thoughtful of me to terminate my life before I reached a decadent condition of helplessness." He told a friend of forty years, "I just don't want to continue to suffer. I've had five operations and now I need another and it's useless because I'm not going to get well."

The police, called to his house by his sixty-five-year-old son, William Meyer III, decided it was a simple case of suicide. However, in August 1994, after several locally published interviews, a magazine in a nearby town printed the son's account of how he had helped his father kill himself. The police came back and arrested him. He was charged with second-degree manslaughter, which carries a ten-year prison sentence.[c]

In his first suicide attempt, the father had taken an overdose of medication and tied a plastic bag around his head with rubber bands. The elder Mr. Meyer tore off the bag in an unconscious reflex.

Though shaken by this failure, they decided to try again another day. This time the son would hold his father's hands, they agreed. And that's how it was done. "He kept reaching up. He kept trying to take the bag off. . . . He struggled for about five minutes." This suggests that they used the wrong drug(s), inadequate dosage, too small a bag, or put the bag on too soon. (See Asphyxia chapter.)

When the author of the *Connecticut* magazine article that attracted the authorities' attention asked Mr. Meyer why he wanted the public and the police to know what he had done, he replied, "Because I think it would be a good test case for the State of Connecticut. . . . I was so frustrated that there is still no answer for all these very anguished people who face painful deaths. . . . They need this issue raised."

"People with terminal illness have a right to make a decision about the end of their lives," he said later. "As helpless as I felt in that jail is not nearly as helpless as those people feel forced to stay alive."[5]

On December 15, 1994, William Meyer III was sentenced to two years' probation. He also agreed to not help anyone else commit suicide, to donate $1,000 in his father's name to a prison youth program, and to drop his membership in the Hemlock Society.[6] Kafka would have loved it.

When patients are close to death, there is a strong tendency on the part of most families, physicians, medical examiners, and police to "look the other way," and not examine the exact cause of death too closely unless their attention is specifically drawn to it. In one series of interviews, only fifteen of 140 non-physician-assisted suicides were even classified as suicides, and none were considered "assisted," though all, in fact, were.[7] In many of these cases there was an active conspiracy on the part of the dying person and his or her doctor, family, partner, and friends: "In forty-one of these remaining 125 deaths, physicians knowingly provided lethal prescriptions, were fully aware of their patients' plans to end their lives, and signed their death certificates claiming 'natural' causes."[8]

Without anything stronger than anecdotal evidence, my sense is that local prosecutors tend to be more hard-nosed, though it may be that we hear mostly of the ones who insist on following the letter of the law, unmodified by either compassion or sense. In the words of the prosecutor in the case of William Meyer, "My decision [to prosecute] was based on whether there was probable cause that a crime was committed. Assisting in a suicide is a crime. The law is the law." And, as Dickens observed, a ass.

In fairness, not all prosecutors are cut from the same cloth. For example, on May 20, 1994, California District Attorney Dennis Sheehy said that Dr. John Coe, who helped a dying AIDS patient commit suicide, would not be prosecuted despite the coroner's verdict that Thomas C. Snell's death was a homicide.[9]

This is an area where the concept of "jury nullification" is real: Although the evidence for such assisted suicide may be overwhelming, juries rarely convict under these circumstance, even if they have to ignore the judge's instructions. One hundred fifty-one "mercy-killing" cases were tried between 1920 and 1985 (70 percent between 1980 and 1985). Only ten people were convicted of (or pled guilty to) homicide and jailed.[10] Even with Dr. Kevorkian, who has rubbed their noses in it, prosecutors have failed to get a single juror in three trials to vote for conviction.[d]

On the other hand, it is always possible to get some combination of ruthless prosecutor, incompetent defense attorney, unsympathetic jury, and hanging judge. On March 4, 1985, seventy-six-year-old Roswell Gilbert was convicted of first-degree murder and sentenced to twenty-five years in prison—without parole—for shooting his wife of fifty-one years, who had Alzheimer's disease (progressive dementia, with no realistic hope for recovery) and osteoporosis (loss of bone strength, leading to multiple fractures and severe pain).

He spent five-and-one-half years in jail before being granted "clemency" due to his age and poor health.

MEDICAL FAILURE IN ASSISTED SUICIDE AND EUTHANASIA

A much more likely problem is the failure of an assisted suicide to go smoothly.[11] One of the few studies of assisted suicide looked at the situation among dying AIDS patients in Vancouver, British Columbia.

Russel Ogden found that half of the thirty-four mostly non-physician-assisted suicides he was able to get details on were bungled, increasing suffering when the aim was to alleviate it. The assisted suicides were carried out by ministers, physicians, social workers, counselors, teachers, and writers.

In six cases, death was from an overdose of barbiturates; in six others, morphine; in two more, heroin; five died from a combination of sedatives and plastic bag asphyxia; one died from a gunshot, one from a razor blade, one from carbon monoxide, and two from injection of an unknown material.

Many of these people took several hours to die. In one case it took four days. "We injected him with massive amounts of morphine and he didn't die," said one of those who assisted in that death. "We used a month's supply of morphine in three days. We were triple-dosing him every hour because the information we had was that eventually the morphine would arrest his respiratory system."[12] One physician felt that the law forced him to secretly kill dying AIDS patients with huge overdoses of their pain medication, morphine, rather than the much faster and more reliable secobarbital (Seconal).

Many of these deaths did not go as planned. In several cases pills were vomited before they could exert their full effects, leading the assistants to finish the job with plastic bags, gun, or razor blade. As one assistant said:

> At least I had an idea of what to do when he died. I had a vague understanding of what would happen and had the phone numbers of who to call. But I was totally unprepared for failure. This would mean that it would officially become a suicide attempt and could implicate the doctor who gave us the prescription. Plus, I didn't know if the overdose would cause serious damage when he recovered. I didn't want to see him in worse shape afterward than he'd been in before.[13]

Ogden, a thirty-one-year-old social worker who spent thirteen months interviewing people, said, "What this study shows is that in the absence of regulation and medical supervision, euthanasia is occurring in horrific circumstances, like back-street abortions."[14] He cited lack of knowledge on the part of the suicide assistants and lack of suitable drugs as the immediate problems, but the failure to legalize assisted suicide as the root cause.

The head of the British Columbia Persons with AIDS Society, Arn Schilder, said the report showed "only the tip of the iceberg." He added, "We have no alternative now to coat-hanger euthanasia."[15]

Based on Ogden's data and another study from the Netherlands,[16] between 10 and 22 percent of AIDS deaths are from assisted suicides. Anecdotal evidence suggests that assisted suicide is particularly common in the gay AIDS community, especially in large cities. In general, there have not been legal repercussions.

What Suicide Methods Are Most Appropriate for a Terminally Ill Person in a Hospital?

I believe that choosing if and how to end your life is your decision to make. On the other hand I also believe that suicide should not be undertaken without a clear medical prognosis and understanding of alternatives nor when in the midst of temporary or correctable depression.

If you're thinking of killing yourself, are all of the following conditions true?[e] If not, some other course of action is indicated.

1. You have advanced terminal illness and/or your "quality of life" is unacceptable (intractable pain, physical or mental disintegration, etc.) *and* without likelihood of improvement;
2. You're of sufficiently clear mind to make rational decisions;
3. You've discussed the diagnosis, situation, and treatment choices with your doctor and are sure that you understand them;
4. You have gotten an independent second opinion;
5. You've considered the alternatives (for example, hospice care, with generally better pain control than hospitals provide);
6. You're not "clinically depressed";
7. You're consistent in your choice;
8. Your physician and family will not help you, or provide you the means, to kill yourself.

Each situation differs, depending on your physical condition and abilities, how and how frequently you're monitored, and other variables that I can't anticipate. (Are you on the first floor or the tenth floor? Does your window open? Can you get out of bed?) In general, your best bet—if you're not continuously monitored—for a quick suicide under these circumstances will be some form of asphyxia: hanging (you don't need to be suspended) or strangulation. These methods take less than fifteen minutes and can be done without leaving bed. Plastic-bag asphyxia usually takes longer and is more prone to error, but may be combined with drug overdose. See chapters on asphyxia, drugs, and hanging for further information.

Drug overdose, by itself, will almost always take too long, and overdose with pain medication will be less effective if you've been using the drug therapeutically and have therefore developed some level of tolerance.

For example, eighty-one-year-old Alice Marks, suffering from degenerative bone disease, injected herself with an overdose of morphine (one of her pain drugs) with the knowledge and in the presence of her son. Believing that she was dead, he called paramedics, who revived her. She was deprived of pain medication in the hospital and was subsequently transferred to a locked psychiatric ward as she was considered a "danger to herself."[17]

If you have an intravenous line, you may consider potassium chloride, found in salt substitutes.[f] This is the method that was used by Dr. Kevorkian in his first assisted suicide.

Janet Adkins was a fifty-four-year-old woman diagnosed as being in the early stages of Alzheimer's. She could still converse and play tennis, but could no longer read. Knowing the grim progression of this disease, she chose to end her life while she was still able to arrange to do so. In June 1990, she went to Michigan, with her husband and three children, and met with Kevorkian. The next afternoon, with the support of her family, she reaffirmed her decision. Kevorkian started an IV line in her arm. When she was ready, she opened a switch that added a sedative to the IV drip and activated a timer that would add the potassium chloride. She soon fell asleep, and shortly afterward, her heart stopped.[g]

Electrocution and drowning are remote possibilities. (See respective chapters on these methods.) The most commonly reported method of suicide among hospital patients is jumping from a height,[18] but the numbers are small (on the order of one per hospital per year, or two per 100,000 admissions) and, in addition to the medically ill, they include "acutely delirious" admissions, and those admitted after a suicide attempt.

Unfortunately, if you don't succeed at first, you may not have much chance to "try, try again." You will probably see access to medications restricted and may even find yourself in restraints—for your own good, of course.

NOTES

[a]More precisely, it is not illegal under any state (or federal) statute, but in some states might be considered a "common law" crime. [Smith, C, pp139-149]

[b]In Germany it is accepted and legal to assist the freely chosen (uncoerced) suicide of

someone who is in possession of his or her mental faculties, that is, a "rational" suicide. However, euthanasia, even on request, is illegal. This position appears to be largely in response to, and from suspicion of, authoritarian medical practices, both past and present. Indeed, due to Nazi-era abuses, even *discussion* of euthanasia is highly controversial (Battin, 1994).

The German language also has one (out of four) words for "suicide" that has a quite positive connotation: *Freitod*, free- or freely chosen death. English has no corresponding (or any positive) term. Thus, English-speakers may have a conceptual problem imagining *Freitod*. "The distinction between suicide as a moral wrong or psychological aberration and as a religiously or altruistically motivated choice is readily marked off in English, but the distinction between suicide as a moral wrong or psychological aberration and an autonomous choice based in personal ideals and values is not" (Battin, 1994; Daube, 1977).

It is ironic that in America, self-proclaimed "land of the free" (not to mention "home of the brave"), patients have fewer civil liberties and choices in end-of-life decisions than do, say, citizens of Holland and Germany.

[c]American (English) law is unusual in that it does not take motive into account in the determination of a verdict. Thus someone who kills their terminally ill parent out of compassion may well be charged with first-degree murder. As a result, American juries, and even judges, have sometimes found confessed mercy-killers "not guilty" by reason of insanity—and then immediately declared them "cured" and free to go. However, this is capricious: Others are sentenced to long prison terms (Battin, 1994, 19-46).

[d]In April 1994, Kevorkian went on trial for assisting the suicide of Thomas Hyde, who was dying of Lou Gehrig's disease (ALS, or amyotrophic lateral sclerosis). You may have seen home videos of Hyde and his wife, taken about a month before his death. Barely able to speak or move, Hyde still made it clear how much he wanted to end his life and medically hopeless suffering. The jury (five members of which had medically related jobs) also saw this footage and returned a verdict of not guilty. Said one, a nurse, "I don't believe it's our obligation to choose for someone else how much pain and suffering they can go through" (Singer, 135).

[e]A broader and more philosophical list of considerations, not focused on terminal illness, can be found in Battin (1994), 272-275.

[f]Depending on your size and the specific salt substitute, you would need to dissolve and administer intravenously one to three teaspoons of salt substitute. Death, due to heart stoppage, occurs in a few minutes. However, this is a painful method without sedation, and you still need to acquire the material. See potassium salts section in Drugs chapter.

[g]As an aside, a survey of geriatricians (physicians specializing in problems associated with old age) found that 49 percent felt that her decision was not "morally wrong" while 29 percent thought that it was; but only 21 percent would consider assisting the suicide of a competent dementia patient. However, 41 percent said they would consider suicide for themselves (39 percent said they wouldn't) under these circumstances (Watts, 1992). This is consistent with several studies showing physicians' greater abstract support of (and interest in receiving) assisted suicide than willingness to perform it.

14
EUTHANASIA IN THE NETHERLANDS

●

I am dying with the help of too many physicians.

—Alexander the Great

The two most prestigious American medical journals have recently addressed assisted suicide and euthanasia in the Netherlands. *Citing the same evidence*, they say: "From our point of view there has been an erosion of medical standards in the care of terminally ill patients in the Netherlands" (*Journal of the American Medical Association*[1]) and "In our view, these data do not support the idea that physicians in the Netherlands are moving down a slippery slope" (*New England Journal of Medicine*[2]).

HISTORY

Euthanasia and physician-assisted suicide have been openly practiced in the Netherlands[a] since 1973, when a doctor received a one-week suspended sentence for ending the life of her severely ill mother.

In 1971, Dr. Geertruida Postma gave her elderly mother a lethal overdose of morphine. Her mother had suffered a brain hemorrhage and was partially paralyzed and deaf. When sitting up, she had to be tied to a chair. She had repeatedly begged her daughter to kill her. Dr. Postma was convicted of mercy-killing, which carries a possible twelve-year prison sentence. Instead, she was given a one-week suspended sentence and a year of probation.

Enough other doctors signed an open letter to the justice minister (comparable to the U.S. Attorney General) stating that they were guilty of the same crime, that the issue could not be ignored. The Dutch Medical Association changed from its previous opposition to assisted suicide, to asking the courts to decide whether physicians had an irreconcilable conflict (force majeure) between their duty to not kill and their duty to relieve suffering by shortening the life of an incurably ill patient.

In 1984, the highest Dutch court made such a ruling. As a result, the justice ministry stopped prosecuting (but continued investigating) both assisted suicide and voluntary euthanasia, as long as the guidelines of the Medical Association were followed. Since then, while there have been a few prosecutions, only one case has resulted in a criminal conviction: nurses who killed (without their consent) several mental patients dying of cancer were sentenced to six months in jail in 1986.

The Dutch guidelines for providing euthanasia or physician-assisted suicide were made explicit in 1984. The patient is supposed to be terminally ill or suffer uncontrollable pain (this has been taken to include emotional pain), and specifically and repeatedly ask for death while rational and free of coercion. There must be no other reasonable way of decreasing the suffering that is acceptable to the patient. Physicians are required to report all such deaths to the medical examiner who, in turn, reports them to the state prosecutor.

In 1993 the law was modified to reflect the experience of the prior decade: Doctors are encouraged, whenever possible, to have the patient administer the lethal medication rather than having the physician do it. This decreases the possibility of misunderstandings, ambivalence, or manipulation—and diminishes the burden on the physician's conscience.[3]

> "This step [assisted suicide] is first a decision of the patient, and eating or drinking the substance is a symbol of the patient's responsibility," said Dr. Robert Dillmann, a member of the ethics commission of the Royal Dutch Medical Association. "It is consistent with the decision. An exception should be made when a very sick person is not able to swallow."
>
> Many doctors find euthanasia an extremely difficult and burdensome action, and the patient's participation diminishes this burden

slightly. In the past we said that all things being equal, there was no
difference between mercy killing and assisted suicide. But in practice, doctors say this is not the same, that there is a difference if a
doctor gives a lethal injection or an intravenous drip and, on the
other hand, if the patient drinks a potion.[4]

Not all doctors agree that the change has been beneficial: "Morally and
emotionally it is equally difficult," says family physician Herbert Cohen.
"You help prepare the patient and the family and you accompany them. A
doctor does not just give a box of pills and walk away." In addition, pills take
much longer than injections, typically hours rather than minutes.[b] Dr.
Cohen continues, "There are risks because people are terribly sick. A patient
can spill the medicine or choke or vomit or fall asleep before the full dose
has been taken. It is never simple."[5]

The 1993 changes also emphasized the duty to get a second, independent,
medical opinion from an experienced, uninvolved physician. While that rule
was already on the books, critics note that doctors often will consult another
physician with whom they work or one who knows the patient well. While
this has some advantages, it also decreases the likelihood of a fresh perspective, which is the primary point of a second opinion.

Although there is widespread agreement in Holland with the current
rules—about 80 percent public and physician approval—there is substantial
dispute about the boundaries: What to do when people have not explicitly
asked for death—for example, in the case of a comatose patient or a severely
deformed newborn. The Dutch Medical Association says that it will address
this issue soon.

How Frequent Are These Practices in the Netherlands?

After a quarter century of more-or-less open practice, euthanasia and assisted suicide remain uncommon.[6] To summarize the numbers of people involved: There were 128,000 deaths in the Netherlands in 1991. An
estimated 25,000 patients began euthanasia discussions with their doctor;
9,000 explicitly requested euthanasia, of which some 2,300 (26 percent of
requests; 1.8 percent of all deaths) were consented to and acted upon by the

physician. In addition, there were about 400 (0.3 percent) PAS (physician-assisted suicides) and 1,000 (0.8 percent) LAWER (Life-terminating Acts Without Explicit Request), that is, nonvoluntary euthanasia.

I do have some concerns with the Dutch process. While there were about 2,700 cases of voluntary euthanasia and PAS (some 4 percent of those who died at home[c7]) carried out each year, government figures show that only about half that number were reported. This is probably because euthanasia is still illegal, and, until 1994 involved police interrogation and the possibility of prosecution; but lack of reporting can also hide abuses. On the other hand, "toleration" does not appear to have set off an avalanche of euthanasia. "Our sense is that [euthanasia] has not increased, but we're not quite sure," said Dillmann.[8] He noted that even with quasi-legalization, there are about three or four requests for euthanasia for each one that was actually carried out. In addition, lives were shortened by less than a week in more than 70 percent of cases.[9]

More troubling, on its face, is the fact that in more than one thousand cases a year doctors had "actively" hastened a death without the patient's request.[10] In about six hundred of these there had been patient discussion of ending life, but no explicit request (as legally required) had been made.

It seems impossible to justify making such a decision on the basis of preliminary or tentative discussions, if the patient was competent at the time a lethal injection was administered. On the other hand, if the patient had become, say, comatose, preliminary talks might be the best or only information about his or her wishes on the matter. According to the main author of the Dutch Commission reviewing these practices (the Remmelink Commission), most of these patients were not competent.[11]

However, about 20 percent of these cases were not discussed partly (10 percent entirely) because the physician thought it not in the best interest of the patient to do so. These were mostly the patients' longtime GPs: "This is perhaps why they more easily assume that they know what is best for the patient or that they will harm the patient by discussing these subjects."[12] I find this ethically unacceptable.

Of the remaining four hundred cases, in all but two there was no discussion because the patient was no longer mentally capable of making decisions or expressing preferences. Relatives were consulted in 83 percent of these circumstances. Thus, while there is nonvoluntary euthanasia being carried out, there seems to be little or no involuntary euthanasia. It is plausible that the increased emphasis on physician-assisted suicide, at the expense of euthanasia, will decrease such abuses as exist, but this remains to be seen.

To put things in perspective, we should also keep in mind that there were many more cases where life-extending treatment was withdrawn or withheld (about twenty thousand cases) without explicit permission than there were euthanasia/PAS cases. In 87 percent, the patients were not capable of being consulted; in 13 percent they could have been but were not.[13]:

In comparison, an estimated 70 percent of deaths in U.S. health-care institutions involve withdrawal or withholding of life-support.[14] This practice, "allowing to die," is considered barbaric by some Dutch physicians, who feel that it prolongs the agony of dying people for no good purpose. Margaret Battin notes that the Dutch are grappling with issues of decision-making for incompetent patients (widely discussed and analyzed in the United States since *Quinlan* and *Cruzan*), while the United States struggles with assisted suicide and euthanasia, with which the Netherlands has twenty-five years' experience.[15] However, the significant differences between the two societies would make it a serious mistake for either one to accept the other's experience as a model to blindly follow.

From my perspective, there certainly is a problem in the Netherlands with what appears to be medical paternalism, but this attitude is widespread throughout the world, and as discussed earlier, is common in the United States as well. As to the question of whether or not this represents the beginning of the "slippery slope," the answer at this time must be: No one knows, if for no other reason than because there is no data on the frequency of these actions prior to the quasi-legalization of assisted suicide and euthanasia.

However, after twenty-five years of more-or-less open practice, assisted suicide and euthanasia in the Netherlands are infrequent and abuses rare.

NOTES

[a]The Netherlands gets all the publicity for its policy allowing both euthanasia and assisted suicide; it's not widely known that assisted suicide—but not euthanasia—is also legal in Germany (Battin, 1991). Euthanasia, under very restricted circumstances, is legal in Japan, and was legalized in Colombia in 1997 (*Washington Post*, August 18, 1997).

[b]In Dutch euthanasia, the most commonly used method is to cause unconsciousness with intravenous barbiturates, followed by curare, which paralyzes the muscles that control breathing. This combination might cause death after about ten to fifteen minutes. Taken by mouth, fast-acting barbiturates such as Nembutal and Seconal typically require two to four hours.

[c]Almost identical numbers of people die at home as in hospital. However, assisted suicide and/or euthanasia at home occurs at about 2.5 times the hospital rate. This is attributed to the generally high level of trust and communication, and long-term relationships between Dutch GPs and their patients. In addition, the patients who choose such deaths often prefer to die at home (Pijnenborg, November 5, 1994).

15
EUTHANASIA AND ASSISTED SUICIDE IN THE UNITED STATES

•

> He had been, he said, a most unconscionable time dying; but he
> hoped that they would excuse it.
> —Macaulay on Charles II, King of England

In November 1994, voters in Oregon narrowly approved an assisted-suicide law, making Oregon the first state in the United States to do so. Similar referenda, with fewer safeguards, were defeated by 54 to 46 percent margins in Washington State in 1991 and California in 1992. However, this is not a new issue. The Ohio legislature defeated a bill to legalize euthanasia in 1906; other proposals failed in Nebraska (1937) and New York (1947).[1]

The Oregon law allows doctors to write prescriptions for lethal drugs to be taken voluntarily by a terminally ill patient. There are four main conditions:

1. The patient must have a life expectancy of six months or less.
2. The patient must ask the physician for suicide help on three separate occasions, the last of which must be in writing in the presence of two witnesses, at least one of whom is not family or employed by the hospital or nursing home, and who does not stand to benefit from the estate.
3. There must be at least a fifteen-day delay between the first request, and a two-day delay between the third request and writing the prescription.

4. There must be second, independent, medical opinion that the patient's judgment is not impaired.

No other forms of mercy-killing or euthanasia are permitted.

Safeguards of this sort cannot be perfect: If they are too permissive, coercive abuses will occur; if they are too restrictive, dying people will needlessly suffer while bureaucratic requirements are met.

Opponents blocked the referendum in the courts until October 1997, when the U.S. Supreme Court declined to intervene in the case. In the meantime, however, the Oregon legislature, not liking the results of this referendum, voted to hold another one on November 4, 1997. The referendum was again approved, and by a much greater margin. Congressional opponents, suddenly claiming federal jurisdiction, got the Drug Enforcement Administration to threaten physicians who wrote such lethal drug prescriptions with loss of drug-prescribing licenses. When this was overturned by the U.S. Attorney General, Janet Reno, they attempted to pass congressional legislation to achieve the same result. The results are not yet in.

As of this writing, only a half dozen people are known to have gotten a physician's help to die by means of this law. However, not only its existence, but the intense debate surrounding its court cases and two referenda, has sensitized health-care workers to the needs of dying patients. For example, between 1994, when the first referendum was passed, and 1997, medical use of morphine has increased by 70 percent, Oregon going from eleventh to first in its retail distribution of this pain medication.[2]

Similarly, deaths in hospitals have decreased dramatically; now 60 percent of people are dying at home or in nursing homes. Hospice use has increased from 21 percent of deaths in 1994 to about 32 percent in 1997, and all of Oregon's fifty-seven hospices now accept patients who say they intend to avail themselves of this new law.

Nevertheless, the debate is certainly not over. Let's look at some of the arguments in more detail.

ARGUMENTS SUPPORTING THE "SLIPPERY SLOPE" THESIS

Most opponents of assisted suicide[a] cite the "slippery slope" argument: Crudely stated, assisted suicide (initially, death in a few sympathetic medical situations for those who have asked for it or on the basis of mercy) makes euthanasia (including death for people who have not expressed such a request) more acceptable, which, sooner or later, leads to the legal killing of people who are considered in some way "defective" or "inferior."[b]

In the words of Bishop Joseph Sullivan,

> If voluntary euthanasia were legalized, there is good reason to believe that at a later date another bill for compulsory euthanasia would be legalized. Once the respect for human life is so low that an innocent person may be killed directly, even at his own request, compulsory euthanasia will necessarily be very near. This could lead easily to killing all incurable charity patients, the aged who are a public care, wounded soldiers, all deformed children, the mentally afflicted, and so on. Before long the danger would be at the door of every citizen.[3]

I think this concern is quite legitimate. I would briefly put forth three arguments supporting and three opposing it.

First, I have no reason to believe that a medical and legal system that is capable of the ethical blindness of torturing dying people by keeping them alive in medically hopeless situations contrary to their desire, is not also capable of erring in the other direction. The shameful Tuskegee syphilis study, the formerly common use of prisoners as medical test subjects, the involuntary sterilization programs associated with the eugenics movement, and a variety of radiation experiments on unwitting subjects show us that American medicine and law can fail and, at times, have failed to protect the people who need protection most.[4]

Two brief examples may be useful: (1) In one study, 525 men with strep throat were *not* treated with penicillin, though the experimenter knew that such treatment would prevent rheumatic fever (with probable severe heart damage). As a result "twenty-five men were crippled, perhaps for life." The subjects were not informed that any experiment was being carried out.[5] (2) Cancer cells were transplanted into a patient's mother, who was told by the experimenter that the purpose was "the hope of gaining a little better understanding of cancer immunity and in the hope that the production of tumor antibodies might be helpful in the treatment of the cancer patient." The daughter died the next day, the mother a little over a year later—from the metastasized transplanted cancer.[6]

Physicians, like other people, respond to financial, legal, and social incentives. I would note that in Nazi Germany, half of the medical doctors in the country were members of the Nazi Party and 7 percent joined the SS, a much higher proportion than that of any other academic profession.[7] And, "the abundant availability of human guinea pigs among people labeled as inferior or subhuman was exploited by doctors as a unique opportunity for scientific research."[8]

Second, the concept of a slippery slope is plausible: Fewer people will go two steps past acceptable behavior than will go one step. If we move the definition of "acceptable" by a step, we have also turned two steps away into one step away. Moving the norms also moves the boundaries.

For example, in 1993 Boudewijn Chabot, a Dutch psychiatrist, was tried on charges of helping a depressed (but physically healthy) patient commit suicide. He was acquitted when the court ruled that intense mental distress might also justify assisted suicide.[9] Thus we have moved from "terminal illness" to "intractable pain" to "intense mental distress."

Third, we are already partway down the slope. Most Americans morally accept killing in self-defense, just war, capital punishment, or abortion. Current American medical practice (if not theory) includes violations of patient autonomy, both in the direction of maintaining life and of ending it. Patients or their surrogates are sometimes pressured to agree to do not resuscitate (no-code) orders. There are reports of no-codes being written into a patient's chart in pencil, to allow erasure.[10] Advance directives are widely ignored.

Arguments Against the "Slippery Slope" Thesis

Counterarguments to the slippery slope thesis might be, first, that numerous societies have practiced infanticide, assisted suicide, or euthanasia without extending the limits of acceptable practices later.

In one study 50 percent of the societies reviewed used some form of hastening death in the elderly.[11] For example, an Eskimo tribe might, during starvation times, abandon some elderly members, asphyxiate them, or encourage them to go outside to die—but murder (though not warfare) was almost unheard of.[12] In nineteenth-century Europe, unwanted babies were given to foundling homes, which often had such high death rates that the people who ran them were called "angel makers."[13] Female infanticide is common in India and China. None of these societies proceeded to build concentration camps or otherwise systematize murder, as slippery slope proponents claim will inevitably happen.

And, despite appalling American examples of abuses of patients in medical experiments, they have become less, not more, frequent. There are few calls to end all human experimentation. Rather, the demands are for an end to the abuses, and this is as it should be.

As the Presidential Commission for the Study of Ethical Problems in Medicine reported,

> ... much more is needed than merely pointing out that allowing one kind of action (itself justified) could conceivably increase the tendency to allow another action (unjustified). Rather, it must be shown that pressure to allow the unjustified action will become so strong once the initial step is taken that the further steps are likely to occur ... [and] such evidence is quite commonly limited.[14]

Second, the Nazis (commonly cited by slippery slope proponents) did not start with voluntary euthanasia from a sense of compassion and slide down the slippery slope to involuntary euthanasia and sterilization, and then to mass murder—all within ten years, mind you. Their rationale had less to do with relieving suffering than with achieving racial purity and medical knowledge.[15]

The slippery slope argument is also weakened to the extent that one can get down the slope while omitting the "first" step. If Stalin's or Pol Pot's concentration camps existed without the prior approval of the practice of assisted suicide and euthanasia, it makes the association, let alone claims of cause and effect, unconvincing.

In any case, the Nazi death camps were certainly not caused by the earlier program of euthanasia; nor does it seem likely that the Nazis would have refrained from mass murder and genocide had they not first implemented their program of voluntary euthanasia for Aryans.[c]

One might make the parallel argument that the Nazi example of sterilization abuses should cause us to forbid voluntary sterilizations lest we slide down this same slope. Involuntary sterilization, including that of children, also took place in this country, before, during, and after the Nazi era; yet such abuses have decreased, rather than becoming the norm, while voluntary sterilization has become more widespread.[16]

The concept of a slippery slope also becomes less persuasive when we realize that it can be—and has been—applied, both honestly and dishonestly, to just about any issue that people care about. Nothing has only one effect, and abuse can follow from any good.

Indeed, one could reasonably argue that the tortures sometimes inflicted through prolonged dying are predictable slippery slope abuses arising from advances in medical technology. Are we prepared to give up the benefits of this technology in order to preclude such abuses?[d]

It is certainly true that if you prohibit all assisted suicide, you will avoid disputes about where to draw the line. But simplicity has a price too, and ignores the hard cases. For example, "[A Dutch] doctor, Henk Prins, will go on trial for ending the life of an infant born in 1992 with severe spina bifida. Though the baby's parents wanted the death, and the infant was in pain, Prins is being charged with premeditated murder in a new test of the limits of the euthanasia guidelines."[17]

As Ronald Dworkin notes, "No set of regulations can be perfect. But it would be perverse to force competent people to die in great pain or in a drugged stupor for that reason."[18]

Other objections[19] to assisted suicide center on the pressure a dying—or merely old and ill—person might feel to make a decision to die. In the American health-care system, that motivation could well be financial. Some sources of this pressure might be:

Family: Herbert Hendin cites a Dutch study to the effect that patients in that country are subject to such family coercion.[20] However, the existence of living wills (valid in every state and affirmed by the Supreme Court), which limit medical care, already make people subject to this kind of incentive.

In any case, it's not clear that this is a significant problem in the United States: "Talking with hundreds of terminally ill over the past few years, I've yet to hear this complaint voiced," notes Stephen Jamison. What he has found, instead, "is an often not-so-subtle coercion by the dying themselves to ensure the participation of others in their deaths."[21] One should also be aware of the possibility of coercion to stay alive, contrary to the patient's wishes.

An institution (for example, hospital, insurance company, HMO, or government agency) concerned about covering its bottom line. Health-care expenditures are 14 percent of the U.S. gross domestic product (GDP) and the highest per-capita in the world. An estimated 30 percent of health-care costs occur in the last six months of life. The proportion of old people is increasing and will numerically peak with a surfeit of geriatric baby-boomers early in the twenty-first century who will be a financial burden to the outnumbered generation Xers. Add these together and you're looking at enormous pressure to keep costs down. The terminally ill and the elderly will likely bear the brunt of any resulting health-care rationing or coercion to die.

In fact, there already is such coercion: Medicaid requires that a person facing a long stay in a nursing home first use up almost all of her assets before becoming eligible for public assistance. While this seems reasonable from one perspective, the quite predictable result is that a person, especially one who is terminally ill, must choose between exhausting these funds for a relatively short extension of life or dying earlier and leaving money for spouse or children.

One suggestion is intriguing.[22] Besides the usual explicit request by the patient and two-independent-physician approval, the patient would be asked, "Is the care you are now receiving adequate?" If the patient or patient's-advocate said no, this situation would have to be rectified before assistance to die could be provided—if it was still wanted. It's possible that such a system might even improve health care for the people who need it most, if it were applied honestly.

In addition, it would be naive to believe that the terminally ill do not face these same issues in the absence of assisted suicide. For example, one study of cancer and AIDS patients found that three-quarters of them wanted to limit medical expenditures: 23 percent would be willing to spend all their resources, while 27 percent would not wish to spend any of it; the average amount to be spent was 43 percent of their life's savings. Unmarried patients were willing to spend 19 percent more than married ones.

When asked about being dependent on family and friends for care, 14 percent said they would want to live as long as possible; but 28 percent said that they would not want to live even one day in that situation![23]

This study does not address whether terminally ill people would feel more or less pressure to shorten their lives in order to limit being a burden on family and friends if assisted suicide/euthanasia were legalized. But it does show that they already make these calculations.

The fact that assisted suicide is illegal, combined with its increasingly common practice, leaves us with the worst of both worlds: It is carried out underground, without supervision or review; sometimes by physicians, but often by people who have limited knowledge of how to go about it. As Lonny Shavelson says, "The present prohibition against legal assistance in suicide has guaranteed that not a single [American] physician has ever assisted in the death of a patient while following set rules, nor under the observation of her peers, nor under the watchful eyes of the law."[24]

In addition, since active euthanasia is more obvious and conspicuous than withdrawing or withholding treatment (both commonly done in the United States and throughout the world), it is less subject to abuse.[25] Making these practices open and legal would compel us to erect protections against abuses, which would, I believe, also lead to better protection and clarity in cases of withdrawing or withholding treatment.

Reasonable people can disagree. For my part, I come out, reservations and all, squarely on the side of assisted suicide. It's not a panacea. People will still kill themselves on account of present misery; but not over fears of future helplessness. Improved medical care—and caring—for the dying would decrease the impetus for suicide, assisted or not. But in the absence of such care, or when it fails, each of us who so decides should have the option of a chosen death.

In the case of terminal illness, there are still choices to be made. A return to health is not one of them. What remains are the choices of how and when to die: What image and memories of yourself to leave behind, what resources to use, and what to pass on to your heirs and society.

Some questions that a dying person who is considering suicide might want to think about:[26]

- Is suicide morally appropriate for me, given my circumstances, values, religious beliefs, suffering, and responsibilities?
- Can I kill myself without assistance? If so, is involving someone else appropriate?
- Who will be harmed by my suicide? How can I minimize this harm?
- Is suicide a rational choice for me? Why do I think so, and what are the counterarguments? Is suicide an attempt to assert some control over an illness that has taken most choices from me? Is it motivated by present suffering or fears of future consequences of my illness?

The methods to achieve these choices include (1) leaving things to chance, as most people do, and trusting "the system" to make the decisions; (2) making advance directives in the hope, frequently unjustified, that they will be followed; (3) committing suicide while still able to do so, sacrificing some time in exchange for control of life's endgame.

Each option has advantages, disadvantages, and risks, and the third option disappears if you are incapacitated. The most flexible individual strategy would seems to be:

1. Find a physician who is open-minded about these issues and willing to talk with you about them;
2. Have a living will and a power-of-attorney document, and a health-care proxy who understands, agrees with, and will carry out what you want;

3. Utilize home-hospice or comfort care;
4. Have a means of killing yourself available if points 2 and 3 fail and you're still able to carry it out;
5. Have someone willing to help you in an assisted suicide, or willing to kill you (if that's what you want) should you become unexpectedly incapacitated during this process and advance directives are being flouted. Be aware that the last two eventualities may well have legal repercussions for your assistant.

It would be far better if suicide were never the best choice or if doctors could be counted on to sensitively guide end-of-life decisions in the interests of the patient, as defined by the patient. Physicians often have a preexisting relationship with a patient that allows an accurate assessment of the latter's prognosis and emotional state. And physicians are in the best position to apply effective and humane methods of assisted suicide or euthanasia. But the law forbids them to offer such help under any circumstances. Until that changes, patients will continue to kill themselves in desperation, assisted suicide and euthanasia will continue to resemble back-alley abortion, and books like this one will continue to be necessary.

NOTES

[a]Some opponents, arguing from a libertarian perspective, oppose assisted suicide because it maintains and reinforces the medical monopoly and requires medical approval for a decision that should not be a doctor's to approve or disapprove.

[b]Or criminals. I would be curious how slippery slope supporters (and opponents) feel about the active role of physicians ("First, do no harm.") in the state-sanctioned execution of prisoners by lethal injection.

Ethicist Daniel Maguire examines the root principle, "life is sacred" and its derivative, "do not kill," and some possible exceptions, such as self-defense, war, abortion, euthanasia, and genocide, in an essay titled "Good Exceptions to Good Principles" (Maguire, 1984, 77-83). He includes a droll parable, in which people put stickers on their carts to show which exceptions they favor:

> Some carts would have inscriptions on one side saying: "Life is sacred; stop the war!" And on the other side: "Liberalize abortion laws!" Other carts urged the people to support "our boys" who were away somewhere killing in the national interest, and, alternately, they would condemn all abortion. The people had good reason to be confused. And so they lived not so happily ever after.

[c]As Thomas de Quincy (1785-1859) satirized it, "If once a man indulges himself in murder, very soon he comes to think little of robbing; and from robbing he comes next to drinking and Sabbath-breaking, and from that to incivility and procrastination" (De Quincy, 1827).

[d]"Associated with" is not the same as "caused by." For example, when comparing various states, strict gun-control laws and high church attendance are associated ("correlated") with lower suicide rates (Clarke and Lester, 1989). However, this does not necessarily mean that a lower suicide rate is caused by church attendance or gun-control laws; they may all be results of some other social variable(s), such as a stable (nonmigratory) population or high percentage of families with children. With social "science," one can't (usually) change one variable at a time and look at the results.

It may be instructive that in 1997 the Centers for Disease Control (CDC) found increased teenage drug use *and* decreased teenage suicide rates. The pundits who, earlier, were quick to claim cause and effect when both rates had increased, have been uncharacteristically quiet.

PART II
•
SUICIDE METHODS

16
HOW DANGEROUS ARE VARIOUS
METHODS OF SUICIDE?

•

You got to be careful if you don't know where you're going, because
you might not get there.

—Yogi Berra

If you torture numbers long enough, they will confess to anything.

—Charlie Thayer

This chapter looks briefly at two questions: (1) How dangerous are various suicide methods?

and (2) can suicide methods be used to predict the likelihood of later suicide among survivors?

There is a huge amount of material on suicide, but surprisingly little information comparing the fatality rates of different suicide-attempt methods. There appear to be only two large studies, one published in 1961 by Edwin Shneidman and Norman Farberow, the other in 1974 by Jaime Card. Their data are generally similar, which gives us some confidence in them. Later chapters will look at individual methods of suicide in much more detail, but this is where you can compare them side by side.

Guns are the most lethal method. Of every ten attempts, eight or nine are fatal. Hanging, drowning, and carbon-monoxide poisoning are almost as deadly; other gases, poisons, and drugs tend to be less so. Attempting suicide by cutting or stabbing are the least dangerous: only one of twenty attempts is fatal. Recent data suggest a fatality rate of 1 to 2 percent in deliberate drug overdoses.

Keep in mind that all of these numbers show probabilities; there are no certainties. Every method may be lethal, and every method has been survived. You should also be cautious because the categories are broad and include differing techniques and intents—cutting one's wrist is not the same as cutting one's throat.

Look at the numbers. Table 16.1[1] shows how lethal various suicide methods are by percentage and by rank. Number one position is held by gunshot, fatal in 85 percent of cases.

Table 16.1 Lethality of Suicide Methods

Method	S/F	Percentage Fatal Card	Weighted Average	Rank
GUN	77.1	91.6	84.7	1
Head wound	[89.2]	—	—	—
Other	[46.5]	—	—	—
HANG	78.7	77.5	78.0	2
CO	75.7	78.0	77.0	3
DROWN	100	66.7	75.0	4
PLASTIC BAG	—	54.8	—	5
IMPACT/JUMP	46.0	41.6	42.3	6
FIRE	—	34.6	—	7
POISON	11.5	23.2	14.5	8
OTHER gas	15.8	8.5	13.4	9
DRUGS	12.2	11.4	11.8	10
CUT/STAB	5.8	4.1	4.9	11
OTHER	5.5	6.3	5.6	—

"Other" includes combinations and unknowns. CO_2-carbon monoxide.
Source: Card (1974) and Shneidman and Farberow (S/F) (1961).

Table 16.2 shows less detailed, but more recent studies from New Zealand (1990) and Hawaii (1990).[1] These are generally consistent with the older U.S. data:

Table 16.2

Method	New Zealand % Fatal	Hawaii % Fatal
Guns	83	73
Hanging	88	81
Car exhaust (CO)	78	na
Drowning	76	na
Jumping	60	87
Drugs/poisons	2	5
Drugs	na	(4)
Poisons	na	(20)
Cut/stab	10	6
Cooking gas	33	na
Other/unspecified	na	13

Source: Langley (1990); Hawaii Dept of Health (1990).

The category showing the greatest difference in lethality between the earlier and the more recent data is drugs/poisons. The decreased fatality percentage is due mostly to the widespread replacement of barbiturates with safer sedatives. Secondary reasons include use of less toxic antidepressants and, perhaps, better hospital treatment.

While not reflected yet in these numbers, carbon-monoxide poisoning by car exhaust is much less likely to be fatal (and will take much longer) because recent low-pollution cars emit far less carbon monoxide than do older cars.

Jumping, in Hawaii, may be singularly dangerous because of the easy availability of cliffs, ocean, and volcanoes, but this is speculation.

How Serious Are the Consequences of Suicide Attempts?

J. J. Card studied 2,729 suicides and suicide attempts from Pennsylvania.[3] In Table 16.3 the actual numbers of deaths and levels of injury associated with each method are shown, because in many categories the numbers are too small to draw statistically reliable conclusions. The possible outcomes, shown across the table, are:

Unknown ("UNK")
Psychiatric commitment ("PSYCH")
1=self or no treatment
2=treated and released
3=detained for observation and treatment
4=admitted to medical unit
5=admitted to intensive care unit
6=dead

The suicide-attempt method used ("METHOD") is shown in the first vertical column.

Table 16.3 OUTCOME of Suicide Attempts

METHOD	UNK	PSYCH	1	2	3	4	5	6	TOTAL
GUN	5	6	5	1	2	11	2	349	381
HANG	12	15	7	6	1	6	2	176	227
CO	10	6	2	4	5	6	0	117	150
DROWN	5	8	0	2	0	0	0	30	45
PLASTIC BAG	9	6	3	1	0	0	0	23	42
IMPACT	31	47	17	23	9	19	4	107	257
FIRE	8	3	2	1	0	3	0	9	26
POISON	6	8	5	15	13	21	5	22	95
OTHER GAS	8	10	6	3	8	7	1	4	47
DRUGS	136	189	80	285	214	278	126	168	1476
CUT/STAB	125	74	21	176	65	72	5	23	561

METHOD	UNK	PSYCH	1	2	3	4	5	6	TOTAL
MISC	4	2	7	0	3	4	0	1	21
COMBINATION	5	12	5	17	11	15	3	9	77
UNKNOWN	36	14	6	4	3	10	2	1	76

"CO"=carbon monoxide. IMPACT is not defined by Card, but is probably jumps/falls.
Source: Card, 1974.

Since raw numbers like these can be confusing, we can try combining them in a variety of ways in order to find patterns. For example, in the next table (Table 16.4), we look at how dangerous the sundry methods were, calculated by two different methods. The first, seriousness of result (column 2) is an average (weighted mean) of the outcomes for each method; the more severe the consequences, the higher the number. This table uses the same 1-through-6 scale as Table 16.3. Gunshot has the highest mean seriousness (5.84); cuts are the lowest (2.81).

Is the fatality rate of a given method a good predictor of the seriousness of survivors' injuries? Not necessarily: Jumping, hanging, and carbon-monoxide poisoning, for example, are more lethal methods than are drugs and poison. Yet the latter two cause more serious injury, as shown in column 3 (seriousness of result in survivors), on a 1 to 5 scale, when number 6, death, is excluded.

Does this tell us that jumping survivors have less severe injuries than do drug overdose survivors? Again, not necessarily; glancing back to the possible outcomes in Table 16.3, we find that there's no information concerning how many of these injuries are permanent or disabling. All we can tell is that a smaller proportion of jumping than drug-overdose survivors were hospitalized or put into the ICU. However, as you will see in later chapters, while drug overdoses may be acutely dangerous and require ICU intervention, jumps are more likely to leave you crippled.

Table 16.4 Severity of Suicide Attempt

Method	Seriousness of result	Seriousness of result in survivors
GUN	5.84	3.76
HANG	5.62	2.45
CO	5.60	2.65
DROWN	5.75	*
PLASTIC BAG	5.30	*
IMPACT/JUMP	4.63	2.58
FIRE	4.67	*
POISON	3.89	3.10
OTHER gas	3.21	2.76
DRUGS	3.51	3.11
CUTTING	2.81	2.60

*=less than 10 survived injuries
Source: Card, 1974.

HOW LETHAL DO PEOPLE BELIEVE VARIOUS SUICIDE METHODS TO BE?

Like carpenters they want to know *which tools.*
They never ask *why build.*

—Anne Sexton from *Wanting to Die*

In the introduction, I said that many people don't have an accurate idea of how dangerous particular suicide methods are. As a result, they may kill themselves when they intend to survive, and vice versa. This lack of knowledge increases the possibility of permanent injury.

In one study, 291 nonexperts and 10 pathologists were asked to estimate the lethality of a number of suicide methods.[4] (The nonexperts, all college students, are probably not typical of suicidal individuals of various ages and backgrounds—but they're easier to recruit.)

The college students:

1. Drastically overestimated the lethality of drug overdose and slashed wrists. For prescription-drug OD, the student estimate was 61 (on a 100 point scale) while the pathologists' estimate was 12; with limb cuts, the respective numbers were 44 and 6.

2. Underestimated danger from gunshot wounds and a cut throat. The student estimate for a shotgun wound to the chest was 77; pathologists said 96.

3. Had a much larger standard deviation[a] (not shown) for their estimates than did the pathologists.

There were often large differences between the student and pathologist estimates for time and pain. However, it may be that the wrong group of experts was surveyed: Big-city emergency-room physicians would have been a better choice since they have considerably greater experience with living suicide attempters than do pathologists.

The implications of this study are important—and scary:

- The medical literature generally considers most overdoses and limb cuts to be "ambiguous," "less serious," or "cries for help" methods, because the fatality rates are low. As a result, survivors may not be taken seriously. However, to the extent that attempters *believe* that these are seriously lethal means—as the student estimators do—using them becomes less a cry for help than an attempt to die. And not being taken seriously may convince someone to try again, using a more lethal method.

- Some people will die because they fatally underestimate the risk of their method; others will survive due to overestimating the danger. Even when the nonexpert's average estimate is reasonably accurate, the large standard deviations mean that many of the individual estimates are far off.

THE CONSEQUENCES OF INTENT

You might suppose that people who make a lethally intended suicide attempt would be at greater risk of later suicide than those whose suicide attempt was a call for help or attention. However, this seems not to be the case.[5] As mentioned earlier, surviving a serious suicide attempt may be therapeutic or cathartic, for a variety of reasons: getting help or punishing oneself, for example. Or it might be so traumatic as to effectively discourage a repeat attempt.

Table 16.5 shows the percentage of suicide-attempt survivors (by each method) who did and who did not subsequently die from suicide. These methods are ranked by risk of subsequent suicide (risk rank) and compared to the lethality of the survived method (fatality rank).

What does it mean? If there were a "strong positive correlation," it would show that survivors of highly lethal methods tended to later kill themselves significantly more often than survivors of low lethality methods. A "strong negative correlation" would show they did so significantly less often. "No correlation" would show a lack of statistical relationship between the two events. What we find is a very low positive correlation (+0.264), which is not "statistically significant"; that is, there is essentially no relationship.

Some high-lethality methods have many subsequent suicides, some have few; and likewise for low-lethality methods. The least lethal method (cuts) is eighth in predicting future suicide; the most lethal (guns) is sixth. The best predictor of future suicide (plastic bag suicide attempt) was fifth in lethality; the worst (fire) was seventh.

From this data we see that we can't predict the likelihood of later suicide based on the method that was survived.

Table 16.5 Risk of Later Suicide After Suicide Attempt

Method	% Later committing suicide	Risk rank for later suicide	Fatality Rank
GUN	6.2	6	1
CO	15.2	2	2
HANG	3.9	10	3
DROWN	13.3	3	4
PLASTIC BAG	21.0	1	5
IMPACT/JUMP	6.0	7	6
FIRE	0.0	11	7

Method	% Later committing suicide	Risk rank for later suicide	Fatality Rank
POISON	6.8	5	8
DRUGS	4.4	9	9
OTHER gas	7.0	4	10
CUTTING	4.8	8	11

The fatality rank differs slightly from Table 16.1, in which the data from two studies are combined.

Source: Card, 1974.

What if we looked, instead, at the likelihood of future suicide in relation to the medical seriousness of the earlier suicide attempt? This is shown in Table 16.6. Of the most seriously injured only 2.67 percent later killed themselves, while 10.84 percent of those who had no- or self-treatment later committed suicide. However, while the correlation is negative (-0.500), it does not reach statistical significance. Still, it's reasonable to wonder if the "more serious" attempt forced family/friends to deal with problems in a way or to a degree that "less serious" attempts didn't; or, perhaps, if being close to death increased the attempter's appreciation for living.[6]

Table 16.6 Risk of Suicide vs. Seriousness of Previous Suicide Attempt

Outcome of prior attempt	Percentage later committing suicide
self or no treatment	10.8
treated and released	4.3
detained for observation and treatment	0.6
admitted to medical unit	7.1
admitted to intensive care	2.7

Source: Card, 1974.

The overall suicide rate among those who have survived a suicide attempt is generally found to be about 1 to 2 percent the first year, and decreases thereafter, with a lifetime risk of 5 to 15 percent.[7]

Some more recent data are consistent with Card's ideas, some are not. In one study of sixty cases of survived suicide attempts, there was no correlation between the seriousness of the intent and the lethality of the attempt.[8] Similarly, of 156 consecutive trauma admissions using frequently lethal methods (that is, excluding drug overdoses and wrist cuts), 24 percent died. These were serious attempts, but there were few—only seven—subsequent attempts among the survivors, none fatal in the 2.8-year average follow-up, and they tended to use less lethal methods (three by drug overdose, three by wrist cut).[9] Similarly, ten-year follow-up on ninety-four people who survived the usually lethal procedure of jumping in front of a train found no higher suicide rates than those who had survived less lethal methods.[10]

However, other data show a different picture. A five-year follow-up of 886 suicide-attempters found that 6.45 percent of those whose try was classified as "serious" killed themselves, compared with 3.1 percent of the "non- or less-serious" attempters.[11] Similarly, in a group of 1,018 people treated for drug/poison suicide attempts, of those who had intended to die 21 percent later killed themselves, almost three times the rate of those whose lethal intentions were assessed as "mild."[12]

From a number of reports, survivors of suicidal drug overdoses often don't fare particularly well. In one Norwegian study, 227 of 1,487 survivors had died over an average of four-and-a-half-year follow-up, compared to an expected thirty-two deaths (based on standard mortality tables). Thirty-nine percent of the deaths were classified "suicide," 44 percent "natural," 9 percent "accidental," and 8 percent "other" (for example, homicide). Each of these categories had more deaths than expected. The suicide death rate was 1.3 percent per year,[13] about sixty times the overall national suicide rate.

Thus, the question of whether a serious suicide attempt is more predictive of subsequent suicide than a less serious attempt—like many other issues concerning suicide—remains unresolved.

NOTES

[a]A statistical measure of variability or scatter of data. In this case it means that the estimates by the pathologists were much closer to each other than were the student estimates.

17
ASPHYXIA

●

Asphyxia is any process that cuts off the oxygen supply to the brain. This includes such seemingly unrelated methods as a plastic bag over the head, suspension hanging, and carbon-monoxide poisoning. All forms of asphyxia are potentially lethal, but they differ widely in how painful they are. Death usually occurs between five to ten minutes after complete asphyxia. Some of these methods are suitable for suicide; none are appropriate for a suicidal gesture.

LETHAL INTENT: High
FATALITY RATE: High; around 80 percent
PERMANENT INJURIES: Moderately likely
PROS AND CONS OF SUICIDAL ASPHYXIA
Pros: • Can be quick and painless, if done knowledgeably
     • Does not require much strength or equipment
     • Some methods can be carried out by a person unable to get out of bed
Cons:• Possibility of brain damage if asphyxia is interrupted
     • Some methods leave a gruesome cadaver

WHAT IS ASPHYXIA?

In the most general sense asphyxia is any condition that causes the heart to stop beating by interfering with the body's capacity to inhale or utilize oxygen. Oxygen is ultimately necessary for all human metabolic activity, and its absence is rapidly fatal. Since the brain is the organ most sensitive to lack of oxygen, as a practical matter asphyxia is anything that cuts the brain's supply of, or ability to use, oxygen. Obviously the rest of the body needs oxygen, too, but the brain responds most quickly and catastrophically to its absence.

Looking at the various causes of asphyxia outlined below, one can begin to appreciate that methods as seemingly dissimilar as carbon-monoxide poisoning, strangling, and drowning are all fundamentally alike in how they kill.

I. Mechanical interference with oxygen uptake
    A. Compression of neck or chest
        1. Ligature
           a. hanging
           b. strangling
        2. Nonligature
           a. compression of chest
    B. Obstruction of airway
        1. External
           a. smothering
        2. Internal
           a. inhaling foreign object
           b. swelling (e.g., from allergic reaction or blow)
    C. Depletion of oxygen (e.g., plastic bag, drowning, vacuum)
II. Chemical interference with oxygen uptake or utilization
    A. Replacement of oxygen by nontoxic gas (e.g., helium, methane, nitrogen)
    B. Depletion of oxygen
        1. Fire
        2. Other oxidation (e.g., rusty SCUBA tank)
    C. Interference with utilization of oxygen at cellular level
        1. Carbon monoxide
        2. Cyanide

Some of these topics are treated separately or in more detail in other chapters (hanging, drowning, carbon monoxide, cyanide); others are too rarely encountered in the suicide literature (allergic reaction, inhalation of foreign object) to be worth looking at in detail.

How Many People Kill Themselves by Asphyxia?

U.S. suicide data[1] for 1994 (Table17.1) follows:

Table 17.1

Method	Total	M	F	WM	WF	BM	BF	OM	OF
Pipeline gas E951.0	9	8	1	8	1	0	0	0	0
L-P gas E951.1	8	8	0	8	0	0	0	0	0
Motor vehicle CO E952.0	1618	1257	361	1222	352	20	2	15	7
Other CO E952.1	393	317	76	308	74	8	2	1	0
Other gases E952.8-9	15	13	2	12	1	0	1	1	0
Hanging E953.0	4073	3555	518	3005	424	340	29	210	65
Plastic-bag asphyxia 953.1	422	214	208	206	199	4	5	4	4
Other related means E953.8-9	249	184	65	169	60	12	4	3	2
Drowning E954	383	254	129	200	107	42	12	12	10

M = Male; F = Female; W = White; B = Black; O = Other

L-P = liquified propane

CO = carbon monoxide

E-numbers are International Classification of Disease (ICD) codes. For cumulative 1979-94 data.

Source: CDC

Hanging and automotive carbon monoxide accounted for the large majority of these suicides. Drowning is a distant third, though its actual numbers may well be a good deal higher than reported, since it's easier to disguise suicidal intent with drowning than with either hanging or carbon-monoxide poisoning. Plastic-bag asphyxia is unusual in that there are as many women as men who use this method.

HOW AND WHY IS ASPHYXIA DANGEROUS?

Death is a process, rather than an event. Different cells and tissues die at different rates; for example, the brain will not normally survive more than a few minutes without oxygenated blood circulation, while connective tissue and muscle cells may remain alive for many hours.[2] This is one reason for the current medical ability to reattach severed limbs, but not heads.

At a basic level, all asphyxial injury is due to cutting off the brain's oxygen supply. This can happen directly, by interference with breathing (for example, from pressure on the chest or on the front of the neck) or by removal of the oxygen from the air. The same results occur indirectly if blood can't pick up oxygen (for example, in carbon-monoxide poisoning), or if oxygenated blood is prevented from reaching the brain (for example, by pressure on the large arteries in the neck). Irrespective of the method,[a] complete asphyxia causes quick—typically within two to three minutes—unconsciousness, followed by brain damage, ending in death. Since the degree of oxygen depletion varies with the method, so does the length of time needed for any given result.

Resuscitation may produce a survivor with brain damage, which is often long-lasting and sometimes permanent. Four to five minutes of circulatory arrest causes brain damage in around half of patients[3] and approximately five to ten minutes of complete oxygen cutoff is generally fatal (unless body temperature is abnormally low, as in drowning in icy water), though the heart will continue to beat for several more minutes.

Let's look at some of the methods in more detail.

STRANGULATION

Strangulation causes asphyxia by means of pressure on the neck from a ligature or from someone's hands. The weight of the victim's body plays no part, which is what distinguishes strangulation from hanging. Since manual self-strangulation is unknown and probably impossible (your hands relax when you become unconscious), all cases of manual strangulation are considered homicides. I suppose this also makes manual self-strangulation the perfectly safe suicidal gesture, but, by the same token, it would not likely be taken seriously.

Pressure on the neck can close the airway (trachea, or windpipe) at the front of the neck or compress the common carotid (right side) and vertebral (back of neck) arteries or jugular vein (left side), or some combination of the above.[b] The jugular vein is easiest to compress, followed by carotid and vertebral arteries, followed by the trachea. (See Hanging chapter for details.) Much more pressure is needed to close the airway than to close the blood vessels in the neck, and is unnecessarily painful. It is entirely feasible to protect the airway with stiff padding, and still kill oneself by tightening a ligature around the neck, thus shutting off blood flow to or from the brain.

Because they operate at higher pressure, the carotid arteries (which regulate blood flow into the head) require more external pressure to compress than does the jugular vein (which takes the blood out). A tight, quickly applied ligature would squeeze both shut, leaving a body with a dusky, blue-tinged (from deoxygenated hemoglobin in the blood) face.

Lesser pressure, compressing the jugular but not the carotid, would allow blood into, but not out of, the head. This would result in a swollen, blue-purple head, often leaking blood. If aesthetics are an issue, protecting the left side of the neck decreases compression of the jugular, allowing blood to leave the head, and thus minimizes engorgement of the head with blood.

Suicidal strangulation is uncommon, but certainly not unknown. It is generally done by one of three means: (1) knotting a rope or piece of cloth around the neck in such a fashion that it will not come undone when consciousness is lost; (2) twisting a stick or rod under the ligature so that it tightens, and then stays caught under the jaw or chin after unconsciousness; (3) wrapping multiple turns of cord around the neck without any knot at all, depending on friction to hold it in place.

Pressure on the windpipe is painful, but even lethal pressure elsewhere on the neck may produce little or no distress; thus, if the front (and, less critically, the left side) of the neck is well padded, none of the following techniques ought to be particularly painful. But all are potentially deadly.

Method one is straightforward: a ligature is wrapped once or twice around the neck and quickly knotted. This often looks similar to a homicidal strangulation, but can usually be distinguished from it by the absence of scratches on the neck (produced either by the attacker or the victim) and of internal neck injuries.

A more-or-less typical case of a suicidal strangulation is described in a forensic medicine text:

> A woman aged seventy-three was lying full length on the floor of a bedroom, which she shared with another patient in a nursing home. The bed clothing had been thrown back in a manner consistent with getting out of bed. There were no signs of any struggle. She was dressed in a nightgown and a brown stocking was round her neck; the fellow of a pair was seen suspended over the head of the bed. The stocking was applied with a half-knot at the nape on the first turn and with another half-knot at the front of the neck. The first turn was tight, but the second, although close to the first, was easily released. There were no other signs of violence, but a little bleeding, which produced a small stain, 1 inch in its diameter, had occurred from the nose; the stain was directly below her nose. Her face and neck, above the ligature, were congested and of purple colour. Bleeding had occurred beneath the conjunctivae [eyelids], but petechial hemorrhages [pinpoint hemorrhages often found in asphyxia] were not seen in the skin of the forehead and face. The tongue protruded, but was not bitten; she had dentures, but these were on her bedside table.

The author goes on to describe the generally mild injuries in detail and concludes, "The cause of death was asphyxia, following the application of a relatively broad, soft ligature to the neck with sufficient force to obstruct the veins and, to a lesser degree, the arteries of the neck; there was also obstruction of the air passages. The mode of application of the ligature was consistent with self-strangulation, as was all the other evidence."[4]

Sometimes it's difficult to determine whether death resulted from suicidal or from homicidal strangulation. For example, a soft ligature applied with skill and removed soon after death will create problems at autopsy. In one case a woman strangled her child with her husband's necktie. She tied no knot and held the ends of the necktie instead, until the deed was done and then removed it.[5] As a result, there was no externally visible neck injury. But she was caught anyway.

It isn't unusual for defense counsel in a case of homicidal strangulation to try to muddy the waters. In one instance, the body of a forty-two-year-old woman was found in a grave in her well-screened back yard. Clothesline was wrapped twice around her neck and tightened with a half-knot. A man was arrested. At trial, the defense described the ligature as more like a "lover's" knot than a murderer's, but had a hard time explaining the presence of a large piece of cloth forced down the victim's throat and several additional injuries. Faced with this evidence, counsel admitted that the injuries were the cause of death, but suggested that they were the results of a violent quarrel. The accused's failure to report the death was attributed to his preference for conducting his own funeral arrangements. His contention, that he wanted to give her a "Christian burial," was described by the prosecutor as one of the worst pieces of hypocrisy he had ever heard. The jury was equally unimpressed by his solicitude and convicted him of murder.[6]

Method two is rather like applying a tourniquet. There is generally a single loop which is attached loosely and usually knotted with a granny or reef knot.[7] A rod (still called a "Spanish windlass" in honor of its former use in that country for judicial executions) is placed under the ligature and twisted to tighten. Tightening needs to be accomplished fairly quickly in order to get a few extra twists in before unconsciousness intervenes. This is done because the twist may partly unwind when no longer held in place—but only partly. Usually the rod hangs up on the side of the jaw and enough compression is maintained to cause death. Occasionally, quite unwieldy rods are used to tighten the ligature, as in a case where a man used a fireplace poker.[8] Items this large will certainly prevent the ligature from untwisting, but are hard to tighten rapidly.

Method three, multiple loops, is the least common since, if the ligature is tight, there isn't time to do very many loops; if it is loose, it's ineffective. In one case, however, a fifty-three-year-old man succeeded despite these difficulties. He wrapped twine around his neck thirty-five times, tied a knot, and tightened it. He then bent forward on his knees with his head down, which increased his neck circumference, and thus, pressure from the twine; this is the posture in which he was found. Since this is an unusual position, the police were initially suspicious. However, there was no internal damage to the fairly delicate anatomical structures in the neck, a fact consistent with suicide, but not murder.[9]

CHOKING

Choking is the blockage of the internal airway by some foreign object. (Choke and sleeper holds, sometimes used by police and muggers, are discussed in the chapter on hanging.) Some examples are:

1. Inhaling vomit while unconscious, typically after drug/alcohol overdose. While this may be the actual cause of death, it is unpredictable and rarely, if ever, the intended method.

2. Aspiration of food. This is a common (and public) enough accidental cause of death that it's been nicknamed the "cafe coronary." The food item is often a chunk of meat, and the victim often is drunk. Sometimes there is no sign of respiratory distress—the victim just sits back on the chair, or falls over, dead. These are cases of cardiac arrest triggered by food stuck in the airway. Choking on food is also occasionally seen among some mental patients who try to "wolf" (a canard—wolves don't eat in this way) down their own and/or other inmates' food.

3. Young children are indiscriminate about what they put into their mouths, and readily insert things that will block breathing if inhaled.

The emergency treatment for life-threatening choking is the Heimlich maneuver widely taught in first-aid courses. It consists of holding the victim from behind and putting sudden pressure on the diaphragm by a quick squeeze with your locked hands. An emergency self-Heimlich can be done (if you don't panic) by quickly shoving your diaphragm (just below where your ribs come together between your chest and belly) hard against the rounded corner of a table, banister, or other sturdy object. Falling onto a round object such as a soccer ball or your fists should be similarly effective.

In any case, the idea is to dislodge the blockage by a sudden increase in exhalatory air pressure. If this isn't done, or fails, the desperate victim tries harder to inhale, which only wedges the object more firmly. Blood pressure and carbon-dioxide levels rise; lack of oxygenated (red) and excess of unoxygenated (blue) hemoglobin causes the victim to turn bluish; convulsions due to insufficient oxygen and too much carbon dioxide often occur; heartbeat races, falters, then stops.

COMPRESSION OF CHEST

If the chest and diaphragm are compressed, the ability to inhale is impaired. Since this can be done with few, if any, external signs of injury, it was once a notorious method of disguising murder. It was popularized[c] by two Ulstermen, William Burke and William Hare, who killed a number of derelicts in Scotland by this means. The motive was money: They committed these murders in order to sell the bodies for dissection at the local medical school.

Hare was keeper of the Log's Lodging House in Edinburgh. He and Burke sold their first corpse, a male who had died a natural death at the lodging house on November 29, 1827, to a Dr. Robert Knox for seven pounds, ten shillings, for dissection at Knox's anatomy school.

Deciding that there was a career opportunity here, over the next eleven months they enticed at least fifteen people (one at a time) to the lodging house, got them drunk, and smothered them. One would hold the victim's legs while the other would sit on his or her chest. Hare testified that, in one murder, Burke, "got stridelegs on the top of the woman on the floor, and she cried out a little, and he kept in her breath. . . . He pressed down her head with his breast. . . . He put one hand under the nose and the other under her chin, under her mouth."[10]

The technique was given the name "burking" in their honor. After they were caught, Hare turned King's evidence, was eventually released, and disappeared with Burke's former mistress, by then Hare's wife. He supposedly died a pauper in London in 1859. Burke was hanged in 1829; the doctor was never charged.[d]

Other than accidents such as car wrecks, construction cave-ins, falling beverage vending machines (surprisingly common, and usually due to people trying to rob the machine, or to irate customers trying to get their money back[e]), and stampeding mobs (most frequently soccer or music fans), the main incidence of fatal chest compression is in the course of police arrests. If a prisoner is facedown on the ground or in the back of a police car, with hands forced behind in cuffs and the weight of the policeman on his back, there may be lethal results. This is especially, but not only, true if the prisoner is struggling violently or has taken alcohol or other depressant drugs.

Compression is also the method used by constrictor snakes to kill their prey: They wrap themselves around their victim, a bit more closely each time it exhales. Inhalations become progressively more difficult until the victim dies of asphyxia. It is not crushed in the sense of having broken bones, except incidentally. There are four recorded cases of deaths due to constrictor snakes in the United States. Three were due to large pet snakes: Two killed infant children of the owners; one adult was killed while sleeping on the floor. The fourth death was that of a zookeeper.[11] None were considered suicides; nor is it a recommended method of suicide.

SMOTHERING

"Smothering" is the blockage of the nose and mouth. This is sometimes seen in homicide since it simultaneously minimizes the injuries that generate suspicion of foul play and noise (screams, gunshots, etc.) that might attract unwanted attention. However, unless there is a major mismatch in strength, the chances of killing someone quickly and without producing visible injury are slim.[f]

In the eighteenth and nineteenth centuries the accidental smothering of infants was common in England.[g] This was called "overlaying" and was attributed to widespread drunkenness among the lower classes, supposedly due to the availability of cheap gin. Since young children generally shared their parents' bed, if the parents were drunk, they might innocently (or otherwise) lie on and asphyxiate a small child. Nowadays, in the United States, infants are usually kept in their own cribs, and their occasional mysterious deaths are attributed to Sudden Infant Death Syndrome or SIDS.

Sometimes people are gagged in the course of other crimes. If the gag slips upward to also block the nose, or is inhaled, death from asphyxia can result.

Suicidal smothering is rare, requiring extraordinary will power, but is occasionally seen among prisoners and mental patients. One prisoner killed himself by stuffing pieces of cloth into his mouth and nose, and holding them in place with a handkerchief.[12] Another was found dead in a mental hospital with a pebble lodged in each nostril and mouth stuffed with cloth.[13]: It's also possible to smother oneself by lying facedown on soft bedding or clothing. This is occasionally the cause of death for people who are drunk or incapacitated for other reasons, but I'm not aware of cases in which a physically and mentally unimpaired adult has committed suicide by this means.

Accidental smothering occurs mostly in small children. Some of these cases are due to an infant being unable to turn over from its stomach. (The recent decrease in SIDS cases in England has been credited to a campaign to get mothers to lay their babies down face up in cribs.[14]) This situation is made more dangerous by the use of waterproof (and thus airproof) bedding covers. There exist "safety pillows" with holes cut throughout, intended to allow breathing even when the sleeper is facedown. In one case of infant asphyxia, such a pillow was used—but covered with a plastic liner.

There have been rare, but well-documented, cases of infants being smothered by cats sitting on their faces or chests. In one instance a five-week-old baby was discovered in her baby carriage with a cat lying on her face. Her father got her breathing again with mouth-to-mouth resuscitation, but she died seven months later. Autopsy showed evidence of brain damage consistent with asphyxia.[15]

Plastic bags, especially the thin, clinging sort used for garments, are notorious for smothering young children. Though flimsy, they tend to, well, cling. Older children and young adults are sometimes accidentally asphyxiated when sniffing fumes (glue, propane, solvents, etc.) from a plastic bag, if they become unconscious. This is in addition to the sometimes-serious toxicity caused by the vapor itself.

In suicide, a small plastic bag is generally placed over the head and tied or taped around the neck. The oxygen in the bag is used up by rebreathing. This plastic bag technique, however, seems unreliable, since most garden-variety bags are more-or-less easily torn in the course of convulsions or semiconscious movement. Plastic bag(s) or sheets may instead be wrapped tightly around the nose and mouth, which is faster, but more traumatic.

A small bag is said to become unpleasantly warm; if so, some ice, wrapped in a towel and resting on the head or neck, should help. My experiments with larger bags have not found heat to be a problem, but one might as well be comfortable.

A more gradual asphyxia can be achieved by use of a large plastic bag. A would-be suicide could combine drugs with this slow asphyxia to cause death less traumatically, more rapidly, and more reliably than either method could do alone.[h] The seal around the neck doesn't need to be painfully tight—rubber bands, elastic, or Velcro will do—and small air leaks are not significant, at least in the thirty-gallon and tube tent sizes. In fact, there are examples of fatalities where the bottom of the bag was not closed at all.[16]

Interestingly, there is often no sign of asphyxia—the faces are pale and un-congested—after plastic-bag suicides. This may be important in assisted-suicide, where the assistant wishes to avoid legal entanglements. It also suggests that the mechanism of death is not always, or not entirely, hypoxia, but rather cardiac arrest set off by hypoxia.[17]

The combination of asphyxia and drugs would decrease one of the major difficulties with drug overdose as a suicide method: Besides being unreliably lethal, most drugs take a long time, opening a suicide attempt subject to in-tervention. But if one were to use a drug(s) that quickly induced uncon-sciousness, simultaneous use of a large plastic bag or a tube tent would substantially increase the chance of a lethal result. (Obviously, this is coun-terproductive if one wants to survive the suicide attempt.)

And the time-window for permanent injury would be smaller than with the drug alone: Done properly, if one were interrupted within, say, twenty minutes, there would be good chance of full recovery (since the drug dosage alone could be sublethal and there would be enough air for about a half an hour in a thirty-gallon bag); after an hour or so, it would be too late.

However, there are some practical problems with combining plastic-bag asphyxia with drug overdose. For example, the huge number of available drugs[i] and doses makes it difficult to know what and how much to use to achieve unconsciousness. In addition, the effects of drugs are somewhat un-certain for many reasons, among which are individual sensitivity and the possibility of vomiting part of the swallowed dose, and most oral drugs are unpredictable in how long they take to cause insensibility.

Thus, simultaneous use of a small plastic bag might cause you to run out of oxygen while still conscious. This is not a big deal if you're alert—open the bag and try again—but may cause panic and bag tearing or removal dur-ing semiconscious movement. Waiting to use the bag until the drug(s) start to take effect does not seem like a entirely reliable alternative, but may be your best bet here, unless you have help available.

Multiple-bagging, thicker plastic, or wearing gloves will decrease the chance of tearing or removing the bag in the course of involuntary move-ments. If you are terminally ill, you may have friends or family who are willing to assist by sealing the bag and restraining your hands after you lapse into unconsciousness; however, this involvement will lead to legal repercussions if discovered.

Since thin plastic bag material tends to fall onto your face (especially if you're lying on your back), wearing a brim-hat or a dust (or painter's) mask (cut holes in it for easier breathing) is recommended.

Most of these problems can be avoided by using a plastic tube tent instead of a small plastic bag: It's cooler, unlikely to drop onto your face, less critically dependent on drug speed, and will cause asphyxial death after roughly four to five hours.

One could even build a coffin with an easily lifted lid. Having taken some unconsciousness-inducing drug, one might lie in the coffin, holding the lid open. Upon losing consciousness, the lid would fall, cutting off the air supply and leading to asphyxial death a few minutes later. If the drug dose was insufficient, or if, for any other reason, one woke unexpectedly, it would be an easy matter to open the lid.

However, note that while the combination of sedative drugs and large plastic bag (or functional equivalent) might seem to allow time and opportunity to change your mind, as a practical matter such drugs will likely prevent you from making, or acting on, any coherent decision once they start to take effect.

EXCLUSION OF OXYGEN

The effects of oxygen depletion have been described as consisting of four distinct stages.[18] However, the following oxygen percentages are only approximate and vary from person to person.

1. Indifferent stage: Arterial blood is more than 90 percent saturated with oxygen; only effect is decreased night vision.
2. Compensatory stage: 82 to 90 percent oxygen saturation; body compensates by increase in heart and breathing rate. This level of oxygen saturation causes no additional difficulties in people in good health; those with heart, lung, or blood problems may show early symptoms of:
3. Disturbance stage: 64 to 82 percent oxygen saturation; increasing air hunger, headache, exhaustion, dizziness, confusion.

4. Critical stage: Less than 60 percent oxygen saturation; unconsciousness in a few minutes, followed by brain damage and death. This corresponds to 6 to 8 percent oxygen in the breathing mixture (normally 21 percent).

Oxygen can become unavailable to the body by four general means:

- It may be replaced by some nontoxic gas like helium;
- It may be removed from the breathing mixture, either physically (for example, vacuum) or chemically (for example, used up by a flame);
- Red blood cells may be prevented from picking up oxygen (for example, by carbon monoxide);
- The ability of cells to use oxygen may be blocked (for example, by cyanide).

Let's examine each of these in more detail.

DISPLACEMENT OF OXYGEN FROM THE BREATHING MIXTURE. Many gases that are more or less nontoxic can cause asphyxia by replacing oxygen from the breathing mixture. Some common ones include acetylene, argon, butane, carbon dioxide, freon, helium, hydrogen, liquified petroleum gas (LPG), methane, neon, nitrogen, and propane. As a result, they are dangerous in enclosed areas or when breathed through a gas mask, but not otherwise. People start showing signs of asphyxia when the concentration of these gases is around 30 percent; severe symptoms at around 50 percent; death at around 75 percent.[19]

In the above list, argon, butane, carbon dioxide, freon, and LP gas are heavier than oxygen, and may displace it from the bottom of closed spaces, and, occasionally, even open spaces that are protected from wind. Tunnels that are open only through manhole covers occasionally contain lethal concentrations of carbon dioxide. Someone entering such a location unknowingly would become unconscious within a couple of minutes—perhaps within seconds[20]—and would be dead after five to ten minutes. A standard gas mask is useless under these circumstances; supplemental oxygen is necessary.

A mass asphyxia occurred near Lake Nyos, Cameroon, in August 1986. A large amount of cold, dissolved carbon dioxide exists in the bottom layers of this volcanic lake water. Probably as a result of turbulence from a mudslide, this carbon dioxide-rich water rose. As a result, the pressure on it from water above was decreased. The result was like opening a soft drink bottle: Bubbles of carbon dioxide gas left the water.

People living in the valley below were engulfed by an invisible wave of carbon dioxide gas, which, being heavier than oxygen, displaced it. There was no warning. Everything that needed oxygen died within minutes: human beings, domestic and wild animals, even insects. Birds that were on the ground or flew too low perished. People dropped like flies (so did the flies) in the midst of whatever they were doing. The human death toll was more than 1,700.

However, for the purpose of suicide, carbon dioxide would be an unpleasant choice, since its presence stimulates both breathing reflexes and the sensation of smothering.

The hydrocarbons methane, butane, liquified petroleum gas (LPG), and propane, while readily available as fuel gases, are normally mixed with bad-smelling "warning" gases (mercaptans), related to skunk scents.

Acetylene is used for gas welding and is easy to acquire, but contains somewhat-toxic acetone. Don't bother making your own acetylene from calcium carbide (formerly and still occasionally used in carbide lanterns for caving), because it contains an ammonia-like contaminant, phosphine (PH_3).

Freon are bad for the ozone layer and neon is expensive.

Hydrogen is flammable (remember the Hindenberg) and raises the pitch of your voice.

The remaining gases—argon, helium, and nitrogen—are your best bets in this category. They are all tasteless, odorless, nonirritating, and under these conditions, chemically and physiologically inert. In fact, nitrogen comprises about 80 percent and argon 1 percent of sea-level air, while a roughly 90 percent helium to 10 percent oxygen mix (precise ratio depends on dive depth) is used for deep-water diving (to avoid the intoxicating effects of high pressure nitrogen, called "nitrogen narcosis" or, more poetically, "rapture of the deep").

Since these inert gases are not poisonous and your lungs have something to inhale, such asphyxias will be minimally traumatic. That is, they will not cause feelings of suffocation (which are due to carbon dioxide buildup, not the lack of oxygen) or hemorrhages (caused by high blood pressure from blocked jugular vein or struggling to breathe against a closed airway).

Most medical use of inert gases is for animal euthanasia,[21] however there have been human fatalities from them, too. For example, airline face masks were mistakenly hooked up to inert gas cylinders instead of to oxygen at least ten times during the 1980s in the United States. The fact that these people died without attracting attention is consistent with nontraumatic death.[22]

Argon is commonly used for inert-gas electric welding and helium for balloons. Nitrogen has a variety of uses and may be purchased either as a gas or as a cold (-196 degrees C or -321 degrees F) liquid. All of these are available from industrial gas suppliers. Helium can also be found at party-supply stores, and argon at welding suppliers. None of these gases are dangerous[j] unless they displace oxygen from the breathing mixture.

Probably the easiest way to use inert gases for suicide is to enter a tube tent with a gas cylinder, flush the tent with any of the three gases, and seal the ends of the tube. The volume of a tent is such that you won't produce enough carbon dioxide to stimulate breathing reflexes before dying. Since there's little or no residual oxygen in the breathing mixture, minimal amounts of carbon dioxide ought to be exhaled, suggesting that a large inert gas-filled plastic bag over the head should work as well as the tube tent.

Only slightly more complicated method is to hook up a gas delivery mask (available at military surplus or medical supply stores) to a cylinder of compressed inert gas. This may, in fact, be the easiest method if you're using supplemental oxygen, and have a gas delivery system already in place.

The main hazard of this (and all) asphyxia is the possibility of brain damage if the process is interrupted due to intervention, running out of gas, or tearing or removing the gas mask, plastic bag, or tube tent while unconscious. This can be minimized by using a high concentration of the anoxic gas, which causes most rapid loss of consciousness. These gases are not a danger to others in anything but a small, sealed space, however it's important that a gas cylinder not be mislabeled, lest it imperil subsequent users.

In experiments, animals (dogs, cats, rabbits, mink, chickens) show little or no evidence of distress from inert gas asphyxia,[k23] become unconscious after one to two minutes, and die after about three to five minutes.[24] Thus, use of any of these three gases, combined with a plastic bag, should be less traumatic than plastic bag asphyxia alone, since there will be little discomfort from carbon dioxide buildup and unconsciousness will be swift.

REMOVAL OF OXYGEN FROM THE BREATHING MIXTURE. Oxygen can be removed either physically, by pumping it out along with the other components of air, or chemically, by combining it with other substances and so making it unavailable to the body.

Physical removal of oxygen may become a means of suicide in the future, if there is space travel through the near-vacuum between planets. I'm not familiar with any use of hard vacuum to commit suicide on earth (though there at least one instance of suicide in a high-altitude test chamber). Don't try to become a footnote in the *Guinness Book of World Records* by being the first: If a vacuum was generated quickly, your blood would boil most unpleasantly from the low pressure before you had time to die from asphyxia.[1]

Using up the available oxygen is often the cause of accidental death, as when children are trapped in abandoned refrigerators and asphyxiate. Despite laws in every state and widespread publicity, the Consumer Product Safety Commission (CPSC) reported seventy-six of these deaths between 1980-88.[25]

Similarly, glue sniffers who use plastic bags are at risk of unexpected unconsciousness, followed by death in the absence of prompt intervention. Rough calculations show that it's possible for much of the oxygen in a SCUBA tank to be used up if the inside of the tank rusts severely; so don't go diving with old air in your tanks. The same hazard exists in other iron tanks, such as ship's holds. Here, also, the damp steel walls can rust enough to use up the available oxygen. Such deaths tend to occur too quickly to be directly due to hypoxia; instead, the immediate cause seems to be sudden cardiac arrest, brought on by lack of oxygen.

CARBON-MONOXIDE POISONING

Until recently, in Europe you could open the oven gas valve (unlit), stick your head into the oven, and be fairly confident of dying quickly. (Death from opening the stovetop valves was much slower since the entire room needed to reach a lethal gas concentration, unless your head was near the unlit burner.) Yet if you tried this in the United States, it would hardly ever work.

The reason was that the United States and Europe used different gases for household heating. In the United States "natural" gas—composed largely of the nontoxic hydrocarbon methane—is cheap and plentiful; Western Europe, until discovery of the North Sea oil and gas fields in the 1960s, had very little. In Europe, the gas generally used was a mixture of hydrogen, hydrocarbons, and (7 to 15 percent) carbon monoxide. The hydrogen is as nontoxic as methane, but carbon monoxide is deadly.[m] This mixture was called "water gas" or "coal gas," and was a perfectly good fuel except for its deplorable tendency to kill anyone in the same (or sometimes even a nearby) room as a gas leak, deliberate or accidental.

As various parts of the world switched from a water gas-based mixture to natural gas (no carbon monoxide), the head-in-the-oven method of suicide became *much* less frequent. For example, between 1946 and 1996, the fraction of U.S. households using natural gas increased from 45 percent to 98 percent. During the same span, the household gas suicide rate decreased twelvefold, from 0.926 in 100,000 to 0.079 in 100,000.[26] In England, the number of suicides due to gas fell from 2,368 (plus another thousand or so accidental deaths) to 11 between 1963 and 1978.[27] Similarly, in West Germany the percentage of suicides by household gas fell from 11.6 to 0.3 percent from 1963 to 1976; meanwhile, however, the percentage of suicides due to drugs/poisons went from 24.4 to 36.5 percent.[28]

It is possible that some Americans (including the poet Sylvia Plath[n]) who were familiar with low-lethality natural gas died by accident/mistake in Europe when they intended a suicidal gesture with methane and died from carbon monoxide. This may also account for the common misconception that natural gas contains toxic amounts of carbon monoxide: It doesn't (though a misadjusted natural gas burner that produces a yellow or sooty flame is *generating* significant carbon monoxide).

There was a bizarre case where a man tried to commit suicide by the head-in-the-oven method. Since the gas was methane, this wasn't working well. After a while, the man got bored, took his head out, and lit a cigarette. The match ignited the gas-air mixture and he was killed by the explosion. The legally interesting question arose, was this a suicide or an accident? The inquest ruled it a suicide.[29]

Household gas does have a bad smelling additive (methyl mercaptan) intended to warn you if there's a gas leak. This mercaptan is also added to bottled gas for the same purpose. However, old and internally corroded propane and butane tanks absorb the mercaptans, leaving an odorless explosive gas, which probably won't be detected if it leaks.

A second factor that lowered the frequency of head-in-the-oven suicide attempts has been the general introduction of ovens containing thermocouples and either pilot lights or electronic igniters. Instead of manually lighting the oven with a match, these devices, unless disabled or defective, will light the oven moments after gas enters it. This makes gas asphyxia unlikely and substantially decreases the chance of an explosion caused by filling a room with an unburned gas mixture waiting only for a spark or flame to blow sky high. However, the stovetop burners will continue to emit gas if, for whatever reason, they fail to light or blow out.

COMPARISON OF CARBON DIOXIDE, CARBON MONOXIDE, AND HYDROGEN CYANIDE: HOW DO THESE GASES WORK?

There's a lot of confusion concerning these poisonous gases. (Also see the chapter on drugs.)

Carbon dioxide (CO_2) is the product of the complete combustion of carbon by oxygen, and is nontoxic at low concentrations. Your exhaled breath is normally 4 to 5 percent CO_2. Inhaling CO_2 does increase the acidity of your blood, and cause you to breathe faster, but at high CO_2 concentrations these don't have time to become serious problems.

CO_2 kills by two different mechanisms: (1) It displaces oxygen (and most other atmospheric gases, since carbon dioxide is denser than almost all of them), leaving you with nothing else to breathe. (2) Carbon dioxide in concentrations of 30 percent or more is also a rapid anesthetic, causing unconsciousness within one to two minutes, and death in about five minutes, without much evidence of distress in experimental animals.[30] It is widely used for theatrical fog (ever notice how it stays near the ground? and a good thing, too) and as a portable refrigerant in its frozen state, dry ice. There is at least one case report of a death from transporting dry ice in an enclosed car. As the dry ice evaporated, a dangerous concentration of gaseous carbon dioxide was created.

In addition to dry ice, CO_2 also is available as a compressed gas. (You need a special CO_2 valve for these tanks, as standard valves freeze up.) Carbon dioxide gas has the further merit of being nonexplosive and cheap and can be made at home by mixing baking soda and vinegar.

Carbon monoxide (CO) is colorless, odorless, and tasteless; it has one less oxygen atom than carbon dioxide (CO_2). It will be produced by any carbon-fueled flame that doesn't get enough oxygen. If a flame is yellow or puts out visible soot, you can be sure it's also generating carbon monoxide; if a flame is blue, carbon dioxide is the principal carbon oxide. You may have noticed that the outer part of a candle flame is blue, while the inside is yellow. This is because the outer portion burns hotter due to its greater oxygen supply.

Carbon monoxide's biological effects are mostly due to the fact that it's 200 to 250 times more strongly attached to the oxygen-transporting molecule in red blood cells, hemoglobin, than is oxygen. And a hemoglobin molecule can't carry both carbon monoxide and oxygen. Thus a low concentration of CO in the air can occupy a large fraction of your hemoglobin. For example, 0.01, 0.02, 0.10 and 1.0 percent CO in the breathing mixture would tie up 11, 19, 54, and 92 percent, respectively, of a person's hemoglobin at equilibrium.[31]

Carbon monoxide is also directly toxic to cells by interfering with their ability to use oxygen, by binding to a number of iron-containing enzymes and other proteins. Carbon monoxide causes blood to be a bright, cherry red, which produces a ruddy corpse. This unusual coloration can be used for preliminary identification of CO poisoning.

The toxicity of carbon monoxide is shown by a case in which a car accident victim was put on a stretcher, which was placed eight to ten feet behind the tailpipe of an idling ambulance while another person was attended to. Upon reaching the hospital, the first man was discovered to be dead from carbon-monoxide poisoning. His other injuries were minor.

Since smoldering tobacco contains about 4 percent carbon monoxide,[32] pack-a-day smokers have 5 to 6 percent of their hemoglobin tied up by carbon monoxide. This level causes small, but measurable, impairment of both physical and mental performance.[33] Frequent cigar smokers have peak carbon monoxide blood levels of around 20 percent.[34] A 50 percent carbon monoxide blood level is often fatal, but levels as low as 15 percent may also kill those with heart or lung problems.[35]

It takes about five and a half hours of breathing fresh air to remove half the carbon monoxide from hemoglobin, another way of showing the high affinity between the two; 100 percent oxygen reduces this to 80 minutes; 100 percent oxygen at three atmospheres pressure gets rid of half the carbon monoxide in twenty-three minutes,[36] but may cause permanent eye damage. However, even twenty-three minutes is often too long: A few minutes of asphyxia is enough to cause brain damage which may be fatal, and has a good chance of being permanent.

These injuries include dementia, psychosis, paralysis, cortical blindness, memory deficits, and Parkinsonism; the latter two are the most common. The frequency of permanent injury from carbon-monoxide overdose ranges from 0.3 to 43 percent in various studies,[37] even if high-pressure oxygen used. "Some survive [in] a coma for weeks or months before succumbing to infection."[38]

Alcohol and other central nervous system depressants (for example, sedatives) may increase the toxic effects of carbon monoxide. A 0.20 percent blood-alcohol concentration combined with a serious (but generally not fatal in a healthy individual) 35 to 40 percent carbon-monoxide saturation of the blood has been fatal.[39] However, this is association is controversial.[40] Carbon monoxide is also hazardous to unprotected rescuers, and will explode if the concentration reaches 10 percent and there is a spark or flame present. This concentration will not be reached from combustion, but may be achieved from compressed CO (in tanks) or chemically generated CO.

Automotive carbon monoxide poisoning is becoming less frequent in the United States. The reason is that car engines are required to get better gas mileage and produce fewer toxic emissions than in the recent past. A new, well-tuned engine may emit 0.06 percent carbon monoxide, compared to 6 to 9 percent from an engine of the 1960s, a hundredfold decrease. As a result, it takes longer to kill yourself by filling a garage with carbon monoxide from a tuned engine. It can be done, but is no longer either fast or certain.

How long does this take? For a given-volume garage, it depends primarily on the age, state-of-tune, and size of the engine. If a "clean" two-liter engine idles at 750 rpm, then it will take about an hour for 20 by 20 by 8 foot garage to reach 0.06 percent carbon monoxide. This is not a reliably lethal concentration.

What would happen if the exhaust gases are piped directly into the car, as is commonly done using a garden or vacuum-cleaner hose? It would take about three minutes to reach 0.06 percent atmospheric carbon monoxide. However, the atmospheric CO concentration can't be greater than that of the exhaust mixture; it just takes less time to get there. Once again, not reliably lethal.

If we had a "dirty" engine of the same size with 6 percent carbon-monoxide emissions (100x clean engine), it would take about thirty-five seconds for the garage to reach 0.06 percent carbon monoxide; 70 seconds for 0.12 percent, 140 seconds for 0.24 percent, and so on. Thus, a lethal concentration of CO would be produced in a minute or two. Death could occur in less than a half an hour. Note that, while running such exhaust into the car would generate a lethal concentration of CO within a few seconds, one would have to continue breathing it for a fatal result.

These calculations are illustrative rather than precise because (a) garages differ widely in size and airtightness; (b) most cars emit somewhere between 0.06 and 6 percent CO.

Alternatively, one may be able to buy a small tank of carbon monoxide from a chemical, science supply, or industrial gas supply company (you will need a gas regulator/valve, too). Loosely sealing yourself in a plastic tube tent, car, or functional equivalent, and releasing the gas should be quickly (five to fifteen minutes) fatal.°

A simple and reliably lethal source of carbon monoxide is a charcoal grill, hibachi, or other burner. If charcoal (or any other handy carbon fuel, like wood or coal) is burned in one, a deadly CO concentration will be quickly generated in any small, enclosed space, such as a tent. Using this method inside a building is a bad idea, both due to fire hazard and because of the CO danger to other people.

Dr. Kevorkian's current suicide apparatus consists of a gas mask attached to a tank of carbon monoxide. The gas flow is controlled by a valve that is opened by the patient, who is wearing the mask. Under these conditions, death should occur in less than five minutes. The advantage is that the gas concentration will probably be higher than with a tent, with faster results. The disadvantage is that the hookup is a bit more elaborate and is correspondingly more likely to require someone else's help.

EFFECTS OF CARBON MONOXIDE

A century ago the eminent British scientist J. B. S. Haldane studied the effects of carbon monoxide on himself—a time-honored, but sometimes hazardous, medical tradition. While sitting and taking notes, he breathed a 0.21 percent carbon monoxide mixture for seventy-one minutes. A summary of his observations follows: After twenty to thirty-four minutes he had a slight feeling of fullness and a throbbing of the head; 17 percent of his blood hemoglobin was tied up by carbon monoxide as carboxyhemoglobin. After forty to forty-five minutes the headache was worse, his breathing was slightly fast and he felt abnormal (39 percent carboxyhemoglobin). After fifty-nine to sixty-five minutes, he was breathing fast, looked pale, was starting to become confused, and couldn't move in his chair without feeling worse (44.5 percent carboxyhemoglobin). After seventy-one minutes his vision was dim, he couldn't get up without help, and he stopped the experiment (49 percent carboxyhemoglobin). There were no long-term ill effects.[41]

As always, there is individual variability: In 7 percent of fatal CO poisonings, less than 40 percent of the victim's hemoglobin was tied up by CO.[42] Another study found that 0.32 percent CO for an hour caused unconsciousness; 0.45 percent caused death.[43]

In animal experiments, carbon monoxide is about as fast as inert gases: unconsciousness occurs in one to two minutes and death after around five minutes, using 4 to 8 percent CO.[44] Death is preceded by convulsions and muscle spasms, but the fact that there are frequent accidental carbon monoxide poisonings among sleeping people shows that it doesn't cause enough discomfort to reliably awaken someone. However, first taking enough of a sedative (for example, alcohol, opiate, barbiturate) to achieve unconsciousness would probably result in an easier death.

If low concentration of CO is anticipated, such as from new car exhaust, it may be useful to premedicate with antinausea (for example, some antihistamines) and antiseizure (for example, Valium) drugs, but this is speculative. Better is to avoid this situation: Don't use CO for a suicidal gesture and don't use low concentrations for suicide.

We close this section with a suicide note from Japan, written while a car was filling with carbon monoxide.[45] The first eleven items of the note were personal messages and instructions for the disposal of assets. The last entries are quoted below, in translation:

> 12. I had attempted suicide with several methods, I could not commit it yesterday. I hope I am successful in killing myself today.
>
> 13. I have written too much.
>
> Finally, good-bye my life! I believe in Rin-ne [Buddhist concept of reincarnation as human or animal, depending on one's conduct in the most recent life.]
>
> [At 6:15 p.m.] The inhalation of exhaust gases is begun.
>
> [After seven minutes] My eyes and throat are slightly irritated. Put on a bathing towel. There are tremendous water drops on the door glasses [This is condensation of water vapor from the exhaust]. The tank is full of gasoline.
>
> [After eight and one-half minutes] Slight shortness of breath. Ha-ha-ha. The powers of Nissan's engine are great!
>
> [After ten minutes] Swallowed a cup of Japanese sake [rice wine]. I could not control myself to stay in the cabin [of the minivan] at this level of shortness-of-breath yesterday.
>
> [After eleven minutes] To the mistress of a grocery store: "Yes, you were right. The size of this hose, 30mm in outer diameter and 25mm in inner diameter, fits the exhaust pipe perfectly.
>
> [After twelve and one-half minutes] Swallowed another cup of sake. I wish I could have a can of beer. I wonder what the concentration of carbon monoxide is now.
>
> [After fourteen minutes] Breathing can only be done by mouth.
>
> [After fifteen minutes] Water is pouring out of the hose.

[After sixteen minutes] Good-bye, Mum and Papa! [and a list of six people].

[After seventeen minutes] Still I am living. It is asthmatic breathing. Now, I will sleep.

This was the last entry.

Cyanide is one of the fastest-acting poisons (see the chapter on drugs for more information), though sources differ with regard to just how long (mostly between one and fifteen minutes in large (1500 mg) doses, longer with lower doses[46]) it takes to kill. The lethal dose is estimated to be 50 to 300 mg;[47] however much larger amounts have been survived with prompt medical attention.

The gaseous forms, hydrogen cyanide and cyanogen, are rarely used in suicide, but should act more quickly than the oral poison; solid cyanide salts (potassium, sodium, and calcium cyanide) are the commonly sold forms, but hydrogen cyanide gas can be easily made by mixing a solid cyanide and a liquid acid (for example, hydrochloric [muriatic] acid); this is what is done in gas chambers.

Cyanide works by causing asphyxia at the cellular level; it binds to iron ions found in some enzymes and makes them unavailable for cellular respiration, essentially choking your cells. The cells try to survive by switching to a non-oxygen requiring metabolic pathway (the same one your muscles use when you're exercising faster than you can breathe in oxygen), but this quickly builds up lactic acid to toxic levels. The fastest-metabolizing cells, brain and heart cells, are most quickly affected; and if they die, so do you. Cyanide also has a direct poisonous effect on the central nervous system and depresses breathing, but this is overkill. As with carbon monoxide, some survivors have permanent nervous-system injury, such as memory deficits and tremor.

If you use cyanide, it would be a thoughtful gesture to leave a conspicuous note to that effect, because of possible hazard to rescuers who might otherwise apply mouth-to-mouth resuscitation—some people lack the ability to detect the almond-like smell of cyanide.

Thus, all three substances, carbon dioxide, carbon monoxide, and cyanide are asphyxiants: Carbon dioxide displaces oxygen, keeping it from getting to your lungs; carbon monoxide prevents your red blood cells from picking up oxygen and also blocks cellular respiration directly; and cyanide stops your cells from "breathing" despite plenty of available oxygen in the air and in your red blood cells.

SUMMARY

1. None of the methods discussed in this chapter should be used for a suicidal gesture; all are potentially lethal and don't give enough warning of unconsciousness to allow you to count on being able to change your mind.

2. Strangulation, like hanging, is quickly fatal. If the front (throat/airway/trachea) part of the neck is well-protected, it should not be particularly painful. Protecting the left side of the neck will minimize compression of the jugular vein and subsequent engorgement of the head with blood. For someone who is terminally ill, has no help available, and is bedridden, strangulation may provide the best combination of speed, ease of application, and lethality.

3. Carbon monoxide is probably the only readily available toxic gas worth considering for suicide, but internal combustion engines are highly variable as sources for this gas. This is relevant either if you are contemplating filling a garage with a lethal carbon-monoxide concentration or running a hose from the exhaust pipe into a sealed car. At the same time, carbon monoxide is both slower and probably more subject to interruption than hanging or strangulation, and has caused brain damage in some survivors.

4. Perhaps the least traumatic of these methods consists of achieving unconsciousness with drugs, combined with plastic-bag, carbon monoxide, or inert gas asphyxia. However, this requires arranging and coordinating two methods, which may be difficult to do without help, particularly for people who are severely ill. Finding the right drug(s)/doses is also sometimes a problem.

In the absence of sedative drugs, either carbon monoxide or inert gas (nitrogen, helium, or argon) will probably make plastic-bag asphyxia less unpleasant since they speed unconsciousness and minimize carbon dioxide buildup.

NOTES

[a]CT (computed tomography, CAT scan) studies find similar hypoxic brain abnormalities after: suspension hanging, drowning, hypoglycemic coma, and cyanide, carbon monoxide, hydrogen sulfide, or methanol poisoning (Aufderheide, 1994).

[b]This, incidentally, is how big cats, such as lions and cheetahs, often kill prey.

[c]But certainly used earlier, as in the seventeenth-century Salem, Massachusetts, judicial punishment called "pressing" (Spitz, 1993).

[d]He was, apparently, an innocent party to the proceedings, but his reputation was not helped by a contemporary doggerel that went, "Burke's the butcher, Hare's the thief, Knox's the man that buys the beef."

[e]You will, no doubt, be fascinated to learn that there have been at least thirty-seven fatalities since 1978 due to toppling vending machines. These are almost all soda machines, which are top-heavy and weigh almost a ton when filled (The Washington Post, January 2, 1996). Help is on the way, however: The Consumer Product Safety Commission (CPSC) has negotiated a tough agreement with the seven U.S. vending machine manufacturers in which the manufacturers have agreed to post warning labels on their machines. A spokeswoman for the CPSC stated, apparently without irony, "This is a terrific example of what we call the safety triangle—cooperation between industry, consumers, and government. The companies were very cooperative."

[f]Death from oxygen depletion is occasionally seen in homicide (as in Poe's story, The Cask of Amontillado, in which the victim, the ironically named Fortunato, is bricked up in a wine cellar).

[g]The first recorded case occurs in the Old Testament, where Solomon has to judge which of two women is the mother of a live baby, the other infant having been "overlain."

[h]Back-of-the-envelope calculations suggest that one could survive for roughly a half hour, sitting quietly, breathing only from a fully inflated 30-gallon plastic trash bag.

For a tube tent 8 feet long with a diameter of 4 feet, volume is about 400 gallons if it's in a typical triangular shape (maximum; less due to pinching of tent ends and volume of occupant). This corresponds to—very roughly—five-hour survival.

In self-experiments, I've found that I become uncomfortable enough, probably from carbon dioxide buildup, to remove a 30-gallon bag after about fifteen minutes. Over that time my breathing rate increases from around eight breaths per minute to around thirty per minute.

[i] See Drug Appendix web site for details and dosages.

[j]There have been occasional reports of cardiac arrhythmias caused by breathing pure helium (usually as a party game), but these are extremely rare. And, obviously, any liquified gas at -200 can cause cold injury.

[k]Rats show some evidence of distress (Hornett, 1984) but other animals don't seem to remember it: Revived cats and dogs showed no subsequent fear of the inert-gas chamber (Quine, 1988). In any case, if this is a concern one can take sedatives while holding a gas valve closed that will open when your hand relaxes. Be aware, though, that presedated animals survived inert gas anoxia far longer (fifty-one minutes in one dog) than did unsedated ones (Quine, 1988).

[l]The vapor pressure of water (blood) at body temperature, is 47 mmHg (torr). This corresponds to atmospheric pressure at around 12 miles (64,000 feet or 19,300 meters) elevation (Hodgman, Charles D., editor-in-chief, *Handbook of Chemistry and Physics*, 37th ed., 2141-47).

[m]This combination was used when it was discovered that if steam (thus the name "water gas") was passed over hot coal ("coke"), the carbon (C) in coal would take the oxygen away from water (H_2O) and create equal volumes of two flammable gases, carbon monoxide (CO) and hydrogen (H_2), which could be sent through pipes into individual homes, unlike the coal itself. And Europe had lots of coal.

[n]The evidence is clear that (unlike her sleeping pill overdose ten years earlier), she did not intend to die. She had scheduled an au pair to meet her at 9 A.M. that morning; there was no answer at the door when the Australian girl knocked and rang. The old man on the ground floor who could have let her enter (and who, Plath knew, rose before nine) was unconscious from escaped carbon-monoxide fumes. Plath's note, "Please call Dr_____," which included the phone number, was thus not seen until she was dead (Alvarez, 33-36).

[o]The smallest size chemical lecture bottle is about 2 cubic feet of gas, which would produce a CO concentration of around 1.5 to 6 percent, depending on the size of the tent or car. Thus even a small lecture bottle of CO will be enough for a quickly lethal concentration.

18
CUTTING AND STABBING

•

I decided I'd better use the bathroom because from what I'd read, that's where everyone kills themselves. Plus if I got the bedroom rug dirty my mother would *kill* me. Then I just started. I cut my wrists. I watched the blood go into the sink, and because the sink was already wet, the blood spread out and I realized how neat it looked. It hurt, but I didn't mind. It was almost as if I wanted it to hurt because I wanted to be tough. Everything in the bathroom is white. White tile walls and white tile floors. I had to keep stopping and cleaning up because I didn't want to make a mess. I poured water in the sink so the blood would go down the drain. I'd rest my arms on my pants to soak up the blood so it wouldn't get on the floor.[1]

Relatively few people commit suicide by cutting or stabbing themselves. However, around 10 to 15 percent of suicidal gestures/attempts are from wrist cutting.[a2] Unlike all-or-nothing methods like hanging and drowning, cutting and stabbing can be made about as lethal as you choose to make it. Nevertheless, mistakes and accidents do happen.

LETHAL INTENT: Variable, mostly low
MORTALITY: Low, around 5 percent
PERMANENT INJURIES: Low
PROS AND CONS OF CUTTING AND STABBING FOR SUICIDE

Pros: • Can be done as a fast (or slow), highly lethal method
  • Knives and razors are readily available
Cons:• Painful
  • Sometimes gory cadaver
  • Consciousness not immediately lost

PROS AND CONS OF CUTTING AND STABBING FOR SUICIDAL GESTURE

Pros: • Can be fairly safe
  • Consciousness not immediately lost
  • Knives and razors are readily available
Cons:• Painful
  • Possibility of scars or permanent injury

DEMOGRAPHICS: WHO, WHERE, AND HOW MANY

The number of cut/stab suicides for 1994 is shown in Table 18.1, as is the rate of such suicides in 1994 and for 1979 to 1994.

Table 18.1 Suicide by Cuts/Stabs, E956			Rate/100,000	
	Deaths,1994	pop (millions)	1994	1979-94
Total	515	260,423,572	0.19	0.18
All male	427	127,118,264	0.33	0.28
All female	88	133,305,308	0.06	0.07
White male	381	106,178,839	0.35	0.30
White female	80	110,371,063	0.07	0.08
Black male	28	15,500,047	0.18	0.15
Black female	3	17,189,697	0.01	0.02
Other male	18	5,439,378	0.33	0.26
Other female	5	5,744,548	0.08	0.13

E-numbers are International Classification of Disease (ICD) codes.
Source: CDC

NATIONALITY. In recent years, about four to five hundred (1.4 to 1.7 percent) of the roughly thirty-thousand suicides in the United States each year die of self-inflicted cuts or stabs. The frequency of cutting and stabbing seems to vary less from country to country than do some other methods, such as gunshot or drowning. For example, cuts/stabs was the method used by 2.25 percent of Swedish suicides between 1973 and 1984,[3] 3 percent in Great Britain between 1975 and 1987,[4] and 1.7 percent of Japanese suicides between 1959 and 1970.[5]

AGE. In the United States, cut/stab suicide rates increase steadily with age, unlike the overall rate, which is remarkably steady between the ages of twenty to twenty-four and fifty-five to sixty-four. This mostly reflects the pattern of white male suicide, which swamps female and nonwhite suicide numbers.

RACE. Whites have about twice the overall suicide rate as blacks, and also twice the cut/stab rate.

SEX. Men killed themselves by cutting/stabbing at a rate about 4.8 times that of women in 1994, which is a bit more than the overall male to female (M/F) suicide ratio of 4.2 to 1. Thus a slightly higher proportion of suicidal men than women killed themselves by cuts or stabs in that year. However, these ratios vary from year to year. The sixteen-year (1979-94) M/F ratio average was 3.6 to 1, similar to the overall suicide ratio of 3.8 to 1 (21.21 in 100,000 for males compared to 5.61 in 100,000 for females).

A comparable sex ratio in cut/stab suicides was also seen in Sweden (3.67 males to 1 female) between 1973 and 1984[6] and Japan (3.4 to 1) from 1948 to 1955.[7] While these data have a surface similarity, the distribution of suicide methods in Sweden and Japan is strikingly different from that in the United States. For example, guns and explosives caused 65 percent of the male and 40 percent of the female suicidal deaths (M/F ratio of 6 to 1) in the United States, but 16 percent of the male and just 1 percent of the female deaths (M/F ratio of 40 to 1) in Sweden. Swedes preferred drugs/poisons, drowning, jumping, and asphyxia. In addition, styles change; the Japanese M/F ratio dropped to 2 to 1 for the years 1959 to 1970.

MOTIVES. U.S. national suicide data don't address motive, so we turn for details to a study from Sweden.[8] This information may be helpful in drawing a picture of some people who killed themselves with sharp objects; however, differences between Swedish and American suicide patterns make any interpretation tentative.

The events or reasons that investigators thought precipitated the suicides are shown in Table 18.2 below.[b]

	Male		Female	
Motive	Number	%	Number	%
Known mental illness	14	20	8	38
Known serious physical illness	6	9	5	23
Emotional loss (death, divorce)	7	10	0	0
Job/school problems	2	3	0	0
Money problems	1	1	0	0
Fear of social disgrace	2	3	0	0
Unknown	36	53	8	38
of "unknown" motive, known alcoholics	15	22	1	5
Total	68		21	

Table 18.2 Motives for Suicide by Cutting/Stabbing in Stockholm, Sweden.

It's curious that all of the emotional loss or social-motive suicides were by men.

Eleven of the 89 (nine in the "known mental illness" group) were known to have made a sucide attempt within the six months prior to their deaths; five of these were within eight days of the fatal attempt. Nine of the eleven had taken a drug overdose in their earlier bid; one had tried hanging, one had used "sharp force" (presumably cutting or stabbing).

The seriousness of these efforts is not reported, but both cutting and drugs are often considered "ambiguous" methods in the suicide literature, because of their low death rates. However, this is only the case in the aggregate: Some overdose or sharp force suicide attempts are deadly serious, some are calls for help, some are a toss of the dice. A knife blade through the heart is every bit as lethal as a bullet in the head.

Most of the "mental illness" suicides occurred several years after diagnosis, and in fifteen of the twenty-two cases the patients killed themselves less than a week after the last treatment session. The nature of these "treatments" (psychotherapy, drugs, etc.) is not specified in the article. Among this same group of twenty-two there were seven alcohol addicts, two addicted to other drugs, and two to both alcohol and other drugs.

The authors point out that only one of these eleven people repeated their previous method. However, this should not be surprising, since (a) drug overdose is used in a majority of all survived suicide attempts, and (b) people intending to kill themselves might understandably choose a method different from one which they had survived. On the other hand, people who carry out a series of suicide attempts/gestures tend to repeat their earlier methods.[9]

REPEATED SELF-CUTTING. Some people have a history of cutting themselves. A majority of repeated self-cutters are young, single, and female. They usually have interpersonal or psychiatric problems, though not necessarily severe ones; rather, they're prone to wide mood swings in response to stress, most often rejection, either real or imagined. Investigators claim that cutting releases this tension and returns them to reality, at least for a while; suicide is rarely intended. Around 70 percent of cutters also have eating disorders: anorexia and/or bulimia.[10]

CARVING. There is a phenomenon seemingly related to self-cutting called carving, where people cut scarring wounds, often, but not always, on their wrists. Usually names, initials (people who go through lots of boy/girlfriends may look like palimpsests), or symbols (crosses are popular, as are names of rock groups) are carved. These cuts, generally done by teenagers, are sometimes confused with suicidal-gesture wrist cutting but are a form of scarification more akin to tattooing. This is not to say that a disproportionate number of carvers don't commit suicidal gestures; they do. But they seem to mostly use medicine overdoses, at least among girls.[11]

Carving, except in this subculture, is generally seen as pathological. However this may be a parochial view: In addition to contemporary cosmetic plastic surgery, there are,

> numerous examples of the widespread human interest in hand-crafting the body which ranges from head-moulding in ancient Egypt, Central and North America and modern Europe, to Chinese foot-binding, which produced feet that were so small

they could not bear their owner unsupported. Other types of anatomical rearrangement in the list include trepanation of the skull (worldwide, prehistoric), finger amputation (Pacific, Africa), and various types of genital rearrangement (Australia, Africa). In fact, [the author of the book cited] concludes that only the eyes and the anus have never been the target of socially sanctioned mutilation....."Such practices fill many Westerners with horror although, it must be said, Western practices of ear- and nose-piercing, circumcision, and skin-bronzing through radiation exposure are rarely abhorred with equal vigour."[12]

How Dangerous Are Cutting and Stabbing Wounds?

Cutting/stabbing looks like one of the safer methods for a suicidal gesture because it has the lowest fatality rate, 4.1 to 5.8 percent. It also has the lowest ratio of fatal to nonfatal injury. It would thus seem to be the "least serious" method. (See Tables 16.1 through 16.4.)

However, as mentioned earlier, all these data combine people intending to die with those wanting help or attention. As a result, they overestimate the danger of cutting as a suicidal gesture and severely underestimate the likelihood of death for those really trying to kill themselves. Cutting and stabbing is used by both groups because, unlike most other methods of self-harm, one can—roughly—predict the degree of injury from a given cut; such graded injury is hard to arrange in, say, drowning or hanging. Generally speaking, the people who cut themselves as a cry for help tend to be younger and female; those who mean to die are more likely to be middle-aged and male.

Methods

Suicidal Cuts

Throat. Cutting the throat is the fastest, most reliably lethal, and perhaps most gruesome of suicidal cuts. However the method is not used as often as formerly, probably because straight razors have been widely replaced by safety razors and electric shavers.

The cut-throat wound usually starts high and (in right-handed persons) on the left side of the neck, goes across the center, and ends lower on the right side. (You might try this—with your finger—to get a better sense of it.) Since the "victim" generally throws his head back, the skin will be under tension and the cut smooth and straight. This may not be the case when the skin is too loose to be effectively stretched tight, as in old age or after recent major weight loss. While most cuts are by razor or knife blade, occasionally broken glass or some other irregular object is used. These also tend to leave jagged rather than straight wounds.

More often than with other methods, the corpse is found in front of a mirror. Perhaps mirrors are used to visually guide the hand. Shallow cuts are often found near the beginning of the wound. These are one piece of evidence a medical examiner will use to distinguish suicide from murder. However, hesitation cuts are occasionally seen in murder, and therefore are not definitive.

Other hesitation cuts are shallow, more or less parallel gashes inflicted before, or in the process of, achieving enough courage for the final wound. These are often seen in wrist cuts. In one study, hesitation/tentative cuts were seen in 80 percent of fatalities; in 20 percent, one resolute cut or stab was sufficient.[13]

It's very rare that the back rather than the front of the neck is the target. In one case, however, "A butcher, who had failed to commit suicide by the usual incision, succeeded on a later occasion by adopting the incision, at the back of the neck, which he was accustomed to use when slaughtering animals."[14]

Sometimes, when another method is not working fast enough, an impatient or desperate person will slash his throat: "A man aged thirty-three ingested a quantity of aspirin. He was found dead in his garage with a superficial cut on his right wrist and a deep cut on his left wrist. There was an incised wound three inches long on the right side of his neck accompanied by tentative, superficial cuts. The major blood vessels were spared but he had severed the right anterior jugular vein."[15] He had taken approximately twenty-five tablets of aspirin. Though these had caused significant bleeding in his stomach, it is not a normally dangerous dose in a healthy adult, as he would have known had he read this book.

Wrist, Elbow, Ankle. Cuts on the wrist, and to a much lesser extent elbow or ankle, are often used to make a suicidal gesture. Such wrist cuts are generally shallow and perpendicular to the long bones of the forearm. They tend to sever the surface veins. Since these veins are not particularly large and do not carry as much pressure as the arteries, such cuts are not usually life-threatening because they can clot before a fatal quantity of blood is lost.

Wrist cuts become more dangerous:

1. If the cuts are more or less parallel to the long bones. In such cases the blood vessels tend to be sliced lengthwise or diagonally, making clotting more difficult and thus allowing more and faster blood loss.

2. If cuts are deeper and near the long bones of the forearm (the thumb-side long bone is the radius; the other long bone is the ulna), they may sever the radial artery or the ulnar artery. These pieces of plumbing *are* under high pressure and cutting them can be fatal unless the bleeding is actively stanched.

There are claims that a single cut across a healthy wrist artery is not dangerous, because the cut artery (which, unlike veins, has built-in muscle) will contract and so limit blood loss.[16] While this protective mechanism does exist, it's not always sufficient: Four of the forty Stockholm deaths due to cuts on the limbs were from just such an injury.

You can find (or usually avoid) these arteries by checking various points around your wrist for a pulse. Without a stethoscope you will only detect one in a couple of spots, for example, where your wrist and thumb come together. You can locate the radial artery fairly near the surface there. The other major wrist artery, the ulnar, runs parallel to the other forearm bone and can be felt near the heel of the hand. Hyperextending the wrist is common, but hides the radial artery around the end of the radius (try feeling for the pulse), and one may end up with only severed flexor tendons.

3. If cuts are numerous. Multiple cuts of wrists, elbows, and ankles, none individually dangerous, may cause enough blood loss to be fatal.

4. If clotting is inhibited. This may be deliberately done by keeping the cut under water. Another way to slow clotting is with drugs. Some drugs, like heparin and coumarin-like compounds,[c] are prescribed specifically to decrease blood clotting in medical conditions like stroke. With other drugs,

the anticlotting ability is usually considered a side effect to its intended therapeutic use. Aspirin, when taken for pain relief, is the most common drug of this sort. Since many people are not aware of these effects, use of such drugs may occasionally turn a suicidal gesture into an accidental suicide.

FEMORAL ARTERY AND VEIN. The femorals are the main arteries and veins to and from the legs. As you might expect, they carry a lot of blood, and an untreated cut to either one is quickly fatal. In one case, a thirty-four-year-old man bled to death from a 2 millimeter (less than 1/8 inch) nick to the femoral vein—and the vein is the low-pressure half of the circuit.[17] They run next to each other, with the artery closer to the front of the leg, and are nearest to the skin at the groin, which makes a tourniquet hard to apply if that's the site of the cut.

While knives can be and often are used on impulse, one case showed the benefits, however temporary, of planning and knowledge. A physician applied a local anesthetic to his leg, and then neatly cut his right femoral artery lengthwise.[18] I estimate that he would have lost a fatal amount of blood in about five minutes. He died quickly, and, probably, painlessly.

STAB WOUNDS. Unlike most wrist cuts, self-inflicted stab wounds are generally intended to be lethal. They are usually aimed at the front of the trunk, with the heart area being the most frequent target. Other sites tend to be scattered near the centerline of the chest, from the neck to the groin; they are almost never seen on the head, back, or extremities.

Death, when it occurs, is generally due to loss of blood if a major vein or artery is cut, or to heart damage, if that vital organ is cut. A heart injury, in turn, causes internal bleeding and/or an inability to pump blood to other parts of the body. Even a relatively small heart wound may be fatal if not promptly repaired, but the severity of a heart wound also depends on its location. If the cut is to the upper chambers, the right ventricle, or the major blood vessels, death is likely; a small cut to the left ventricle wall is sometimes survived, since the thick muscle there may seal the wound when the heart contracts.[19] However, this is not something you should count on.

OTHER WOUNDS. There are occasional reports of unusual sites or methods. One woman cut off her arm just below the shoulder, using a small kitchen knife with a six-inch blade.[20] Another held a knife to her back and ran backwards into a wall. One man stabbed himself in the chest with a chainsaw while it was running.[21]

LOCATION AND NUMBER OF WOUNDS

In the previously mentioned eighty-nine Swedish suicides, the most common sites were wrists, throat, and heart area; less frequently chosen were the inside of the elbow and the abdomen. There were no wounds of the head, face, shoulders, or back, and very few of the legs.

In forty people the only injuries were to the arms and/or legs; in four of these a single cut of the radial and/or ulnar artery caused fatal hemorrhage. The chest area was the target of thirty-four people, but there were often additional injury sites. With five of these thirty-four, such force was used that the sternal (breast) bone or ribs were cut through. This requires a good deal of pressure. Most of the other thrusts in this region went between the ribs; only three were blocked by them, thus requiring a second site. If bones are missed, little strength is needed: "The skin offered a little resistance, but that being overcome, the blade went deep into the chest with alarming ease."[22]

This is not to say that multiple cuts or stabs were rare. Quite the contrary. Thirty-four of the forty suicides with injury only to arms and legs had multiple cuts. In deaths that included chest or abdominal stabs, only nine of thirty-one were from single thrusts. One person stabbed himself in the chest area over the heart fifteen times. Ten of these went through the chest wall but only one pierced the heart; the others were too low. The largest number of stab wounds in and by a single person was thirty-one, by a twenty-eight-year-old woman who probably was hyperactive due to thyroid disease.

Suicidal stab (as opposed to cut) wounds to the neck are unusual. One instance was by,

> a labourer aged fifty-eight who for two years had suffered from emphysema; during the seven weeks prior to his death his condition had worsened and he had been unable to work; he slept downstairs. On the day of his death his wife had left the house to go shopping at 10:30 A.M. She left him in bed and locked both of the house doors. On her return, an hour later, he was not in his bed;

she thought he had gone upstairs to dress. Since he did not appear and she heard no sounds of movement she went upstairs to find him. He lay dead on the floor and had fixed a "suicide note" on the door. (She identified the writing as that of her husband.) The man lay on the floor fully clothed. The handle of a knife protruded from the right side of his neck and the point emerged by ¼ inch on the left side. There had been no struggle and no one had entered the house. The knife was nine inches, and its blade was 4¾ inches long. It had entered the neck an inch below the lower jaw on the right side and emerged 1½ inches below the external opening of the left ear. . . . The blade had severed the right sterno-mastoid muscle, right common carotid artery and internal jugular vein.[23]

Suicide, Homicide, or Accident?

How does a medical examiner determine if a cut or stab wound is self-inflicted? Since a blade is generally held differently in suicide and homicide, the resulting wounds tend to be different. For example, in homicides, three-fourths of stab wounds to the heart are vertical or slant upwards and to the right; among suicides only one-fifth have those characteristics.[24]

Similarly, in sixty-five of the sixty-nine suicides (94 percent) where information was available, clothing had been removed or pushed aside from the target site prior to the injury. This is similar to the situation found in suicidal gunshot wounds, but differs from most homicidal cuts and stabs.

In homicide, since the skin is not normally stretched, a cut tends to be more jagged than in suicide.

Instantaneous rigor is the immediate stiffening of the body occasionally seen in cases of quick and traumatic death. If the fatal weapon is found firmly held in the victim's hand, that weapon was held at the time of death and is very strong evidence of suicide. Gunshot and a cut throat are two suicidal methods in which instantaneous rigor is occasionally seen. This phenomenon is infrequent, its mechanism is unknown, even its existence is disputed, and there are no known instances of it being successfully simulated after a homicide.

Obviously, injury to a site that can't be reached by the victim argues strongly against suicide, but there are rare instances of suicides imitating a homicidal wound, for example, the previously mentioned knife-in-the-back case.

Similarly, if there are many potentially fatal wounds, suicide is unlikely. Multiple severe stab wounds are common in homicides. This "overkill" may be due to rage or to wanting to be sure that a lethal stab was administered or to expedite the death of the victim.

There are enough other differences that it is unlikely that a competent medical examiner will be fooled into confusing the cutting and stabbing of suicide with simulated suicide (murder).

Fatal cuts and stabs that are accidental are rare but fascinating. In one such case, a woman was seen carrying ducklings in a box covered by a piece of glass. She reached a fence and collapsed. By the time medical help arrived, she was dead. She had apparently shattered the glass against the fence and a shard had penetrated her chest and heart. A piece of glass that fit the wound was found nearby, and there was a fresh cut on her finger that probably occurred when she pulled the glass dagger out of her heart.[d25]

Another case was a medical whodunit:

> While the *Deblin,* a Polish ship, was sailing . . . in international waters, a member of the crew was found lying injured on the starboard side; he lay in a space between the superstructure and deck cargo. Blood was freely distributed on the deck and adjacent parts of the ship in the form of pools and some splashes. The appearances were those of venous rather than arterial bleeding. He was carried below and laid in his bunk. The Captain summoned a doctor from Grimsby [England] but by the time he had boarded the ship the patient had died. Inspection of the body disclosed a stab wound in the left groin; it was deemed to have been homicidal. The police were summoned when the ship docked in Hull and the crew were submitted to interrogation. One member whom they wished to interview had locked himself in his cabin and refused to see them. In another cabin they found freshly washed outer garments and a red-brown stain on the cabin door. At this juncture the atmosphere was distinctly tense.
>
> The postmortem examination confirmed the presence of a

punctured wound in the left groin. Its course was upwards and backwards. It was elliptical but had a small secondary side cut at its inner end. Nearby, on the outer side of the wound there were two superficial abrasions. He also had a laceration under his chin and a scratch above his left eyebrow. Dissection demonstrated a pointed fragment of glass in the thigh wound. The front of the femoral vein had been punctured and opened for a distance of one third of its circumference; the femoral artery was intact. The blood in the deck had come, in the main, from the injured femoral vein.[e] Inspection of the clothing disclosed several fragments of glass in the left-hand trouser pocket. Some of these bore pieces of the label of a bottle of vodka. Several of the fragments were sharply pointed and dagger-like. There was a recent cut in the lining of the pocket, and trouser leg.

This was the result of an accident. He had been below drinking with friends and had gone on deck to get more drink for the party. He was not drunk but might have been under the influence of drink. On his way back to the party he had put a bottle of vodka in the left-hand pocket of his trousers. When on deck, either because of his condition or because the ship had suddenly pitched or rolled, he had fallen. In consequence the bottle of vodka was shattered and one of the fragments had punctured his thigh. He had also struck his chin during the fall.[26]

And thus an international incident was averted.

Often a difficult case arises from a single stab wound sustained in a fight. The defense frequently makes the claim that the victim ran onto the blade. The medical examiner must then consider the angle of the wound, presence or absence of defense wounds on the hand and arms, and other such factors. In one instance of this sort, analysis of the deceased's clothes showed that the knife hole in his jacket was lower than that in his shirt, which was lower than the wound in his body. There were also two knife holes in the vest. This pattern is inconsistent with running onto a blade, but quite consistent with being held by the shoulder, and thus having the clothing pulled upwards at the moment of the stabbing. Guilty.[27]

We close this side tour with an unusual murder from 1978.[28] Georgi Markov was a forty-five-year-old Bulgarian political exile and dissident living in London. He had defected from Bulgaria in 1971, and began to broadcast a mix of satire and criticism home on the BBC World Service.

On September 7, while waiting for a bus, he felt a sharp jab in the back of his right thigh. Looking around, he saw a man who mumbled an apology, dropped an umbrella and hopped into a waiting taxi. Within a few hours Markov was ill and had a fever. His condition worsened and he was hospitalized the next day. He continued to deteriorate and died three days later.

Autopsy found a platinum-iridium (a noncorroding alloy, stronger than steel) ball in the center of the inflamed area on the back of his thigh. It was about the size of a pinhead and had two channels drilled into it. The ball had been spring-loaded in the sharpened tip of the abandoned umbrella, and was used to administer poison, carried in the tiny holes.

The poison was never directly identified. In a curious way, this helped implicate ricin (a toxic protein extracted from castor beans), because ricin is broken down in the body after doing its damage, and since virtually nothing else would have killed in such small dosage.[29] The Bulgarian secret police were thought to be responsible. Later information confirmed the identities of both the perpetrators and the poison.[f]

CAUSE OF DEATH

A cut-throat wound most often causes death by hemorrhage. Severing either of the two carotid arteries on the right side of the neck or the jugular veins on the left will cause fatal blood loss within about five minutes. Since blood flows into the head via the carotid, unconsciousness might occur a couple of minutes after cutting it; perhaps a minute or two longer if the jugular veins are sliced instead.

Since the trachea (windpipe) is usually also cut, blood may be inhaled, making asphyxia a secondary factor. If the trachea is partially cut while the carotid arteries and jugular veins are missed, inhalation of blood (asphyxia) may be the actual cause of death, but this is unusual. In one case of this sort, the victim died after about thirty minutes.[30]

Very occasionally, the trachea is completely severed without major blood vessel damage. This can cause the lower part of the trachea to fall into the thorax (chest cavity), followed by unsupported soft parts of the neck. This results in mechanical obstruction of the airway and subsequent asphyxia. It's conceivable that an upside-down posture would permit breathing under these circumstances, but this is mere speculation.

It's also possible, but rare, that when the external jugular vein is partly cut and open to the air, enough air gets into the damaged blood vessel to cause a fatal air embolism: A large air bubble enters a major vein and is sent to the heart, which isn't designed to pump gases. It's a bit like getting air in your car's brake lines, which is also designed to pump only liquids.

Injecting air into a vein has been suggested (and tried) as a suicide method; it's not a good one. Since the output of the heart is around 70 milliliters per beat, you would probably want to inject at least twice that volume of air to make sure your heart developed the cardiac equivalent of vaporlock. This would require something like a bicycle pump and you would be conscious for at least the first three to five minutes.

How Long Does It Take to Bleed to Death from Cuts to Limbs?

When death occurs after wrist, ankle, or elbow cuts, it is almost always from loss of blood and shock. How long does this take? Obviously, it varies, depending on which vessels are cut, at what angle they're cut, and where your body is sending blood at the time.[g] A very rough estimate of blood loss would be: 2–3 ml/beat × 70 beats/min = 140-210 ml/min; × 12–18 min = around 2500 ml, which is half your blood supply, and about the limit of what you might survive without prompt medical help. Add another five to twenty minutes to die, for a total of seventeen to thirty-eight minutes; but this is just a ballpark figure and could easily be off by a factor of two or more.

If avoiding discomfort is a priority, be aware that severe loss of blood causes a physiological anxiety response.

Cut/Stab Wounds to the Chest

With suicidal chest stabs, death is usually due to either (1) injury to a major vein or artery leading to fatal blood loss or (2) injury to the heart itself or to the sac surrounding it, the pericardium. If the heart is sufficiently damaged, it will hemorrhage and be unable to pump blood. But even if the heart itself is untouched, blood may fill the pericardium faster than it can drain out (or a blood clot may block outflow). This will eventually leave the heart with no room to expand, and thus keep it from filling (and thus pumping) properly ("cardiac tamponade").

In one case a forty-four-year-old man stabbed himself six times in the chest with a seven-inch-long kitchen knife. He then washed and returned the knife. After changing his clothes a number of times, he had lunch with his aunt who apparently didn't notice anything unusual. He collapsed about two hours after stabbing himself and died shortly after reaching the hospital. The pericardial cavity was found to have 300 milliliters of partly clotted blood; another 410 milliliters was in the chest cavity. The heart muscle received cuts, but the cause of death was cardiac tamponade.[31]

Types of Weapons Used

In Sweden, kitchen knives were used in about one-third, razor blades in another third, and other knives in one-fifth of cutting and stabbing suicides. There is similar data from Japan, where the same three categories accounted for 78 percent of cutting and stabbing suicides.[32]

The length and shape of the wound track usually give a good, but not infallible, reflection of the weapon used. Obviously a wide blade cannot make a narrow wound track, but a slim blade is certainly capable of expanding a narrow cut into a wider one. Similarly, a four-inch blade cannot make an eight-inch-deep cut, but an eight-inch knife can easily make a shallower cut by the simple expedient of not thrusting to the hilt. It is possible for the track to be an inch or more longer than the blade: If the thrust is made with enough force, it will compress the body. This was the situation in a fatal stabbing in the heart with a small pocketknife.[33] In stabbings where the weapon was thrust with great force, there is also usually bruising around the injury site(s), the pattern matching the shape of the weapon's hilt, or sometimes the assailant's fist.

COMBINATION OF CUT/STAB WITH OTHER METHODS

Cuts and stabs are sometimes combined with other methods. For example, one forty-two-year-old woman was found with her head submerged in the bloody water of her bathtub, with hesitation cuts on her wrists, ankles, and neck and a "star-shaped bullet wound on her forehead." She had also consumed a fatal dose of sleeping pills.[34] (Clearly, she intended to die.)

Another woman, a forty-nine-year-old alcoholic, tried to hang herself from the electric cord of an overhead light, using a twisted bedsheet for a ligature. When the noose broke, she stabbed herself in the chest with glass from the broken lamp diffuser; and when that failed to kill her, she grabbed a kitchen knife and fell on it, ramming it deeply—and fatally—into her chest.[35]

Others leave more doubt about their intentions. One thirty-two-year-old woman was found dead in a motel room she had checked into twenty-four hours earlier with a male companion. "A blanket was neatly folded under the arm to absorb the expected bleeding, and the bloodstained razor blade was placed on a handkerchief on the dresser." However, there was little blood at the scene, and the autopsy showed that only one medium-sized superficial vein had been severed. She had died of acute alcohol intoxication.[36]

HOW TO DO IT; HOW NOT TO DO IT

SUICIDAL GESTURE:

- Avoid alcohol, and drugs that interfere with blood clotting, such as aspirin.
- Clean skin on wrist with alcohol swab for one minute (you wouldn't want to die of infection).
- Optional: anesthetize skin. The most readily accessible local anesthetic will be a "freeze" spray commonly used for athletic injuries. It works by evaporating so quickly that it chills and numbs the sprayed area. One particular product is Cold Spray. These are short-acting products, but should not be used on skin once it's cut or broken. If you have access to "caine" anesthetics (lidocaine, procaine, cocaine) you may prefer to inject one of these into the target site, since they are more effective and longer-acting. However, you need to know

what you're doing since these drugs can be dangerous if poked into a vein or artery, or if you're allergic to them.

- Sterilize (or buy sealed and certified-sterile) a razor, scalpel, X-acto knife, etc. If it's not already sterile, heat the blade to a dull red color using a propane torch, or gas or electric stove rather than candle or match—the latter two may not be hot enough and/or may leave unsightly deposits on the blade. Let the blade air-cool or set it on a sterile surface. Chemical sterilization is less reliable than heat. If you want to use razor blades, get single-edge; the double edge are both flimsier (they flex at inopportune moments) and much harder to hold and control when slippery with blood.
- Have sterile gauze dressing, tourniquet, and tape available.
- Cut across (not lengthwise) the large surface vein that goes diagonally across your wrist, or the thumb-side vein that goes along the inside of the wrist (the one that IV lines are often stuck into). You may want to have a tourniquet around your upper arm both to make the vein stand out more and to limit blood loss. Don't go deeper, or closer to bones, and avoid cutting anything that looks or feels like a tendon or like a pulsing blood vessel (artery).
- Get help. After all, what's the point if nobody knows? You probably shouldn't walk to the hospital if you don't have to—you could pass out on the way and people might ignore "another drunk" while you bleed to death. Driving yourself is also a bad idea, since an impaired driver puts others at risk. Better to have a friend (make sure they're home first) take you or call for ambulance or rescue squad. Avoid Friday and Saturday nights—they're busy ER times.

If you do this carefully, you will (almost) certainly survive with nothing more than a scar or scars on your wrist. However, be prepared for unexpected behavior from family and friends and don't count on much medical sympathy.[37] In addition there is the problem that the safer you make the suicidal gesture, the less "seriously" it may be taken. This should not be the case, since about 10 percent of people who do "safe" suicidal gestures eventually go on to kill themselves.[38]

You may prefer to use an ankle vein in order to avoid wrist scars, and subsequent tedious cocktail-party conversation.

SUICIDE

If you really intend to kill yourself by cutting and stabbing, there would seem to be no particular point to sterile technique. But you might as well do it that way on the off chance that you're rescued. It's also a good idea to have tourniquet, tape, gauze, and a telephone next to you just in case you have a belated change of heart.

WRIST. Since you're trying to kill yourself by bleeding to death, your preparations should be directed toward keeping your blood from clotting. To this end you might eat a few (four to eight) aspirin about an hour before the main event. Can't hurt, might help. It also might decrease the pain a bit.

An excellent meal, hot bath and a glass or two of good wine—after all, you won't get another chance—should be pleasant and relaxing. The alcohol and hot bath will also have the effect of increasing your near-the-skin blood flow. More importantly, since our blood has a hard time clotting in water, keeping a sliced wrist submerged increases blood loss.

Using a properly aimed spray of water from a shower head is even more effective because the motion of the water and mechanical action of the drops further interfere with clot formation. It also improves the visual aesthetics, for whoever finds your body, not to have a tub filled with blood. You may want to rig a "stand-off": something to keep your wrist from falling against your body or the tub and thus slowing blood loss; or use blood vessels in your ankle instead of, or in addition to, your wrist.

Now, the best preparation in the world won't do the job if you don't cut yourself adequately. To lose a lot of blood in a hurry you need to either cut a good artery or two or several veins. As discussed in more detail above, you can feel the arteries on the insides of the wrist near the long forearm bones. Cutting them lengthwise is more effective, but either way should work. If the blood spurts out you've hit a gusher of an artery; if it flows, you got a vein. Cutting several times across the underside of the wrist may well get you enough veins and small arteries to do the trick, but if you want to be faster and more certain, go for the radial or ulnar arteries.

On the other hand, maybe there's no hurry and you want to savor the slowly spreading pool of red in the tub. Fine. Just be aware that you will eventually lose consciousness and that a bit later you will have a "window of opportunity" for brain damage from lack of oxygen before you die. That would not be a good time to be rescued. On the third hand, it's entirely possible that you will slide underwater when you become unconscious and thus drown before you can bleed to death. I suppose if you wanted to make this more likely you could use an air pillow to support your head above the water: You hold the air valve shut by hand; when you lose consciousness your hand falls, the valve opens and lets out the air. Or perhaps this is getting too complicated.

An alternative method has been suggested.[39] It consists of running an IV line into your favorite elbow vein, using a big-bore needle (say, 16 gauge), taping it into place, and letting it drip away. Call the Red Cross for details, though they may suggest a better use for your blood. I'm not aware of any cases using this technique. It would certainly be slow, and probably subject to clotting, but I don't know this for a fact.

The femoral arteries and veins, going through the groin to the legs carry a lot more blood than does the wrist plumbing. Cutting them is thus more quickly fatal. It also allows use of both hands and avoids wrist tendons, but is hard to stanch or tourniquet should you change your mind after the fact.

THROAT. If you're going to cut your throat, the three major structures that are commonly injured are the carotid artery, the jugular vein, and the windpipe. These are all accessible from the front of the neck, but the major blood vessels are partly protected by the sterno-mastoid muscles nearby. (Turn your head to the side and feel them.) The large carotid is on the right side under the angle of the jaw (where you can feel your pulse). It's most accessible by cutting in between the trachea and the sterno-mastoid muscle. Completely severing it will cause unconsciousness in a couple of minutes and death in about five. Not pleasant, but fast. Throwing the head back moves the carotids under the sterno-mastoid muscles and may require deeper cuts or limit damage to the trachea or larynx.

Cutting the jugular vein on the left side of the neck causes death almost as quickly, but you may remain conscious a minute or two longer, since blood continues to enter the head. Similarly unpleasant.

Cutting into the windpipe is not generally life-threatening unless it is either cut all the way through or a lot of blood enters it. In fact there is a surgical procedure for cutting a passage into the trachea near the breastbone (tracheotomy) in order to bypass an obstruction to breathing.

If you insist on cutting your throat, go for either of the major blood vessels: the carotid (on the right side of the neck) or the jugular (left side of the neck). No extra credit for cutting both. If the trachea is also cut it won't make much difference, but it shouldn't be the target.

TRUNK. The only target worth aiming for is the heart: Single-stab injury to other organs is too slowly fatal unless you happen to hit a major blood vessel. The heart is somewhat protected by the cartilage and/or bone structures of the chest and ribs. The ease of getting through varies a lot from one location to the next. To most reliably reach the heart may require either a strong thrust through the chest wall—falling onto a knife will be more than enough—or an upward stab from between a pair of ribs. In either case, it is easier to get through if the wide part of the blade is held horizontally rather than vertically.

Death from heart wounds can be fast, slow, or, occasionally, not at all, depending on the nature and extent of the injury. If it occurs, death can take from a couple of minutes to several hours (and, rarely, longer). However, remarkable feats are sometimes seen, despite fatal injury: One man, though shot through the heart, ran sixty to eighty yards and then took part in a fight before collapsing.[40]

SUMMARY

The fact that only about 4 to 5 percent of suicidal cutting and stabbing are fatal should not leave you with the impression that they are safe. They are about as safe or as dangerous as you make them.

The most quickly fatal suicidal cut is one that severs the carotid artery and/or jugular vein. An untreated stab to the heart is usually lethal but not always as swiftly as one might expect. In addition, many people are unclear about where the heart actually lies; they tend to aim too far to the left and sometimes too high, and may miss altogether, a telling commentary on the sorry state of modern science education. The danger from wrist cutting varies from trivial to deadly, depending on the circumstances, as discussed in detail above. If you're in a hurry, but don't want a gaping gash in your neck, you might want to consider the femoral artery, whose pulse you can feel just below the crease in your groin.

As a suicidal gesture, a single wrist or ankle cut is pretty safe if you avoid tendons and the two major arteries, don't cut deeply, and have a tourniquet in place (you can always hide it when the rescue squad arrives).

As methods of suicide, cutting and stabbing have little to recommend them: Compared to lower-trauma asphyxias (see Hanging and Asphyxia chapters) they are, generally, more painful and no faster or more reliable. Their major advantage is that (depending on site and method) you may, after the injury, have some time to change your mind.

NOTES

[a]"Gesture" is not the precise word, as it implies lack of serious intent; "attempt" is not precise either, since it implies lethal intent. The reality is that some people fall into the gesture category, some into attempt, some into neither (for example, those who leave it to chance).

[b]It is difficult, if not impossible, to make valid comparisons between various studies' data on motive. First, people usually have multiple and complex problems and motivations. Second, different researchers use different criteria. The closest to an objective category is "known serious physical illness" and even here researchers report data that differ by factors of three to five: in other studies, 25 to 70 percent of suicides had physical medical illness; for 11 to 51 percent this was an "important" contributing cause; however, only around 5 percent were terminally ill (D. Clark, 1992; T. B. Mackenzie in Blumenthal, 205-32).

[c]Coumarin-derived drugs, such as Warfarin, are also used as a rodent poison because they are slow-acting: Most rats are smart enough to avoid fast poisons after a few of their friends and family go into postprandial convulsions. Coumarin was discovered in the process of tracking down the then-mysterious deaths of cows from hemorrhage. This bleeding was eventually found to be caused by eating spoiled, moldy hay; the blood-clotting inhibitor is produced by a mold.

[d]In general, it's better to leave a penetrating object in place, to minimize bleeding, until medical help is available.

[e]This would have been survivable had anyone put pressure on, or a tourniquet above, the wound.

[f]In January 1992, Gen. Stojan Savov, sixty-eight, a former Bulgarian interior minister who was accused of complicity in the assassination of Markov, was found dead two days before he was to go on trial for this and other crimes. Savov apparently committed suicide (*Boston Globe*, January 7, 1992).

[g]Blood flow to a muscle can increase by a factor of twenty, from resting to working hard.

19
DROWNING

•

A man who is not afraid of the sea will soon be drowned, he said, for he will be going out on a day he shouldn't. But we do be afraid of the sea, and we do only be drowned now and again.

—J. M. Synge

Now would I give a thousand furlongs of sea for an acre of barren ground.

—Shakespeare

Drowning is an effective and quick means of suicide, usually taking between four and ten minutes. Whether or not it is a low-trauma death, as some have claimed, is in dispute. Drowning is responsible for only 1.3 percent of official suicides in the United States, land of the handgun, but is much more common in many other parts of the world. It is a distinctly poor choice for a suicidal gesture.

LETHAL INTENT: High
MORTALITY: High, 67 to 75 percent
PERMANENT INJURIES: Moderately likely
PROS AND CONS OF DROWNING AS A MEANS OF SUICIDE

Pros: • Requires no equipment or expertise
   • Is generally quick
   • May be low-trauma, especially if combined with drugs
Cons:• Difficult to use by someone confined to bed
   • Potential for lung and brain damage if interrupted
   • Possibility of revival for up to half hour in very cold water

PROGNOSIS FOR DROWNING: FACTORS DETERMINING SURVIVAL

The chances of surviving submersion depend mostly on how long some-one has been breathing water. Secondary factors are water temperature, age of the victim, and whether the water is salt or fresh.

SURVIVAL TIME. Though the medical sources differ, they generally cite some-where around four to ten minutes as minimum-fatal and maximum-surviv-able times. Even though the heart may continue to beat weakly for several more minutes, there is little chance of recovery.

TEMPERATURE. People can swim much longer in warm than in cold water (see Hypothermia chapter). However, very cold water substantially increases the time during which a drowned person can be successfully revived. This is because quick chilling of the body retards cellular damage and death. This, in turn, is due to the fact that at lower temperatures all chemical processes, including metabolism and decay, are slowed. For example, at 20 degrees C (68 degrees F), metabolic rate, as measured by oxygen consumption, drops to about one-fourth that of normal body temp (37 degrees C, 98.6 F).[1]

Recoveries after as long as twenty to thirty minutes in very cold water are not uncommon.[2] The longest documented submersion without brain dam-age is sixty-six minutes (body core temperature was 66 degrees F [19 degrees C]).[3] However, two-thirds of these recoveries are in children under eight years of age[4] though only about 20 percent (about 865 out of 4,200 in 1988) of accidental drownings are in this age group.

The reasons for this high survival rate seem to be: (1) Children cool more rapidly, since they are smaller; (2) they are protected by a phenomenon called the "mammalian diving reflex," which is strongest in kids up to two to three years old.[a] When such a child falls into water, more blood is sent to her brain and heart, the heart slows to just a few beats per minute, and the glottis (vocal cords) closes, preventing water (and air) from entering the lungs.

INJURY. Survival rates after near-drowning are around 90 percent.[5] However, even someone who seems to have been successfully resuscitated may have suffered permanent or even fatal injury: Pneumonia can develop, especially from contaminated water; temporary kidney failure sometimes occurs, caused by the red blood cell destruction following massive absorption of fresh water; heart failure and/or brain damage due to lack of oxygen may be seen. The frequency of brain damage reported in near-drowning cases ranges from 2 percent to over 30 percent.[6] If near-drowning is defined as having impaired consciousness on arriving at the hospital, the latter figure is probably more realistic. Recovery may take weeks or months and may be incomplete.

WHAT IS DROWNING?

The short answer is: Drowning consists of filling the lungs with liquid so that oxygen cannot be absorbed. To the extent that this is the direct cause of death, drowning is another form of asphyxia. Further, inhaling water can cause the airway (larynx) to spasm shut or the heart to suddenly stop. In addition, both fresh and saltwater damage the blood, lungs, and heart, though some medical consequences of drowning depend on whether saltwater, fresh water, or some other liquid is inhaled.[b]

Here's the long answer: Someone who is conscious can hold his breath until carbon-dioxide buildup in his blood stimulates the brain's respiratory center, which overrides any voluntary breath-holding and forces an inhalation: You *can't* not breathe. If the mouth and nose are under water at this moment, water is inhaled. This in turn causes reflex coughing, gagging, vomiting—and additional inhalation, often of more water. This cycle continues until consciousness is lost, generally within two to three minutes, due to lack of oxygen. Convulsions and cessation of breathing follow quickly, which is followed more slowly by heart failure. Brain damage, then death, usually occurs within four to ten minutes.

Foam frequently comes from the mouth and nose of a drowning victim,[7] but sometimes this is not visible until pressure is applied to the chest in a resuscitation attempt. The foam is usually white, but may be bloodstained and may persist for several days (depending on temperature) on a corpse in the water.[8] It is produced by a mixture of air, water, mucous, and other components, whipped into a froth by desperate respiratory activity. It may be more frequent in accidental than in suicidal drowning, if in the latter the person is less likely to struggle, but this is speculation based on the fact that people who are already unconscious when they drown don't produce this foam.[9]

The presence of foam is normally accepted as proof that drowning was the immediate cause of death. Thus, bloody foam at the mouth and nose of Mary Jo Kopechne[c] led (or allowed) the judge at the Chappaquiddick Island inquiry on her death in 1969 to refuse to order an autopsy, ruling that it was sufficient evidence that death was due to drowning.[10] However, fluid in the lungs (pulmonary edema) from illness or injury can also cause similar foaming.

The more graphic description of drowning that follows came from observations on dogs that were tied up and held under water until they were dead.[11] The first stage was described as "surprise" and lasted a few seconds. This was followed by violent agitation in which the dog tried to escape its bonds and reach the surface while holding its breath. This lasted about a minute. The third stage, also about one minute long, consisted of deep inspirations of water and expiration of white foam. Mouth and eyes were open, and body movements decreased. In the fourth stage, breathing motions stopped, pupils were dilated, and corneal reflexes disappeared; another minute. In the last stage, lasting thirty seconds, there were three or four respiratory gasps and a few spasms around the lips and jaws.

These observations were later confirmed when a man who had drowned his pregnant wife gave a detailed description of her death in very similar terms.[12]

In general, and not surprisingly, near-drowning victims show less in the way of severe biochemical imbalances than do drowned bodies. For example, a study of eighty-three near-drowning cases showed none with life-threatening salt imbalances.[13]

Curiously, 10 to 30 percent of drowning victims' lungs are found to be fairly dry on autopsy.[14] There are physiological processes that could account for this phenomenon: Since the heart can continue beating for a short time after respiratory reflexes have ended, water absorbed from the lungs into the bloodstream can be distributed to other parts of the body. Meanwhile, little additional water will reach the lungs; hence a drowned body with dry lungs.[15]

An alternative explanation is that these people died suddenly from a process called "vagal inhibition." The vagus nerve, which normally slows the heart in response to an increase in blood pressure, can also be triggered by inhaled water or by pressure on the side of the neck (see the Hanging chapter). It can cause the heart to stop from relatively small amounts of inhaled water, thus resulting in sudden death with few signs of drowning. In one case,

> A boy, aged two and a half years fell head first into a drum which contained some chalky, sooty water; the water level was only six inches above the bottom of the drum. The child was removed at once, but prompt resuscitation was of no avail; the child was dead. It was readily possible to trace the internal distribution of the water by its sooty content. Soot was present in the nasal cavities; there was a little in the larynx and traces of soot adhered to the vocal cords and the wall of the trachea, but there was none in the lungs. The child had swallowed about an ounce of the water, but there was no soot in his mouth. The level of water in the drum was too low for any of it to have entered except by the nose.[16]

A third possibility is that when water starts to be inhaled, it causes a powerful reflex closing of the epiglottis[17]—one of the protective actions of the previously mentioned mammalian diving reflex—but this cuts off air as well as water and people start to asphyxiate. When this occurs, the face looks like that of a typical asphyxia victim: bluish color with pinpoint hemorrhages often visible on the eyelids and face. After two or three minutes, carbon-dioxide buildup in the blood overcomes this protective reflex; of course, if this "terminal gasp" occurs while the face is submerged, the lungs fill with water anyhow.

While there is evidence for each of these mechanisms, there seems to be no general agreement among the medical experts as to their relative importance or frequency.

The notion that a drowning person rises and sinks three times before finally going down has no basis in fact. However, it is true that:

- Unless someone is very fat, his dead body will sink in fresh water; most will also sink in ocean water, which is about 2 percent denser at a given temperature;
- Since your head is your densest part,[18] you'll end up head-down at the bottom;
- Drowned bodies sink and then rise to the surface some time later due to gases formed during putrefaction How much later depends mostly on water temperature. In New York, for example, about half the annual floaters come to the surface in April and May: "If somebody jumps in the water in the summer, they'll be up the next day, but if somebody jumps in November, they won't come up until the spring. The deeper the water, the longer they take to come up" (Sgt. Jim Cowan, New York City Police harbor diver).[19] A secondary factor is that snow melt and spring rains can churn up the bottom and release bodies that are snagged on submerged tree limbs and other debris at the bottom of rivers.

FRESH VERSUS SALTWATER DROWNING

Surprisingly, the standard forensic texts differ considerably in their assessment of the relative dangers of inhaling fresh versus saltwater. For example, one says that drowning in saltwater is twice as lethal as in fresh[20] (but doesn't define "twice as lethal"). Another says that saltwater drowning is "likely to be more amenable to resuscitation than drowning in fresh water."[21] A third claims that drowning takes four minutes in fresh water and eight in saltwater.[22]

While these experts reach different conclusions, there is general agreement on some fundamentals:

PHYSIOLOGY. Lack of oxygen (asphyxia) is the primary cause of death in drowning. However, in people who are rescued, the effects of salt- and fresh water on the heart and lungs differ significantly, changing both the optimal treatment and the likelihood of survival.

What accounts for these differences between the effects of salt- and fresh water? Did you ever do a school biology lab exercise in which you looked through a microscope at red blood cells that had been put into fresh and saltwater? If so, you may remember that the cells in fresh water expand until they break up; those in saltwater shrink and wrinkle. The reason is that these cells are semipermeable; that is they let water through the cell wall, but not (much) salt. This means that a bit more water is constantly entering a cell (0.9 % salt) which is in contact with fresh water than is leaving it. As a result, the cell expands and finally ruptures.

In saltwater the principle is the same, but the net direction of water flow to/from the cell is reversed because most ocean water is more than 3 percent salt and thus only around 97 percent water. That is, more water will leave than enter a cell, which will shrivel. Not surprisingly, this is less damaging to a cell than is bursting.

Lung cells are also semipermeable, but instead of bursting from absorbing too much fresh water, they're able to channel most of the excess into the bloodstream, with which they're in intimate contact. This happens very quickly: Within three minutes or so, half the liquid in the bloodstream may be from inhaled water.[23]

While temporarily protecting lung tissue, this has some undesirable effects:

- It decreases the concentration of sodium and calcium in blood serum which interferes with nerve and muscle function;
- The serum dilution causes red blood cells to expand and break up and increases the volume (while decreasing the concentration) of blood. This increased volume makes the heart pump harder, which forces fluid into the lungs—which, as you may imagine, hardly need more liquid. Thus even if someone is rescued and has her lungs drained, pulmonary function may be impaired due to the additional fluid pushed into the lungs from the diluted blood.

Meanwhile, the heart isn't getting enough oxygen, primarily because the water-filled lungs can't provide it, secondarily because the concentration of functioning red cells is low, while, at the same time, the heart *needs* more oxygen since it's working harder. Under this combination of circumstances (aptly described as "a serious biochemical insult,")[24] the heartbeat quickly becomes irregular, blood pressure drops to dangerously low levels, and ventricular fibrillation (unsynchronized contraction of heart muscle) causes death within three to five minutes.[25] The experts disagree about the relative importance and frequency of these mechanisms.

In fresh water drowning, the breakup of large numbers of red blood cells decreases the blood's ability to transport oxygen and also releases the cells' contents into the circulation. The most immediately significant component is potassium ions, which can cause the heart to fibrillate and fail.[d] This is offset, to some degree, by the initial absorption of water, which dilutes the released potassium.

As an aside, normal blood volume is around five liters. In fresh water drowning, this can be diluted by several liters of water, so measurement of alcohol or other drug levels must be adjusted to take this into account.

After resuscitation from saltwater drowning, pulmonary edema also quickly occurs, but by an entirely different mechanism—the salt remaining in the lungs "pulls" (by osmosis) water from the lung tissue into the air spaces, thus filling the lungs and preventing them from picking up oxygen.

The net water loss from the lung cells in turn draws water out of the bloodstream and into the lung cells. However, the amount of blood volume lost is less than the amount absorbed in fresh water drowning.[26] Since the resulting blood electrolyte imbalance is also less, the often-lethal heart arrhythmias seen in fresh water drowning are infrequent in saltwater drowning. Heart failure, from the combination of lack of oxygen and the increased viscosity of water-depleted blood, takes longer to be fatal and is more likely to permit effective medical intervention.[27]

Thus saltwater drowning victims don't die as quickly as those in fresh water, and there is a better chance of reviving someone drowned in saltwater.

CHLORINATED WATER. Pulmonary edema also occurs after drowning in chlorinated swimming pools, in part because chlorine irritates lung tissue.[28] Indeed, chlorine was the first poison gas to be used in warfare (1915, Ypres).[e]

TREATMENT OF DROWNING

The first and most important thing to do is to perform immediate artificial respiration;[29] even a few minutes' delay will be fatal. Mouth-to-mouth resuscitation is the most effective low-tech method; attention to other injuries must wait. If medical care is available, defibrillation and blood transfusion may help in fresh water drowning; repeated lung suction may be needed for saltwater cases; adjustment of blood electrolytes (salts: mostly sodium, calcium, and potassium) may be useful in both fresh- and saltwater victims.

HOW DANGEROUS ARE SUICIDAL DROWNING ATTEMPTS?

Tables 16.1 through 16.4 show that drowning is a quite lethal means of suicide: The fatality rate was 67 percent and 75 percent in two large studies. The lack of minor and moderate injury results is further evidence that it's not a good choice for a suicidal gesture.

DEMOGRAPHICS: WHO COMMITS SUICIDE BY DROWNING?

In 1994 there were 3,942 (3,179 male and 763 female) drownings in the United States listed as "accidental" and 383 (254 male; 129 female) attributed to suicide. This is 1.2 percent of the 31,142 official suicides in that year and is similar to the worldwide frequency of suicidal drowning: 1 to 2 percent.[30]

Suicide by Drowning, E954*			Rate/100,000	
	Deaths,1994	Population (million)	1994	1979-94
Total	383	260,424,000	0.14	0.19
All races, male	254	127,118,000	0.20	0.23
All races, female	129	133,306,000	0.10	0.15
White Male	200	106,178,839	0.18	0.21
White Female	107	110,371,063	0.09	0.15
Black Male	42	15,500,047	0.27	0.39
Black Female	12	17,189,697	0.06	0.11
Other Male	.12	5,439,378	0.22	0.15
Other Female	10	5,744,548	0.17	0.15

*E-numbers are International Classification of Disease (ICD) codes.
Source: CDC

However, local rates may vary substantially. For example, 22 of 207 (8.5 percent) suicides in the Province of Newfoundland died by drowning,[31] as did 7.3 percent of Japanese suicides,[32] 15 percent of Norwegian,[33] and 4.5 percent of suicides (70 of 1,569) in Dade County, (Miami) Florida,[34] which is about three-and-a-half times higher than the U.S. national rate. These higher percentages are likely due to lengthy ocean coastlines and/or a long nautical tradition.

The suicide rate from drowning decreased by almost half between 1979 and 1994; from 0.25 in 100,000 per year to 0.14. Drowning is also the only method in which black males have higher rates than white males: 0.39 versus 0.21 (1979 to 1994).

Some more-detailed information is available from Dade County, Florida. Sixty of 70 suicidal drownings (85.7 percent) there died of simple drowning; three (4.3%) had "contributory drug overdose," which does not include alcohol. Three had contributory self-inflicted injuries (for example, cutting one's wrist or throat just to "make sure"; four (5.6%) had contributory illness/disease (serious physical illness that may have been the impetus for suicide).

During the same five-year period the total official number of drowned people in Dade County was 521. Thus the seventy Dade suicides were 13.4 percent of all drownings there.[f] Seventy percent of the seventy suicides were attributed to depression, most to depression caused by poor health, imminent blindness, and death of a spouse or other significant person.

The reasons cited for the suicides follow in Table 19.1.

Table 19.1

Reason cited for suicide	Number	Percent
Depression (total number)	49	70
Due to:		
Poor health/going blind	11	
Death of spouse/significant other	6	
Financial problems	3	
Chronic pain	3	
"Tired of living"	3	
Death of child	2	
Recent divorce	2	
"Nerve problem"	1	
Felt self to be a burden	1	
Spouse in hospital	1	
"People killing others in the world"	1	
Alcohol problem	1	
Death of sibling	1	
Sale of home	1	
Marital problems	1	
"Broke up with boyfriend"	1	
Loss of children by custody proceedings	1	
Argument with landlord over pet dog	1	
Recently confessed to murder	1	
Not otherwise specified	7	
Psychiatric history, not otherwise specified	8	11.4
Recently acting in a bizarre manner	3	4.3
Recent religious cult activity	1	1.4
Unknown	9	12.9

Source: Copeland, 1987.

It is, of course, simplistic to believe that most suicides have a single cause, but the urge to look for simple answers to complex problems is widespread.

Most Florida drownings occurred in lakes, rivers, canals, bays, the Atlantic, or the Gulf of Mexico, but a dozen (17 percent) occurred in swimming pools and five (7 percent) in bathtubs. Twenty (28.6 percent) left suicide notes and eighteen (25.7 percent) gave a verbal equivalent; thirty-two (45.7 percent) did neither.

A British study of 536 "probable suicides" found that drowning was the single most underreported method: Only 24 percent had been officially designated as suicides.[35] Reasons for this include: (1) Unless there is unambiguous evidence, a verdict of suicide will rarely be rendered; (2) many drowning victims, both accidental and suicidal, are drunk ("Bacchus hath drowned more men than Neptune"[36]), which makes it easy to attribute the death to alcoholic mishap; (3) where the victim was known to have a medical condition such as epilepsy or heart disease that *could* have caused unconsciousness, the drowning will almost always be declared "accidental" absent strong evidence, such as a suicide note, to the contrary.

ACCIDENTAL DROWNING

In accidental drowning a large majority of every age group, even infants, was male. This male to female ratio has been attributed to greater mobility, energy, and exploratory behavior in infant males, and increased risk-taking and generally stupid behavior later.[37]

It should be noted that the five-gallon buckets widely used for paint, pre-mixed drywall compound, and many other things, are extremely hazardous to curious toddlers, who tend to fall in head-first and are then unable to get out. About fifty kids annually drown in them in the United States.[g38]

An aside on some accidental drowning: It's not generally known that every year there are a number of unexplained drownings, mostly of young males between fifteen and twenty-four years old engaged in underwater endurance contests, along the line of seeing who can swim further while submerged. Since most swimmers are aware that one can hold one's breath longer after hyperventilating, the evidence associates hyperventilation followed by exercise, with unconsciousness, leading to drowning, even in fit, competitive swimmers.[39]

A possible explanation is that hyperventilation depletes blood of dioxide. Since the urge to breathe is due to CO_2 buildup (not lack of oxygen), it may be, when exercising and holding one's breath, that one runs out of oxygen and becomes unconscious before the breathing reflex kicks in. Another expert thinks that these deaths are due to reflex inhalation upon hitting cold water.[40] The same researcher has found that sudden immersion in cold water causes an increase in blood pressure that can trigger heart failure.[41]

WHAT DO DROWNING PEOPLE THINK ABOUT?

In popular lore, drowning persons (besides invariably going down three times) spend their last moments reviewing their lives. Sometimes this appears to be what happens. As a youth, a British sailor named Beaufort (not the same Beaufort for whom the wind scale is named) fell overboard into the sea. Years later he wrote about the experience to an acquaintance. After swimming for a while he lost all hope, he said, and, "From that moment all exertion ceased, a calm feeling of the most perfect tranquillity superseded the previous tumultuous sensations. It might be called apathy, certainly not resignation, for drowning no longer appeared to be an evil. I no longer thought of being rescued, nor was I in any bodily pain."

He compared his feeling with the state just before sleep: senses dim but mind active. He thought about his family, his last voyage, and adventures he had experienced. He was rescued and went on to an eminent naval career, ending as an admiral.[42]

Another man related similar experiences: While half-conscious and lying at the bottom of a river, he felt no pain, but he had colored vision and ringing in his ears. He visualized his friends and relatives attending his funeral, even dirt dropping on his coffin. He lost consciousness and woke up on the riverbank, "being subjected to the disagreeable process of restoration of life."[43]

Not everyone's near-drowning experience is so tranquil. One woman described it thus: "I sank again and gasped involuntarily. Then all other senses were overpowered by the agonising scorching pain which followed the rush of saltwater into my lungs. From that moment I was conscious only of the burning suffocation, and the intense desire that the others might know what had become of me. Except for that one thought my brain was dulled."[44] She, too, heard roaring in her ears and saw through a colored (red) mist. She was unconscious when rescued.

WAS IT SUICIDE, HOMICIDE, OR ACCIDENT?

This is often a difficult call since there are no reliable physical signs in or on the body that, alone, would allow a verdict. This differs from, say, knife wounds, which are generally quite informative. In addition, the body may not be found before decay and scavengers make it difficult enough to figure out who, let alone why.

There is a further diagnostic problem: Did the person actually die from drowning or from some other cause? As mentioned previously, sometimes the lungs are dry in known drownings, and lungs can become waterlogged after death, at least in turbulent water. In addition, even the presence of sand and seaweed in the lungs and stomach are not proof of drowning: Both were found in the body of a young woman discovered on a deserted beach with a contact bullet wound in the center of her forehead.[h45]

The visible characteristics of drowned bodies (wrinkled skin, goosebumps, diatoms in the lungs, retracted penis and scrotum) are also found in other submerged bodies, and the levels of blood electrolytes are affected by postmortem biochemical changes. Because of these uncertainties, the most reliable evidence for drowning is still the presence of white foam around the mouth and nose of the victim.

SUICIDE

Suicidal drowning is not very common in the United States, but is certainly underreported. Drowning is a convenient way for a suicide to look like an accident: One simply doesn't come back from a swim, or perhaps one drives the car off the road into water. Skid marks add verisimilitude, but even without them it would be difficult to prove suicidal intent without other evidence.

Most drownings in bathtubs are suicides; in a series of forty-two cases only nine were accidental or due to illness;[46] thirty were suicides (twenty-one female, nine male). A majority of people who commit suicide by drowning are partly or fully clothed; whether they are frequently under the influence of alcohol or other drugs is in dispute[47]

Obviously if someone is unconscious or unable to move, the depth of the water they fall into makes little difference. For others, while deep water provides more certainty, even shallow water may be fatal. For example, a fifty-year-old woman committed suicide by sticking her face into a bowl of water only six inches deep. She was found dead in bed with the bowl still in her hands.[48] In another case a baby was drowned by his father, who held the child's face under a running water spigot. Death was due to absorption of water from the lungs into the circulatory system.[49]

Sometimes more than one method is used:

> A sixty-five-year-old woman with multiple blunt injuries and her throat cut was found in a shallow river. Bloodstains were found on a small bridge crossing the river and on the ground of the adjacent terrain. Following the stains, the police found a large pool of blood at a place 50 meters [55 yards] from the bridge. The police wanted to know if the woman could have cut her throat herself at this place and walked to and jumped into the river afterward. The autopsy showed that the cause of death was drowning and that the blunt injuries in all probability stemmed from collision with stones on the river bottom. The cut throat was the result of two superficial cuts, and only the superficial jugular vein was severed. It was concluded that she could have walked the distance in question after her throat was cut.[50]

HOMICIDE

Drowning a resisting, healthy adult in shallow water is difficult, and to do so without causing suspicious-looking injuries is even harder. One man, George Joseph Smith, did manage to drown three wives (one at a time) around 1910 by lifting their feet while they were bathing, thus minimizing their visible injuries.[51] These were the notorious Brides of the Bath murders. Despite his efforts to disguise the crimes, Smith was caught and executed.[i]

Naturally, it's easier to drown someone if they're incapacitated first. In one case, a nurse injected his pregnant wife with insulin; when she lost consciousness, he put her into the bathtub and drowned her.[52] She had believed that the injection was to induce an abortion.

SUMMARY

This is not a complicated means of suicide. Pretty much all that's needed is some water and a few minutes without interruption. Reports from near-drownings are contradictory concerning pain. To minimize it, one may take enough alcohol or sedatives to become unconscious while swimming or bathing. To decrease chances of unwanted resuscitation, avoid drowning in freezing water.

Drowning is a fairly quick and frequently lethal—two-thirds to three-quarters of such attempts are fatal—means of suicide, usually taking between four and ten minutes, but there is some danger of brain damage if you're rescued after being unconscious. Drowning is a very poor choice for a suicidal gesture.

NOTES

[a]This is crucial for marine mammals, such as whales. Upon diving, the reflex closes air passages and decreases blood flow to muscles and organs other than the heart and brain (Guyton, 64). This permits these mammals to stay underwater without breathing for up to half an hour. The existence of the diving reflex in humans is an argument in favor of the theory that Homo sapiens evolved in shallow coastal water rather than in the savannas. For a well-written book presenting this thesis, see *The Descent of Woman* by Elaine Morgan.

[b]There exist artificial liquids that are nontoxic and contain enough dissolved oxygen to be successfully breathed, at least for a while (Chang, 897).

[c]She was a passenger in a car driven by Sen. Edward Kennedy. Some people believe that the events surrounding her death have never been satisfactorily explained.

[d]Intravenous potassium ion is used to stop the heart in judicial "lethal injection" executions. (See Drug chapter for details.)

[e]Chlorine was first used by the Germans, initially with devastating effect. Since it's denser than air it accumulated in the trenches. Its use decreased as the Germans (and the Allies) discovered that winds shifted unpredictably, often sending the gas back toward their own lines. Gas masks were reasonably effective against chlorine, but other, more toxic, substances were soon introduced (for example, mustard gas), which also blistered, or were absorbed through, the skin. Interestingly, during WWII both sides refrained from the (military) use of poison gases.

[f]U.S. data for 1979–86 show 9.2 percent (4,181 of 45,275) of drownings as suicides. By

comparison, 17.9 percent (51 of 285) of drownings in Finland between 1978 and 1986 were suicides (Auer, 1990).

[g]Late news flash: The Consumer Products Safety Commission has given up—for the moment—on redesigning the five-gallon buckets. It will, however, require them to carry warning labels that will, no doubt, be of significant benefit to literate toddlers (*NY Times,* January 11, 1992).

[h]The possiblity that the bullet was fired *after* she had drowned is not discussed by the author. While that seems pretty far-fetched, stranger things have happened.

[i]He was caught because the father of one of his victims read a news story describing an "accidental" bathtub drowning that sounded identical to his daughter's death. The victim was also a wife of George Smith. Apparently the same technique had been used in an Egyptian murder in 1909, but it's unknown if Smith knew of this (E. R. Watson, cited in Polson, 444).

20
DRUGS, CHEMICALS, AND POISONS

●

> All things are poisons, for there is nothing without poisonous quali-
> ties. It is only the dose which makes a thing poison.
>
> —Paracelsus Theophrastus

From my own attempt experience with sleeping pills, I can tell you to avoid any that have aspirin/ibuprofen/acetaminophen in them—as tempting as it may be to go with a label that says "Takes away the pain." (Which is I presume what you're trying to do, take away the pain.) Painkillers in high doses can cause liver damage, and this is anything *but* a painless experience . . .

Be warned of one other thing, though: All those people you see on TV and in the movies that use sleeping pills to off themselves, they seem to take the pills and then fall asleep right away. It doesn't work that way. More sleeping pills will not make you fall asleep faster—just deeper. You will have as much as a half an hour, once those pills are in your stomach, to contemplate exactly what it is you've just done.

"Impulsivity and lack of knowledge about the dangers of drugs can sometimes result in an unintended fatal outcome."[1] Or an unintended survival. Or permanent injury. A drug overdose can be a fairly safe suicidal gesture, if you pick the right drug, right dose, and right circumstances—and there are no unexpected problems. Otherwise you can be dead within minutes or permanently injured.

The focus of this chapter is to provide information on the toxicity of some commonly used drugs and household chemicals. It is meant to help those who want to survive a suicidal gesture pick a relatively safe drug and dose; those who intend to die pick a drug with a more or less acceptable combination of lethality, speed, and unpleasantness.

There is also material on: (a) practical issues, such as acquiring and administering drugs; (b) demographics—who tends to take overdoses; (c) the effects of drug overdoses; (d) what drugs are most often used in suicide attempts.

LETHAL INTENT IN DRUG OVERDOSE: Highly variable, from nil to very high
FATALITY RATE: Low, 1.2 to 11.4 percent
FREQUENCY OF PERMANENT INJURIES: Variable; mostly low
PROS AND CONS OF DRUGS AS A MEANS OF SUICIDE OR SUICIDAL GESTURE
Pros: • Drugs often readily available.
  • Can choose high or low toxicity drugs.
  • Doesn't require physical strength or dexterity.
  • Easy to do.
Cons:• Most drugs take hours to be lethal (a possible advantage if you change your mind) but the toxicity of some is not reversible (a distinct disadvantage if you change your mind).
  • Most people have no clear idea about the lethal or safe dose of the drug(s) they take.
  • There are no "guaranteed safe" or "guaranteed lethal" doses, for reasons discussed in detail later.
  • Many of the drugs/poisons people use are painful and lethal and some may cause (if survived) permanent damage.
  • Easy to act on impulse.

DEFINITIONS

I use the term "drugs" to mean substances that are generally or commonly used as medicines. Examples are: aspirin (acetylsalicylic acid), propoxyphene

(Darvon), and meperidine (Demerol). Generic names (for example, aspirin) will generally be used in preference to trade names (for example, Anacin) because there are usually many trade names for a single drug. However, if a single trade name has widespread recognition (for example, Darvon), this name may be used. Chemical names (for example, sodium hydroxide) and any equivalent common name (for example, lye) will be used for nonmedical chemicals.

"Chemicals" refers to substances whose use, packaging, and distribution are primarily nonmedical. Examples are: ethylene glycol (the most common type of car antifreeze), methanol (wood alcohol; solvent and windshield washer liquid), and lye (usually sodium hydroxide; one type of caustic drain cleaner). Drugs are, of course, chemicals, but a medical/nonmedical-use distinction is useful.

A poison is just a chemical or drug in a toxic dose.

DEMOGRAPHICS: WHO, WHERE, AND HOW MANY

We'll start with a brief look at the overall suicide rate, and the suicide rate from the use of solid and liquid poisons in selected countries, as reported to the World Health Organization (WHO). Be aware that these numbers must be taken with several grains of salt (sodium chloride), because these data are notoriously unreliable due to the social (and sometimes legal) stigma attached to suicide in many societies.

For example, in one British examination of 536 "probable suicides," only 60 percent had been given that verdict and thus appeared in official suicide statistics. Of those who had taken poison, the figure was 40 percent. Since women use more underreported methods than men do, their suicide rate is also more underreported (in this study, 51.7 percent of female suicides were reported, compared to 64.5 percent of males'.)[2]

In the United States (1994 data), suicide by use of solid and liquid poisons (including drugs) occurred at a rate of 1.16 in 100,000 population per year as part of an overall rate of 11.95 in 100,000 per year. These poisons accounted for about 10 percent of the total number of U.S. suicides, but more than 20 percent elsewhere in the world.

Of ten European countries, plus Australia, Canada, Japan, New Zealand, Venezuela, and the United States:

- the average (unweighted mean) suicidal poisoning rate, by solid or liquid poisons, was 3.0 in 100,000;
- the average overall rate was 14.9 in 100,000;
- the highest value for solid/liquid poisoning was 9.9 in 100,000, in Denmark (overall rate of 31.6 in 100,000);
- the lowest was 0.7 in 100,000, in Italy (overall rate of 7.4 in 100,000);
- the highest percentage of suicides by solid or liquid poisons was in England and Wales (37 percent) (overall rate of 8.7 in 100,000);
- the lowest was in Japan (6 percent) (overall rate of 17.6 in 100,000).

For the most part, suicide rates in these countries increased from 1960-64 to 1980 and decreased slightly by 1988-91, while there was a slight increase in the use of poisons from 1960-64 to 1980. These solid and liquid poisons do not include gaseous poisons (generally carbon monoxide); these gases cause about another 1.1 deaths per 100,000 population per year in the United States.

Suicidal poisoning in the United States decreased by one-third, from 17 to 10.3 percent of suicides from 1970 to 1994, while the total suicide rate increased from 11.8 to 12.0 per 100,000, the difference being made up primarily by an increase in gunshot suicides.[3] Historically, these numbers vary considerably both between countries and over time.

Furthermore, when particular methods of suicide are minimized (for example, by banning some drug or removing carbon monoxide from household gas), other methods tend to increase.[a] For example, when prescribing barbiturates was restricted (in 1979) in New Zealand, barbiturate overdose deaths dropped by two-thirds, but deaths due to tricyclic antidepressants increased sixfold.[4] Even without significant prescribing restrictions, the same phenomenon occurs as drugs go in and out of style: Barbiturate suicides decreased 80 percent while antidepressant suicides increased fivefold in the United States between 1968 and 1979.[5]

PEOPLE WHO POISON THEMSELVES—U.S. DATA

Men kill themselves around four times as often as do women (about 25,000 male [80 percent] and 6,000 [20 percent] female) by all suicide methods combined. Using drugs/chemicals/gases, 3,208 men (about 13 percent of male suicides) and 2,065 women (about 35 percent of female suicides) killed themselves in 1994, a ratio of roughly three to two. However, women make twice as many pharmacological suicide attempts (116,000 versus 57,000 in 1991) that are treated in emergency rooms.[6]

More detailed U.S. data follow:

Table 20.1 Suicide by drugs			Rate/100,000	
	Deaths 1994	Population (millions)	1994	1979-94
Total	3022	260,423,572	1.16	1.21
All races, male	1443	127,118,262	1.13	1.07
All races, female	1579	133,305,308	1.18	1.31
White male	1301	106,178,839	1.22	1.17
White female	1455	110,371,063	1.31	1.45
Black male	104	15,500,047	0.67	0.45
Black female	84	17,189,697	0.48	0.51
Other male	38	5,439,378	0.69	0.54
Other female	40	5,744,548	0.69	0.78

Suicide by solid and liquid poisons			Rate/100,000	
	Deaths 1994	Population (millions)	1994	1979-94
Total	207	260,423,572	0.08	0.10
All races, male	161	127,118,206	0.13	0.14
All races, female	46	133,305,308	0.03	0.06
White male	136	106,178,839	0.13	0.14
White female	35	110,371,063	0.03	0.06
Black male	18	15,500,047	0.11	0.10
Black female	6	17,189,697	0.03	0.03
Other male	7	5,439,378	0.12	0.18
Other female	5	5,744,548	0.08	0.09

Suicide by gaseous poisons   Rate/100,000

	Deaths, 1994	Population (millions)	1994	1979-94
Total	2044	260,423,572	0.79	1.02
All races, male	1604	127,118,206	1.26	1.53
All races, female	440	133,305,308	0.33	0.53
White male	1559	106,178,839	1.46	1.75
White female	428	110,371,063	0.38	0.61
Black male	28	15,500,047	0.18	0.25
Black female	5	17,189,697	0.02	0.05
Other male	17	5,439,378	0.31	0.30
Other female	7	5,744,548	0.12	0.13

Suicide by poisons and by all methods   Percentage of suicides by specified methods

	All Methods, 1994		drugs	s/l chem	gases	all poisons
	Deaths	Rate				
Total	31142	12.0	9.7	0.7	6.6	17.0
All races, male	25174	19.8	5.7	0.6	6.4	12.7
All races, female	5968	4.5	26.5	0.8	7.4	34.6
White male	22581	21.3	5.8	0.6	6.9	13.3
White female	5395	4.9	27.0	0.6	7.9	35.6
Black male	1922	12.3	0.6	0.9	1.5	7.8
Black female	349	3.9	7.9	1.7	1.4	43.0
Other male	671	12.4	35.6	1.0	2.5	9.2
Other female	224	2.0	4.9	2.2	3.1	23.2

Rate is per 100,000 per year. S/l chem=solid and liquid nonmedicinal poisons; gases include pipeline and automotive gases.
Source: Centers for Disease Control

We can see that women tend to use medical drugs; men are more likely to go with gases (generally carbon monoxide) and nonmedical chemicals. But even in these latter categories, the proportion of men is less than with all methods combined, because 60 percent of American males' suicides are committed with guns.

While, overall, blacks commit suicide in numbers roughly half those of whites, their suicide rate by drugs, chemicals, and gases is around 0.77 in 100,000 compared to the white rate of 2.2 in 100,000, or about one-third the white rate.

Curiously, the age group with the highest suicide rate for men, eighty-five and older, has one of the lowest rate for adult women. There is a second peak for men, ages thirty-five to forty-four; for women, the highest rate is between forty-five and fifty-four years.

As with other methods, older people who attempt suicide by drug/chemical overdose achieve more lethal results: while only 40 percent of overdose suicide attempts were by people over thirty years old 71 percent of poisoning deaths were in this age group.[7]

How Lethal Are Suicidal Drug Overdoses?

This simple question doesn't have a simple answer. Estimates of fatality rates range from around 1.2 to 11.4 percent, if we consider all the people who die or are hospitalized after taking drugs with the intention of suicide, self harm, or as a cry for help. The fatality rate from suicidal use of non-medical poisons is about two times, and from carbon monoxide five times, the medical drug rate.

For the United States, a plausible fatality rate estimate—there are no comprehensive national data—might be 1.8 percent for intentional overdoses. The basis for this figure are the NIDA (National Institute on Drug Abuse) 1991 reports: There were around 400,000 (extrapolated) "drug abuse episodes" seen in hospitals in 1990. Suicide was cited as the motive in 43.8 percent of these, or for around 175,000 people. About 0.3 percent (some 525) died.[b] Since there were 3,143 drug overdose deaths in 1990,[8] presumably the remainder, 2,618 (1.5 percent of suicidally intended overdoses), died before reaching hospital. This is consistent with evidence that around 80 percent of overdose deaths are dead at the scene or dead on arrival[9] and with hospital data from around the world that generally report fatality rates between 0.6 and 6 percent for overdoses.[10]

However, these numbers don't include people who weren't hospitalized or whose overdoses were not reported. In addition, these data combine people intending to kill themselves with those wanting to survive. Thus they overestimate the danger of drugs/poisons as a suicidal gesture—for those who know what they're doing—and underestimate the likelihood of death for those really trying to kill themselves.

Drugs are used by both groups because, like wrist cuts, but unlike many other methods of self-harm (for example, hanging or drowning), one can roughly estimate the degree of injury from a given drug and dose. However, the results of drug overdoses are less predictable than those from blade injuries.

Not surprisingly, overdoses with suicidal intent are more dangerous than accidental poisonings.[11] While only about 7 percent of the incidents reported to the American Association of Poison Control Centers (AAPCC) involve suicide attempts, at least 53 percent of the deaths were from suicide (63 percent if the "reason unknown" group is dropped or divided proportionately).

In terms of percentage of fatalities from overdoses, death occurred in:[c]

0.310 percent of suicidal overdoses
0.091 percent of "therapeutic misuse"
0.434 percent of "psychotropic misuse"
0.007 percent of accidental poisonings
0.057 percent of adverse reactions

The actual percentage of deaths is certainly higher, since the AAPCC data would not normally include those dead at the scene or dead on arrival, which account for around 80 percent of suicidal poisoning deaths. So, multiplying the suicide figure in the above table by five would probably yield a reasonable estimate of the real fatality rate: about 1.5 percent.

The AAPCC numbers differ from data in a frequently cited comparative-method report by J. J. Card (Tables 16.1 through 16.3). Of 1,476 suicidal drug overdoses there were 168 (11.4 percent) deaths.[12] Card also found that 22 of 95 (23.2 percent) people who took nonmedical chemicals died, as did 117 of 150 (78 percent) who used carbon monoxide.

Why such a large difference between these two inquiries? Fatality rates have decreased since the date of Card's study (1974) because of some improvements in medical care, but mostly as a result of (1) the general replacement of barbiturates by less toxic sedatives; and (2) the decreased amount of carbon monoxide in newer cars' exhaust, due to more stringent air pollution standards. In addition, the real fatality rate is lower than shown here, because minor injuries tend to be underreported. This is true for all methods, but is proportionately more frequent for the less lethal ones: There are more unreported overdoses than unreported gunshot injuries.

WHAT IS THE RELATIONSHIP BETWEEN SERIOUSNESS OF INTENT AND THE LETHALITY OF DRUG USED?

> The ingestion of 100 5-mg [milligram] diazepam [Valium] tablets is probably more serious [an intention of suicide] in a pharmacologically naive person than in a pharmacologist. Conversely, ingestion of a bottle of acetaminophen [Tylenol, paracetamol] with bourbon may well be a serious attempt in a pharmacologically sophisticated person, but may be intended as a manipulation in a naive attempter (Miller/Micromedex).

Do people who take drug overdoses know what they're doing? Often not: There are an astonishing number of suicide attempts, using potentially lethal doses of poison, carried out by people who did not want or intend to die.[13]

In a study of 100 consecutive overdose survivors from Belfast, 30 percent of these people said they would not have taken the drug had they known it might kill or otherwise harm them; 52 percent said they would have; 19 percent didn't know; 49 percent took someone else's drugs.[14] Of course, we have no way of telling how many people who die fall into each of these categories.[d]

In another study, of adolescent drug-suicide attempters, out of fifty teenagers (forty-five female, five male), half reported thinking seriously of suicide for less than fifteen minutes; eight for between fifteen minutes and one hour; only four thought about it for more than twenty-four hours before making their attempt![15]

In four of these cases (8 percent) physicians thought the drug/dose had a greater than 50 percent chance of being lethal if untreated; only one of these four said that she wanted to die, and in none of these did psychiatric assessors think there had been serious suicidal intent. Similarly, in a larger study, two-thirds of 522 fatal self-poisonings in Scotland were described as "impulsive."[16]

In a survey of adolescents' knowledge of acetaminophen toxicity, it was found that 40.5 percent underestimated the lethality of this drug and 17 percent thought that one could not ingest enough to cause death.[17] This is a drug that, some years, is the number-one suicidal poison, and is generally among the top three.[e]

There are around 49,000 annual emergency room visits due to overdoses among twelve- to seventeen-year-olds; 68.2 percent (34,000) are suicide attempts/gestures.[f] Extrapolating the British numbers to the U.S. data, if 8 percent of these 34,000 people took a dose/drug that was more than likely lethal if not found and treated, we have 2,700 potentially dead teenagers. Fortunately, most of them don't die, but their survival depends on timely intervention; if such help is delayed or absent, an unintended death may well result. The number of these is not known. Impulsiveness and ignorance are a lethal combination.

Looked at as a practical matter, unless you know what you're doing, drugs, alone, are usually a poor choice for those intending suicide: Most drugs take hours—sometimes days with medical intervention—rather than minutes to be fatal; the effects are often unpredictable and tend to be more traumatic than generally appreciated; too often they result in permanent injury in survivors; and the death rate is low.

WHAT ARE THE SHORT-TERM MEDICAL CONSEQUENCES OF DRUG/POISON OVERDOSE?

It's a common misconception that all poisons have antidotes.[18] In fact, antidotes exist for only about 10 percent of poisons.[19] Most treatment consists of removing as much toxin as possible and trying to keep the person alive long enough for the body to repair itself.

What are the effects of drug/chemical toxic overdoses? Not surprisingly, it depends on drug, dose, and individual sensitivity.

Unlike in the movies, few drugs cause one to go peacefully to sleep, never to wake again. More often, they generate some combination of pain, vomiting, fever, convulsions, respiratory depression, organ failure, heart arrhythmias, and other serious unpleasantries.

Let's now look at the overdose experience of one hospital, to see what drugs were used and the medical consequences and complications of the overdoses.[20]

In a review of 419 consecutive acute hospital admissions for drug/chemical overdose, 71 (17 percent) needed intensive care unit (ICU) treatment; 45 in 71 (64 percent) of these more seriously poisoned people were female; 90 percent of them (64 in 71) were suicidal; 8.4 percent (6 in 71) were drug addicts with accidental overdose; one was an accidental poisoning. Multiple drugs were found in 55 percent. There were two deaths in the ICU group (2.8 percent).

The most common problem was respiratory depression. This required mechanically assisted breathing, or intubation (an oxygen tube run into the trachea), which is not a great deal of fun. Subsequently there are a lot of lower respiratory tract infections in these people, probably related to inadequate or absent cough and gag reflexes, which may have allowed vomit to enter the lungs. Serious cases show abscesses and necrotizing (tissue-destroying) pneumonia, which is as unpleasant as it sounds.

Next in frequency was fever. Usually occurring on the second day, these often are not garden-variety fevers, but high-temperature ones, 105 degrees F (40.5 degrees C) or above, with the potential for causing seizures, brain damage, and death.

Since most of the drugs taken suppress cough reflexes, aspiration pneumonia is a frequent complication; either through inhalation of vomit by unconscious person, or through medical procedures intended to remove the drug. This may also lead to bacterial pneumonia.

Thus we see that only a small percentage of those who were alive when they got to the ICU died, but that many of the survivors had serious injuries.

LONG-TERM MEDICAL CONSEQUENCES

Some drugs damage specific organs. For example, acetaminophen is mainly toxic to the liver; the herbicide paraquat targets the lungs. More often, overdoses cause general respiratory and/or cardiac depression. The resulting lack of oxygen, in turn, causes acid/base imbalance and further heart damage, because heart muscle tends to become arrhythmic (it beats irregularly and thus does not pump blood) under these conditions. In turn, lack of oxygen can cause permanent brain damage and multiple organ failure.

How Frequent Are Severe Effects After "Intentional" Drug/Poison Overdoses?

Of people in the United States who were alive when they reached the hospital (and for whom we have data), 27.4 percent suffered no ill effects, 55.6 percent had minor effects, 13.2 percent moderate effects, 3.3 percent major effect, 0.45 percent died.[21] Of those with major effects, about 2 percent had permanent injury.[22]

The following table (20.2) shows the distribution in severity of effects of "intentional" (suicidal, therapeutic, and recreational) overdoses in the United States in 1991 and 1992.

Table 20.2 Results of Intentional Drug/Poison Exposure: AAPCC Data

	1991		1992	
Result[8]	Number	%	Number	%
No effect	33,870	17.4	34,484	17.2
Minor effect	68,088	35.1	70,668	35.3
Moderate effect	16,179	8.3	16,813	8.4
Major effect	4,091	2.1	4,128	2.1
Death	576	0.30	541	0.27
Suicide	408	0.210	395	0.198
Accident	168	0.087	146	0.073
Unknown	71,393	36.8	73,316	36.7
Total	194,197		199,950	
Source: AAPCC (Litovitz, 1992, 1993)				

We can see that there are seven or eight people in the "major effect" category for every death. How many of these result in permanent injury is unknown.

This is substantially different from the older data in Card (see Table 16.3), which shows 1.4 to 2.0 "major effect" cases per death. I don't know why; perhaps because fewer people are dying, more survive to be in the major effect category.

Since the AAPCC injury data lump together suicidal and other intentional drug uses, it is less helpful for our purposes; however, from the next table, we can get data that, combined with the above, show that 67.4 percent of the reported cases intended suicide (1991 and 1992 combined), while 71.9 percent of the fatalities (table above) were due to suicide. This suggests that suicide attempters had similar consequences as those who otherwise intentionally overdosed.

Table 20.3 Reason for Intentional Exposure

	1991	1992	Combined %
Suicide	131,707	133,822	67.4
Therapeutic misuse	27,581	29,544	14.5
Psychotropic misuse	18,884	20,808	10.1
Unknown	16,025	15,776	8.1
Total	194,197	199,950	

Source: AAPCC (Litovitz, 1992, 1993)

What else can we learn from these data? If we look at the number of deaths as a percentage of the "moderate," "major," and "death" categories—the ones most likely to be admitted to a hospital—we find that the death rate was 2.6 percent, which is within the suicidal-poisoning death rate of 0.6 to 6 percent generally reported from hospital admissions.[h23]

WHICH DRUGS ARE USED IN SUICIDES AND SUICIDE ATTEMPTS?

The answer depends on both when and where (and who) you ask. Fashions in poisons change:[24] In one hospital in Sweden, barbiturates (for example, Seconal) caused 60 percent of fatal adult poisonings in 1962; by 1976 tricyclic antidepressants (TCAs) (for example, Elavil, Tofranil) were the largest group,[25] despite the fact that the death rate for TCA overdoses fell from 15 to 1.7 percent between early 1960s and 1977.[26] In Switzerland (1983) benzodiazepines[i] (for example, Valium) were the drugs of choice.[27]

The Brits seem to prefer ending it all with acetaminophen.[28] In Australia, for a while chloral hydrate was the most-used single drug.[29]

In Singapore, Thailand, and Sri Lanka agricultural chemicals are popular.[30] In Sri Lanka more than half of *all* suicides use agricultural chemicals. "Almost every rural grocery store has shelves full of many brands of pesticides in bottles of various sizes. Over one hundred chemicals—including malathion in more than two hundred formulations—are sold. Liquid preparations of pesticides can be lethal in minute doses."[31]

These data reflect prescribing practices, lethality of available drugs, and availability of alternative chemicals and methods.

In the United States, antidepressants and pain relievers run neck and neck in number of fatalities—about seven hundred a year for each—but antidepressants are about five to six times as lethal per overdose.[32] In 1990 amitriptyline (for example, Elavil) accounted for only 3.7 percent of suicide attempts, but for 12.7 percent of 1,492 deaths from drug overdose that were classified as suicides.[33] Some years amitriptyline was the most often prescribed drug in the United States.

Antidepressants, ironically, were responsible for the greatest number of drug-suicide deaths (723), followed by narcotics (461), cocaine (342), and tranquilizers (322).

Alcohol, which causes an estimated 4,000 acute and 200,000 chronic deaths a year[34] is ignored except as a contributor to another drug's toxicity. Tobacco, with some 390,000 annual notches on its belt, is not mentioned at all. These omissions are presumably the result of NIDA's pharmacologically irrational focus on "illegal drugs" rather than "dangerous drugs."

The other problem with their data is that "mentioned" only means that the drug was mentioned by the reporting hospital. This implies, and usually means, a significant or lethal amount—but not necessarily. These may be drugs found in the toxicology screen or even remaining pills in a bottle.

For example, as far as I've been able to determine, there are *no* reports of fatal marijuana overdoses *anywhere* in the medical literature; yet NIDA cites thirty-one marijuana "mentions" in just one year's suicide overdose statistics.

Table 20.4 Drugs Found in Suicides and Suicide Attempts (1991) (percentage greater than 100% due to multiple drug use)

DRUG CLASS	SUICIDES		SUICIDE ATTEMPTS	
	Number of times mentioned	% of deaths mentioned	Number of times mentioned	% of attempts mentioned
Tranquilizer	322	21.6	35,257	20.0
Diazepam (Valium)	146	9.8	8,791	5.0
Alprazolam (Xanax)	31	2.1	11,607	6.6
Chlordiazepoxide (Librium)	27	1.8	2,155	1.2
Chlorazepate (Tranxene)	1	0.1	1,020	0.6
Lorazepam (Ativan)	13	0.9	5,093	2.9
Meprobamate (Miltown)	14	0.9	285	0.2
Other/unknown	90	6.0	6,307	3.6
Narcotic pain reliever	461	30.9	14,166	8.0
Heroin/morphine/others	157	10.5	1,176	0.7
d-Propoxyphene (Darvon)	121	8.1	5,060	2.9
Methadone	21	1.4	129	0.1
Oxycodone (Percodan)	17	1.1	2,394	1.4
Codeine	108	7.2	926	0.5
Meperidine (Demerol)	9	0.6	550	0.3
Hydromorphone (Dilaudid)	7	0.5	97	0.1
Other/unknown	21	1.4	3,833	2.2
Non-narcotic pain reliever	190	12.7	48,259	27.3
Aspirin	53	3.6	17,076	9.7
Acetaminophen (Tylenol)	109	7.3	24,669	14.1
Pentazocine (Talwin)	1	0.1	215	0.1
Butalbital combinations	-	-	1,409	0.8
Other/unknown	27	1.8	4,891	2.8

DRUG CLASS	SUICIDES		SUICIDE ATTEMPTS	
	Number of times mentioned	% of deaths mentioned	Number of times mentioned	% of attempts mentioned
Non-barbiturate sedative	95	6.4	15,240	8.6
Methaqualone (Quaalude)	1	0.1	364	0.2
Flurazepam (Dalmane)	32	2.1	2,338	1.3
OTC sleeping pills	1	0.1	5,494	3.1
Ethchlorvynol (Placidyl)	8	0.5	160	0.1
Glutethimide (Doriden)	-	-	-	-
Chloral hydrate	-	-	399	0.2
Other/unknown	53	3.6	6,395	0.7
Antidepressants	723	48.5	29,755	16.8
Amitriptyline (Elavil)	190	12.7	6,401	3.7
Amitriptyline combos	1	0.1	1,146	0.7
Doxepin (Sinequan)	100	6.7	3,146	1.8
Fluoxetine (Prozac)	58	3.9	5,855	3.3
Imipramine (Tofranil)	51	3.4	2,852	1.6
Desipramine (Norpramin)	97	6.5	1,717	1.0
Other/unknown	226	15.1	8,639	4.9
Antipsychotics	57	3.8	10,363	5.9
Chlorpromazine (Thorazine)	12	0.8	1,310	0.7
Thioridazine (Mellaril)	18	1.2	1,991	1.1
Haloperidol (Haldol)	4	0.3	2,009	1.1
Trifluoperazine (Stelazine)	2	0.1	935	0.5
Other/unknown	21	1.4	4,119	2.4
Barbiturate sedative	196	13.1	3,716	2.1
Phenobarbital	61	4.1	2,275	1.3
Secobarbital/amobarbital	-	-	16	-
Secobarbital (Seconal)	46	3.1	269	0.2
Pentobarbital (Nembutal)	26	1.7	-	-
Other/unknown	63	4.2	1,015	0.6

DRUG CLASS	SUICIDES		SUICIDE ATTEMPTS	
	Number of times mentioned	% of deaths mentioned	Number of times mentioned	% of attempts mentioned
Amphetamine	68	4.6	906	0.5
Amphetamine	27	1.8	483	0.3
Methamphetamine	40	2.7	405	0.2
Other/unknown	1	0.1	18	-
Hallucinogen	15	1.0	606	0.3
PCP/PCP combos	14	0.9	223	0.1
LSD	1	0.1	234	0.1
Other/unknown	-	-	-	-
Other drugs				
Alcohol-in-combination	525	35.2	48,521	27.7
Cocaine	342	22.9	6,703	3.8
Marijuana/Hashish	31	2.1	1,280	0.7
Codeine combos	-	-	5,831	3.3
Diphenylhydantoin (Dilantin)	302.0		1,985	1.1
Diphenhydramine (Benadryl)	107	7.2	5,400	3.1
OTC diet pills	-	-	640	0.4
Inhalent/solvent/aerosol	21	1.4	356	0.2
Methylphenidate (Ritalin)	1	0.1	308	0.2
All other drugs	322	21.6	82,265	46.6
Drug unknown	11	0.1	8,940	5.1
Total Drug Mentions	3,517	235.7	320,498	182.9
Total Drug Suicides	1,492	100.0		
Total Drug Suicide Attempts			175,203	100.0

Source: NIDA, 1991

More detailed, but less comprehensive, data on fatal poisonings from the AAPCC found that roughly half of drug-suicides took single drugs, half multiple drugs.

Older data[35] from state and county death records have found (1) fatal acetaminophen (Tylenol), codeine, chlordiazepoxide (Librium), diazepam

(Valium), ethchlorvynol, flurazepam (Dalmane), meprobamate (Miltown), methadone, and aspirin overdose are usually found in multidrug deaths; (2) cyanide, TCAs, and carbon monoxide tend to be single-drug deaths. This reflects the greater toxicity and speed of the second group of substances.

NONMEDICINAL POISONS USED IN FATAL SUICIDE ATTEMPTS

In the U.S. nonmedicinal poisons are responsible for about one-fifteenth as many suicide deaths as are medical drugs. The most common poisons are: automotive antifreeze (ethylene glycol), rubbing alcohol (isopropyl alcohol), acid toilet bowl cleaner (sodium hydrogen sulfate), corrosive drain unclogger (lye, sodium hydroxide), windshield fluid (methanol, wood alcohol), metal plating chemicals (cyanide), and pesticides.[36]

WHAT ARE THE MOST DANGEROUS POISONS?

That depends on how you define "dangerous." You might base it on the smallest amount of chemical needed for a lethal effect (botulinum toxin). Or perhaps how quickly fatal it is (cyanide, nicotine, nerve gases). Or how many people a year die from its effects (tobacco, alcohol). Or the smallest ratio of therapeutic-to-toxic dose (lithium). Or the hardest to detect.

For botulinum toxin, the lethal dose in mice is 0.03 ug/gm (microgram of poison per gram of mouse), or about one-seventh that of the most poisonous North American snake (Mojave rattlesnake); it was the first bacterial protein ever crystallized. The discoverer whimsically described it as a "white odorless protein of high molecular weight and unknown taste."[37] However, the venom of the beaked sea snake is about five times more poisonous than the Mojave rattler and within spitting distance of botulinum protein. Another snake, the Taiwan Banded Krait (Bungarus multicinctus), may be even more poisonous.[38]

For medical drugs, one intuitively appealing measure of "dangerous" is the death rate per prescription. On one scale, the highest rate (for quinalbarbital) was defined as 100, rather like octane rating for gasoline; others are relative to it (the absolute number for quinalbarbital was 698 deaths/million prescriptions).

The idea is simple enough: To measure the real-world lethality of prescription drugs by the ratio of deaths from their use to the availability of the drug.[k] Note that this does not mean that a drug with a low fatal toxicity index (FTI) is safe; only that it is not used, for whatever reason(s), with fatal results very often, in relation to the number of its prescriptions.

Besides important safety information for physicians (and users), more recently developed antidepressants produce a lower death rate than either older TCAs or (most) MAOIs; they're less toxic—there are few overdose deaths using these as the only drug—and probably more effective against suicidal behavior.[l]

WHY ARE RESULTS OF DRUG OVERDOSE UNPREDICTABLE?

If you hang or shoot yourself properly you will almost certainly die; if you take a handful of pills you might die or you might be okay or you might be permanently injured. Why is this, and what can you do to maximize the chance of a predictable outcome?

BIOCHEMICAL INDIVIDUALITY

Biochemically, each of us is similar—and different. That's why some people are fatally allergic to penicillin or bee stings; why organ transplants require close tissue matches; why fingerprints are unique; why effective concentrations of medication vary from person to person. The range of biochemical individuality is not widely appreciated. For example, the rates at which people metabolize frequently used suicide drugs, tricyclic antidepressants (TCAs), vary ten- to thirtyfold.[39]

Additionally, individuals' size and health vary. Since drugs/poisons require a certain *concentration* for their effects, the same *amount* will be less effective when distributed throughout a large person than a small one, all else being equal.

But "all else" is rarely equal. For example, brains are fairly similar in size irrespective of whether one is a beefy 300-pound football player or a scrawny 150-pound writer. Thus a drug that is concentrated in the brain would require a reasonably similar dose for people of different size while a muscle-bound drug would require substantially different doses.

And there are further complications. For example, most drugs are metabolized and inactivated by the liver. However, prior chronic use of some drugs (for example, barbiturates, alcohol) revs up the liver, which then metabolizes drugs faster. This may have a protective effect against a subsequent drug—unless that drug is metabolized *into* its active form (for example, aspirin, heroin).

And, of course, someone in poor health may well die from a dose that wouldn't have a serious effect on someone in good health. Thus, the same dose that would cause permanent injury in one person might make another vomit and be okay and a third one die.

Further, multiple drugs are often taken, either therapeutically or suicidally. Sometimes these interact in unpredictable ways.[m] For example, an antiulcer drug, cimetidine (Tagamet), decreases the body's ability to metabolize some other drugs, like theophylline (for example, Theo-Dur), increasing their toxicity. The medical literature is full of case reports citing novel or unusual drug interactions; there are ten thousand drugs currently in use and more new ones every year.

SEX DIFFERENCES

While women and men absorb, distribute, and metabolize most drugs similarly, sex-related differences in drug clearance (removal from bloodstream) of over 100 percent are well known.[40] The cause of such variation is that women are more subject to internal cycles and changes: menstrual, pregnancy, and menopause. These disparities are mostly seen with psychotropic (mood/thought-effecting), heart/circulatory system, and antiinflammatory drugs, and are one reason why blood levels of drugs are increasingly often monitored.

UNCERTAINTIES ABOUT LETHAL DOSES

If you think about how the data are acquired, added uncertainties arise concerning the reliability of the published toxic/lethal doses. Animal test data often vary widely from one species to the next. For example, the lethal concentration of botulinum toxin is a thousandfold higher for rats than for mice. Thus, extrapolation of data from one species to another must always be tentative.

Botulinum toxin is pretty strong stuff, deadly at one part in 33 million for mice.[41] For a 70 kg human, that would be about 2 milligrams (the standard aspirin tablet has 325 milligrams of aspirin, plus filler).

Since there is sometimes a reluctance to poison large numbers of people acutely[n]—or at to least publish the results—human poisoning data frequently are presented as single case reports, resulting from accidental or deliberate overdose. Many times, the amount of drug taken is uncertain,[42] and about half of overdoses are drug mixtures, further confusing the toxicity picture. The concentration of the drug varies between tissues and over time. Some analytical techniques measure drug metabolites, some don't. The underlying health of different subjects is highly variable, as is the speed and quality of medical treatment.

As a result, the lethal doses cited in medical reviews are generally in the form of a range of values rather than a nice, misleadingly simple single number. Furthermore, even this range differs from one authority to another. For example, the lethal dose of the familiar and thoroughly studied short-acting barbiturates is estimated to be 3-6 grams,[43] 2-10 grams,[44] 1-2 grams,[45] and 1.6-2.2 grams[46] by four different authorities. Adding more uncertainty, much larger overdoses are sometimes survived—20 grams of amobarbital in one case.[47] Less common drugs/chemicals often have even wider ranges of human toxicity cited, because the data are too scanty for much precision.

Finally, some individuals will have adverse reactions to normally safe amounts of drugs/chemicals. An estimated 80 to 90 percent of drugs can cause a potentially fatal reaction in some people at therapeutic doses.[48] A few of the more common ones are: penicillins, aspirin, ACTH (hormone), allergen extracts, nuts (food), eggs (food or in vaccines), milk (food), iodine mixtures (used in X-ray and other diagnostic testing), animal sera (vaccines), and procaine or lidocaine (local anesthetics). Approximately 1 to 3 percent of the AAPCC poisoning deaths were due to adverse reaction, that is, an unexpected lethal reaction to a normally safe dose.

Thus, the best anyone can do is to provide the range of toxic and lethal doses cited in the medical literature. Even so, there is no guarantee that any given dose of a particular chemical will have its predicted or intended effect.

MORE PROBLEMS

As if this weren't enough, there are a large number of additional sources of uncertainty. For example, many drugs (for example, opiates, most antispasmotics, some antihistamines) slow the gastro-intestinal system. These drugs thus slow their own absorption, as well as that of other drugs. On the other hand, a few drugs (for example, the antivomiting drug metoclopramide, and cathartics) speed gastric motility.

If many tablets are swallowed at the same time, they may clump together in the stomach or intestine in an unabsorbed lump, called a bezoar.

Both these problems may have occurred in a death described by Steven Jamison:[49] Bill was dying from AIDS and was told he had only weeks left. After arranging to get a prescription for a narcotic skin patch, he invited his family to his house to say good-byes. After two days with them, he said it was time, and went to his bedroom with his brother and his partner. He filled six syringes with Demerol (another opiate) to be used by them after he was unconscious, and applied twenty skin patches. He then swallowed over two hundred tablets of sedatives (Valium, Soma, Halcyon) and pain relievers, including morphine.

He quickly lost consciousness and three hours later his brother injected the Demerol into Bill's thigh muscle. Seven hours later, Bill woke up and vomited, and fell into a light sleep. Probably the narcotics had slowed or stopped his digestive system, and the large number of unground pills may have formed a bezoar. In addition, the Demerol was not injected into a vein, because of his brother's fear of contact with Bill's blood.

The family tried to decide what to do next; Bill's father wanted to use the plastic trash bag that Bill had prepared as a back-up. The brother disagreed, arguing that Bill would wake up and fight to remove it, but eventually agreed to give it a try. Bill did wake up, but they calmed him down. He said one last word, "okay," and died without a struggle.

Such botched deaths—and there was no single cause here—are common in amateur assisted suicides.[50] Even physician-assisted suicides are prone to failure where they're illegal. This is primarily because doctors fear that a large prescription for barbiturates—probably the best oral suicide drugs—will have legal or professional repercussions if their patient uses it for that purpose.

The sum of all these uncertainties is that you can't count on any drug to be either 100 percent safe or 100 percent lethal.

How Can We Distinguish Among Suicidal, Accidental, and Homicidal Poisonings?

Murder by poison has a long and fascinating history. Not surprisingly, many of the leading practitioners have been physicians. This is because doctors have a tempting combination of knowledge, access to drugs, and, in some cases, the hubris to believe that they're smarter than the police.

Between 1979 and 1995 the United States averaged forty-six homicidal poisonings per year. One reason for this low number is that there are very few, if any, poisons that break down fast enough or are lethal in low enough concentration to be undetectable by current analytical methods. Thus there is little likelihood of such a murder slipping by as a natural-causes death, if a complete autopsy is done. Poisoners who have specific victims in mind generally need access to the victim's food, drink, or medicine. Since the number of people with such access is usually small, the police can concentrate their efforts, with better than normal results.

Homicidal poisoning comprised 0.16 percent of U.S. murders between 1980 and 1984. The British incidence of homicidal poisoning is fourteen times that of the United States (2.22 versus 0.16 percent). However, in England and Wales the total number of homicides between 1972 and 1982 (eleven years) was 5,323; this average annual rate of 0.8 per 100,000 is about one-tenth of the American rate.

U.S. Homicides, 1980-1984, by Weapon[51]

Weapon	1980	1981	1982	1983	1984
Poison	17	12	19	20	6
Narcotics	12	20	16	17	19
Guns, total	13,650	12,523	11,721	10,895	9,819
handguns	10,012	9,193	8,474	8,193	7,277
rifles	1,124	968	1,017	831	763
shotguns	1,636	1,528	1,377	1,243	1,154
other/not stated	878	834	853	628	628
Explosives	21	16	12	5	8
Cutting, stabbing	4,212	3,886	4,065	4,075	3,540
Clubs, hammers, etc.	1,094	1,038	957	1,062	973
Hands, feet, etc.	1,282	1,132	1,298	1,280	1,090
Fires	192	258	279	216	192
Drowning	49	51	52	40	44
Strangulation	401	337	359	376	317
Asphyxiation	104	150	108	123	111
Other	727	630	599	564	570
Total°	21,860	20,053	19,485	18,673	16,689

Second, contrary to TV shows and crime novels, it is difficult to slip most poisons into someone's drink such that they will swallow it because: (1) many poisons are hard to dissolve; (2) they often taste terrible. Try dissolving some of your medicines in water or booze; if you succeed, taste the resulting drink. Not very encouraging for would-be poisoners, especially considering the amount needed. Arsenic is unusual in being almost tasteless and easy to obtain. Regrettably (for murderers), it is *very* easy to detect, both at the time and even years later.[P]

Third, undiscovered poisonings don't show up in the statistics. In recent years only around 10 percent of deaths in the United States have been autopsied, and not all of these include full toxicology screens. If a person with a serious preexisting medical problem dies in a manner consistent with the illness, a complete autopsy is highly unlikely. This is particularly true if the deceased is old, unless there are suspicious circumstances.

Distinguishing between suicide, accident, and homicide is generally more difficult in overdose cases than with gunshot, stabbing, or hanging. This is because, with the latter groups there are frequently differences in the size, shape, angle, and location of the injury, depending on whether it was self-inflicted or not. For example, the bodies of most people who cut their own wrist or throat show evidence of "hesitation cuts": shallow wounds that often precede lethal ones. There may also be physical evidence, for example, gunpowder residue or rope fibers on the hands of a suicide. This sort of information is rarely available with overdoses. And so the determination of suicide, accident, or homicide in these cases is more often based on circumstantial evidence and a "psychological autopsy."

PRACTICAL STUFF

Recommended drugs; drugs to avoid; drug mixtures; tolerance; sources of drugs/chemicals.

SOURCES OF DRUGS[52]

Your best source of prescription drugs is usually your doctor. If you are terminally ill, some physicians will prescribe enough pain medication to allow you to take a lethal overdose. Others, however, have ethical, professional, legal, or religious scruples against suicide even under these circumstances and will not help you. In that case, you may want to consider finding another physician: The last thing you need, in my opinion, is to have no choice about being kept "alive," hooked up to a mechanical ventilator, blood pressure maintained only by intravenous drugs, lungs vacuumed every hour, tubes in every orifice, until your body can't be flogged any further. This kind of torture continues to be seen, sometimes despite explicit instructions of patients and their families.

You can easily obtain almost any medical drug in some countries: Brazil,[53] Spain, Singapore, and Hong Kong have been recommended.[54] Others have suggested Cyprus, Ecuador,[55] Panama, and Mexico. Nevertheless, this seems like going to a lot of trouble since finding a sympathetic doctor is not difficult. And a piece of rope or a plastic bag are workable alternatives (see Hanging and Asphyxia chapters).

While you can buy just about any drug you want on the street, you can't be sure of what you're getting or how much it has been diluted or adulterated. As a result, the street is usually your least reliable source of suicide drugs.

If you're a packrat, check the medicine cabinet; you might be surprised. You may also want to ask friends and family, if appropriate, for donations. Most—but not all—drugs are effective for at least a year beyond their expiration date if kept in a cool, dark, and dry place,q though you might take a bit more to compensate for deterioration. If you're on good terms with a pharmacist, you may want to ask about the expected loss of strength of a particular expired drug that you have available.

However, it is unrealistic to assume that eating even the entire contents of a medicine cabinet will necessarily be lethal, if for no other reason than the sheer variety of available drugs.

WHICH DRUGS TO USE, WHICH TO AVOID

What follows are general observations. See Table 20.4 for the frequency that some common drugs are used in suicide and suicide attempt.

"SAFE" DRUGS AND CHEMICALS.

To survive a suicide attempt with least likelihood of permanent injury,

1. Find a well-known drug that has relatively low lethality and few severe effects. Some examples are: acyclovir (Zovirax); aspirin (in low doses *only*: less than 150 mg/kg, which is thirty-two 325-mg standard tablets for a 70 kg (154 pound) person; caffeine; diazepam (Valium) and chlordiazpoxide (Librium) (*don't mix the last two with other drugs*); steroids; diuretics; NSAIDs (for example, ibuprofen); and ACE inhibitors (for example, captopril).
2. *Don't take more than half the lowest known fatal dose*—almost all of these drugs have killed people—and hope you don't set a new record.

3. Arrange to be found quickly, and avoid holidays when hospitals are short-staffed and are busy patching up drunk drivers and their victims. But there are no guarantees. Remember: 1 to 3 percent of drug-caused deaths are due to adverse reactions to *normal* doses.

Ballpoint pen inks, bathtub floating toys, body conditioners are of the type of commonly available substances that are generally considered nontoxic in acute overdose. This does *not* mean that it is impossible to ingest a toxic or even lethal amount; only that it is difficult to do so. *Anything* is toxic if ingested in large enough quantity or concentration (oxygen, water, sugar, salt—even chocolate). In addition, some of these household items may be toxic after *chronic* ingestion, for example, hair dyes or saccharin. And there is always the possibility of an individual's hypersensitivity to any particular substance. Finally, some can cause *mechanical* injury: One can choke on a chemically nontoxic golf ball or die of lung damage from inhaling baby powder—both of these have been done.

LETHAL DRUG OVERDOSE

If you really want to kill yourself using drugs, your best bet for a low-trauma overdose is probably a central nervous system (CNS) depressant drug. These include opiates, barbiturates, and alcohol. Combining these with some fairly safe other drugs (among which are major tranquilizers, sedatives, and muscle relaxants) makes a mix that is considerably more lethal than either component separately.

You should be aware that drug tolerance, the need for increasingly large doses to achieve the same effect, is especially common in drugs that affect the nervous system. This includes opiates, barbiturates, alcohol, tranquilizers, and sedatives (as well as stimulants such as amphetamine and hallucinogens like LSD).

If you have been using any of them for a while, you will require a larger—possibly much larger—dose of that drug for any given effect, therapeutic or suicidal. This is a significant problem for dying people who are getting lots of pain medication and want to kill themselves with an overdose of the same drug. The lethal doses listed in medical literature will be underestimates in these circumstances; how much of an underestimate can't be predicted.

Martin Delaney, the director of Project Inform, an advocacy group for people with AIDS, notes that he has seen situations where dying patients try to take enough intravenous morphine to kill themselves. "The problem is, they tend to do it gently and gradually and hope they will fade out without pain," he said. "Instead, they can develop tolerance, enormous tolerance. I'm talking about bags of morphine going into people."[57]

Some drugs, especially those affecting the central nervous system, also show cross tolerance: use of one drug generates tolerance not just to itself but, to a lesser extent, to similar drugs. Generally speaking, the more closely related the drugs (or the mechanism of their action), the more cross tolerance.

BARBITURATES. Barbiturates, especially the shorter-acting ones, are highly lethal in overdose, but are rarely prescribed since there are safer drugs with many of the same therapeutic effects. However, if you are terminally ill, it should be possible to find a sympathetic physician who will prescribe these for "insomnia."[58]

On the other hand, you should not wait too long to start inquiries since many doctors will first prescribe benzodiazepines (for example, Valium, Dalmane) or SSRI antidepressants (for example, Prozac). In addition, many pharmacies no longer routinely carry any barbiturates other than phenobarbital (a long-acting antiepilepsy drug), adding further delay.

Since the physician will probably want to protect herself, she will likely prescribe much less than a potentially lethal quantity. Thus it may be necessary to get several refills.

These drugs were quite popular with suicidal doctors: In 1974 almost 70 percent (139 of 203) of physician suicides via drugs/poisons used barbiturates.[59] They invariably used short-acting varieties and/or mixed them with other short-acting CNS depressants, notably glutethimide (Doriden), a sleeping pill.[60]

But there's no need to be picky: All CNS depressants and sedative-hypnotics increase the toxicity of barbiturates. A few examples of these are: alcohol, opiates, diezepam (Valium), meprobamate (Miltown), and antihistamines.

The organization *Compassion in Dying* (CID) recommends 6,000 to 9,000 mg (6 to 9 grams; 60 to 90 100 mg capsules) of Nembutal (pentobarbital) or Seconal (secobarbital)[61] broken apart and mixed and suspended in about one cup of applesauce or melted ice cream. Barbiturates are bitter, so adding some sugar, honey, or artificial sweetener may be helpful. Half an hour before the main event, *Compassion* suggests three antinausea pills (for example, promethazine)[r] and beta-blocking heart medication (for example, 80 mg propranolol), the latter to further decrease blood pressure.

The barbiturates must be eaten quickly, lest one fall asleep before swallowing a lethal quantity. Alcohol, taken after the barbiturates, will increase their toxicity. At these barbiturate doses, this is probably unnecessary, but, with smaller amounts, may be important. CID reports that sleep occurs in five to seven minutes; death in twenty-five minutes to ten hours. There is no evidence of discomfort. Unless vomited, this is a reliably lethal dose; however, concurrent use of a plastic bag or tube tent may hasten death. (See Asphyxia chapter.)

In the Netherlands, about four hundred people a year receive oral drugs for assisted suicide from physicians. The lethal ingredient is also pentobarbital (Nembutal), typically 9 grams (9,000 mg). But even with this large dose about 25 percent of the users survive for between two hours and four days.[62] This may be another argument in favor of the simultaneous use of plastic bag/tube tent.

ORPHENADRINE (Norflex, Disipal), an antihistamine, has been used in the Netherlands for euthanasia, mostly as an adjunct to barbiturates. By itself, orphenadrine is moderately but unpredictably toxic and quite unpleasant, and should not be used either for suicide or for a suicidal gesture.

PROPOXYPHENE (Darvon), an opiate-like drug, has also been used with barbiturates in the Netherlands. It's more toxic than orphenadrine, but shows cross tolerance with morphine and other opiates, and is thus less effective with people who are taking large amounts of narcotic pain drugs.

ASPIRIN AND ACETAMINOPHEN. Both aspirin and acetaminophen are commonly found around the house and are dangerous in overdose, but neither is quick or painless. Acetaminophen has a specific antidote (n-acetyl cysteine), but it has to be administered prior to the development of fatal liver damage. There was at least one instance where this wasn't done because blood levels of acetaminophen seemed nondangerous, probably due to the overdose being from the sustained-release form of the drug.[63]

TRICYCLIC ANTIDEPRESSANTS (TCAs). Overdosing with antidepressants kills a lot of people, but if you're using them therapeutically, it may suggest that your decision on important topics like, say, suicide should wait until your judgment is not depression- or drug-influenced. Besides, "the first two to three weeks of treatment are the most critical, when the depressed patient experiences little benefit but maximum [unpleasant] side effects."[64] And also has the largest supply of drug available.

There are three broad classes of antidepressant drugs: TCAs, which are fairly effective, but also quite toxic in overdoses; mono-amine oxidase inhibitors, MAOIs (rarely used anymore); and serotonin-specific reuptake inhibitors, SSRIs, which are similar to TCAs in effectiveness against depression, but are much less frequently used to commit suicide.

TCAs have a multitude of other medical uses: insomnia, headaches, chronic pain, bulimia, and bed-wetting, among others. As a result, only a minority of their prescriptions are written by psychiatrists. This widespread availability, combined with their high toxicity—there's a 7 to 10 percent overdose death rate[65]—makes them the prescription-drug group with the highest suicide body count.[s] Amitriptyline (for example, Elavil) holds the recent single-drug record, primarily because it's more widely used than other TCAs; but dibenzepin has about twice the death rate per prescription.

TCAs are absorbed fairly quickly. Onset of convulsions generally occurs within three hours of overdose. Death, when it occurs, is usually due to some combination of heart failure, respiratory depression, and uncontrollable seizures. Lethal cases average around six hours between hospital admission and death.[66]

BETA-BLOCKERS AND CALCIUM-CHANNEL BLOCKERS are fairly lethal in overdose and are the primary drugs in around three hundred suicides per year. However, their availability is limited since they are prescription-only heart drugs.

POTASSIUM. If you have access to intravenous equipment and know what you're doing, you can kill yourself quickly with potassium ion. Cardiac toxicity predominates, with results resembling a heart attack.[20]

1. Potassium chloride (KCl) is a handy source of potassium because it's available in grocery stores as salt substitute, but read the label to make sure the formulation hasn't changed, as in "New and Improved."

Salt Substitute	approximate mEq potassium per teaspoon
Adolph's Salt Substitute (unseasoned)	65
Morton's Lite Salt	38
Morton's Salt Substitute	72
No-Salt	64
Nu-Salt	67

   The lethal intravenous dose is 0.34 to 0.41 milliequivalents (mEq) per pound (0.75 to 0.90 mEq/kg).[67] This corresponds to about two teaspoons of Morton Lite or one teaspoon of the others. The minimum lethal volume is 12 to 14 ml (1 teaspoon is 5 ml, 1 tablespoon is 15 ml) saturated KCl solution for a 70 kg (154 pound) person; however, it's more reliable to use excess.[u]

   You can make a saturated solution by mixing about 40 grams (1.5 ounces) of KCl into around 100 ml (4 ounces) of water. The quantities here are not critical. Stir for at least five minutes, or until no more seems to dissolve. Pour the liquid solution into an IV bag. Don't drink this though; it's not reliably lethal by mouth and will certainly make you very sick.

2. Run an IV line into a handy vein; attach this to the potassium solution bag with a "dead man" clamp—one that allows flow only when you relax pressure on the clamp.

3. Take depressant/sedative drugs, such as alcohol or morphine, by mouth, injection, or by another IV line or Y connection; potassium chloride causes muscle paralysis without unconsciousness, and is thus, by itself, an unpleasant way die. It also produces severe pain at the injection site (pain can be decreased by an ice pack or local anesthetic).

4. When you lose consciousness and let go of the clamp, the intravenous potassium drip will begin, and, your heart should stop in a few min-

utes, if nothing goes wrong. This is more or less what is done to prisoners who are killed by judicially ordered lethal injection. They also get a muscle paralyzing drug similar to the poison-arrow drug, curare. You'll probably have to settle for a muscle relaxant like Valium.

The most likely problems include getting an IV line started or having it pull out. You can minimize the likelihood of the latter by taping it down.

This is a relatively complicated method that may be difficult for someone to do alone, particularly if she is debilitated. It is, however, quick and lethal, and may be useful for someone who is bedridden and has a semipermanent intravenous line.

APPLE SEEDS. If you really can't get what you need, as a last resort you might consider . . . apple seeds. If you crush a fresh apple leaf (or cherry, plum, pear, and some others) between your fingers, you should be able to detect the faint odor of almonds. This is the smell of cyanide. Apple seeds average around 0.6 mg hydrogen cyanide (HCN) per gram of dry seed. Since the lethal dose of HCN is estimated to be about 50 mg, you need around 85 grams (3 ounces) of dry seeds. This is around half a cup, which requires a *lot* of apples. However:

1. Plants are variable; eat enough—at least three times the minimum dose: Cyanide is not a drug on which to skimp, since it can cause brain damage in sublethal doses (see Asphyxia chapter for details).
2. The HCN must be liberated from the sugar it's chemically attached to.[v] This occurs when the moistened seed is crushed, releasing an enzyme, emulsin, which does the job. Apparently this also occurs in the stomach, due to the hydrochloric acid there. In any case, you need to crush and eat these seeds fairly quickly, both to avoid evaporation of cyanide from the crushed seeds, and so as not to lose consciousness before ingesting a lethal dose. A blender or coffee grinder would be a good way to break up the seeds.
3. There are around 150 plants known to contain cyanide (vegetarians note!). Many of them have it in higher concentration than do apple seeds. For example, bitter almond seeds average around 3 mg/grams

(range 0.9 to 4.9), or five times the apple seed concentration. Cassava root is also quite poisonous unless processed to remove its cyanide. (I wonder how this was originally discovered.)

4. Cyanide, in the form of the alkali potassium salt is available as a metal plating solution, for example, "Cy-An-In"; the lethal dose of the sodium, potassium, and calcium cyanide salts is estimated to be 200 to 300 mg (0.07 to 0.11 ounce).

5. The use of cyanide is controversial: Some claim it is painless and quick, others that it is painful and quick.[68] For what it's worth, cyanide is commonly used by suicidal chemists but rarely by physicians. However, this may reflect their respective easy access to different poisons rather than any other basis for preference.[w]

The German Euthanasia Society recommends 1.5 grams potassium cyanide—about seven times the lethal dose—dissolved in a glass of cold water. Don't use fruit juice or soft drinks; their acid releases HCN prematurely (not that it will matter if you drink it quickly). Kool-Aid has been recommended for those who don't like plain water.[69]

The same folks suggest placing 1 gram of a cyanide salt into a gelatin capsule and putting that inside a larger gelatin capsule. The idea is for at least the inner capsule to reach the gut before dissolving and releasing the cyanide. This is claimed to minimize stomach pain.[70]

Sodium cyanide works every bit as well as the potassium salt; calcium cyanide decomposes in water, but should do the job if used quickly.

Effects are fastest if the stomach is empty and gastric acidity high. With minimally lethal doses, death may take up to an hour. Symptoms include a bitter, burning taste; constriction or numbness of the throat; nausea and vomiting; disorientation; irregular breathing; unconsciousness; violent convulsions; protruding eyeballs; foam, often bloody, around the mouth.[71] All in all, not a particularly peaceful exit, it would seem.

6. If you're in a hospital, and wired to monitoring devices, this (and most drugs) won't work fast enough and you'll probably be "saved"; but, if you're considered mentally competent, you can check yourself out "against medical advice" (AMA) and take care of business at home.

7. Unlike most drugs/poisons, cyanide has a reasonably specific set of antidotes that are usually effective if administered quickly enough: amyl nitrite by inhalation; sodium nitrite and sodium thiosulfate, intravenously.

SIGNIFICANT DETAILS

If you're trying to kill yourself be aware of the following:

- Many drugs cause vomiting in overdoses. To limit this, you can eat lightly and take one to four antinausea/travel sickness tablets about an hour before the main event. Promethazine (Phenergan) is a common antinausea drug. The presence of food also increases the rate at which stomach contents are released into the small intestine, where most food/drug absorption takes place.

- If the drugs are in tablet or gelatin capsule form, you may want to grind or break them open and then try to dissolve them. A blender works well if there's other material (for example, milk) in it, but a coffee bean grinder or mortar and pestle is better if you're chopping pills dry; however, you'll probably still need to dissolve or suspend them in a liquid in order to swallow them. Powdered or dissolved drugs will be absorbed faster in your digestive system. As a result, it's important to drink the concoction quickly—within two to five minutes—to minimize the chance of losing consciousness before ingesting the entire dose.

   On the other hand, some may be too bad-tasting to easily swallow in this form. Test with a single tablet/capsule to determine this. Most solids will dissolve better in hot liquid than cold; some dissolve better in a mixture of alcohol and water than in water alone, but this varies from drug to drug. Experiment. Melted ice cream in a blender is a often a good choice because it will dissolve both fat- and water-soluble drugs as well as mask some bad taste. Remember that alcohol is a central nervous system (CNS) depressant and will increase the effect of other depressants.

- If you have the "slow-release" formulation of a drug, grinding it to powder will usually be necessary.

- The full lethal dose must be taken quickly; many suicides have failed when the attempter has lost consciousness before swallowing enough drug to finish the job.
- If an overdose causes convulsions, the noise may attract attention. The frequency of convulsions varies, but is always a sign of severe toxicity.
- If you use CNS depressants you may want to put a large plastic bag over your head, and fasten it (airtight, but not painful—rubber bands work well) around your neck; you will likely die of asphyxia. This combination of drugs and asphyxia substantially increases both the speed and likelihood of dying.

A thirty-gallon trash bag holds (very approximately) enough air for half an hour. (*Important*: See Asphyxia chapter for more information.) You may want to wait until you begin to feel the effects of the drugs, but this increases the chance of falling asleep before applying the bag. It's better to use a larger bag or a tube tent. The latter, in particular, will minimize the chance of running out of air while still conscious. Whatever you use, it's also a good idea to practice with the plastic bag/tent until you're confident you can put it on and seal it—or remove it—when needed.

TREATMENT OF DRUG OVERDOSE

For most drugs, the standard treatment of choice consists of getting as much drug out of the stomach as possible, before it's absorbed. If the patient is awake and alert (and has not taken a drug likely to change that state within a half hour), 15[72] to 30 ml (1 to 2 tablespoons) syrup of ipecac (*not* "extract of ipecac", which is fourteen times more concentrated) should be swallowed along with at least one glass of water or clear soft-drink. This can be repeated after fifteen to thirty minutes if there has been no vomiting and no change in consciousness.

Syrup of ipecac[x] is the emetic-of-choice: It is more effective (but slower) than mechanical methods, and safer than chemical alternatives: saltwater, apomorphine, and copper sulfate. Liquid detergents (for washing by hand *only*; don't use liquid automatic-dishwasher or washing machine detergent) are a safe alternative if ipecac is not available. A dose of about 30 ml (2 tablespoons) of detergent caused vomiting in 83 percent of volunteers, compared to 97 percent with ipecac.[73]

Vomiting occurs an average of eighteen minutes after ipecac administration, but 11 percent do not vomit for more than thirty minutes.[74] This can be important since only 30 to 60 percent of a drug dose is recovered in experimental animals when ipecac is given right after various drugs, and falls to 15 to 30 percent recovery after a one-hour delay in giving ipecac.[75] In cases of large overdose of seriously toxic material, it's also appropriate (*if* there is no reason to avoid vomiting, see below) to try mechanical (fingers down the throat) induction of vomiting: It is important to get rid of as much poison as quickly as possible to prevent its absorption.

However, vomiting is a potential disaster in unconscious or convulsing people, since inhaled vomit will cause lung damage and may be fatal. Inducing vomiting in people whose gag reflex is depressed may cause similar problems, and gag reflex may be chemically depressed or absent in alert patients. This is no joke. Some drugs that rapidly cause seizures or coma in overdose are: TCAs, strychnine, camphor, chloral hydrate, and isoniazid.

The use of some other poisons also contraindicates vomiting: in general, if the poison is likely to do more damage from coming back up than from staying in the stomach a few more minutes, vomiting should not be induced. Poisons that fall into that category are (1) *caustics*: lye, automatic-washing detergents, most drain cleaners, strong acids; and (2) *liquid hydrocarbons* (furniture polish, gasoline, oils).

If induced vomiting fails or is inappropriate, gastric lavage ("stomach pumping") is often used. This is done by running a lubricated 1 cm tube through the nose into the stomach. Small volumes of water (50 to 100 ml) are pumped in (to avoid pushing drugs into the small intestine) and pumped back out. The process is repeated until the removed gastric contents are drug-free.

Use of "activated" charcoal (not what you use for barbecues) seems to be more effective than syrup of ipecac for limiting absorption of many chemicals and is the home remedy of choice in parts of Europe.[76] It is of little or no value against mineral acids or alkalis, cyanide, elemental metal ions, many pesticides, and wood alcohol, among others. It is effective against many medical drugs, including TCAs, aspirin, acetaminophen, and barbiturates. Since activated charcoal absorbs drugs, it should not be used at the same time as ipecac or specific drug antidotes, such as n-acetyl cysteine (an antidote for acetaminophen).

Because it is safer than either ipecac or stomach pumping, and most overdosed people get to the hospital too late to remove much drug by any of these methods, activated charcoal is becoming the standard treatment in U.S. hospitals as well.

Activated charcoal is probably best acquired as a commercial, premixed slurry. It can be mixed at home from powder and water, but must be mixed thoroughly. Flavoring may be added to improve palatability. Dose is 1 gram/kg of body weight (70 kg equals 154 pounds). This is a good thing to keep around the house.

Cathartics (diarrhea inducers) are often used to decrease drug absorption by limiting the time it remains in the gut, but the effectiveness of gut decontamination more than one hour post-ingestion is unclear.

In one study of suicidal overdoses, people got to the emergency room an average of 3.3 hours post-ingestion, ipecac did not significantly change the outcome for those in whom it was used[77] (people who were alert), and stomach pumping only helped when done within an hour of ingestion.

More invasive methods may be tried in cases of severe toxicity. One of these is "forced diuresis," which pushes the kidneys to pass more urine (and drug), typically by diuretic drugs or by fast intravenous fluid infusion. If there is kidney failure, hemodialysis may be necessary.

Each of these procedures has hazards associated with its use, the details of which are available in any medical text on poisoning.

SUMMARY

All in all, drugs can be—if you know what you're doing—a reasonably safe suicidal gesture roughly on a par with nonlethally-intended wrist cuts. Pick a low-toxicity drug, preferably one you know you're not allergic to; take a dose that won't do major damage even if help is delayed; call for help before the drug affects you; have activated charcoal available.

If you're trying to kill yourself, be aware that most drugs take hours to be fatal—but you can't rely on it—and are not pleasant. Read the list of symptoms again. Convulsions, which are common, may make noise and attract attention. Spontaneous vomiting, if it occurs, may leave you with few further ill effects; or with an almost-lethal dose and permanent injury; or you may choke to death.

Central nervous system depressants are probably the least traumatic, though not particularly fast, lethal drugs. Since these depressants cause unconsciousness, they may be combined with plastic-bag or inert-gas asphyxia, drowning, intravenous potassium chloride, or carbon monoxide for a faster and more certain death.

NOTES

[a] This assertion is disputed, particularly by some gun-control advocates. The majority of the evidence I have seen supports the "substitution of methods" argument. However, I would not deny that if easy and impulsive methods are made less available, fewer people will use them, but I would also argue that anyone who really wants to kill himself can and will do so.

[b] AAPCC data is similar to NIDA's: Both show a death rate of 0.3 percent among those hospitalized after suicidally intended overdose.

[c] Definitions: (1) *Therapeutic misuse*: improper, incorrect, or mistaken use of a drug(s) for a medically approved purpose. (2) *Psychotropic misuse*: use of drugs for pleasure. Officially disapproved drugs, that is. For example, in the U.S. use of marijuana is labeled "psychotropic misuse," while use of the far more dangerous drug, ethanol (alcohol), is not. (3) *Accidental*: unintended ingestion or absorption of a chemical or drug. (4) *Adverse reaction*: rare or unexpected response to a prescribed or OTC drug.

[d] The question of why, then, they took these overdoses is not addressed in this paper. Nevertheless, these data suggest that increasing "toxicity awareness" would decrease intentional overdoses. However current OTC drug labels are uninformative (for example, "In case of accidental overdose seek professional assistance or contact a poison control center immediately") and prescription drug labels don't even say that much. Given space limitations on labels, school and the media may be more fruitful avenues for dissemination of such information.

[e] Interestingly, when acetaminophen became an over-the-counter (OTC or non-prescription) drug in Denmark in 1984, it did not lead to an epidemic of fatal overdoses, as had been the case in Great Britain a decade earlier. Apparently the Danish formulation didn't include the analgesic dextropropoxyphene (Darvon), which was part of the available combination in England and which is also quite toxic (Ott, 1990).

[f]The limitations of this information are: (1) About one-third of the data are from nonsuicidal "intentional" poisonings; (2) only a small fraction of drug/poison suicides were reported to the poison control centers; (3) we don't know if the reported cases are representative. They may be typical of intentional poisoning, but are probably not representative of suicidal poisonings since some 80 percent of fatal overdose suicides die before getting to a hospital (Chafee-Bahamon, 1983; in Ellenhorn, 8). Also, in more than one-third of these overdoses the result was not reported to AAPCC.

[g]AAPCC definitions: (1) No effect. (2) Minor effect: some minimal symptoms, usually of skin, mouth, eyes, or nose. Symptoms resolved quickly and without permanent injury. Often no treatment needed. Examples of minor symptoms: dizziness, nausea, drowsiness, skin irritation. (3) Moderate effect: more systemic, more severe, or more prolonged than minor effects. Treatment was appropriate, but symptoms were not potentially lethal. No permanent injury. Examples: seizures that are readily treated or spontaneously subside, severe nausea and vomiting leading to dehydration, temporary kidney failure not needing dialysis, brief high fever, disorientation. (4) Major effect: symptoms were life-threatening or caused permanent injury. Examples: coma, severe cardiac dysrhythmias, multiple seizures, respiratory depression requiring mechanically assisted breathing. (5) Suicide: includes suicides, suicidal gestures and attempts. However, it clouds the issue to combine in a single category people who intended to die with those who intended to not die. (6) Accident: unintended poisoning.

[h]If we consider all suicidally intentioned poisonings reported to AAPCC, deaths constitute only 0.30 percent. However, this includes people with no, or minor, injuries who were sent home; and it is unlikely that these data include many people who were dead on arrival or dead at the scene.

[i]Benzodiazepines are not highly lethal by themselves, but become much more so when mixed with other depressant drugs, like alcohol, sleeping pills, or opiates. It's been jokingly said that the only way to die from Valium (diazepam) is to get run over by the truck delivering it. Yes and no: While just two of some 1,200 Valium-only ODs were fatal, there was a 30 percent death rate when Valium was part of a mixed-drug overdose (Finkle, 1979). Curiously, the study's author reached the opposite conclusion: He asserted that the best test of a drug's toxicity in mixed-drug OD is the toxicity of the same drug alone. Since Valium alone is fairly safe, he concluded that the drug-cocktail toxicity is mostly due to the other drugs.

[j]These numbers are subject to considerable dispute. One typical study of fatal drug/poison (including carbon monoxide) overdoses found that 23 percent of the deaths were due entirely to alcohol, and in another 13 percent a combination of alcohol and other drug(s) was lethal (Dukes, 1992).

[k]As usual, nothing is simple, and there are problems with this approach:

(1) Different uses of similar drugs: Most phenothiazines (for example, chlorpromazine [Thorazine]) are used as major antipsychotics at single doses of 25 to 200 mg; a few (for example, promethazine [Phenergan]) are used—at much lower doses (1 to 25 mg)—as, among other things, antinausea drugs. Unsurprisingly, chlorpromazine is found to have a higher death rate per prescription than promethazine. But this index does not show the intrinsic toxicity of the drugs, but rather their toxicity modified by the dosage of the prescriptions available and by what population (in this case, people either psychotic or seasick) they're

prescribed to. Does a change in prescribing alter the drug's intrinsic toxicity? Obviously not, but if the use or dosage shifts, so will the fatal toxicity index.

(2) The toxicity index does not take into account the age, sex, or condition of the patient; a particular drug may, for example, be used by more severely depressed people, which would skew the index (Kelleher, 1992).

(3) Half of drug suicides involve drug mixtures, so which particular drug should get credit?

Despite these limitations and complications, these data are useful, particularly for physicians wanting to prescribe a less toxic member of a more or less interchangeable class of drugs, for example, antidepressants. Such data also may be interesting and relevant for the suicidally inclined.

[l]At least one drug, clomipramine, has both a higher heart toxicity along with a low toxicity index; that is, it kills fewer people than expected, based on the number of prescriptions, despite being quite toxic.

Why is this? It turns out that clomipramine is used more often in obsessive-compulsive patients than in (more suicidal) depressed ones, and tends to be used more with hospitalized patients, who are under closer supervision, than with outpatients. Thus its low toxicity index seems to be due to its prescribing profile (Farmer, 1989).

This example of a mismatch between "toxicity" and "toxicity index" also supports the notion that some other drugs' high toxicity index might not be due to high intrinsic toxicity, but rather to the drug provoking its own use in suicide. There have been claims that this occurs with fluoxetine (Prozac) and maprotiline (Ludiomil), but the evidence is controversial (Baldwin, 1991; Frankenfield, 1994).

However, since there is good rank-order agreement between fatal toxicity index and the lethal dose in mice (Molcho, 1992)—in whom provocation of suicidal behavior is not a serious problem—it seems likely that most of the higher toxicity index for TCAs is due to their higher inherent toxicity compared to other antidepressants.

[m]A principle of pharmacology is that "the response to multiple drug therapy is not equal to the sum of the known responses to separate administration of each drug" (Sigell, 1970). This is similar to the everyday situation where two well-known chemicals are mixed; the result may be a dangerous surprise. For example, people sometimes figure that since ammonia is a good cleaner and chlorine bleach is a good cleaner, the combination should clean even better. Unfortunately, mixing bleach and ammonia will produce poisonous chlorine gas, which has killed a few fastidious toilet scrubbers. When these chemicals are poured together in a toilet bowl, and the seat put down, a dangerous concentration (denser-than-air) chlorine gas can form. If someone subsequently lifts the lid and places their head near the water, they may inhale a lethal amount of chlorine.

[n]Alcohol and tobacco corporations need their addicts alive.

[o]Just for perspective, the number of motor-vehicle-related deaths in the United States is around 40,000 to 50,000 per year.

[p]"Able was I ere I saw Elba." There were longstanding rumors that Napoleon, while exiled on Elba, was poisoned by arsenic on orders of the British government. (Then, as now, people who believe they're Napoleon tend to get put away, one way or another.) Recently, a bit of Napolean's hair was examined by a highly sensitive method called neutron activation

analysis: It had around thirteen times the normal amount of arsenic. Perfidious Albion! Well, maybe; however, arsenic was part of many medicines of the time, so may have been taken innocently. It may also have been taken prophylactically, since low doses of poison were thought to protect against higher doses. And sometimes they do.

qIf you keep drugs in the refrigerator, seal them thoroughly since it's a moist environment; it's also a good idea to add a small packet of dessicant, for example, silica gel or calcium chloride.

rIn the Netherlands, premedication with the antinausea drug metoclopramide (also available in the United States) is taken twenty-four hours before the euthanasia drug (Kimsma, 1996). In the United States, Dramamine (dimenhydrinate), Compazine (prochlorperazine), and Marezine (cyclezine) are often used for nausea.

sThis weasely wording lets me avoid mentioning alcohol and tobacco here.

tDon't bother trying this method to commit murder; blood potassium levels are routinely and easily measured.

uSorry about the messy units; life's easier in metric.

vPits have mygdalin, a cyanide-containing sugar, which gives off cyanide when exposed to the enzyme beta-glucosidase in the gut.

wIn U.S. physician suicides, 55 percent used drugs, 12 percent guns; of ninety-three police suicides, 90 percent used their issued revolvers (Colt, 235); of U.S. general population suicides, 60 percent used guns, 10 percent solid and liquid poisons, mostly drugs.

xIpecac is extracted from the roots of a couple of tropical New World shrubs (Cephaelis ipecacuanha and C. Acuminata, in case you were wondering) and contains several alkaloids, most notably emetine and cephaeline. Syrup of ipecac is sold OTC in 15 and 30 ml sizes.

21
ELECTROCUTION

●

Electrocution is an effective, but infrequently used, method of committing suicide. It is not a good choice for a suicidal gesture. The potentially lethal effects of electricity on the body include heart stoppage, respiratory failure, and burns.

LETHAL INTENT: High

MORTALITY: 40 to 90 percent

PERMANENT INJURIES: Moderately likely

PROS AND CONS OF SUICIDE BY ELECTROCUTION

Pros: • Not much physical strength or dexterity needed
  • High fatality rate
  • High (not household) voltage and current usually causes quick unconsciousness

Cons:• Scarcity of data on suicidal electrocution—most of our information is extrapolated from accidents
  • Frequent permanent injuries from high-voltage accidents
  • Electricity is mysterious to many people
  • May be hazardous to innocent bystanders or rescuers

The major topics of this chapter are the medical and physiological effects of electricity. Also discussed are sources and types of electricity, as well as methods and impediments to suicidal electrocution.

How Dangerous Is Electricity?

This may seem a silly question, but electricity is usually invisible and, for many people, mysterious. As a result, it's not widely known that consequences of electric shock often depend on how quickly help is available. This is because death is commonly due to the shock-induced stoppage of heartbeat or breathing—which are frequently reversible if there is prompt medical intervention, usually CPR (cardio-pulmonary resuscitation).[a]

The medical literature cites a wide range (5 to 50 percent) of mortality rates in known electrical accidents,[1] but since minor shocks are rarely reported, the accuracy of even this figure is questionable. In one recent study only 3 percent of hospital patients admitted with injuries from high voltage (greater than 1000 volts; found in high-power transmission lines and some industrial uses) died.[2] But this didn't include those dead at the scene or dead on arrival.

There is about a 90 percent fatality rate in suicidal electrocution attempts using household and high-voltage current.[3] Use of electric stunning devices is about 40 percent fatal.[4]

The frequency of long-term injury is unknown with suicide attempts, but occurs fairly often in accidents. Much depends on the type and duration of electric shock. The three most common sorts of long-term injury are:

- burns, typically from high-voltage power transmission;
- direct neurological (brain/nervous system) damage, generally from lightning or high-voltage power transmission;
- indirect brain damage resulting from breathing paralysis, which can be caused by high- or low-voltage power, or lightning.

There's more detail on these in the section on long-term injury.

History

There are records of lightning strikes from as early as A.D. 77 Pliny the Elder described the survival of a pregnant woman, but the death of her fetus, after they were hit by lightning[b5]

The invention of the Leyden jar, an early type of capacitor, in 1746 first permitted electricity to be collected and stored. Word of this simple device spread quickly and electric shocks became a popular novelty in fashionable circles. Kings had their own court "electricians." In one spectacle, seven hundred monks were connected to each other and to a Leyden jar. When the jar was discharged, they jumped into the air "with a simultaneity of precision out-rivalling the timing of the most perfect corps de ballet."[6]

Benjamin Franklin proved that lightning was identical to electricity from the recently invented Leyden jar (and not a gas explosion, as previously believed) in his famous kite experiment—flying a kite in a thunderstorm and getting a spark from the ground end of the kite-string (attached to a metal key) to charge a Leyden jar—the repetition of which electrocuted a number of less fortunate subsequent experimenters.

DEMOGRAPHICS

SUICIDE. Suicide by electricity is rare: There were fourteen known suicidal electrocutions in the United States in 1994; the 1979 to 1994 average was eighteen, which is 0.06 percent of the roughly 30,000 official suicides annually. Of 220 electrocutions in Dade County, Florida (Miami), 217 deaths were accidents, 2 suicides (0.9 percent), and 1 a homicide.[7]

ACCIDENTS. Electrocution is the fifth leading cause of occupational fatalities among men in the United States;[8] power lineworkers are electrocuted at a rate of 33.4 per 100,000 per year; electricians 8.3 per 100,000 per year.[9] Construction workers are also at high risk for electrocution. The overall accidental electrocution rate is approximately 0.54 per 100,000 per year (1 per 185,000) in the United States.[c10] Nonlightning electrical deaths per year in the United States have decreased steadily from 1,140 in 1970 to 640 in 1990,[11] but about 3 to 5 percent of burn center admissions in the United States are caused by high-voltage electricity.[12]

While a large majority of severe electrical injuries are due to high voltage, about half the deaths are from low voltage (arbitrarily defined as anything less than 1,000 volts). This low voltage is generally household (wall outlet) current, 110 to 120 volts A.C. (or 220 to 240 volts A.C. for electric clothes dryers, larger air conditioners, etc.) at 60 hertz (cycles per second) in the

United States; 240 volt power will produce twice the current as 120 volts at any given resistance, and is thus, generally, more dangerous.

Telephone or doorbell voltage and current are too low to be hazardous except occasionally as an unintended electrical conductor during a lightning strike.[d] In about 15 percent of electrical accidents there are also injuries from falls.[13]

LIGHTNING. Lightning strikes the earth around one hundred times per second. There were seventy-four deaths due to lightning in the United States in 1995; the 1979 to 1995 average was eighty-three.[14] Lightning kills around 40 percent of the people it hits.[15] Nonfatal injuries are discussed later in this chapter.

The speed of sound in air is around 1,100 feet (335 meters) per second; thus the time difference betweeen seeing a lightning flash and hearing the shock wave is about five seconds per mile (3 secs/kilometer). If you don't hear the thunder, either the lightning's very far away or you got hit by it.

FAMILIARITY-BREEDS-CONTEMPT DEPARTMENT (Part one).The use of household appliances in the bathroom, especially hair-dryers, is a common cause of electrocution.[e]

(Part two). Not unplugging electrical devices under repair can be fatal. A study found that, "About half the [electrocution] deaths of women over sixty were due to the use of metal scissors in the investigation of connectors of electric irons and kettles."[16] One woman who was killed in this manner *had* pulled the plug from the wall socket; unfortunately, her three-year-old son had reinserted it.[17]

EFFECTS OF ELECTRICITY

There are three types of fatal injury directly caused by electricity (an electric shock may also kill by knocking people off ladders or otherwise into danger):

- Burns;
- Interference with heartbeat or breathing by means of continuous small electric shocks, none of which may be individually harmful;
- Paralysis of heartbeat or breathing from a single large electrical jolt.

Lethal burns are most often due to high electrical current passing through the body. Such current is most commonly found in power lines and some factories. Household-voltage electricity rarely kills by this means, though it may cause burns, even charring, if there's prolonged contact.[18]

Low A.C. voltage causes repeated muscle contractions while the electrical circuit is complete, which may prevent effective breathing and heartbeat. Such shock can make various areas of heart muscle beat without coordination (fibrillation). Breathing usually resumes when electrical contact is broken, but the heart is more sensitive to electrical interference and generally does not recover spontaneously from ventricular fibrillation (uncoordinated contractions of the portion of the heart muscle which pumps blood through the body).

Promptly applied cardiac defibrillation ("electroconversion") may restore normal heartbeat,[f] but is rarely available soon enough to make a difference. In the absence of CPR or spontaneous recovery, a fibrillating heart starts to die in sixty to ninety seconds.[19] CPR extends the possible intervention time by at least a few minutes.

A single large electric shock can paralyze the heart, the muscles responsible for breathing, or the respiratory-control center in the brain. This can occur from lightning, or high-voltage power lines/sources. Prompt CPR can maintain many such people until their own heart and breathing restarts. Such recovery is much more likely than in cases of ventricular fibrillation.

The following table summarizes the types and severity of injury from electricity.

Table 21.1

	Burns	Stops Breathing	Stops Heart	Ventricular Fibrillation
High voltage				
A.C.	+++	+++	+++	−
D.C.	++	+++	+++	−
Low voltage				
A.C.	++	++	−	+++
D.C.	+	−	+	−
Lightning	+	+++	+++	−

+++ = very likely or severe
++ = moderately likely or severe
+ = not very likely or severe
−= unlikely

ELECTRICAL PATH. To achieve (if that's the right word) electrocution, the electrical current pathway must go through organs that are both vital and susceptible to electrical disruption. The ones that best fit this description are the brain, spinal column, heart, and respiratory muscles in the diaphragm.

The electrical pathway is thus critical: Head-to-limb is always dangerous because it goes through the brain, and, depending on which limb, possibly the heart. Similarly, a right-hand-to-right-foot pathway is less hazardous than a left-hand-to-left-foot or a hand-to-hand circuit, since the latter two are more likely to go through the heart.

CELL AND TISSUE DAMAGE. At a cellular or tissue level, electricity causes damage by two mechanisms: (1) It depolarizes (fires or sets off) nerve and muscle cells by mimicking normal nerve and muscle electrochemical conduction, but does so with greater intensity, so that both nerve and muscle tissue may be overstimulated, and exhausted or injured. Direct current (D.C.) generally causes a single muscle contraction and/or nervous system depolarization; alternating current (A.C.) does this repeatedly.

This depolarization is not directly fatal or even necessarily injurious. However, since the impulse to breathe is sent out by the brainstem, transmitted by nerves, and carried out by muscles, prolonged electrical interference with any of these could be lethal. Similarly, a big electrical shock may severely depolarize and paralyze the heart muscle. Lesser, but continuing, shock can interfere with the exquisitely synchronized flow of nerve impulses within the heart, and cause its muscle cells to beat chaotically, and thus be unable to pump blood. And we're back to fibrillation, which is fatal unless quickly reversed. (2) Electric current moving through resistance generates heat. This heat causes cell and tissue damage, similar (but not identical) to fire burns. More on this later.

HOUSEHOLD (A.C. OR ALTERNATING CURRENT) ELECTRICITY

To be electrocuted, three things must happen at the same time: (1) There must be an electric charge or current, (2) the electric charge must go through you, and (3) the electric charge must return either to "ground potential" or complete the circuit by returning to the source. Thus a bird can land on an uninsulated high-voltage wire with no ill effects because each of its feet is at the same voltage, that is, there is no voltage difference.

ELECTRICAL GROUND. What is "ground"? It is something that has the same electrical level ("potential") as the earth. Grounds or grounding paths are conductors that are physically connected to the earth, either directly or through other electrical conductors. Examples are metal (but not plastic) pipes, damp concrete, radiators, grounded appliances, water, etc. If you are connected to any of these, electricity can flow through you to the earth with potentially lethal results. If there is no such connection, you are insulated and pretty safe. Thus someone wearing thick boots might pick up a (single) bare wire carrying 120/240 volts with no ill effects—unless the boots were steel-toed, used metal nails, had worn-down soles, or were wet.

HOW SMALL A CURRENT CAN YOU FEEL? The threshold for feeling household (60 cycle-per-second) alternating current, is between 0.5 and 2.0 milliamps (mA), depending on individual sensitivity. This minimal current feels like a tingle and causes no direct injury, but may startle someone into losing balance or dropping an electrified object into a more dangerous position, for example, into the bathtub.[20]

WHAT ARE THE EFFECTS OF INCREASING AMOUNTS OF CURRENT? A little more current can cause numbness (2 mA),[21] pain (1-4 mA),[22] and muscle spasms (5 mA).[23] Somewhere between 6-22 mA, these muscle contractions are uncontrollable and the victim cannot let go of a grasped object, often the electrical conductor.[g] The fundamental reason this happens is that voluntary muscles, like those in your hand, normally contract in response to small electrical signals transmitted through the nervous system; the hundred-times-stronger external electrical signal totally overwhelms the nervous system's control.

This current level is sometimes called, rather confusingly, both the "let-go current" and the "no-let-go current," as well as the "hold-on current." Whatever the name, it occurs because the grabbing muscles (flexors) are stronger than the releasing muscles (extensors), as can be easily demonstrated with your hand: Make a fist; now wrap the other hand around the fist and use it to try and keep the fist from opening. This is also why an alligator's jaws, which are strong enough to crush bones, can be kept shut with bare hands.

Some electricians and repair people—most older ones—have the habit of touching any possibly-live electrical device with the *back* of their hand before attempting to pick it up: Even if they get a shock, they won't involuntarily grasp it and be unable to let go.

Since other muscles also go into involuntary contractions from electrical overstimulation, people will die from inability to breathe (tetanic asphyxia) if a low current path goes through the respiratory muscles (head-to-leg, arm-to-arm, or arm-to-opposite-leg).

Thus, not being able to let go of an electrical conductor may well make such relatively small current more dangerous than a larger current that knocks you away from the conductor. In one instance a 21 volt A.C. microphone electrocuted a pastor who was waist-deep in a water-filled concrete baptismal fountain. Death was attributed to drowning, as a result of electrical paralysis.[24]

However, the most common reason for death from low-voltage (household) alternating current is ventricular fibrillation.[25] This is caused by somewhat higher current, starting around 100 mA for one-tenth of a second,[26] which will induce the different parts of the heart to beat out of synch with each other, as normal nerve conduction within the heart is disrupted.

This quivering, uncoordinated mass of heart cells cannot pump blood, and unless some circulation is restored quickly (within approximately five min-utes[27]) by CPR or defibrillation (a big electrical jolt, typically five amps at 440 volts D.C. for 0.25 seconds, that makes all the heart cells simultaneously contract, and thus "resets" them to the same state), brain damage and death follow. CPR will extend the time during which defibrillation can be suc-cessfully applied, but hearts in ventricular fibrillation rarely convert sponta-neously to normal rhythm.

The minimum amount of current needed to provoke fibrillation depends on both individual sensitivity and on how long the current is applied. One source[28] calculates the minimum current as 116 mA multiplied by the square root of the current duration. Thus a four-second shock could result in fib-rillation with a current of as little as 58 mA, while 116 mA would be needed for a one-second shock. By way of comparison, the current going through a small 7.5 watt lamp at 120 volts is 62.5 milliamps; 625 milliamps is drawn by a 75 watt lamp. The liklihood of fibrillation increases with current, up to the point where the heart stops altogether.

A 2,000 mA (2 amps) or greater jolt can make the heart, basically, stop (cardiac standstill). However, it will often restart spontaneously when the current stops. Thus, higher amperage current, which can cause the heart to stop, will be less dangerous than lower amperage, which sets off fibrillation.

Fifteen amps of current passing through the diaphragm (muscles below the lungs) can paralyze breathing (respiratory arrest),[29] but paralysis also depends on the electrical path; lesser current through the head may have the same effect by knocking out the respiratory center in the brainstem. In both cardiac standstill and respiratory arrest, CPR has a good chance of maintaining circulation long enough for breathing and heart function to restart.

BURNS DUE TO HOUSEHOLD ELECTRICITY

The third mechanism of death from electricity is burns. Most low-voltage burns are due to an inability to let go of the electrical conductor. Such pro-longed muscle contraction is typically a problem with A.C., but not D.C. current. In one study, fourteen of fifteen low-voltage burns occurred for this reason.[30]

CONTACT AREA WITH THE ELECTRICAL SOURCE. If the electrical conductor touching the body is small, for example the end of a wire, the current enters the body at a correspondingly small site and with high current density, which promotes local tissue damage. Sometimes this looks like a bullet wound or a thermal burn.

If the electrical contact is over a large area, as is the case in most bathtub electrocutions, there may be no external mark at all. This is because (1) water conducts electricity over much of the body, thus lowers electrical density; (2) the water acts as a heat sink, absorbing most of the heat produced by electrical resistance, at least with low voltage.

HIGH-VOLTAGE A.C. ELECTRICITY

"High voltage" is arbitrarily defined as more than 1000 volts. Power lines into houses are generally 220/240 volts A.C.; high-power lines in residential and industrial areas are often at 7,620 volts A.C.; power lines from generating plants sometimes carry over 70,000 volts A.C.

In high-voltage shocks (for example, from high-voltage transmission lines or lightning) death is most often due to respiratory paralysis, and/or heart stoppage, while ventricular fibrillation is infrequent.

Most characteristic of high-voltage electrocution is the presence of burns: 96 percent (89 in 93) of high-voltage deaths in one study had visible burns (compared to 57 percent of deaths from electrocution due to less than 1,000 volts).[31] In the survivors, burns are often the most severe injury, especially with A.C. current. In one case,

> ... a man aged twenty-two was electrocuted while attempting to steal copper cable. He was found at the foot of a high-tension pylon with a pair of wire cutters beside him. He had been seated on an iron bracket at the top of the pylon and had already cut several lengths of wire. He had worn thick PVC gloves to protect himself from the 6,000-volt supply. Arcing occurred and he sustained grave burns of his body especially of the wrists, upper arms, and chest. Although his clothing had been damp it was set on fire from the flash. This had probably been the cause of the thermal burns of

his abdomen and thighs. Although he had fallen about 20 feet this had not caused additional injury as the ground was soft.[32]

Sometimes the temperature exceeds the flash point of muscle, which then ignites and burns, rather like a piece of meat over a hot charcoal fire. As you might suspect, such electric current through the skull is particularly gruesome. In some cases, the skull splits open, and the eyes are blown out of their sockets by the steam pressure from the boiling brain.

The tetanic contraction can be so severe that it is capable of causing bones to break and muscles to tear from their attachment points in bones. The upper arm bone is most frequently broken.[33]

Despite the above, the actual cause of death in the majority of high-voltage electrocutions is paralysis of the respiratory center of the brainstem, which keeps you from breathing on your own, and results in asphyxia.

LIGHTNING INJURY

Lightning bolts average around 30,000 amps, millions of volts, and 20,000 degree C temperature,[34] but only 1/10,000 second duration.[35] Paralysis of the heart, and/or of the respiratory center in the brainstem, are the most dangerous lightning injuries. Either of these will cause death in about five minutes in the absence of CPR. Since CPR keeps some oxygenated blood moving, it significantly increases chances for spontaneous recovery, especially if it is started quickly, say within a minute. About one-third of the people struck by lightning die within a few minutes;[36] relatively few die later of their injuries.

Severe burns are infrequent from lightning strikes, despite the several-thousand-degree temperatures involved, because of the short duration of the strike doesn't transfer much heat.[h] However, there is a curious and characteristic faint burn pattern found about half the time in lightning victims, called "arborescence"; the pattern is fern-like. Experts disagree concerning how it's formed. Some claim it's caused by heat damage (denaturing) to red blood cells in veins or arteries;[37] others argue that it marks the trail of nerve damage.

More serious burns can occur if the victims are wearing, or are near, metal (coins, jewelry, belt buckles, fences, etc.) when struck (iron and steel objects may become magnetized), or if their clothing ignites. On the other hand, if the skin is wet with rain or sweat, clothing tends to be blown off by the explosive evaporation of the liquid.

Nervous system injuries, such as blindness, confusion, amnesia, and tinnitis (imaginary ringing sounds), are common, but usually not permanent. In one study, 86 percent of surviving lightning victims had amnesia and 19 percent were temporarily paralyzed.[38]

There is a certain capriciousness to lightning injuries:

> When two men were driving in a dog cart during a storm, the vehicle was struck and both men fell out of it. Five minutes after the flash their bodies were found lying side by side on the road. The seat of the cart was beneath them and the driving apron was still around their legs. One of the men had an extensive burn over his chest and abdomen, and circular holes of from $\frac{1}{16}$ to $\frac{1}{4}$ inch in diameter scattered over the burnt area. His metal collar stud had fused and the underlying skin was deeply burned. The other victim had no external injury. The horse was uninjured and trotted home.[39]

High voltage is not in and of itself particularly dangerous; amperage is much more significant. For example, the output voltage from an automobile ignition coil is, typically, between 15,000 and 50,000 D.C. volts, but the current is less than 1 milliamp. As anyone who has been shocked by spark plug voltage can attest, it is an unpleasant jolt—your eyes light up like a pinball machine—but not normally a killer.

Direct Current

Direct Current (D.C.) electricity occurs naturally in lightning, static electricity, and electric eels; somewhat less naturally in batteries, capacitors, electric trains, and other human artifacts. Direct current is less dangerous than A.C. for two reasons: (1) It does not cause multiple tetanic muscle contractions; thus one can let go of a D.C.-energized wire (though the single jolt it does cause can result in broken bones from the force of the contraction, injury from falls, burns, cardiac standstill, or respiratory arrest); (2) It is less likely than A.C. to cause ventricular fibrillation. As a result, D.C. current of less than 80 mA is claimed to have no harmful physiological effects.[40]

The lowest D.C. voltage that has caused death (from external contact[i]) seems to be 24 volts. This is the voltage of two car batteries in series (end to end). A man was found on the wet ground under his battery-powered milk truck. He had two small electrical burn marks, one on the right shoulder, the other on the right hip. The death remains a bit of a mystery, since the batteries, when examined, only leaked 5 mA, far below what is considered dangerous. Nevertheless, the fact remains that a previously healthy man died under circumstances and with signs of electric injury, and nothing else of significance was found on autopsy.

Arc Current

Air is a poor electrical conductor, but sufficiently high voltage will jump across an air gap; the higher the voltage, the larger the gap that can be jumped. This phenomenon accounts for the spark in a spark plug; why static electricity will jump from one person to another without them touching; and, of course, what occurs in lightning. The approximate air gaps are about 30,000 volts per cm[41] with round electrodes, and around 12,000 volts per cm with needle-point electrodes.[j42]

In other words, you can get zapped by being close enough to a high-voltage source; physical contact is not necessary. "A man was loading hay on to a stack in damp conditions; there were frequent showers. As the stack grew, the man came nearer and nearer to overhead cable, carrying 20,000 volts. His clothing was damp. Arcing occurred and he fell off the stack and broke his neck. He had not touched the cable but there was an electric entrance mark behind the tip of his right ear."[43]

As anyone who has done arc welding knows,[k] sustained electric arcs produce sufficient heat to melt metal. The temperatures can reach 4,000 degrees C (7,200 degrees F). This is hot enough to vaporize most metals, which condense on the first cooler object they touch, and so a characteristic of arc burns is the "metallization" of nearby skin. Since the bright light of an arc causes the eyelids to close reflexively, there may be metal-vapor crow's feet visible around the eyes. Once an arc is established, it can be made longer without additional voltage. Thus, falling down might not break the electric circuit. These arc burns are some of the most traumatic of injuries.

In addition, arcing heats the nearby air, which rapidly expands causing an explosion, that is, thunder. A 25,000 amp arc generates a pressure of almost 500 pounds on someone two feet away.[44] Burns from such an arc—remember, this is *hot* gas and metal vapor—can be fatal even several feet away, and severe burns from even ten feet away are common.[1]

LONG-TERM INJURY

There are three common types of long-term damage from electricity:

- Tissue damage and destruction from burns;
- Direct neurological damage;
- Indirect neurological damage.

TISSUE DAMAGE AND DESTRUCTION FROM BURNS is most common with high voltage, but can also occur with low-voltage A.C. after prolonged contact. Arterial injury may occur and the resulting hemorrhages can be both sudden and severe, because (a) the damaged arteries are brittle and can't be clamped off without breaking, and (b) the arteries are sometimes damaged beyond areas of obvious tissue injury.[45] Eye damage, including corneal burns and optic nerve injury, may be permanent. Cataracts (clouding of the lens of the eye), probably caused by heat, may appear from weeks to years after high-voltage contact to the head.[46]

Interestingly, electrical burns tend to heal better than similar nonelectrical ones, and they are somewhat less painful because of greater nerve damage from electricity.[47] Nevertheless, such burns may be severe enough to require amputation of the affected limb; this occurs in 18 to 45 percent of high-voltage injuries.[48] As with thermal burns, infection is the most common cause of delayed death.

DIRECT NEUROLOGICAL DAMAGE. Loss of consciousness occurs in an estimated two-thirds of high-voltage and one-third of low-voltage accidents.[49] This typically lasts five to ten minutes but may continue for several days. Not surprisingly, it is most frequent when the head is in the electrical path. However, there are cases where significant early and delayed brain injury occur even though the brain is not in the current path. These injuries may persist for more than a year.[50]

Amnesia and confusion are also common. Personality change and deafness have occurred,[51] as has spinal cord damage, leading to paralysis.[52] In one study, eleven of twenty-two patients with low-voltage burns had neurological symptoms, generally temporary.[53] However, another study found that twelve in sixteen survivors of electric-current injury had neurological problems after one year, while only four in eighteen who had flash or arc injuries "without passage of current" had long-term damage.[54] By comparison, in the high-voltage group, only twenty of sixty-four recovered completely. Injury symptoms include paralysis, anxiety, depression, outbursts of aggression, difficulty with writing and/or speech, and loss of taste.[m55]

INDIRECT NEUROLOGICAL DAMAGE. The brain is very sensitive to lack of oxygen. If the oxygen supply is cut off due to heart or breathing stoppage, brain tissue starts to die within five minutes or so. Even if heartbeat and breathing are restored, such brain damage tends to be persistent. For more details, see chapters on hanging and on asphyxia.

Since there's little information on suicidal electrocution injuries, we are pretty much limited to accident data. In a large study of electric-lineworker injuries in France:[56]

- 2.4 percent were immediately fatal; another 0.9 percent died later as a result of their injuries;
- 7.2 percent lost consciousness;
- 93 percent suffered burns;
- 19 percent of survivors had disabling or disfiguring scars;
- 7.3 percent had neurological or psychological damage;
- 21 percent were permanently disabled.

This suggests that unplanned high-voltage electrical injury is neither reliably lethal enough for suicide, nor sufficiently nontraumatic for suicidal gestures.

JUDICIAL EXECUTION[57]

The State of New York introduced electrocution in 1890.[n] In the first execution, electrodes were attached to the victim's head and lower back, salt solution was utilized to improve conduction, and a 1,600 volts A.C. at 150 cycles-per-second (hertz) current was applied. After seventeen seconds the man was declared dead. Congratulations were premature, however, since thirty seconds later, he began to breathe again, followed by "groaning and foaming at the mouth." The current was restarted and kept on until the "body of the victim steamed"[58] and he finally died. Other early attempts were similarly bungled.[o]

The procedure was gradually "refined" so that in our present enlightened day, one electrode in the shape of a helmet is attached to the head, the other to the right leg. 2,000 volts at 60 Hz are applied for three to five seconds (intended to cause unconsciousness), followed by 250 to 500 volts (to cause heart and/or respiratory stoppage) until death ensues. At the site of the electrodes, third-degree burns may occur, producing smoke and charring.[p] In prompt autopsies, the brain steams and has a temperature as high as 63 degrees C (145 degrees F) and the cortex is covered with blood from ruptured vessels.[59]

SUICIDE BY ELECTROCUTION

Suicide attempts by electricity, though rare, are about 90 percent successful. Some methods that have been used to commit suicide follow:

1. Climbing a high-voltage pylon or pole and grabbing (or attempting to grab—see section on electric arcing) a high-voltage wire. Typical injuries include burns, heart and/or respiratory stoppage, and injuries from the fall. The initial jolt causes unconsciousness, and death is highly likely.

A variation on this is sometimes used by people who don't like heights: Rather than climbing, they wrap a wire around some part of their body (often around a wrist, but in at least one case, around the neck) attach a weight to the other end of the wire and toss the weight over a high-voltage line, which is an uninsulated, bare wire. In this situation there is no fall from a height, but the electrical contact is prolonged. Bare feet and damp soil are helpful but generally not necessary. Enough heat is generated to often amputate the wire-wrapped part of the body. A thin wire is at risk of melting before you do, so it's important to use the thickest one you can handle.

There are occasional reports of people being electrocuted as a result of urinating onto the high-voltage electric train rail, though these are probably not deliberate suicides.[960]

Despite its high lethality, people sometimes survive high-voltage suicide attempts with nothing but third-degree burns and permanent injuries to show for their trouble.

2. A simple electrocution method using household current is to remove the insulation from the end of an extension cord, plug in the extension cord, and grasp the two bare wires, one in each hand. Alternatively, one can hold one wire and touch a grounded item (for example, an exposed metal pipe) to complete the circuit. This requires the black (hot) wire to be held—if a polarized plug is used and the wiring has been installed correctly. Or, if the circuit/outlet has an on/off switch, one can wrap the bare ends of the extension cord around two different limbs (no chance of letting go) and flip the switch. For example,

> A few weeks after his wife had been accidentally electrocuted in her bath, a man, aged fifty-eight, was found dead in his locked bathroom. He was seated on a chair, his feet were bare and in a bowl of water on the floor [probably unnecessary]. His wrists were wired to the domestic supply. He had ... burns around each wrist. He had threatened suicide and left a "suicide note." It appeared that he had felt himself responsible for the faulty condition of the heater which had caused his wife's death.[61]

There are many other ways to do this, limited only by your imagination. But don't leave an electrically live (albeit biologically dead) corpse for someone to blunder onto; to avoid this, you could incorporate a timer into the circuit. You should also leave a prominent sign telling people not to touch *anything* before turning off main fuse or circuit breaker.

It might seem that this sort of electrocution would be an option for a terminally ill person in a hospital. However, if the circuit is protected by a "ground fault circuit interruptor,"[r] as it should be, this will not work. In addition, resuscitation equipment is generally nearby, making electrocution more difficult.

3. Dropping a 120 volt electric appliance into a bathtub containing water (and you) should do the job, especially if you're also touching metal, for example, a spigot or drain. Even if the device is turned off, the terminal of its attached electric cord is still "live." Estimate of the current involved: 120volts/1,000 ohms equals 0.12 amps (120 mA), which is not enough to trip a standard fuse or circuit breaker; however, you should try it first with an unoccupied tub. Once again, if the device is plugged into a circuit with a GFCI, this will not work; but obviously, one could plug into a non-GFCI circuit.

Of forty-eight cases of bathtub electrocution studied, nineteen were judged suicides (three females to one male ratio); electrical marks were seen in eight. The calculated amperage was 100 to 250 milliamps, which is in the ventricular fibrillation range. Fourteen also showed evidence of drowning.[62]

EMERGENCY TREATMENT OF ELECTRICAL INJURIES

1. Safely switch off electric power if victim is still attached to current source. If it is necessary to disconnect someone from an electric circuit and you can't turn off the power at a switch or (better) circuit-breaker/fuse box, a bare, dry, wooden pole (power company uses fiberglass, which is less conductive) can be used to push the wire away from the victim. However, while this is generally safe with household wiring, fallen power lines may be "springy" or coiled, and thus dangerous to move, and high voltage (if it's a high-voltage line) can more easily be conducted by dirty or damp wood than can lower voltage.

2. Call for help.

3. If victim is not breathing and/or has no heartbeat, administer CPR as soon as possible, and for as long as death is not certain. There are cases of recovery after as long as six hours of apparently fruitless resuscitation.[63] Success is most likely if CPR is started within a minute of cardiac or respiratory stoppage. Prolonged (more than about five minutes) heart or respiratory stoppage will generally cause permanent brain damage or death due to lack of oxygen to the brain and

heart. Thus it will be more useful to do CPR, if going off to call for help would take too long.

Summary

High-voltage electrocution is a gruesome and traumatic method of suicide, but it is quick and usually lethal. While it might be considered when a lengthy uninterrupted time cannot be assured, there seems little advantage to it compared to other methods. Unconsciousness is quick, but injuries in survivors are often severe and may be permanent.

Low-voltage (household) electrocution is neither quick nor painless, but is also fairly lethal. It is not a recommended choice for either suicide or a suicidal gesture.

Notes

[a]CPR consists of alternately breathing into the victim's mouth to get air into his lungs and pressing on the victim's chest, which circulates some oxygenated blood. The details are important and should be learned through a first-aid course or equivalent.

[b]Fetuses seem to be much more sensitive to electric injury than are their mothers; many are spontaneously aborted or are stillborn after lightning strikes (Polson, 312), and there is often fetal injury or death from minor nonlightning shocks to the mother (Strong, 1987).

[c]New technology produces new hazards. People have gotten electrical burns when their high-tech carbon (graphite) fiber fishing rods touched high-voltage overhead lines (Logan, 1993). Carbon (in the form of graphite, but not as diamond) conducts electricity readily, which neither bamboo nor fiberglass rods do.

[d]Or unless you're doing something really stupid: I got quite a jolt from a phone wire I was stripping of insulation with my teeth, when someone called in on that line.

[e]Because of the dangerous proximity of electricity and water, some European building codes forbid wall switches in bathrooms and require that lights have outside switches or string-pulled switches.

[f]There's also a case of a nurse applying a 5,165 volt defibrillator to his own head in a suicide attempt. He survived (Grumet, 1989).

[g]Since both A.C. and D.C. high voltage can generate enough heat to melt tendons, a hand grasping a high-voltage object may thus remain attached.

[h]Temperature and heat are not the same thing; for example, it takes 100 times as much heat to boil 100 gallons of water than to boil one gallon, but they will boil at the same temperature.

[i]Death from defective implanted (that is, low resistance, around 500 ohms) medical devices has been seen with lower voltage. There was also a fatality from a toy train transformer (20 volts D.C.) used by a masochistic forty-eight-year-old who inserted the two output

wires into his chest (Camps, 362). This voltage has also been known to cause deep burns, if applied for sufficient time (Benmeir, 1993).

[j]This difference in shape is why "precious metal" (gold or platinum) spark plugs, which use needle-like electrodes, can have larger gaps (and thus better burning) for a given voltage than can conventional (thicker electrodes) plugs. Going back a step further, thin electrodes can be used because gold and platinum are less prone to erosion at combustion-chamber conditions than are copper and other metals used in standard spark plug electrodes.

[k]Some other people know it, too.

[l]It may be of some minor historical interest to note that Joan of Arc (a French descendant of Noah) was described as "electrifying her countrymen" several hundred years before Thomas Edison.

[m]Sometimes manifested as a sudden craving for Muzak.

[n]This was despite the best efforts of Westinghouse and other electrical-device manufacturers to short-circuit the execution. They bankrolled the legal appeals of the defendant, a fruit peddler named William Kemmler, to the tune of over $100,000—in 1890 dollars (Laurence, *A History of Capital Punishment*). This was undoubtedly due to their corporate love of justice, possibly augmented by a fear of bad publicity for things electric.

The situation was actually even more byzantine: Thomas Edison (dc current) and George Westinghouse (ac current) were fighting over control of electric power transmission technology. Edison wanted to show how dangerous ac electricity was; besides publicly electrocuting an elephant as a demonstration, he had an associate make sure that a Westinghouse generator was used for Kemmler's execution—and wanted to use the term "Westinghoused" for "electrocuted." [Reynolds, 1989]

[o]In a recent (March 1997) Florida execution, the prisoner's head caught on fire, allegedly due to the use of a new and more flammable damp sponge (the old one having become aesthetically unappealing), used to conduct electricity from "Ol' Sparky's" helmet to the victim's head.

[p]Each state has its own favorite recipe. For example, Alabama prefers 1,800 volts for twenty-two seconds, followed by 700-800 volts for twelve seconds, then 1,800 volts for five seconds. 1,800 volts produces around 7 amps.

[q]The electric current climbs the stream of urine which (unlike distilled water) is highly conductive. This is eerily reminiscent of the behavior of a tiny South American catfish, the candiru, which swims up a urine stream and lodges inside the victim's urethra with its sharp spines, requiring surgical removal (of the fish). The candiru is normally a parasite in larger fish's gills, and feeds on blood.

[r]If a wall outlet has a properly installed and functioning ground fault circuit interrupter (GFCI) (often found outdoors and in newer bathrooms, sometimes in kitchens), any electrical leakage greater than 4 to 6 milliamps will cause a magnetic switch to disconnect the circuit in about 1/40 of a second and become, generally, nonlethal. In addition, all recent (since 1991) listed hair dryers are supposed to incorporate an "immersion detector" or GFCI in their circuitry to break the circuit if the device is dropped into water (D. Shapiro). However, compliance with the CPSC standard is voluntary. You can tell if you have one of the protected models, because they have a rectangular box built into the cord or the wall plug. Before GFCIs were used in hair-dryers, there were an average of eighteen electrocutions a year from these appliances; this has since fallen to two per year. (*Washington Post,* May 14, 1997).

22
GUNSHOT WOUNDS

•

Guns don't kill people; people kill people.

LETHAL INTENT: High
MORTALITY: High, around 80 percent
PERMANENT INJURIES: Likely
PROS AND CONS OF GUNS AS A MEANS OF SUICIDE
Pros: • Usually fatal
 • Often fast
 • Generally easy to obtain firearms (in United States)
Cons: • Easy to act on impulse/no chance to reconsider
 • Survivors often have severe and permanent injury
 • Sometimes gruesome cadavers
 • Less reliable than one might expect, due to bad aim, bullet deflecting from bone, or defective gun/ammunition

Shooting yourself is a generally effective—76 to 92 percent mortality rates are reported[1]—but frequently messy method of suicide. About 60 percent of the suicides in the United States are by means of gunshot; four out of five of these are head injuries.[2] Suicidal gun wounds to the head tend to be quickly fatal: 70 to 90 percent of people with such injuries die before getting to a hospital,[3] but there is a 3 to 9 percent survival rate, and these people often have brain damage or disfiguring injuries. Wounds to other parts of

285

the body are less likely to be lethal. Gunshot is a method that can be, and all too often is, used impulsively, as it doesn't require much planning or allow time to reflect on other possibilities.

How Dangerous Are Suicidal Gunshot Wounds?

Tables 16.1 through 16.4 show guns to be the most lethal common means of attempting suicide: The fatality rate in Card's study was 92 percent, though the actual rate is undoubtedly somewhat lower, since minor injuries are less likely to be reported than fatal ones. The lack of minor injury results further suggests that it's not your best bet for a suicidal gesture. But you probably already knew that. One can reach the same conclusion by noting that guns accounted for 34 percent (1974 data; up to 60 percent by the 1990s) of Card's suicide fatalities but only 1.4 percent of nonfatal injuries.

While this study is old, it is in agreement with more recent data from the United States and Finland. Washington State hospital and death certificate data from 1989 to 1995 show an 89 percent fatality rate from gunshot suicide attempts.[a4] This was the same as the rate in Finland, where 1,205 of 1,356 gunshot suicides were fatal.[5] Eighty-one percent of these people (1,101 in 1,356) died before getting to a hospital. For people still alive when they reached the hospital, American data show a 76 percent fatality rate from gunshot suicide attempts.[6] The corresponding Canadian death rate was 79 percent.[7]

Demographics: Who and Why?

Availability of guns

More Americans commit suicide by gunshot than by all other methods combined. Roughly 18,000 of some 30,000 suicides a year in the United States (7.6 per 100,000) are by means of firearms.[8] It should be no surprise that the high rate of American firearm suicides is a function of the widespread availability of guns in this country: 45 to 70 percent of Americans have them in their homes (up to 90 percent in parts of the West).[9]

In areas of the world where guns are hard to obtain, people tend to use other methods.[b10] For example, firearms are used by less than 5 percent of male suicides in England and Wales, and by almost no women,[11] probably because handguns are severely restricted.[c] Shotguns, on the other hand, are commonly used in hunting, and shotgun suicides are more frequent than those by means of handguns.[d12] In India, where factory-made guns are relatively expensive and many people work on farms, poisoning by pesticides is the most common suicide method.

On the other hand there are obviously important factors other than gun availability that affect firearm suicide rates. For instance, Australia, as well as Great Britain, has strict handgun (but not long gun) control laws.[13] Yet the Australian gun-suicide rate is around ten times that of England and Wales, while its overall suicide rate is twice that of England and Wales.[14]

In parts of the world where civilian handguns are difficult to acquire, a much larger percentage of men than women shoot themselves. Thus, in Sweden, 16 percent (2,203) of male suicides but only 1 percent (55) of female suicides between 1973 and 1984 were by guns.[15] This is probably because most of the available firearms are either military or hunting weapons, which are generally more accessible to and commonly used by men. Because of size, men also could be expected to find long guns somewhat easier to use than women would. For example, of 1,200 gunshot suicides in the Dallas area, the ratio of male-to-female handgun users was 3.66 to 1 (703 to 192); with long guns the ratio was 12.26 to 1 (282 to 23).[16]

In the United States more than one-third of female suicides are by gunshot, while about two-thirds of the men who kill themselves use guns.[17] Again, there are other factors at work, as shown by the fact that in Canada, with a national suicide rate similar to that of the United States, only about 2 percent of female suicides were by gunshot, both before and after guncontrol legislation.

SUBSTITUTION OF METHODS

Whether restricting gun availability decreases the suicide rate or merely causes people to use other methods is in dispute.[18] Overall, the evidence seems to favor the switch-to-other-methods position. For example, the Seattle and Vancouver metropolitan areas are similar—almost identical—in most socioeconomic aspects, such as income, education, and population. They differ on gun control: Guns are easily available in Seattle; handguns are essentially banned in Vancouver (and the rest of Canada). Not surprisingly, the handgun suicide rate in Seattle was 5.7 times higher than that in Vancouver. However, the overall suicide rates were the same (15.1 in 100,00 in Seattle, 15.5 in Vancouver), because Vancouver had about 1.5 times Seattle's rate for other methods. On the other hand, among those in their teens and early twenties, the Seattle handgun suicide rate was 9.6 times higher than the Vancouver rate, and this was not entirely offset by the higher Vancouver nonhandgun rate.[19]

Certainly there are countries that have low rates of gun ownership along with low (Great Britain, 8.8 in 100,000 per year), medium (Japan, 17.6), or high (Denmark, 31.6) suicide rates;[20] others have high gun ownership along with low (Israel, 6.0), medium (United States, 11.8), or high (Switzerland, 25.7) suicide rates. Obviously there's much more to suicide rates than mere gun ownership. Just what that "more" might be remains controversial, but generates lots of journal articles and books.

In any case, fewer than 10 percent of gunshot suicides buy a gun for that purpose. Even fewer buy one shortly before killing themselves. Thus, a "waiting period" to buy guns will have little effect on suicides.[21]

On the other hand, when someone makes an impulsive suicide attempt with a gun, the results tend to be a lot more lethal than had she taken a handful of random pills. And young people tend to be most impulsive. According to former Surgeon General Everett C. Koop, almost all of the increase in the adolescent suicide rate is by means of firearms.[22]

One thing that is clear is that the suicide rate is significantly higher in homes that contain guns than in homes that don't. To put this risk into perspective, some (there are many others[c]) variables associated with increased suicide risk are shown in Table 22.1 below.

Note that "associated with" does not necessarily mean "caused by." For example, not graduating from high school probably doesn't cause many people to kill themselves. But it's also statistically associated with lower economic and social status, more beer drinking, fewer symphony visits, more likely ownership of American cars, more cigarette consumption, and so on—some part or combination of which does increase chances of suicide. Table 22.1 shows the "adjusted odds ratio," which is a statistical measure of how much more (or less) likely suicide is for someone with a particular characteristic, such as alcoholism, compared to a "similar" person without the trait. An odds ratio of 2.5 makes the claim that a person with the attribute is 2.5 times as likely to kill himself than one without it; 0.5 is half as likely.

Table 22.1 Some Social Variables and Their Odds Ratios in Suicide

Social variable	Odds ratio
Didn't graduate from high school	4.1
Lives alone	5.3
Drinks alcohol	2.3
Previous hospitalization due to drinking	16.4
Psychotropic medication prescribed	35.9
Active use of illicit drugs	10.0
Guns kept in the home	4.8
handgun	5.8
rifle or shotgun	3.0
kept loaded	9.2
kept unloaded	3.3
kept unlocked	5.6
kept locked	2.4
no gun in the home	1.0
suicide by other than firearms	0.7
Source: Clark and Lester p 52-61	

Thus, keeping guns in the house is associated with slightly higher odds of committing suicide than not having graduated from high school and slightly lower than living alone. Looking on the bright side, the availability of a gun in the home decreases the odds of committing suicide by other methods.[24]

With regard specifically to adolescents, the presence of *any* firearm in the home was associated with a doubled suicide rate. There were no distinctions between types of stored weapons or methods of storage; storing guns locked or separate from ammunition didn't make much difference. But, lest gun-control advocates get too optimistic about the benefits of restricting hand-guns, (a) almost half of adolescent gun suicides used long guns, and (b) those with access only to long guns killed themselves at the same elevated rate as those with handgun access.[25]

U.S. firearm-suicide data are shown below in Table 22.2. As with most suicide methods, the highest death rates are associated with older white males.

Table 22.2 Suicide by Guns and Explosives, E955			Rate/100,000	
	Deaths	1994 Population (millions)	1994	1979-94
All	18,778	260,423,572	7.21	7.26
All male	16,298	127,118,264	12.83	12.72
All female	2,480	133,305,308	1.86	2.07
White male	14,761	106,178,839	13.90	13.81
White female	2,258	110,371,063	2.04	2.27
Black male	1,227	15,500,047	7.91	7.02
Black female	167	17,189,697	0.97	0.97
Other male	310	5,439,378	5.69	5.25
Other female	55	5,744,548	0.95	0.90

E-numbers are International Classification of Disease (ICD) codes.
Source: Centers for Disease Control

Between 1953 and 1988 the U.S. suicide rate by firearms increased from 4.9 per 100,000 to 7.4 per 100,000, while other methods remained stable.[26] Many observers have suggested that this increase is due to the parallel increase in the number of guns owned by Americans.[27] However, while the number of guns per person has risen, the percentage of gun-owners has not; that is, the same (or a slightly lower) percentage of Americans own more guns.[28] Thus the increase in the number of guns is not, in itself, a plausible cause for the increased gun-suicide rate.

On the other hand, the percentage of handguns *has* gone up (rifles the same, shotguns fewer), and handguns are used at a disproportionately high rate in gun suicides.[29] Thus the increase in the gun-suicide rate (but not the overall suicide rate) is correlated with the higher availability of handguns, rather than guns in general.

There have been numerous other theories as to the reason(s) for the increase in gun suicides. One frequently cited notion is that television and movies unrealistically portray life as perpetually exciting and shootings as quick, clean, neat, and painless.

> While parents spend an average of two minutes a day communicating with their child, the television spends an average of three and a half hours a day with their child. The average child will watch more TV by the time he is six than he will spend talking to his father for the rest of his life.... By the time he graduates from high school, he will have logged twenty thousand hours in front of the TV, compared to eleven thousand in the classroom...."TV bombards kids with the glamorous and the thrilling, and then they have to go out and live their lives, and their lives are not glamorous and thrilling," says high school counselor George Cohen. "TV doesn't help kids understand that life on a day-to-day level can be boring and mundane and upsetting. Being held up to that image when you have to face the realities of your life can be discouraging, if not depressing." And on TV no problem is so great that it can't be solved in half an hour.[30]

In addition, the TV actors who are killed in one show turn up alive on another show, increasing the unreality of killing.

It is interesting that young women, who as a group tend to use nondisfiguring methods,[f] increased their gunshot-suicide rate by 50 percent between 1970 and 1980.[31] This rise continued for 10- 14-year-old girls (but not other young women), going from 18 (0.20 per 100,000) in 1980 to 47 (0.50 per 100,000) by 1995. Similarly, in one study the ratio of women-to-men in psychiatric referrals for (survivors of) self-inflicted gunshot wounds more than doubled, rising from one in seven to one in three between 1977 and 1987.[32] Over the same time period, the percentage of women in this study who had owned a gun for more than a year went up by over 50 percent, suggesting, plausibly enough, that increased availability of and familiarity with guns tends to increase their use.

Also consistent with this are epidemiologic studies which claim that states with stronger gun-control laws have a lower rate of firearm suicides.[33] However, data from Canada and elsewhere show that the decrease in firearm suicides in these places was approximately equalled by an increase in other methods, particularly jumping. For example, between 1973 and 1977 there were 117 suicides by gunshot and 80 by jumping among Canadian males. Between 1979 and 1983, after national gun-control legislation, there were 80 gunshot and 111 jumping suicides.[34] But, as noted earlier, Canadians and Americans may differ in relevant ways.

Perhaps one reason that these studies come up with differing results is that the net is too big: It includes all motivations, whether they involve impulsive or resolute behavior, terminal or mental illness, alcoholism or whatnot. It may well be that some impulsive people will kill themselves if a gun is handy, but not otherwise. It may also be that a terminally ill person or prisoner will readily substitute any reliable method. For example, the suicide rate among judicial and psychiatric prisoners is several times that of age-matched nonprisoners, despite staff surveillance and lack of availability of most lethal methods.[35]

WHAT PORTION OF GUNSHOT DEATHS ARE SUICIDES?

U.S. data from 1988 show 18,181 (54.2 percent) suicidal, 13,666 (40.7 percent) homicidal, and 1,694 (5.1 percent) accidental deaths caused by firearms (and explosives). Numbers from 1987 and 1989 were almost identical for suicide, but increased from 12,657 (1987) to 14,464 (1989) for homicides. By 1994 there were 18,765 (49.8 percent) suicides, 17,532 (46.6 percent) homicides, and 1,356 (3.6 percent) accidental firearm deaths.

COST

Estimated costs for a fatal gunshot suicide are $21,700 in medical expenses and $848,000 in lost productivity. For a survived attempt, average medical expenses were $28,000, lost productivity totaled $42,600 (1992 dollars).[36] These figures do not take into account pain, suffering, and lost quality-of-life.

FIREARM INJURIES: SUICIDE, HOMICIDE, OR ACCIDENT?

A twenty-four-year-old woman was found in her bedroom wedged between her bed and dresser. On the bed were male undershorts smeared with blood. Near the body on the floor was a male shoeprint pointing away from the body. A .38 caliber Colt revolver was in her left hand, the index finger on the trigger guard. A near-contact gunshot wound was present on the right cheek. On the palmar surface of the hand, just below the index finger, were two parallel, ¼-inch-long pinch marks surrounded by faint-brownish discoloration due to gunsmoke. The fired cartridge in the cylinder of the revolver was at six o'clock. The weapon was clean, apparently freshly oiled.

The boyfriend, a gun collector, free on probation, was seen driving away from the house after a shot was heard, and he was not apprehended until late that night. He stated that they had had an argument following which she shot herself. He took the weapon from the pool of blood on the floor and wiped the blood on a pair of shorts. When it occurred to him that possession of the gun might incriminate him in a murder charge, he cleaned and oiled the weapon, *then placed it back into her hand.* [italics added] His statement sounded credible. When the cocked gun was held in the right hand with the thumb pulling the trigger and the muzzle pointing toward one's own cheek and the left hand was placed over the cylinder to steady the weapon, the downing hammer inflicted a pinch of the same appearance and in the same location as on the left hand of the deceased.[37]

Score one for good forensic investigation.

When a gunshot victim is found, what kinds of things do the police and medical examiners consider in determining whether it was a suicide, homicide, or accident?

PSYCHOLOGICAL AUTOPSY. If the situation is murky, frequently they carry out a "psychological autopsy." This includes talking to friends and neighbors, checking medical and psychiatric records, and attempting to determine the state of mind of the deceased.

PREPARATION. A suicide note is strong evidence of intent, but only around one in five suicides write them, and a forged note, or one written under duress, is always a remote possibility.

There is sometimes evidence of preparation, as in the case of a man who put the butt of his gun in the stove grate, lit a fire, and sat down in front of the barrel to wait.

PROXIMITY OF WEAPON. In suicide, the weapon is almost always at the scene and near the body. There are exceptions, however. Occasionally a fatally wounded person can walk a substantial distance before collapsing, but the trail of blood can be followed back to the place where the injury occurred. A handgun is sometimes thrown some distance by the fatally injured suicide, for no known reason.

More frequently, the weapon is removed by a friend or relative who wants to avoid a verdict of suicide, often for either financial (many life insurance policies will not pay, in case of suicide, unless the policy is more than two years old) or social ("What will the neighbors think?") reasons.

INSTANTANEOUS RIGOR. In rare cases, there may be "instantaneous rigor" (a.k.a. "cadaverous spasm"), where the hand firmly holds on to whatever it was grasping at the time of death. Removing a loaded semi-automatic pistol in such a situation is something of a challenge. Instantaneous rigor, though of unknown cause (and even disputed existence), is considered conclusive evidence of suicide, since placing a weapon into a dead person's hand does not achieve the same effect and there's no known—or at least published—way to simulate it.

CONTACT WOUND. A contact, or near-contact, wound is one where the muzzle of the weapon was touching, or almost touching, the victim when fired. Evidence for such proximity may include gunpowder residues on the hand and the wound, singed hair near the wound, blood in the gun barrel, the cherry-red color characteristic of carbon monoxide (caused by the incomplete burning of the gunpowder) in blood or tissue, and sometimes massive tissue damage from the expansion of hot gases at the muzzle. These gases, sometimes combined with the forceful ejection of wadding, is how people have been killed by "blanks." There may on rare occasions be a muzzle-shaped abrasion around the entrance wound, caused by the impact between gun barrel and skin.

Occasionally (most often with rifles and shotguns, rather than handguns), the muzzle is held in place with one hand while the other hand pulls the trigger; this can cause a contact wound to the hand rather than to the fatal site. Overlooking the hand wound might lead an investigator to think that the bullet had been fired from further away, mistakenly suggesting murder.

While a contact wound doesn't eliminate the possibility of murder, a distant wound, in the absence of clear evidence to the contrary (for example, a gun held in a vise and fired with a long stick), does eliminate a verdict of suicide.

FINGERPRINTS. If the only fingerprints on the gun are the victim's, it is, obviously, consistent with suicide. However, murderers have been known to wipe off a gun and place it in their victim's hand in an effort to disguise the crime. There has even been a case where a murder defendant claimed that his fingerprints on the gun were due to his attempt to prevent the suicide.[38]

INDIRECT TRIGGERING. When a long-barreled weapon is used, often a stick, rod, string, or other means of pulling the trigger is found at the scene. In their absence, the victim's arms are measured to estimate the likelihood of his being able to reach the trigger. If the suicide is barefoot, the possibility that he used a toe to push the trigger has to be considered.

WHAT CAN THE SITE OF THE WOUND TELL US?

The distribution of fatal wound sites can be informative. In a study of 175 self-inflicted lethal gunshot wounds to the head or neck:

- Most of the self-inflicted gunshot wounds to the forehead are right on the midline.
- Fatal neck wounds were all in the front.
- There were no wound sites behind and under the ear: Such a wound, especially one under the left ear for a righ-handed person (or vice versa) is very likely—but not certainly—murder.

It's commonly thought that when people shoot themselves in the head, they pick the side that is the same as their handedness. Indeed, Seattle investigators found that all five of the left-handed people who shot themselves in the side of the head picked the left side of the head—but so did five (9 percent) of fifty-five right-handed people. Similarly, data from Dallas[39] showed that 7 of 141 (5 percent) suicidal shots to the head were to the left temple by right-handed people. This suggests that there should be only a minimal suspicion of foul play in what would otherwise be unquestionably a suicide if the "wrong" side of the head was injured. On the other hand, a fatal hand-gun wound to the abdomen, eye, or back of the head is more suspect because of its rarity in suicide.

In suicidal wounds through the mouth, the mouth is generally open and the tongue depressed when the shot is fired. If there's damage to teeth and tongue, it's probably homicide. However, the absence of such damage does not necessarily mean suicide, since occasionally a murder victim has been forced to open his mouth or is in the process of screaming or shouting when shot.

> I have *not* had a fall. I was writing a letter to Mrs. Anderson and a pis-tol went off under my ear.
>
> —Mrs. Bertha Merrett (Murphy 1985)

> The site of the wound may be an important issue in a trial, as in the case of J. D. Merrett in 1927. He was accused of the murder of his mother by shooting her with an automatic pistol; his defence was that she had shot herself. The wound was situated at the back of the right ear, immediately behind [the ear]; the bullet had passed forwards to the base of the skull and lodged ... without causing injury to the brain; she died, about a fortnight later, from meningitis. The site of the wound is unusual for suicide but Sir Bernard Spilsbury [the most eminent forensic pathologist of the time], who gave evidence for the defence, believed that this site and the direction of aim were not inconsistent with suicide. He instanced a similar case of his own in which the victim was found with the weapon firmly grasped in his hand ["cadaverous spasm"]; death had been instantaneous and there was no doubt that the circumstances were then those of suicide. In the Merrett case, a verdict of "Not Proven"[g] was due, in the main, to the fact that the medical witnesses were unable to agree.[40]

Due to the serendipitous nature of research, I ran across further references to this case while looking into something else. To make a long story short, Spilsbury made an inexcusable mistake, because he had carried out his tests using a different gun and powder. Merrett went on to a life of crime, and eventually brutally murdered his ex-wife and mother-in-law for money.[41] Having been seen by neighbors, and realizing that the police were closing in, he fatally shot himself in the head.

CAN A GUNSHOT SUICIDE FIRE OFF MORE THAN ONE ROUND?

Multiple gunshot wounds understandably raise suspicion of foul play, but they also occasionally occur in suicides. There were fifty-eight multiple-shot suicides, or 1.6 percent of all firearm suicides in North Carolina from 1972 to 1978.[42] The distribution (mostly middle-aged white males) by age, race, and sex was somewhat different from single-shot suicides (mostly older white males) in the state and nation. A majority of these shot themselves at home.

Only 15 percent had alcohol (quantity unspecified) in their bodies, substantially fewer than the approximately 40 percent of the total gunshot suicide group who had been drinking before killing themselves. One might speculate that absence of alcohol improves the eye-hand coordination needed for a second shot. This, however, might be a hard hypothesis to test.

In Seattle there were three of 223 (1.6 percent) suicides by multiple—in this case two—gunshot wounds, consistent with the data from North Carolina indicating that the existence of such wounds does not necessarily imply murder. The Chief Medical Examiner in North Carolina also mentions multiple suicidal wounds in a warning against the mistaken prosecution of an innocent "perpetrator."[43] (There is more detail on multishot suicide later in this chapter.)

Multiple injuries have been occasionally described in the medical literature. In one case, four gunshot wounds were found in a suicide. Two, presumably the first two, were flesh wounds to the head; the latter two were fatal shots to the heart. In another instance a man shot himself in the neck with a shotgun, suffering severe damage. He then walked back to where his ammunition was, reloaded, returned to the scene of the first shot, and shot himself in the head, this time fatally.[44]

There are even cases of multiple suicidal shots to the brain.[45] One man shot himself upward through the mouth, injuring an optic nerve and temporal lobe (front) of the brain. He then drove home and shot himself in the temple. He lived two days.

Another man shot also shot himself through the mouth, but aimed too low and a bit off to the side, slightly damaging his spine. His second shot was through the right temple and injured the temporal lobe. A third shot, through the left temple, was fatal.

In both of these cases low-energy ammunition (.25 and .22 caliber respectively) were used.

The record for this sort of thing seems to be held by a young man who killed his lover and then shot himself in the head seven times before giving it up as a bad business and hanging himself.[46]

RESULTS: HOW AND WHY ARE GUNSHOT WOUNDS FATAL?

Obviously, gunshots can cause severe tissue and organ damage. Death, when it occurs, usually results from loss of blood leading to irreversible shock, or from injury to a vital organ(s), such as the brain or heart.

BLOOD LOSS. Injury to a large artery or vein can cause death within minutes. Such vessels are to be found in every major region of the body. Some well-known vessels include the carotid artery and jugular vein (in the neck and head), aorta, pulmonary and thoracic artery (chest), hepatic (liver), femoral (thigh/groin), and brachial (shoulder).

The mechanism of shock from blood-loss is interesting. An adult normally has about five liters (5.3 quarts) of blood. If you were to lose one liter (about twice what you give as a blood donor) what would happen? Nothing much; your body is very good at compensating—up to a point.

The drop in blood pressure due to blood loss increases the heart rate from the normal 70 as high as 200 beats per minute. Tiny arteries and veins constrict, especially in the limbs, making more blood available to the major vessels and organs. This raises blood pressure, and everything is okay, other than having cold hands and feet.

However, if blood loss is great enough (more than about two liters), there is progressive and eventually irreversible deterioration. Because there isn't enough blood left, the heart muscle doesn't get adequate oxygen and nutrients, and beats more weakly. Because the cardiac output thus decreases, less blood gets to the lungs to pick up new oxygen. The lack of oxygen weakens the heart muscle further, a downward spiral that ends in death. (Things are actually a good deal more complicated, but this gives the basic picture.) If blood is replaced soon enough, the process can be reversed, but if delayed, even adequate transfusion will only postpone death for an hour or two, since the heart muscle has been irreversibly damaged.

HEAD INJURY. A contact shotgun blast to the temple or cheek causes damage from the shot, the wadding, and the propellant's hot gases. The skull may burst and pieces of scalp, bone, and brain be scattered over several feet. Eyes may be blown out of their sockets. Damage may be so severe that inexperienced medical examiners have been known attribute suicide by shotgun to an axe murder.[47]

A shot upward through the mouth is less likely to produce an exit wound, since the hard palate absorbs some energy and decreases the residual force of the explosion. The nose, sinuses, and nearby blood vessels are demolished. Which part of the brain receives the brunt of the damage depends on the position of the barrel when the trigger is pulled. The skull is often cracked, but sometimes the more elastic scalp remains intact.

High-powered rifles cause similar injuries if the bullet shatters, mushrooms, or tumbles, which is usually the case when it hits bone. Occasionally, survivable injuries are produced by a bullet that exits intact and undeformed, but this should not be relied on.

Low-powered rifles and handguns generate a few nonlethal head injuries, most often when the low-energy bullet is fired at an oblique angle to the skull and is deflected. On the other hand, such a bullet that enters the skull will generally fragment, tearing multiple tracks through brain tissue—and is very unlikely to have enough energy to make an exit hole.

CHEST AND ABDOMEN INJURY. If a bullet injures the heart, death is usually swift. This is because either the heart muscle is too damaged to pump blood or the major blood vessels near it are destroyed. The results are the same: hemorrhage, shock, and death. Wounds elsewhere in the chest and abdomen may or may not be survivable, often depending on whether a major artery or vein is severed, and the availability of quick medical help.

Less common injury can also occur. For example, bullets or their fragments and shotgun pellets occasionally lodge in an artery or vein, causing an embolism (blockage), with sometimes fatal results. In one case a man shot himself in the chest and the bullet entered the lower right heart chamber (right ventricle). It eventually migrated to the main artery of the lung (right pulmonary artery) where it caused massive lung damage (infarction) due to interruption of the lung's blood supply. The victim survived nineteen days.[48] In another unusual case, a woman died of lead poisoning after several years of carrying a bullet lodged in her knee.[49] While rare, there have been similar cases, both fatal and nonfatal.[50]

Another uncommon, but well-documented, source of gunshot injury is the hot and expanding gases that enter a contact-wound site along with the bullet or shot. In two cases a shotgun contact blast to the temple injected enough high-pressure gas that it blew a half-dollar-sized hole through the front of the skull, directly between and slightly above the eyes.[51] The initial wound was one that would be instantly lethal, so the existence of what appeared to be a second site (in a suicide) was at first perplexing. Autopsy resolved the issue.

There is even an instance of a man who was killed by a shotgun blast even though none of the pellets or wadding hit him. The shot had passed between his chest and left arm. He suffered broken ribs, lacerations of left chest, inner arm, and lung, and massive bleeding in his chest cavity—the last being the fatal wound; death was from blast injury due to expanding gases.[52]

SURVIVAL TIME AND MOBILITY AFTER INJURY

> Death does not occur instantly except under a few circumstances. Death obviously does not occur in the way many television programs would have us believe.[53]

In most cases of fatal (nonfatal wounds will be discussed in the next section) gunshot wounds to the head or heart, collapse is rapid but death may not be. In one study of fatal brain gunshots, 98 percent of victims found alive maintained vital functions (heartbeat, blood pressure, breathing) long enough to reach a hospital and be evaluated.[54]

In one case a Finnish man committed pistolshot-to-the-head suicide—in front of a movie camera he had set up. There was immediate collapse, but just before the four-minute film ran out, he opened his eyes and raised his head; how long he survived and his capabilities before dying are unknown.[55]

Specific regions of the brain control particular functions. For example, the brain stem, at the base of the skull, is responsible for maintaining, among other things, breathing, while the cerebral cortex, just behind the forehead, is the seat of intellectual abilities. Thus, someone with a wound that is limited to the cerebral cortex may well remain mobile (and sometimes even coherent) for minutes or hours. Similarly, a bullet that travels from temple to temple may miss the brain entirely, passing beneath it, possibly cutting the optic nerves and causing blindness, without producing immediate collapse. On the other hand, a shot to the brain stem is quickly fatal.

"One-shot" targets are those where a bullet wound is instantaneously incapacitating and quickly fatal. These are: brain stem, basal ganglia, medulla oblongata, and spinal column in the neck.

"Rapidly fatal" targets allow ten to fifteen seconds of voluntary action after a gunshot wound. These are the heart and the large blood vessel above it, the aorta. Injury to other organs, though often lethal, allows more time before incapacitation.

A gunshot to the front of the head may fall into any of these categories, depending on the bullet's angle and how far it penetrates. Large caliber and high-velocity bullets are most likely to be immediately disabling, but there are no guarantees.

The ability to function despite soon-to-be-fatal brain injury is remarkable:

> An elderly man left his hotel one evening and did not return that night. This occasioned no comment because he was accustomed to absent himself without notice. He returned at 7:30 A.M. and when seen by the maid at the door, he had his umbrella over his arm and his hat on his head. The maid, however, noticed bloodstains on his face and called her mistress. The man placed his umbrella in the hall, took off his overcoat and then, saying "I will just go upstairs," did so. He was found unconscious in the bathroom and transferred to hospital, where he died three hours later. He had a bullet wound of entry at a point beneath the chin two inches to the left of the middle line. ... The bullet had traversed the base

of the tongue, the frontal and temporal lobes of the brain, which were extensively damaged, and had left the skull at the left side of the frontal bone; the exit wound was that of a .45 [caliber] bullet which had turned on its side inside the skull. A .45 revolver, the property of the deceased, was found in some gardens, near the hotel. Investigation of the scene showed that the man must have shot himself before 6:30 A.M. and, for some time, had walked about before he returned to his hotel, when he still appeared to be reasonable and intelligible.[56]

A study of such unusual cases found that 70 percent were associated with low-energy ammunition (small and/or slow bullets); most of the remaining bullets were antique or homemade. None involved shotguns or center-fire rifles from close range.[57]

There is also a good deal of variability in the outcomes of similar injuries. In one instance of a self-inflicted shotgun wound to the head, the family insisted on no treatment, and none was given. Nevertheless the victim lived forty-five hours. Another person with a similar injury died within five minutes.

While data on suicide are meager, about half the people who die of homicidal handgun wounds do so within ten minutes of being shot; another third die within a day.[58]

Injury Sites in Gun Suicides

If you wanted to kill yourself with a gun, what part of the body should you aim for? Head or heart give the best (though not 100 percent certain) targets for quick and fatal injury. An abdominal shot is a very poor third, since you are both less likely to die and more likely to take a long time in doing so. Single pistol shots to limbs are generally not fatal, though it's always possible to bleed to death from a severed artery or die of infection.

Exactly what parts of the head and body do suicides aim for? First we'll look at fatal wounds; later we'll compare them with nonfatal ones.

FATAL GUNSHOT SITES

Numbers on the left numerical column in the following Table 22.3 are from a study of 223 suicidal gunshot deaths in King County (Seattle), Washington, from 1976 to 1978;[59] in the center column are less-detailed data from 1,200 Dallas-area suicides;[60] the right column shows data from fifty-seven head-wound (only) suicides in Bangkok, Thailand, between 1983 and 1986.[61]

Table 22.3

Target Site	Seattle number (%)	Dallas number (%)	Bangkok number (%)
Total head	165 (74)	857 (71)	57 N/A
Right temporal (temple)	87 (39)		23 (40)
Left temporal (temple)	11 (5)		3 (5)
Right parietal (top and side)	6 (3)		14 (25)
Left parietal (top and side)	1 (0.5)		2 (3.5)
Occipital (back of head)	1 (0.5)		1 (2)
Mid-frontal (forehead)	18 (8)		3 (5)
Other frontal	3 (1)		——
Orbit (eye)	2 (1)		——
Nose	1 (0.5)		——
Mouth	20 (9)	59 (4)	2 (3.5)
Chin	2 (1)		——
Submental (under chin)	7 (3)		——
Right head, no site specified	2 (1)		——
Left head, no site specified	4 (2)		——
Right ear region	——		5 (9)
Right side of face	——		3 (5)
Right eyebrow	——		2 (3.5)
Neck	10 (4)	17 (1.4)	
Total chest	40 (18)	246 (20.5)	
Presternal (center of chest)	13 (6)		
Precordium (in front of heart)	20 (9)		
Other chest	7 (3)		
Total abdomen	8 (4)	21 (2)	
Epigastrium (stomach)	5 (3)		
Other abdomen	3 (1)		

From Seattle and Dallas we see that almost three-quarters (71 to 74 percent) of all fatal wounds were shots to the head. The most popular single site was the right temple (39 percent), followed by mouth (9 percent), heart (9 percent), mid-front or forehead (8 percent), and presternal or center of chest (6 percent) areas. The "no site specified" is listed because, in six cases, there was such extensive damage as to prevent identification of the entrance wound. Like I said, messy.

Comparing this with the data from Bangkok shows that the distribution of head injuries is roughly similar. However, there are some differences: More Thais shot themselves in a region from behind the temple to the back of the head, while more Americans chose the front of the head.

SEX. Seventy-two percent of fatal suicidal gunshot wounds, among Seattle women, were to the head.[62] This 72 percent figure is higher than the numbers cited in most earlier papers.[63] Since head wounds are often disfiguring, the authors of this study suggested, perhaps facetiously, that Seattle women might be less vain than those elsewhere. However, this increasing proportion of fatal suicide shots to the head among women has also been found in Dallas where 69 percent (78 in 113) chose that site, as did 80 percent of men (427 in 537).[64]

GUNSHOTS TO THE HEART. Most bullets that enter the heart are swiftly fatal, though one lodged in the left ventricle may take a long time (minutes to hours) to kill if the muscle seals around it. A more common, though still rare, reason some shots aimed at the heart are survived is that the bullet may be deflected a few degrees by the ribs. To avoid this, one can aim under (or between) the left-side ribs, with an upward trajectory toward the right side of the neck.

Even if you don't cause fatal heart damage, there's a fair chance that the bullet will hit the aorta (the largest artery in the body), one of its major branches, or the vena cava (the largest vein) with lethal results.

Curiously, in many suicidal gunshot (and knife) wounds of the chest, the victim first lifts or removes his shirt, perhaps to bring the muzzle into closer contact with the skin, or out of some final fastidiousness.

NONFATAL GUNSHOT WOUNDS

In the next sections we look at the following questions:

- What are the demographic and psychiatric characteristics of suicidal-gunshot survivors?
- What are the target sites chosen by these survivors?
- What are the medical consequences of their attempts?

CHARACTERISTICS OF SURVIVORS OF SUICIDAL GUNSHOT WOUNDS

SEX AND RACE

In the Lexington, Kentucky, metropolitan area, which is about 80 percent white, 88 percent of 260 gunshot-suicide survivors were white, 12 percent black. Seventy-seven percent of the whites and 67 percent of the blacks were male. This is in line with the fact that, in all age groups, whites have a higher suicide rate than blacks, and males a higher rate than females. Age distribution was generally consistent with nationwide data on completed suicide, peaking in the twenties. Table 22.4 summarizes a number of their characteristics:[65]

- The male/female ratio in survived gunshot wounds is higher (3:1) than that for completed gunshot suicides (2:1). This "excess" of male survivors is a bit surprising since, in general, men's suicide attempts tend to be more lethal than women's. However this notion may reflect men's preference for more lethal methods (for example, guns rather than drugs) rather than more lethality within a given method.
- Shotguns and rifles accounted for 5 percent of the weapons used by these survivors, compared to 36 percent of weapons chosen by fatally wounded suicides in Seattle. Given that all types of guns are readily available in both areas, it seems reasonable to conclude that, in suicide attempts, shotguns and rifles are more lethal than handguns.

Table 22.4 Characteristics of 260 Patients Referred to Psychiatric Consultation After Self-inflicted Gunshot Wound

	number	percent
Male	198	76
White	(176)	
Black	(22)	
Female	62	24
White	(51)	
Black	(11)	
Method: handguns		95
rifle, shotgun		5
Site of wound: abdomen	88	34
head	62	24
chest	58	22
limbs	35	13
shoulders	16	6
Marital status: single	106	41
married or living with other	96	37
divorced	34	13
widowed	13	5
separated	11	4
Previous suicide attempt	17	7
Previous suicide attempt by gunshot	1	0
Past psychiatric history	39	15
Left suicide note	3	1
Acquired gun specifically for suicide attempt	5	2
Significant alcohol consumption within 24 hr of suicide attempt (BAC of .10 or more)		25
Premeditation before suicide attempt (leaving note, buying weapon for suicide, writing will or distributing assets, behaving in ways to decrease the chances of rescue, or having persistent thoughts or conversations about the suicide attempt in the preceding days)		20

Source: Frierson, 1990

- Head wounds were far less common (24 percent of the survivors in Lexington) than in fatal gunshots (74 percent of fatal wounds were to the head in Seattle); abdominal wounds far more common (34 percent versus 4 percent of fatal wounds in Seattle). These data are consistent with the much higher lethality of gunshot wounds to the head than to the abdomen.
- Distribution of wounds between head, chest, and abdomen was roughly equal; this is consistent with other data.[66]
- Alcohol use was similar to that in completed suicides.

What I find most striking about these data is how little premeditation there seemed to be: 80 percent of the suicide attempts were described by the researchers as "impulsive" (regrettably, undefined). A number denied that they had really intended suicide. Two even initially claimed to have been shot by someone else. Equally remarkable is that only 7 percent had made (or admitted to) a previous suicide attempt before trying a highly lethal method, gunshot. Thus, apparently one cannot count on a "warning" attempt prior to a gunshot suicide attempt.

The two most common psychiatric diagnoses in this group of 260 people were major depression (40 percent) and continuous alcohol abuse (20 percent).

Marriage or relationship difficulties were the most frequent reasons cited for the suicide attempts, but many attempts were by severely depressed individuals with less specific problems. (Or more specific problems: Four shot themselves after killing their spouses.)

MEDICAL CONSEQUENCES OF NONFATAL GUNSHOT INJURIES

What are the medical consequences of surviving a self-inflicted gunshot? A gunshot wound, particularly at close range, is often disfiguring or permanently damaging. Since many suicidal people are already seriously depressed and have poor self-image, this is not helpful, and they may become even more withdrawn. On the other hand, at least one study claims that, emotionally, survivors of suicidal head wounds do relatively well after (if) they get out of the hospital.[67]

The fact that there is little or no correlation between the severity of a suicide attempt and the likelihood of a subsequent attempt also suggests that coming close to death may be catharic (or may increase family or social support). Nevertheless, this seems like a hazardous way to find out.

And the physical effects can be catastrophic. Looking again at the 260 Lexington residents who survived self-inflicted gunshots, many were left with permanent injuries: forty people (15 percent) with colostomies, fifteen (6 percent) with brain damage, twelve (5 percent) with repeated seizures; ten (4 percent) with wound infections, and ten (4 percent) needing limb amputations.[68] Since this group included some (presumably less serious) accidents as well as suicide attempts, one might expect that suicidal injuries would be even more devastating than these data indicate.

NONFATAL GUNSHOTS TO THE HEAD

Not all gunshot wounds to the head are equally dangerous. Since the "old" or "primitive" parts of the brain are responsible for maintaining and regulating basic functions like breathing and temperature, injury to these areas tends to be quickly fatal. It's not a coincidence that many executions are carried out by a single shot to the base of the skull. This part of the brain is located at the lower back of the head, near where the spinal column meets the skull. Shots into the base of the skull damage this tissue (brainstem), as do shots straight through the mouth from front to back.

Shots to the front of the head may cause unexpected problems:

The cerebral cortex, directly behind the forehead doesn't control any vital functions, so injury there is not directly life-threatening, but may well result in intellectual and personality deficits.

Firing a gun, especially a shotgun or rifle, with the muzzle under the chin or aimed at the face, is somewhat less likely to be fatal than one might expect. Apparently, people tend to flinch or tilt their head back at the moment they pull the trigger, changing the direction of bullet entrance and decreasing the chances of fatal brain damage while increasing that of massive facial injury. This is generally not a problem when the muzzle is in the mouth: Using 12-gauge shotguns in this manner caused the head to burst open in 74 percent of cases; only 9 percent of such wounds with a 20-gauge shotgun[h] resulted in similar injury. Shotgun wounds from a .410 were similar to 20-gauge; 16-gauge was in between 12- and 20-gauge in its ability to rupture heads. A 12-gauge was the most commonly used shotgun (69 percent), followed by 20-gauge (18 percent), .410 caliber (10 percent), and 16-gauge (3 percent).[69] However, rest assured that even a 20-gauge or .410 wound of this sort is quite fatal. There are claims that a low-velocity bullet, like a .22, is more lethal than a high-velocity one, like a .357 magnum, because a low-velocity round will not have enough energy to make an exit wound in the skull,[i] and will thus rattle around in the cranium, turning your brain into something resembling scrambled eggs. There may be some truth to this, since there is little correlation between the caliber of the bullet and the lethality of the resulting head wound. However, with a low-energy (see ammunition section) round there is also the chance that the bullet won't penetrate the skull. In light of this consideration, I think the most reliably lethal combination is a high-energy bullet/shell aimed at the brainstem, either from the back or through the mouth: If that target is hit, it won't matter (to you) that the bullet will also blast an exit hole.

OUTCOMES OF NONFATAL GUNSHOT WOUNDS TO THE HEAD

These are some of the most disfiguring of injuries. Quoting from a typical case report:

> This twenty-year-old man attempted suicide with a 12-gauge shotgun that was placed under his chin and directed to the left side. He sustained a large soft tissue loss [part of his face was blown off], facial nerve injury, loss of vision, and multiple fractures of the mandible [lower jawbone], maxilla [upper jaw], nose, zygoma [cheekbone], and orbit [eye socket]. The patient was treated with tracheostomy [breathing hole in neck], wound debridement [dead tissue removal], and a neck flap. Mandibular reconstruction with a hip graft was complicated by osteomyelitis [bone infection] and a nonunion [bones didn't join]. Two years later he was referred for treatment of a severe facial deformity, facial paralysis, depressed malar eminence [collapsed cheekbone], nonunion, and ankylosis [inability of a joint to function] of the mandible. Inferior rectus entrapment, [eyeball muscle stuck in the wrong place] visual loss, and lacrymal disfunction [inability to produce enough tears to keep the eye moist] were also present.[70]

Functionally, there may be permanent damage to vision or hearing, and when the brain is also involved, behavior, speech, and balance may be affected. Seizures and/or tremors are not uncommon. In a study from Houston[71], of the 48 survivors of gunshot wounds to the head, 32 (67 percent) were eventually considered to be in "good" condition and went home; 14 of 48 (29 percent) were described as "moderately impaired," and 2 of 48 (5 percent) "severely impaired." Nine of these required continued acute care at a hospital and five went to a rehabilitation center. (What happened to the other two is not explained.) This is similar to results from a smaller study in Germany in which about one-third (5 of 16) of survivors needed permanent care.[72] However, less than one-third (13 of 40 or 32 percent) of Phoenix, Arizona, survivors came out in "good" condition.[73]

These studies do not include the approximately 70 percent who die before they ever get to the hospital. It's clear that suicidal gun wounds to the head are more lethal than assault or accidental ones,[74] but length of hospitalization is similar in suicidal and assault gunshot wounds.[75] Note also that the survival rate for attempted suicides (22 percent) was only about half that of assault victims (43 percent) in Houston and (30 percent versus 79 percent) in Phoenix. These figures suggest that only about 3 to 9 percent of people with suicidal gunshot wounds to the head will live to get out of the hospital, and that a majority of the survivors will be permanently impaired.

Specific medical outcomes found in eleven survivors included:[76]

Outcome	Number of patients
Full recovery	2
Blindness	4
Hemiplegia [one-sided paralysis]	1
Hemiparesis [one-sided paralysis]	3
Aphasia [can't speak]	1
Dysphasia [impaired speech]	1
Dysgeusia [can't taste food]	1
Seizures	1
Facial reconstruction*	2

(The total is greater than eleven because some survivors had more than one medical result.)
*Both shotgun survivors.

Looking on the bright side, there is one case that I'm aware of where a gunshot wound to the head was therapeutic. A nineteen-year-old man was so obsessive-compulsive that he spent many hours every day washing himself and cleaning around him. He was unable to continue at school or hold a job, and had no social life. Drug and psychiatric therapy were not effective. His mother threatened to have him committed, and at one point said, "Go and shoot yourself." Five minutes later he did so.

He fired a .22 caliber rifle through his mouth and into his brain, but survived the experience. The bullet was found at the base of the left frontal lobe of the cerebral cortex. He had essentially done a self-lobotomy. Upon recovery, his compulsive rituals soon decreased to about fifteen minutes a day, and his obsessions became much milder: He merely insisted on a spotless kitchen and bathroom. Interestingly, his IQ increased significantly, he didn't show the common effects of "therapeutic" lobotomy,[j] and his life much improved. Before you rush out to try this, note that elective psychosurgery by means of bullets does not have a great track record.[77]

ABDOMINAL INJURY

The previously described study from Lexington[78] looked at 260 survivors of self-inflicted (suicidal and accidental) gunshot wounds. In contrast to fatal wounds which, as we have seen, were largely head injuries, the most common nonfatal site was the abdomen, with 34 percent of the total. Combining this piece of information with the 95 percent handgun-use in these survivors and the low incidence of fatal abdominal handgun wounds from Seattle, it seems that abdominal handgun wounds (at least with the weapons used by these people) were not often a successful means of suicide.

As an aside, it appears that some authors (and readers) of forensic medicine books may be led a bit astray by their general focus on completed, perhaps to the neglect of attempted, suicide. Thus we read, "Our experience confirms the infrequent choice of an abdominal site by the suicide . . .",[79] which is true not because the site is infrequently chosen, but because it is infrequently fatal.

However, abdominal bullet wounds are not trivial. Injury to the large or small intestine may involve removal of the affected area. These colostomies and ileostomies require lifetime limits and changes in activities—for example, the use of colostomy bags—which tend to be unpleasant and depressing. In one study of three hundred consecutive hospital admissions (85 percent male) for penetrating abdominal gunshots, most patients had more than one organ damaged;[80] the average was 2.1 among survivors and 4.0 in those who died. About 10 percent of the survivors had major postoperative complications including hemorrhage, infection, and abscess. Of the colon injuries, 72 percent were repaired, and 26 percent required colostomies. The overall survival rate for all abdominal gunshot wounds was 88 percent—of those who were alive on reaching the hospital.

In suicide attempts, one would expect the survival rate to be lower than in accidents because (1) the guns are generally held nearer to the body, permitting more energy to be transferred by the bullet, and (2) the shots are presumably fired with lethal aim and intent; the three hundred wounds in this series include accidents without aim or intent, and assaults with (one would suppose) lethal intent but not necessarily good aim, as well as suicide. On the other hand, in assaults there is more likelihood of multiple shots and wounds.

A very rough estimate of survival rate for suicidal abdominal wounds might be 50 percent overall and 75 percent of those getting to the hospital alive. These percentages would tend to be higher when handguns were used and lower for rifles and, especially, shotguns.

WOUNDS TO LIMBS AND SHOULDERS

These accounted for 19 percent of all survived wounds in the Lexington study. They can result in permanent, partial, or complete loss of function; occasionally amputation is necessary. In one review of shotgun wounds, three of twenty-two (14 percent) injured limbs had to be amputated.[81]

The list below shows the estimate of survival from attempted-suicide gunshot wounds to various body sites from a single round from handgun, rifle, and shotgun.

	Handgun	*Rifle*	*Shotgun*
head	10 percent	5 percent	1 percent
heart[k]	10 percent	5 percent	1 percent
chest	40 percent	20 percent	10 percent
abdomen	80 percent	50 percent	20 percent
limbs	95 percent	90 percent	80 percent

WEAPONS: WHAT TYPE OF GUN SHOULD YOU CHOOSE?

> The combined effects of the entry of the shot and the products of detonation, i.e., injury by shot and blast, produces gross disruption of the tissues. The scalp and skull may be burst open and parts of the scalp, skull, and brain blown from the body for a distance of several feet.[82]

Not all firearms are equally lethal. Lethality depends on several physical factors: (1) Speed of the bullet (we will include shotgun pellets under the term "bullet"); (2) weight of the bullet; (3) type of bullet; (4) size of the gun. In general, the order of most to least lethal weapon in contact wounds is: (1) shotgun, (2) high-velocity rifle, (3) large or high-powered handgun (.45 caliber or .357 magnum), (4) small caliber (.22) rifle, (5) small caliber (.22) handgun. However, there are some exceptions and complications.

ENERGY (optional section for math-phobics). Tissue damage is roughly proportional to the amount of energy the bullet transfers to the struck body. Energy, in turn, depends on the velocity and mass of the bullet when it hits. Specifically, $Ek = \frac{1}{2} mv^2$ where Ek=kinetic (motion) energy (m=mass, v=velocity, ^2=squared).

Thus, a bullet's energy depends more on its speed than its mass: If you double the mass of a bullet, you double its energy; double its velocity and you increase its energy by a factor of four. There are practical limits to this, since the gun barrel must be strengthened to withstand the increased pressure needed to propel a heavier bullet to higher speeds.

MASS OF BULLET. Since doubling the mass of the bullet doubles its energy at any given speed, a .45 caliber which has about twice the diameter of a .22 caliber ought to pack four times the energy (volume of a cylinder is proportional to the square of the diameter) if all else (velocity of bullet) were equal. This is one of the reasons that lead is used for bullets: It weighs about 1.5 times as much as does the same volume of steel. Also, since lead is quite soft (you can scratch pure lead with a fingernail), it does minimum mechanical damage to the bore of the gun, though it may clog rifling grooves.

"Depleted" (of bomb-grade U-235) uranium is used in armor-piercing artillery shells, partly because it is considerably denser than lead (18.9 gm/ml vs 11.4), and therefore a given-sized shell packs more energy at the same speed. Besides, you wouldn't want to use soft lead against armor plate. However there are even denser, albeit more expensive, metals.[1]

SPEED OF BULLET. The speed of sound is about 1,100 feet (340 meters) per second (fps). The muzzle velocity of high-velocity rifles is around 2,400 to 4,000 fps (730 to 1,200 meters); handguns are mostly 350 to 1,500 fps (100 to 460 meters).

Low-velocity (less than the speed of sound) bullets crush or push aside tissue; the wound track is not much wider than the bullet (unless it mushrooms or tumbles). High-velocity bullets are used in military-type rifles and some semi-automatic pistols and have a lead core surrounded by a harder copper-alloy jacket. They are designed to not jam automatic loading mechanisms common in military weapons, and to survive rough field conditions; on striking a body, they are less likely than lead to flatten and more likely to drill a clean hole. Quite sporting. However, if jacketed bullets hit bone or develop a wobble while going through flesh, they can cause extensive damage along the wound track.

High-speed bullets send a shock wave of compression ahead of the laceration track. This can tear and even shatter organs, both nearby and, (transmitted through liquid, of which we are mostly composed) distant ones.[m]

High-velocity bullets also cause "cavitation." The bullet accelerates tissue radially away from the wound track at a high rate of speed. This generates a temporary cavity that can be much larger then the diameter of the bullet. The resulting near-vacuum also sucks clothing fibers and other sources of infection into the wound.[83]

If a bullet exits the body at high speed, it has not transferred maximum destructive energy. Thus, various attempts have been made to prevent the bullet from leaving. Without going into the fine points, these methods include:

- using a hollowed out bullet tip, which tends to mushroom upon hitting tissue, and thus slow down;
- using a tip that is softer than the body or jacket of the bullet;
- using so-called "dum-dum" bullets with deformed tips, again intended to cause mushrooming;
- using multiple small bullets, as with a non-rifled shotgun;

- using explosive-tipped bullets, which are supposed to detonate on contact. Like mushrooming bullets, they were banned by the Hague Convention of 1899.

The direct damage from the explosive tip is relatively small; the major effect is, once again, to distort the bullet, causing more of its energy to be absorbed by, and thus damage, the body. It may be of some interest that John Hinckley shot then-president Ronald Reagan with an explosive-tipped .22 caliber bullet—that failed to explode.[n]

OLD AMMUNITION. An occasional complication in gunshot suicide is the use of old ammunition. Bullets that have been sitting around for years, especially in damp conditions, tend not to reach their rated velocity (and therefore energy) when fired.

SIZE OF GUN AND TARGET SITE. The size of the gun is also relevant in choosing a target. This is because a handgun can be easily aimed at almost any part of the body, while rifles and shotguns (typically 40 to 48 inches, or 102 to 122 cm, long) are more difficult to fire into the side and back of the head than into the front of the head or body.

Consistent with this is data from fatal suicidal gunshot wounds in Seattle. In head wounds caused by *handguns*, temple and side injury sites (67 percent) were more than four times as common as frontal (forehead, mouth, and under chin) locations (16 percent). For *rifles*, frontal sites were slightly more frequent (32 percent versus 28 percent) and with *shotguns*, considerably more frequent (29 percent versus 17 percent).

The side of the head, including temple, was the overwhelming favorite among handgun aficionados (62 percent) but to a much lesser extent rifle (28 percent) and shotgun (17 percent) users. With shotguns, the middle and left part of the chest was preferred, and non-head sites were over 50 percent of the total, compared to 33 percent for rifles and 18 percent for handguns.

In addition to the ease-of-aim considerations mentioned previously, I think that the major reason for these differences is that shotguns are simply more lethal than handguns, and thus a larger percentage of people survive handgun wounds to the body. A related possibility is that shotgun users are less discriminating about their target because they are aware that their weapons are highly lethal when fired into just about any essential part of the body. Since the data in these studies were limited to sites of *fatal* gun wounds, they provide us no is information on this point, or about nonfatal suicide-attempt gun injuries.

The Lexington study is more helpful in that regard. Here, the authors looked at 260 people who *survived* a self-inflicted gunshot wound.[84] The age range was fifteen to eight-one, and averaged thirty-five, for both women and men. Twenty-four percent were women, 76 percent were men. Handguns were used in 95 percent of these nonfatal wounds, compared to 64 percent of fatal wounds in Seattle. This is consistent with the notion that the lower energy of handgun bullets (generally lower muzzle velocity compared with rifles and lower mass compared with shotgun loads) causes less damage than rifles and shotguns.

MEDICAL OUTCOME AND TYPE OF FIREARM

It would seem intuitively plausible that higher-energy guns should be more lethal than lower-energy ones. The limited available evidence° seems to support this, but not as clearly, or by as large a margin, as one might expect.

In Mobile, Alabama, 68 percent (62 of 91) of gunshot suicides used handguns, compared with 80 percent (16 of 20) of survived attempts, where the weapon was known; 13 percent (12 of 91) of suicides (5 percent of survivors) used shotguns; 19 percent (17 of 91) used rifles (15 percent of survivors).[85] This is consistent with shotguns being higher energy weapons than most civilian rifles, which in turn are somewhat higher than most handguns. However there is substantial overlap between the bullet energy of various handguns and rifles.

	Handgun		Shotgun		Rifle	
	percent	n	percent	n	percent	n
Suicide	68	62/91	13	12/91	19	17/91
Suicide attempt	80	16/20	5	1/20	15	3/20
Ratio of percent fatal/non-fatal	0.85		2.6		1.27	

Looking only at head wounds the higher-energy weapons—9mm, the magnums, the .45, and the shotgun—as a group were no more lethal than the lower-energy ones (.22, .25, .32, .38 caliber): 67 percent dead compared with 72 percent dead. This may be because higher-energy weapons leave fewer victims alive long enough to reach the hospital, but this is speculation. Some other studies have also found little or no difference.[86]

What about the condition of the survivors? In the Phoenix study of gunshot wounds to the head,[87] the patient outcome was compared to the type of weapon used. Of one hundred people who were alive when admitted to the hospital, the type of gun was known in fifty-five cases (presumably, mostly suicides), giving the data in Table 22.5. Again, there is no clear correlation between type of weapon and outcome, but the numbers are very small.

Table 22.5 Long-term Patient Outcome from Gunshot Wound to the Head

Weapon	Dead	Vegetative or Severely Disabled	Moderately Disabled or Good Outcome
Handgun			
0.22 cal	14	0	4
0.25 cal	3	1	4
0.32 cal	4	0	2
0.38 cal	6	0	4
9 mm	1	0	0
0.357 magnum	4	0	0
0.44 magnum	1	0	0
0.45 cal	1	1	1
Rifle			
0.22 cal	3	0	1
Total	37	2	16

Source: Grahm, 1990

MULTISHOT SUICIDES

TYPE OF GUN USED IN MULTIPLE-SHOT SUICIDE. In the North Carolina data on multiple-shot suicides, .22 caliber handguns were used by half (29 of 58) of this population, reflecting both the popularity of this cheap gun and the low energy of the bullet, which necessitated an occasional second shot. But even much more powerful firearms sometimes needed more than a single shot: One man lived for ten days after two shotgun blasts to the epigastrium (stomach region); another died of a shotgun wound to the epigastrium after first shooting himself in the chest, but at such an angle that the first shot would not have been fatal.

WOUND SITE IN MULTISHOT SUICIDE. Autopsies were performed on twenty-seven of the fifty-eight bodies. They showed that almost 10 percent of the bullets missed hitting any important organ or blood vessel. Even with fatal injuries, loss of consciousness was not instantaneous except, presumably, in some head wounds. In one case, three .22 caliber bullets hit the victim's heart, two penetrating and one grazing it. Despite this, investigation of the scene showed that he had remained conscious for several minutes. (How this was determined is, regrettably, not described.)

Thirty-five of the fifty-eight (60 percent) fired both shots into the same region of the body, but none chose exactly the same spot.[p] The data are shown in Table 22.6.

Table 22.6 Wound Entrance Sites in multi-shot suicides, North Carolina, 1972-78

	Head	Chest	Abdomen	Neck	Limbs
Head	7	14	4	1	0
Chest		25	2	0	2
Abdomen			2	0	0
Neck				1	0

The most popular mixed pair was head/chest, with fourteen of fifty-eight (24 percent), and the head wound was not always the lethal one. Survival of an initial head wound was due to either a failure of the bullet to penetrate the brain (low energy weapon, old ammunition, oblique firing angle, deflection off bone), missing vital centers (even major trauma to the cerebral cortex and frontal lobes is not necessarily fatal), or missing the brain entirely (a temple-to-temple shot may go under the brain, if the bullet remains intact).

Typically, 60 to 75 percent of fatal gunshot wounds are to the head; in this study of multiple wounds the figure is less than 25 percent, the majority, instead, being to the chest, aiming for the heart. Fifty-four of the fifty-eight (93 percent) suffered two gun wounds; four (7 percent) had three wounds.

SUMMARY

About 60 percent of suicides in the United States are committed with firearms; 76 to 92 percent of suicidal gunshot attempts are fatal. Eighty percent of those who survived acted on impulse, many (25 to 40 percent) while drinking.

The chances of living through a self-inflicted gunshot wound depend on many variables: type of weapon, site of injury, availability of medical help, age and physical condition of the shooter.

The most lethal site is the head, followed by heart, chest, abdomen, leg, and arm, in that order. *Many survivors suffer permanent injury.*[q]

This is not a recommended method for either suicide or suicidal gesture, primarily because (1) the chances of surviving with permanent injury are too high and (2) it's altogether too easy to pull the trigger on impulse.

NOTES

[a]The fatality rate in gunshot assaults was 34 percent, and in accidental shootings, 4 percent (Cummings, 1998).

[b]These concepts of "displacement" and "risk homeostasis" show up in many other areas (Jones, 1979). For example, as cars and roads are made safer, driving behavior tends to become riskier (Wilde, 1986).

[c]Currently (June 1997) limited to .22 caliber or smaller, and requiring a hard-to-obtain permit signed by the local police chief. The current Labor government proposes to ban all civilian handguns.

[d]However, shotgun weddings are, inexplicably, rare.

[e]For example, looking at international data, a few factors that are positively correlated

(that is, where one is high or low, so is the other) with national suicide rates are: gross-do-mestic-product/capita, life expectancy, percentage of unionized workers, calories-con-sumed/capita, employment, alcohol consumption, and literacy ("Better read, then dead"). Obviously, these factors, as well as the ones below, are not necessarily independent.

Some negative correlations with suicide rates are: infant mortality, births to unmarried mothers, working children, population growth rate, and percentage of Muslims.

Some that have no statistically significant correlation are: percentage of Christians, unemployment rate, political freedom, and corn consumption. This last item is not quite as off-the-wall as it sounds: The neurotransmitter serotonin (low levels of which are associated with suicide) requires the dietary amino acid tryptophan, which is particularly scarce in corn; hence the imaginative notion that high corn consumption might be associated with suicide; neat idea, but no cigar. (On the other hand, decreased dietary consumption of tryptophan *is* associated with depression (K. A. Smith, 1997). For lots more of this stuff (plus discussion), see Lester, 1996, chapter 5, from which this was taken.

[f]Plutarch says that the Elders of Miletos extinguished a (hanging) suicide epidemic among young women by decreeing that their bodies be put on public display (Alvarez, 104).

[g]In Scottish law, in addition to the possible verdicts of "guilty" and "not guilty," there is also "not proven," when the preponderance of evidence points to guilt, but not beyond any doubt. The existence of such a "Scotch verdict" is one reason the Libyan government has insisted on Scottish jurisdiction for any trial of the Libyans accused of blowing up Pan-Am Flight 103 over Scotland.

[h]Shotguns are most often described by the diameter (bore or gauge) of their barrel. The more modern unit-of-measure is the inch or millimeter. Thus, a .410 shotgun has a barrel with a 0.410 inch (about 11 mm) diameter. The more charmingly archaic unit calculates how many lead balls that exactly fit the barrel can be made out of one pound of lead. In this system a 12-gauge shotgun has a diameter such that 12 balls (each with a diameter of around 0.729 inches, or 18.5 mm) could be made from a pound of lead, while with a 16 gauge, 16 balls (of diameter 0.65 inches, or 16mm) could be made. A variant of this screwy system is used for sizing carpenters' nails.

[i]There was one amazing case where the ricocheting bullet exited from the entrance wound (Grey, 1993).

[j]This is called "frontal-lobe syndrome" and consists of loss of social inhibitions (people become quarrelsome and tactless) and loss of ambition or drive. This was first described in a railroad construction worker in the mid-nineteenth century. A railway tie spike hit him in the head, penetrated his skull, and caused frontal lobe damage. To the surprise of his doctors, he not only survived the injury, but seemed to be not much the worse for it. Eventually, however, it was noticed that his behavior and personality had changed for the worse. Similar results were seen when lobotomy became a widely used form of psychosurgery, in the 1930s.

[k]People don't always know quite where their heart lies; there is a tendency to aim too high and too far to the left side. This estimate is for the lethality of shots aimed at the heart, rather than those actually hitting it.

[l]As Hilaire Belloc wrote:

I hunt the hippopotamus
With bullets made of Platinum

Because if I use Leaden ones
His hide is sure to flattenum.

[m]Longstanding rumors have been recently confirmed that 7.62 mm NATO ammunition usually breaks apart upon striking a body at close range, causing additional injuries and, incidently, contrary to the 1899 Hague Declaration—never signed by the United States—which, in the name of "humane" warfare, outlawed, among other things, mushrooming and fragmenting military bullets (Knudsen, 1993).

[n]Such a defective bullet is a hazard to remove surgically, since it can be set off by contact with an instrument, or even by attempts to find it with diagnostic methods such as ultrasound imaging.

[o]For a discussion of why reliable gunshot data are so lacking, see Riddick, 1993.

[p]Germans are neater and more orderly about such things: Two of seven dual-shot suicides fired the second shot directly into the site of the first wound (Betz, 1994).

[q]If you really want to kill yourself, there's something to be said for redundancy. One man put a noose around his neck and then shot himself in the head; had the gun wound not been fatal he would have quickly died of asphyxia. Another woman shot herself through the chest on a pier and fell into the water. When the body was recovered, it was found that the bullet had missed all vital organs; she had drowned (di Maio, 337).

23
HANGING AND STRANGULATION

●

We must all hang together, or assuredly we shall all hang separately.
—Ben Franklin

Hanging and strangulation are effective methods of suicide. Both can be carried out by people with limited physical abilities. Hanging doesn't require complete suspension. Death occurs within about five to ten minutes after cutoff of oxygen or blockage of blood flow to the brain (anoxia); however, convulsions are common and the noise may attract attention. Pain can be minimized by protecting and padding the front of the neck. Since finding the body will probably be traumatic, care should be given to choosing a location. These are highly lethal methods and cannot be done safely as a suicidal gesture.

LETHAL INTENT: High
MORTALITY: High, around 80 percent
PERMANENT INJURIES IN SURVIVORS: Moderately frequent
PROS AND CONS OF HANGING AS A MEANS OF SUICIDE
Pros: • Quick unconsciousness
　　　• Fairly quick death
　　　• Easily accomplished with materials found around the house
　　　• Can, if necessary, be done without leaving bed
Cons:• Possibility of brain damage if interrupted

- Sometimes a gruesome cadaver, which may be upsetting for whoever discovers the body

Suspension hanging is often lumped (and confused) with judicial-type ("drop") hanging, suffocation, strangulation, and even choking. This is entirely understandable, since the subject is confusing, but there are some important, and sometimes critical, differences between them. Brief definitions of these terms may be helpful in making sense of what follows.

1. *Suspension hanging*: suspension by the neck, with little or no drop. Death is due to compression of the airway (trachea, or windpipe) and/or the major blood vessels connecting the heart and the brain. These latter are the carotid and vertebral arteries, and the jugular vein. We will use "hanging" to mean "suspension hanging" unless otherwise specified.
2. *Judicial-type (drop) hanging*: a several foot drop, with rope attached to the neck. If everything goes right, death is due to a broken neck. While this is quicker than suspension hanging, it may or may not be less traumatic.
3. *Strangulation*: manual compression of the airway and/or blood vessels to/from the brain. In suicide, this generally requires a ligature (rope, wire, cloth, etc.). In homicide, there may be a ligature or there may be direct pressure from hands or forearm on the neck.
4. *Choking*: blockage of the airway by mechanical obstruction, for example, a lump of food.
5. *Suffocation or asphyxiation*: interference with the ability to take in or use oxygen; related to choking, suspension hanging, and strangulation, in that oxygen is prevented from reaching the brain in each case; however, there is no direct pressure on the airway in suffocation or asphyxiation. Examples are, use of a plastic bag or carbon monoxide (see Asphyxia chapter).

DEMOGRAPHICS: WHO AND HOW MANY?

About 4,000 people hang themselves annually in the United States.[1] More than 95 percent of these are suicides. This is similar to the hanging rate in Great Britain, though the overall British suicide rate is about 50 percent lower than in the States.[2]

U.S. NATIONAL STATISTICS

There are roughly 30,000 suicides per year in the United States. The annual average number of suicides by hanging, strangulation, or suffocation between 1979 and 1994 was 4,270. This is about 14.4 percent of official U.S. suicides for those years. Sex, and racial data for U.S. 1994 and 1979 through 1994 are presented below.

Table 23.1 Suicide by Hanging, E953.0   Rate/100,000

	Deaths, 1994	population (millions)	1994	1979-94
Total	4073	260,423,572	1.57	1.62
All male	3555	127,118,264	2.80	2.77
All female	518	133,305,308	0.40	0.47
White male	3005	106,178,839	2.83	2.82
White female	424	110,371,063	0.38	0.48
Black male	340	15,500,047	2.19	2.16
Black female	29	17,189,697	0.16	0.19
Other male	210	5,439,378	3.86	3.62
Other female	65	5,744,548	1.13	1.34

Suicide by Plastic Bag Asphyxia, E953.1   Rate/100,000

	Deaths, 1994		1979-94
Total	422	0.16	0.12
All male	214	0.17	0.12
All female	208	0.16	0.13
White male	206	0.19	0.14
White female	199	0.18	0.14
Black male	4	0.02*	0.02

Suicide by Plastic Bag Asphyxia, E953.1			Rate/100,000
	Deaths, 1994		1979-94
Black female	5	0.03 unrel.*	0.01
Other male	4	0.08 unrel.*	0.05
Other female	4	0.07 unrel.*	0.05

*="unreliable"; E-numbers are International Classification of Disease (ICD) codes. *Source:* Centers for Disease Control.

Interestingly, the average (mean) age for suicidal hangings in the United States. is 34.5 years. In Great Britain it's 50.2 (with a peak between 50 and 59)[3] and in Denmark, 53.[4] The reason for these differences is that older people tend to use more lethal methods for suicide attempts. In the United States, that's guns; in Europe, where civilian guns are much less common, it's hanging. Consistent with this notion are data from New York City, where guns are restricted. The N.Y.C. age distribution for hangings was similar to that in Great Britain and Denmark, with a mean age of around 54 years.[a5]

Since U.S. notional data are not detailed, to find out more about those who hang themselves, we can take a look at some data on age, sex, race, site, and motive on hanging suicides in parts of Seattle (1978 to 1982) and Atlanta (1979 to 1984).

The Seattle region surveyed had about twice the population as that in Atlanta (1.26 million versus 0.62 million). The Seattle suicide rate was 14.0 in 100,000; Atlanta averaged 14.6. (The U.S. national rate was around 13 in 100,000.) Hangings were 9.3 percent of suicides in Seattle and 10.7 percent in Atlanta (14.4 percent in U.S., 1982). The population of the Atlanta area covered was 51 percent black, 49 percent white; 53 percent female, 47 percent male. In Seattle, the population was about 80 percent white, 8.5 percent black, and 11.5 percent other (mostly Asian or Native American).

The Seattle age range was 14 to 89; average (mean) was 41.3 and median (half above, half below) was 37. A note was found associated with 22 of 61 hangings (36 percent), considerably higher than the 10 to 20 percent of suicides in general. The peak at age 60 to 69 was attributed to people with health problems.

The study from Atlanta[6] was a bit more informative in that it compared hangings with other suicides. Age ranged between 12 and 88 years. Average (mean) age was unspecified and median was 31 years, six years less than for all suicide victims. Notes were found in 10 of 56 cases (18 percent), one as a computer screen display.

In Atlanta, black men hanged themselves at twice the rate they used other suicide methods; white women tended to use different means. White men and black women hanged themselves at rates corresponding to their overall suicide frequency.

The reason(s) for these differences are unknown, according to the authors of this study. However, as they also point out, 60 percent (9 of 15) of jail hangings were committed by blacks, and twice the percentage of blacks as whites who hanged themselves did so in in jail (38 percent versus 19 percent). Since (a) the Atlanta jail population is disproportionately black; (b) the suicide rate among prisoners in the United States is several times higher than that of the general population;[b] and (c) about 90 percent of prison suicides are by hanging, this could account for some of the unusual hanging data for black men in Atlanta.[7]

Fifteen of the total of 56 hangings (28 percent) took place in jails.[c] Another 24 (43 percent) hanged themselves at home, 5 (9 percent) in woods, 4 (7 percent) in hotels, 3 (5 percent) in health-care facilities, and 5 (9 percent) elsewhere.

In looking at the "reasons mentioned," we find that the reasons/motives are roughly similar to those cited for other suicides, except for the disproportionate number of "arrest" (jail) hangings.

Alcohol use seems to be less common in hanging than in some other, for example, gunshot or leaping from height, suicides. In one study, only 11 percent showed "legal intoxication."[8] Another report showed 18 percent legally drunk.[9] A third cited alcohol in 34 percent, but included levels well below intoxication.[10]

By contrast, between 25 percent and 40 percent of gunshot suicides have legal intoxication levels above 100 mg alcohol/100 ml blood. Possibly, greater manual dexterity is needed to tie knots than to pull a trigger, or it may be harder to work up the courage to shoot than hang yourself without alcohol— somehow it seems more final. Or, as always, perhaps "none of the above."

How Dangerous Is Hanging Compared to Other Methods of Attempted Suicide?

Tables 16.1 through 16.4 show that hanging is one of the more lethal methods of attempting suicide, with reported fatality rates of 78 to 88 percent. However, since minor injuries tend to be underreported, the actual fatality rates are lower (but not equally for all methods) than the figures cited.

Somewhat more recent (1978 to 1990) data give similar results: Of 306 hangings (92 percent were suicides), 59 percent were found sufficiently dead at the scene that paramedics weren't called; another 19 percent were declared dead at the scene by paramedics; 22 percent were transported alive to hospitals, of whom more than one-third (8 percent of total) died. The overall fatality rate was 86 percent (263 in 306). Almost all the deaths were due to asphyxia, rather than spinal cord or neck injury.[11]

Physiology: What Is Hanging, and How Does It Kill?

Hanging can kill by four distinct mechanisms: compression of the carotid arteries, compression of the jugular veins, compression of the airway (trachea), and breaking the neck. The first three can result from suspension hanging; the last from drop hanging.

Carotid artery. On the right side of your neck, just under the side of the jaw, is your carotid artery. Put your fingers there and gently feel your pulse. It should be quite strong. (If you can't find one, either you're looking in the wrong place or you don't need this book.) The carotid artery carries much of the blood to your brain, which uses around 15 percent of the entire blood supply of your body.[12] Anything which interrupts that blood-flow for more than a few seconds will cause loss of consciousness.

Jugular vein. On the other side of the neck, under the left side of the jaw is the jugular vein, which carries the "used" blood back to the heart. If the jugular is blocked, blood backs up, much like water in a stream that has been dammed. The carotid and jugular can be compressed with just a few pounds pressure; a moderately tightened rope will do nicely. Death occurs within a few minutes. There does not need to be any pressure on the airway (trachea, or windpipe), though there often is.

Trachea/airway. The airway, down the front-center of your neck, can be blocked internally, (by inhaling a foreign object) or externally (by a ligature). When the interference is internal, it is termed "choking." In either case, obstruction of the airway takes a good deal longer to produce unconsciousness than does carotid pressure, and is much more painful. (Details are in the Asphyxia chapter.) Sometimes choking is the cause of accidental death ("cafe coronary") when a piece of food lodges in the airway and can't be dislodged. So learn the Heimlich maneuver, don't make a pig of yourself when eating, and chew your food thoroughly—your mother was right about some things.

"Suffocation" is related to choking, but is an interference with successful breathing, rather than direct blockage of the trachea. Examples include smothering with a pillow or plastic bag and being killed by a boa constrictor. (See the Asphyxia chapter.)

Pressure on the neck is sometimes a method of homicide, typically by the use of two thumbs against the airway and the other fingers grasped round the back of the neck. If the neck constriction is due to the body's weight pulling on a ligature, it is called "hanging"; otherwise it is some form of strangulation. This is of some practical significance, since almost all hangings are suicide, accident, or judicial, while most stranglings are homicide.

HANGING. Judicial (drop) hanging is quite a different kettle of worms from suspension hanging. In a (properly done) judicial-type hanging, the victim falls several feet before coming to an abrupt halt at the end of a rope. Often, this is the bitter end. Such a precipitous change in velocity is supposed to cause a broken neck and quick unconsciousness and death. However, exhumation of judicial hanging victims has shown that a broken neck was frequently not the cause of death.[13] An excessively long drop can result in separation of head from body, and is considered bad form by professional hangmen.[d]

Suspension hanging can cause compression of the carotid, jugular, and/or airway, depending on how it is carried out.

There are similarities between suspension-hanging and choking, as well as the previously mentioned differences. Your blood carries oxygen and nutrients to your brain. Enough pressure on the airway compresses it and prevents oxygen from reaching the lungs. Your body has built-in reflexes to keep this from happening: pressure against your trachea causes quick pain, and you have an irresistible urge to back away and cough; one reflex (pain) gets your attention and moves you away from the stimulus—say, someone's thumbs—and the other reflex (cough) attempts to clear the airway. If these attempts are unsuccessful, blood will continue to be pumped to the brain (and elsewhere) by your heart, but it won't carry enough oxygen and you will lose consciousness in a couple of minutes.

TIME TO DEATH. As asphyxia proceeds, first temporary, then permanent, brain damage from lack of oxygen will occur. Death follows in five to ten minutes (ten to twenty minutes, according to Polson;[14] however, his number seems to be based on the fact that the heart may continue beating for up to twenty minutes after judicial hanging,[15] and ignores that the heart may continue to beat after brain death. While human data are lacking, unanesthetized dogs die after around eight minutes of asphyxia[16]). On the other hand, it's also true that unconsciousness and death will be delayed if blood flow to/from the head is only partially obstructed, as is sometimes the case.

CAROTID REFLEXES. Curiously, you don't have the same protective reflexes along the carotid artery, so that pressure sufficient to block the artery doesn't elicit much in the way of defensive reaction. In fact, one of the reflexes that is present may be counterproductive: Near where the carotids divide are some nerve cells, the "carotid sinus." These nerve cells have the normally useful function of maintaining blood pressure at a steady level. They respond to a decrease in blood pressure (for example, when you stand up) by constricting arteries and telling the heart to beat harder. Without this, you might pass out every time you stood up suddenly, because not enough blood was reaching your brain. (The dizziness many people feel when they stand up suddenly is another way of appreciating how quickly and exquisitely sensitive your brain is to absence of enough blood.) Similarly, the carotid sinus responds to an increase in blood pressure by relaxing the arteries and inhibiting the heart.

So far, so good. The problem arises because these pressure-receptor nerves aren't smart enough to tell the difference between blood pressure and externally applied pressure—for example a forearm or billy club across the right-front side of the neck.[e]

"SLEEPER" HOLD. Those of you who are wrestling (TV variety) fans are probably familiar with the sleeper hold; it is nothing more than a forearm pushed against the carotid artery, compressing it, and cutting off blood flow to the brain (see Asphyxia chapter). This causes unconsciousness in about eight[17] to fifteen[18] seconds.[f]

The sleeper hold is forbidden in tournament wrestling and is faked in the TV stuff. The reason is that the amount of pressure needed to compress the artery is enough to cause the carotid sinus to kick into overdrive and send the heart a priority message to slow down, which is sometimes enough to stop the heart altogether. Despite being quite aware of this, some police departments continue to use this hold to restrain people they arrest, with the altogether predictable result of infrequent, but entirely unnecessary, deaths.[19]

Another hazard with the sleeper hold is that, during a struggle, the constricting forearm can shift from the side to the front of the neck, compressing the airway and becoming a "choke hold." This requires greater pressure than the sleeper hold, with a corresponding increase in injuries to neck structures, for example, fracture of the thyroid cartilage. More dangerously, the lack of oxygen to the heart muscle can trigger fatal cardiac arrest.

In one case, a man's wife

> sought an involuntary psychiatric commitment order because of his withdrawn behavior and refusal to take medication. The order was granted and two police officers were dispatched to his residence to bring him to the hospital. Coaxing by the police officers proved futile. In an attempt to overcome and handcuff him, one police officer stepped behind the victim and grabbed him about the neck. The hold intended by the officer was the carotid sleeper with the neck of the victim in the crook of the arm and forearm of the officer. After a brief but violent struggle during which both the officer and the victim fell to the floor, the victim became lifeless. He did not respond to cardiopulmonary resuscitation. An electrocardiogram taken during resuscitation showed cardiac arrest. Witnesses, including family members, stated that the entire struggle lasted only a short time with the neck hold in place several seconds. . . . An inquest jury ruled that the death was natural because of the victim's previous cardiac history and the brief time during which the neck hold was applied.[20]

PRESSURE NEEDED TO COMPRESS THE CAROTID. How much pressure is needed to compress the carotid? Surprisingly little. To quote the eminent Doctors Polson and Gee,

> By experiment I have confirmed that the carotid artery is appreciably obstructed by a ligature under low tension. Having first established free flow of fluid between the common carotid artery, exposed in the upper chest, and the internal carotid artery, seen inside the skull after removal of the calvarium, I then applied a ligature with a running noose round the neck. Weights were added and injection was repeated, below the level of the ligature. The tests showed that a pull of as little as 7 lb (3.2 kg) was sufficient to reduce free flow through the artery to a mere trickle.[21]

Obviously, this will vary from person to person, and also with the width of the ligature; other published values are as high as 11 pounds (5 kg).[22] Two problems with these calculations are that, in a living person, (a) the carotids are located deeper in the neck than jugular vein and are shielded by a living sterno-mastoid muscle; (b) blood pressure might open the compressed artery on each heartbeat. More on that in a moment.

PRESSURE NEEDED TO COMPRESS THE JUGULAR. Since veins operate at lower pressures than do arteries (if you cut an artery, blood spurts out; blood only flows from a severed vein) one might expect the jugular vein to be more easily compressed than the carotid artery. Experimentally, this is exactly the case, with only around 4.5 pounds (2 kg) pressure needed to block the jugular.

PRESSURE NEEDED TO COMPRESS THE AIRWAY AND OTHER ARTERIES IN THE NECK. About 33 pounds (15 kg) will compress the airway, and 66 pounds (30 kg) the vertebral arteries leading to the face.[23]

What this means, practically speaking, is that someone who wants—or wants to avoid—a lethal result should be aware that full suspension is quite unnecessary. Death will occur after only a few pounds of pressure on a neck ligature; a sitting or semireclining position is sufficient.

SUSPENSION HANGING

Hanging does not have a very good image. For example: "The discovery of a grotesquely hanging corpse whose swollen, sometimes bitten tongue protrudes from a bloated blue-gray face with hideously bulging eyes is a nightmarish sight upon which only the most hardened can gaze without revulsion."[24] However, while some look livid, about 60 percent of hangers have a "pale and placid" face.[25] Some have small hemorrhages, caused by capillaries leaking (due to high blood pressure in the absence of oxygen), on the face, eyelids, and/or scalp; others don't.

What accounts for these differences? Basically, it's a question of how quickly and totally the ligature cuts off blood circulation to and from the head. If suspension is fast and complete, the blood supply both to and from the head will be cut off simultaneously, so there is no excess blood or blood pressure in the head, and thus a more or less normal-colored corpse. Similarly, activation of the carotid sinus pressure receptor would cause a decrease in blood flow to the head, leading to paleness in the cadaver.

If, on the other hand, the pressure on the neck gradually increased as consciousness was lost, it's probable that the jugular vein was shut off before the carotid artery (and almost certainly before the hard-to-clamp vertebral arteries), since it requires less pressure to do so. Thus, in this case blood would continue flowing into the head while having no way to leave it; hence engorgement and blue/purple color. This is most likely when the suicide is in a sitting or lying position, because there is less (and less sudden) pressure on the neck than when he is completely suspended.

PLACEMENT OF THE LIGATURE. An additional variable is the placement of the ligature. The least pressure corresponds to the location of the knot in the rope, since that point is pulled up and away from the neck. Depending on the knot's site, it is thus possible to miss the jugular (if the knot's on the left), carotid (knot on right), or trachea (knot along the centerline of the face).

Further complications arise because the noose can be placed high or low on the neck, with potentially different intermediate results. When high, it is less likely to compress the airway because some of the pressure from the ligature may be transferred to the jaw or skull.

DO PEOPLE DIE FROM AIRWAY BLOCKAGE OR FROM CUT-OFF BLOOD CIRCULATION TO THE BRAIN? Bodies with little weight on the ligature, that is, which are prone or seated, have a greater chance of death from asphyxia, according to a standard forensic text. Since the jugular vein (blood out) is easier to compress than the carotid artery (blood in), enough blood accumulates in the head and neck to compress the airway, leading to asphyxia.[g26]

Medical experts disagree about the frequency and importance of airway blockage in hangings. For example, one says, "Occlusion of the air passage by constriction on the neck is probably extremely rare if existing at all."[27] Others hedge their bets: "Suicidal hanging is earmarked characteristically as causing death by compression of the anatomic airway and the blood vessels in the neck."[28] Or cover all the bases: "Reports in the forensic literature have stated that death may be due to either asphyxiation, coma, carotid artery or jugular vein injury, or any combination of the above."[29] Certainly, airway blockage is not essential to successful hanging. In one case a woman with a tracheotomy[h] killed herself despite attaching the ligature *above* the site of the breathing hole. She would have continued breathing until dying from lack of blood to her brain.

Airway blockage is more likely when:

- the ligature knot is toward the back of the neck. In this situation the maximum pressure from the rope is then on the front of the neck, where the airway is.
- the person is seated, semireclining, or prone. Due to little weight on it, the rope tends not to slide up the neck. Were it to move up, it would end up being partially supported by the chin, relieving pressure on the airway.
- the ligature is thin or attached with a running noose. Such a ligature tends to clamp in place.
- the ligature is placed low on the neck, where it tends not to slide up high enough to be supported by the chin.

WAS IT SUICIDE, HOMICIDE, OR ACCIDENT?

A farmer who, living at a distance from his cattle herd, came to tend the herd alone, [found] the submersible pump in the well which supplied them with water to be broken. He used a piece of angle iron as a bridge across the well head, and a peculiarly flimsy and inadequate piece of rope to lower himself into the well to retrieve the pump: the rope broke and he was drowned—or at least this was the story received by telephone from the local coroner. When the body was received for autopsy the first finding was a ligature mark around the neck; I telephoned the coroner to point out with some acerbity that this was an obvious suicide. "But Doc," the coroner replied, "that was the only way we could pull him out of the well!"[30]

There are four possible definite verdicts in a hanging death: homicide, accident, judicial, or suicide.

HOMICIDE

Homicidal hanging is very rare because there are many easier ways to commit murder. Simulating suicidal hanging is generally done to disguise a murder, often an impulsive one. It is also unusual, mostly because it is difficult to pull off without leaving signs of drugging, struggle or improbable injury.

For example, in a notorious case from Great Britain, Sergeant Emmett-Dunne killed a fellow soldier, Sergeant Watters, by a karate-chop to the throat and then suspended the body from a staircase to make it look like a suicidal hanging.

Autopsy showed an unusual fracture of the cartilage around the thyroid gland and vertical tears in the carotid artery that are typical of drop-type (but not suspension) hangings where there is sudden force applied to the neck. Despite this, a verdict of suicide was rendered by an inexperienced army pathologist due to lack of any other suspicious circumstances.

Nevertheless, military gossip persisted about a relationship between Emmett-Dunne and Watters's widow, which was reinforced when, six months later, they married. It was not until a year later that the military police reopened the investigation (as well as the body). Photographs of the original scene showed that blood had pooled both above and below the ligature, in the head, neck, and upper chest regions, which is inconsistent with hanging. There were no tiny hemorrhages, which are often found in cases of asphyxiation.

Under questioning, Emmett-Dunne's half brother (Emmett) came undone and confessed to helping Emmett-Dunne suspend the body. Further circumstantial evidence was discovered, and Emmett-Dunne was convicted of murder and sentenced to life imprisonment.

He was saved from hanging because of jurisdictional quirks: He was a citizen of the Irish Republic serving in the British army. The crime had taken place in Germany. The question arose as to where, and under what laws, he should stand trial. Eventually it was decided that there was no authority to send him to England; he was tried, convicted, and sentenced to death by British military court in Dusseldorf in June 1955. However, there was no death penalty in the Federal Republic of Germany (though there was in England at that time), nor, by treaty, could military executions be carried out in German territory. The sentence was commuted to life in prison; he was, however, released after seven years, when passions had cooled.[31]

ACCIDENT

How often are hanging deaths due to accident? Combining four studies of hanging[32], we find that 96 percent (range 94 to 98 percent) were suicidal, and 4 percent (range 2 to 6 percent) accidental.

Of the nineteen accidental deaths, five involved children. For the most part, they were toddlers snagged by crib slats and/or their own clothing. The remaining fourteen were all males who had gotten wrapped up in autoerotic asphyxiation. To quote from an unusual review of hanging:

> Add sexual perversion to the woes of mankind. When men or women try to improve on nature's biological methods, they not only become frustrated, but worse, act unnaturally, and usually to their own detriment. Any sexual behavior that strays from the confines of normal physiological compatibility is considered to be a perversion. . . . One may add to the list another deviation, described by the Marquis de Sade: self-induced asphyxia as a means of ejaculatory gratification in the form of masturbation. . . . When propelled by concupiscence, the unfortunate person with autoerotic propensities does not suspect that death lurks nearby.[33]

It seems that increased sexual gratification can be had by partial interruption of oxygen to the brain. There may also be elements of masochism here. Whatever the motivation, the trick is to make sure the interruption is, and remains, partial. The problem is that unconsciousness can occur without warning; if it does, and if the ligature doesn't slip off or loosen, death follows.

These are accidental deaths. The victims are alleged to share some psychological traits with suicides: depression, death fixation, and isolation.[34] However, the circumstances and details of the hangings are usually quite different; in autoerotic hanging:

- there are often signs of masturbation;
- women's clothing, either worn by the victim or found near him, is common;
- erotic literature is frequently found at the site;
- there is often a history of successful partial hangings, evidenced by a diary, a collection of ligatures, or wear marks from the rope on the rafter, door, or other attachment point;
- typically, the neck is protected by padding;
- feet are usually on the floor and/or there is furniture nearby for support;
- there are sometimes mirrors or cameras for viewing the (often bound) genitalia;
- generally, there is no history of suicidal attempts;
- the victims are almost always (more than 99 percent) male, for reasons unknown.[i]

These people die because they lose consciousness quickly and unexpectedly.[35]

Some of the case reports are truly bizarre.[36]

Interestingly, asphyxia as a means of sexual arousal is a centuries-old practice documented by anthropologists.[37] For example, Eskimos (Inuit) apparently choke one another as part of their normal sexual repertoire, and Eskimo children suspend themselves by the neck in play.

The state of unconsciousness is so important and so familiar to the Eskimos that even the children play at it. It is a favorite pastime of theirs to hang themselves by their hoods. When these tighten about their necks, the blood is kept from their heads, and in time they lose consciousness. The other children in the house take them down when their faces turn purple. But they say that the state of unconsciousness is so delightful that they play this game over and over again.[38]

LEGAL CONSEQUENCES. The distinction between suicidal and accidental hanging (or other means of death) has legal, as well as emotional, ramifications. Most life (that is, death) insurance policies, understandably enough, have limitation or total exclusion of payments for suicidal death, at least for the first two years.

Some pay extra in case of accidental death, for no obvious reason.[j] Is autoerotic hanging an accident or suicide? We must go back to the definition of "accident." To quote an attorney:

The legal definition of accident has not always been the same. Variations have been stated legally in different court decisions. Among these are that an accident is:

1. Any event that take place without the foresight or expectation of the person acted upon or affected thereby;
2. A happening or coming by chance or without design; casual, fortuitous, taking place unexpectedly, unintentionally, or out of the usual course of events; and,
3. Something unforseen, unexpected, or extraordinary.

The word, accident, is derived from the Latin verb, *accidere*, signifying "fall upon," "befall," "happen," "chance," or "unexpected." In a etymological appraisal, anything that happens can be interpreted as an accident. In its more formal accepted meaning, accident is defined as a fortuitous circumstance, event, or happening. It is an event happening wholly or partly through human agency, an event which, under the circumstances, is unusual and unexpected by the

person to whom it happens. An accident is an untoward occurrence in the usual course of events. It may be without known or
assignable cause. In its proper use, the term excludes negligence.[39]

After all this, it should be no surprise to learn that insurance companies differ as to whether autoerotic hanging qualifies as an "accident," and will examine such a death very closely. So, if you go in for that sort of thing, read
your life insurance policy carefully.

Should you be in the military, "If the injury or death was incurred as a result of erratic or reckless conduct or other deliberate course of conduct without regard for personal safety,[k] or the safety of others, it was incurred not in
the line of duty, but was due to misconduct" then the deceased can expect to
be court-martialed for destruction of government property.

JUDICIAL HANGING

My father could dispatch a man in the time it took the prison
clock to strike eight—leading him from his cell on the first stroke
and having him suspended dead on the rope by the last stroke.
That seemed a very worthy intermediate ambition for me.[40]

One hesitates to ask what his ultimate ambition was. Albert Pierrepoint followed in his father's footsteps and became one of the small number of "qual-
ified executioners" in Great Britain.

The art of hanging was taught both by apprenticeship and by schooling at
some British prisons. There was widespread need for this skill, since as late
as 1832, 220 separate crimes, including poaching and picking pockets, were
punishable by death. Hangings were public cautionary spectacles and were
covered by the newspapers. There are accounts of executioners—sometimes
family and friends—pulling on the legs of young boys who were not heavy
enough to be successfully hanged in order to add sufficient weight to strangle them.

The theory of deterrence by example was in vogue. It was satirized by a
contemporary painting of a public hanging in which a pickpocket was working the crowd.[41] As a result of critical newspaper reports of botched hang-

ings, the Home Office prepared a standard table of drops in 1888. The formula was basically:

$$\frac{1260}{\text{weight of prisoner in pounds}} = \text{length of the drop in feet}$$

For example, the calculated drop for a 154 pound person would be 8.2 feet, a bit less than the 9 feet in the drop table shown below.

Another source[42] provides similar data:

Hanging Drop Heights

Culprit's Weight	Drop
14 stone (196 lbs)	8ft 0in
13.5 stone (189 lbs)	8ft 2in
13 stone (182 lbs)	8ft 4in
12.5 stone (175 lbs)	8ft 6in
12 stone (168 lbs)	8ft 8in
11.5 stone (161 lbs)	8ft 10in
11 stone (154 lbs)	9ft 0in
10.5 stone (147 lbs)	9ft 2in
10 stone (140 lbs)	9ft 4in
9.5 stone (133 lbs)	9ft 6in
9 stone (126 lbs)	9ft 8in
8.5 stone (119 lbs)	9ft 10in
8 stone (112 lbs)	10ft 0in

These numbers apply to people of average build with no unusual physical characteristics. The author (James "Hangman" Barry) noted that when executing "persons who had attempted suicide by cutting their throats . . . to prevent reopening the wounds I have reduced the drop by nearly half." This would probably not cause a broken neck, however, and the victim of Mr. Barry's aesthetic sensitivities would then be left to strangle, very unpleasantly, over several minutes.

Pierrepoint notes, "A master executioner is responsible for every detail of his craft. He has to come to his own decision on the length of the drop based on the Home Office table, varied by his own experience, and adjusted to the weight of the prisoner, his height, his age, and an estimate of the musculature and tensile strength of his neck."

In order to carry out a perfect hanging, the noose must, of course, be properly applied:

> Draw it firm and tight with the free end of the rope emerging from the metal eye just under the jawbone. There is no knot. That fancy cowboy coil of a "hangman's noose (knot)" is something we abandoned to the Americans a hundred years ago. In Britain, the rope runs free through a pear-shaped metal eye woven into the rope's end, and the operative part of the noose is covered with soft wash-leather. Always adjust it to the left, because with the pull of the drop the noose gyrates a quarter-circle clockwise and the tug of the rope finishes under the chin. This motion throws the neck back and breaks the spinal column, separating it at about the third vertebra of the neck. Adjust it on the right and it gyrates to the back of the neck, throwing the head forward, not breaking the neck, eventually killing by suffocation.

At this point I should mention that one had best not use mountain-climbing rope for a drop hanging, since it is designed to stretch in case of a fall. Thick manila rope is a much better choice.

It is commonly believed that a black bag is placed over the condemned's head just before execution. Alas, contrary to all the movies, the bag is white.

Actually, there's a bit more to say about it. The bag

> has been used in British executions from the later days of batch-strangulation[l] in public, long before the introduction of the long drop designed to sever the cervical vertebrae and cause spontaneous death. Its original purpose was to mask the contortions of slow strangulation, which were considered too horrible even for the ghoulish British public to witness, although the logic that public executions were a public deterrent against crime might have been followed strictly by exposing the ultimate horror in order to achieve the maximum deterrence.[43]

The number of capital crimes was reduced to fifteen in 1837, and, "In 1861, the death penalty was reduced to the offences of murder, treason, piracy with violence, and arson in the Sovereign's vessels, arsenals, or dockyards." Further restrictions ended judicial executions in 1964.

More recent events, especially those related to Northern Ireland, have led the British public to favor the reintroduction of the death penalty for terrorism and other violent crimes. Interestingly, this was rejected by the House of Commons despite the largest Conservative majority in modern parliamentary history and the support of then-Prime Minister Margaret Thatcher (who, it should be noted, freed members of her party from party discipline—she wasn't known as "The Iron Maiden" for nothing—to vote their consciences). The result was due to an unusual alliance between those opposed on humanitarian grounds and those who wished to avoid producing martyrs for the IRA.[44]

Pierrepoint looked back on his career with very mixed emotions:

> I believed with all my heart that I was carrying out a public duty. I conducted each execution [about four hundred] with great care and a clear conscience. I never allowed myself to get involved with the death penalty controversy. I now sincerely hope that no man is ever called upon to carry out another execution in my country. I have come to the conclusion that executions solve nothing and are only an antiquated relic of a primitive desire for revenge which takes the easy way and hands over the responsibility for revenge to other people. It is said to be a deterrent. I cannot agree. There have been murders since the beginning of time and we shall go on looking for deterrents until the end of time. If death were a deterrent, I might be expected to know. All the men and women whom I have faced at the final moment convince me that in what I have done I have not prevented a single murder.

SUICIDAL HANGING

Since more than 95 percent of nonjudicial hangings are suicides, there is sometimes a predisposition on the part of investigators to see hangings through suicide-colored glasses. This can lead to overlooking or misinterpreting evidence. The previously mentioned case of Emmett-Dunne is cautionary.

Most suicidal people are not very picky, and use whatever is handy. Household clothesline remains a big favorite.[45] On the other hand, use of electric cords sometimes takes up the slack. Articles of clothing are also perennially popular. People have used belts, suspenders, shoelaces, scarves, handkerchiefs, neckties, shirtsleeves, pantlegs, and undershirts, among other things.

As previously noted, death occurs after five to ten minutes of complete brain anoxia. A broad ligature, such as a pant leg, may not produce enough pressure to fully cut off blood flow to the brain, let alone air through the trachea, and thus may take much longer to be fatal.

Though a forensic medicine text warns, "Unusual ligatures arouse suspicion [of foul play],"[46] it is not clear why that should be so, given the tendency to use whatever is available at the moment. Indeed, the same authors cite a case of a man who hung himself using some of the roots of a pine tree as the ligature, looped over a low branch of the same tree.

Two studies, one of sixty-one consecutive hanging deaths in Seattle[47] and the other of 106 hangings in New York City[48] show the range of materials used:

Table 23.2 Ligatures Used in Suicidal Hangings

Material	Luke, 1985 Seattle n =61 Number	Luke, 1967 New York City n=106 Number
Rope or clothesline	32 (52%)	49 (46%)
Leather belt	8 (13%)	15 (14%)
Soft belt or necktie	7 (11%)	7 (7%)
Length of sheet or other cloth	6 (10%)	7 (7%)
Electric cord		8 (8%)
String or twine		5 (5%)

Material	Luke, 1985 Seattle n =61 Number	Luke, 1967 New York City n=106 Number
Not specified by coroner		8 (8%)
Other (dog leash, venetian blind cord, clothing, etc.)	8 (13%)	7 (7%)
Width		
One inch or less	46 (75%)	
More than one inch	7 (11%)	
[Not reported]	8 (13%)	
Number of wraps around neck		
One	52 (85%)	
Two	6 (10%)	
Three or more	3 (5%)	

If the suspension point is inconveniently high, ligature material, similar or dissimilar, may be tied together. For example, bed sheets may be torn into strips and connected by knots.

Usually a single simple loop is used, but multiple loops are not grounds for suspicion; quite the contrary, for the presence of more than one loop is unusual in murder, taking longer to apply and being harder to tighten.

TYPE OF KNOT. Most common are the running noose (loop at one end, through which the other end is pulled) and the fixed noose with a granny or reef knot. Multiple knots are uncommon: "A ligature which is knotted firmly at the first turn and then knotted again after a second turn is unlikely to have been applied by a suicide; it is possible but rare."[49]

POSITION OF THE KNOT. The location of the knot is just about evenly distributed between left side, right side, and back of the neck; rarely is it in front. Some data on this are shown in Table 23.3.

Table 23.3 Location of Knot in Suicidal Hangings[50]

Left side of neck	20 (33 percent)
Right side of neck	17 (28 percent)
Back of the neck	17 (28 percent)
Front of the neck	3 (5 percent)

In one case, a fifty-seven-year-old man hanged himself with a rope whose knot was in the front of the face at eyebrow level. All of the pressure was thus on the back, and to a somewhat lesser extent, sides of the neck. The exact cause of death was not clear: There was no sign of asphyxia, which is understandable since the airway was not obstructed, but pressure on the carotid arteries probably cut off the blood supply to the brain; or pressure on the carotid pressure receptors might have caused the heart to stop.

The position of the ligature around the neck provides some distinction between hanging and strangulation, and thus clues to distinguish suicide (mostly hanging, rarely strangulation) from murder (almost always strangulation). In most suicides, the victim's weight causes the ligature to slide up to the top of the neck, under the jaw. Exceptions can usually be accounted for if:

1. The position of the body doesn't put much weight on the ligature. This can occur if the body is partially supported by, say, a chair. Similarly, if the victim was in a reclining position, there is little tendency for the ligature to move toward the top of the neck.
2. The victim has a particularly large thyroid cartilage (Adam's apple), which will limit the upward movement of a ligature.
3. A quickly tightening running noose, or a thin ligature, may clamp down pretty much where it was originally placed.

In two studies of 279 suicidal hangings, the ligature was above the thyroid cartilage in 215 (77 percent), at the level of the thyroid cartilage in 43 (15 percent), and below in 19 (7 percent).[51]

Suicidal hanging typically causes a caret- (inverted V) shaped ligature mark. The tip of the caret is at the site of the knot, since the weight of the body normally causes the knot to be the highest point of a loop around the neck. This will not be seen if the body was at a reclining angle, and the ligature mark will make the death look like a strangulation. A running noose can also produce a horizontal mark, because it tightens quickly. If a soft, wide ligature is used, for example, a T-shirt, and the victim is cut down soon after death, there may be no visible external marks at all.

Legal consequences can hinge on the ligature marks. In one case a man walked into the house and found his wife had hanged herself. To avoid the social stigma of suicide, he cut her down and hid the cord, before calling the police and telling them that he had found her collapsed on the floor. Had the rope marks on her neck not been clearly suicidal, he might well have been charged with murder.

The ligature does not have to go entirely around the neck, as long as it compresses either the sides (blocks blood circulation to the brain) or the front (blocks airway) of the neck. In fact, there does not need to be a flexible ligature at all: People have died from resting their necks on stair tread edges, car steering wheels, and sofa or chair arms.

In one case a sixty-year-old man was found dead in a kneeling position with the bottom of his chin balanced on the arm of a chair. The compression mark on his neck matched the chair arm, and extended to the carotid arteries. There was no bruising of neck muscle or injury to neck cartilage or bones. There was no evidence of alcohol or other drugs, nor of injury or debilitating illness. He had a history of severe coughing, and death was attributed to an attack of violent coughing or choking that had caused him to crouch down and then be unable to rise.[52]

POINT OF SUSPENSION. As with their indiscriminate choice of ligatures, suicidal people suspend themselves from whatever site is handy. Stair rails are popular, as is tying one end of the ligature to a doorknob and tossing the other end over the top of the door. Hooks and nails are useable, but may bend or pull out if not sturdy and firmly attached. Often a chair that the victim stood on is nearby, but total suspension is quite unnecessary; a majority of such suicides have their feet touching the ground.[53]

It's not generally appreciated that even low suspension points are sufficient; a table leg, doorknob, or bedpost have all been used. In one case a seventy-seven-year-old woman hanged herself from the leg of a table, with the rope tied only 17 inches off the floor. She was found lying facedown.[54] In another case, of a completely suspended woman, the seeming absence of a platform caused the police to suspect her husband. Luckily, the victim's footprints were found on top of a sewing machine near the body.[55]

POSITION OF THE BODY. In one study, 37 percent (30 in 80) of hanging victims were completely suspended; 63 percent (50 in 80) were in contact with the ground[56] This is credible, since all it takes to carry out a standing hang is to bend the knees enough to tighten the ligature. In 261 cases of incomplete suspension, 64 percent (168) had both feet touching the ground, 16 percent (42) were on their knees, 11 percent (29) were lying down, 7 percent (19) were sitting, and 1 percent (3) were huddled or squatting.[57]

SUICIDE PACTS AND HANGING. While suicide pacts are not uncommon, dual hangings are rare. In one case, two men were found dead in their hotel room, one on either side of the closet door. The bedsheet had been tossed over the door and opposite corners tied to their necks. Each had been on a chair and had stepped off simultaneously.[58] In another instance a woman and a man, despondent lovers, tied a rope to a branch of the tree under which they were sitting. They attached the free ends to their necks and leaned back.[59] Acts like these require planning, coordination, and trust.

SUICIDE BY HANGING COMBINED WITH OTHER METHODS. There exist several reports where a person attempted to commit suicide by one method, became impatient, and finished the job by hanging. In one instance a man drank ammonia (not recommended) and then hung himself. Presumably the ammonia was too slow or too painful.[60]

In another case, a fifty-three-year-old woman was found hanged in a loft. There was considerable blood, widely scattered, from a depressed skull fracture and other scalp wounds. She had apparently first cut herself with a knife, which was found in her pocket, followed by a blow to the head from the butt of a hatchet. Bleeding profusely (scalp wounds tend to be messy), she found a rope, formed a running noose, and hanged herself.[61]

Finally, there was a forty-eight-year-old man who slit his left wrist and throat. The wrist injury was deep but the throat cuts were too shallow to be fatal. He followed this by two gunshots, one through his left palm and the other to the right temple. This latter bullet did not penetrate the skull. Understandably frustrated, he then hung himself from the stairs.[62]

STRANGULATION

Strangulation is defined as pressure applied to the neck without suspension of the victim. It is uncommon in suicide, but not unknown. Nevertheless, most strangulations are homicide, and will be treated as such by medical examiners and police, in the absence of clear evidence to the contrary. Strangulation was used as a method of execution in some countries, for example, Turkey and Spain. In Spain, the sitting victim was tied to a post. A metal collar was placed around the neck and the post, and then tightened. In one version, a metal spike stuck out of the post and was forced into the base of the prisoner's neck by the pressure of the tightened collar.

The physiology of strangulation is essentially the same as that of suspension hanging and needs not be treated separately. In self-strangulation, the ligature is applied more slowly and less tightly than in suspension hanging. As a result, the jugular veins are more constricted than are the carotid arteries, leading to a blue, swollen head. Neck injuries, however, are rare. Because the ligature cannot slide up the neck or be supported by the chin, compression of the airway is more likely than in suspension hanging.

In suicidal strangulation, people generally use the materials at hand. Women tend to use stockings or scarves; men most often use cord. In one case a man strangled himself with two bowties.[63] In another instance, a man wrapped thirty-five turns of twine around his neck, tied a knot, and attached the free end to his right thumb in order to increase pressure. His blood alcohol level was 0.26 percent.[64]

Two or more turns tied with a half-knot or half-hitch (double knots are more characteristic of murder) is strong evidence of suicide, but there are exceptions. The murdered forty-two-year-old woman described in the Asphyxia chapter was such a case.

More typical of self strangulation were two women who killed themselves with stockings. In one case, a seventy-three-year old woman, depressed and about to be committed to a mental hospital, wrapped a stocking twice about her neck. There was a half-knot at each turn. Because the ligature was only tight enough to compress the jugular vein (blood out) but not the carotid artery (blood in), her face was purple and congested. In the other example, a similar stocking was pulled more tightly and the face was not engorged or cyanotic.

It's possible for a person to strangle him/herself with one arm: A woman with incapacitating burns on her right hand rolled a shawl and scarf into a ligature, wrapped it two-and-a-half times around her neck and tied two knots.[65]

Another method is use of a tourniquet. A single loop of rope is loosely tied around the neck with a good knot, for example, a square or reef knot. A rod is put between the ligature and the neck and is then twisted until the desired degree of tightness is achieved. The rod tends to unwind a bit when the suicide becomes unconscious, but usually snags on the side of the jaw, maintaining enough tension to cause death. (See Asphyxia chapter for details.)

Consequences: What Are the Effects of Hanging?

There is not much information from survivors for two reasons: (1) There are not many survivors, and (2) often, survivors have more or less complete amnesia. In one case, a woman tried to hang herself from the foot of her bed, while in jail. She was saved by a fellow prisoner. She later mentioned having had severe pain, followed by unconsciousness.[66]

In another instance a public entertainer, who hung himself briefly as part of his act, made a mistake of timing. He said (afterwards) that he could not breathe—quite understandable, under the circumstances—and felt as if a heavy weight was on his feet. He lost consciousness before he could move his hands to release himself.[67]

There is additional information from experimental hanging. In one description, the subject mentioned flashes of heat and light, and deafening sound. Legs were numb and weak. Pain was not severe and unconsciousness was sudden.[68]

More detailed information came from another self-experimenter named Minovici. With 5 kg (11 lbs) pull on the ligature, loss of consciousness was rapid. When he leaned on the rope (incomplete suspension), within five or six seconds his eyes blurred, he heard whistling, and his face turned red-violet. With the knot on the side instead of the back of the neck, these effects took eight or nine seconds to appear.

When he tried complete suspension, as soon as he left the ground, he couldn't breathe or hear his assistant. He experienced such severe pain that he immediately stopped the test. Within ten minutes, many small hemorrhages could be seen near the site of the rope; these remained visible for eight to eleven days. For ten to twelve days later he had watering eyes, trouble swallowing, and a sore throat.[69]

After unconsciousness, convulsions follow. In thrashing around, the victim may make enough noise to attract attention, wanted or unwanted. For instance,

> A man aged twenty made a noose with a silk stocking and hung it on a hook behind the door of his room. He climbed on to a chair, put his head through the noose and stepped off "to see if his feet would touch the floor." He found his feet were a few inches short. The slip knot tightened and he was unable to release the pressure on his throat. During his struggles he kicked a chair over and, when his mother heard the noise, she went to discover the cause. The man was then unconscious but she had the presence of mind immediately to cut the stocking. After a brief stay in hospital he was able to return home.[70]

EXTERNAL APPEARANCES. The face color can range from pale to cyanotic blue, depending on whether or not much blood was trapped in the head region. If the ligature put only enough pressure on the neck to close the jugular vein but not the carotid artery, a swollen, blue, blood-congested face is the result.

The tongue may be swollen for similar reasons. In fourteen of forty (35 percent) cases, the tongue protruded from the mouth.[71]

The small hemorrhages previously mentioned occur in about 10 percent of cases, generally the same ones that have blood-engorged faces.

Interestingly, the faces of many (twenty-one of forty) hanging victims were described as placid, in contradistinction to those strangled, choked, or smothered.[72] And, curiously, sometimes the right eye stays open and has a large (dilated) pupil while the left eye is closed and pupil constricted.[73] The reason for this is not understood.

CONSEQUENCES: WHAT HAPPENS TO HANGING SURVIVORS?

DROP (JUDICIAL-TYPE) HANGING. There are no survivors of a properly done drop hanging; the broken neck (similar to some car-crash neck injuries) is invariably fatal. Even when the neck is not broken, injury is severe and debilitating.

SUSPENSION HANGING. Since only around 1 percent of suicidal hangings are of the drop type,[74] there are correspondingly few spinal cord injuries. In suspension hangings, damage to neck structures occurs about one-third to one-half of the time, but is not normally life-threatening.

Both death and permanent injury are due to cutting the oxygen supply to the brain. The severity of brain damage depends on how completely and how long the brain is oxygen-starved. Mild hypoxia (not enough oxygen) causes behavior resembling drunkenness: physical and verbal incoordination, but no permanent harm.

With complete anoxia (no oxygen taken in, but heart and blood circulation uninterrupted), unconsciousness occurs after about two minutes and coma in about five. If blood circulation to the brain is totally stopped, loss of consciousness follows in eight to fifteen seconds.[75] Recovery may take minutes to days, and may not be total. After about four to five minutes of anoxia, permanent brain damage becomes increasingly likely.[76] Five of thirty-nine people rescued from near-hanging had such persistent injury.[77]

On the positive side, there are rare, but well-documented, cases of spontaneous remission of depression after near-hanging.[78]

DROP HANGING. Drop hanging may not be instantly fatal and, "the possibility of briefly retained consciousness in some cases appears quite real."[79] You might be wondering how this was determined. In a study of thirty-four skeletons of people who had been judicially hanged between 1882 and 1945, a substantial number did *not* have a broken neck. Interestingly, the average drop for this group was 83 inches; for those whose neck was broken the average drop had been only 74 inches[80] Thus, "the length of the drop, though important, does not produce expected or consistent results."[81]

In the event of miscalculation leading to an inadequate fall, the victim will undoubtedly suffer some more or less severe neck injury, but will die within five to ten minutes of asphyxiation, carotid/jugular compression, or tears of the vertebral arteries (leading to massive hemorrhage).

SUSPENSION HANGING. In addition to brain damage, there may be heart and/or lung injury. For example, there is a syndrome found, among other cases, in hanging survivors; it's called adult respiratory distress syndrome (ARDS) and is characterized by progressive respiratory failure that is hard to treat and is not helped much by supplementary oxygen administration. The cause is not well understood: It may be due to brain injury from lack of oxygen; an alternative explanation is that fluid fills the lungs (edema) because of the high negative pressure in the lungs due to trying to inhale against a blocked airway; other possible mechanisms have been proposed.[82] In any case, various types of lung damage are the most frequent cause of delayed death in near-hangings.[83]

Some case reports may be useful.

1. A thirty-three-year-old man was jailed for shoplifting. He tried to hang himself with his shirt and was cut down after an undetermined time. Examination two hours later showed deep coma, which did not change over twelve hours. Gradual improvement occurred over the next two days, and he became awake and alert; however an EEG (electroencephalogram) after five days showed residual brain injury. On the seventh day, lung damage appeared; potentially fatal infection followed quickly. Two weeks of intensive care saved his life. A month after the initial admission he was committed to a state mental hospital.[84]

2. A twenty-nine-year-old man was jailed for assault on his ex-wife and a police officer. Later that night he hung himself with a T-shirt "for several minutes" before being cut down. He was also in a deep coma and unresponsive to deep pain. On the second day he began to improve, but his speech was, and remained, halting and often incoherent. After twelve days he was committed to a state mental hospital.[85]

3. A fourteen-year-old boy was found hanging from bleachers by (means of) a jacket he had wrapped around his neck. He was released after being suspended for an estimated five to ten minutes. He opened his eyes sponta-

neously, but had no verbal or motor response to painful stimuli. In the hospital his coma score improved (he reacted to pain), but lung damage quickly appeared. After four days he was transferred to another hospital, but his neurological improvement at that time was limited to opening his eyes when told to.[86]

4. Finally, there is a fascinating case in England from 1650.[87] Anne Green was a twenty-two-year-old maid in the house of Sir Thomas Read. She became pregnant by Sir Thomas's grandson, Geoffrey, and gave birth to a stillborn boy. She hid the baby's body, was discovered, convicted of murder, and hanged. She was suspended for half an hour during which time some of her friends were "hanging with all their weight upon her legs, sometimes lifting her up, then pulling her down again with a sudden jerk, thereby the sooner to dispatch her out of her pain," until forced to stop by the undersheriff who was worried about the rope breaking. When she was considered dead the body was removed, put into a coffin, and taken to a nearby house.

When the coffin was opened, she was seen to take a breath. The physicians, intending a dissection, tried to revive her instead. Because of (and despite some of) their efforts, she recovered fully, except for amnesia about some of the events of the hanging. She was subsequently pardoned, in an attempt to cooperate with what was taken to be divine intervention. She eventually went back to the country, taking along her coffin as a souvenir. She married, had three children, and lived another fifteen years.

PRACTICAL MATTERS: HOW TO DO IT

If you intend to hang yourself, the next major decision is whether to do a drop (judicial-type) or suspension job. Each has some advantages and disadvantages.

HANGING

SUSPENSION: (1) Can be done with a wide range of ligature materials—most anything will work; (2) can be carried out by invalids, without leaving their room; (3) is fairly quick, probably not painless (but unconsciousness is rapid), but may have severe consequences—brain damage—if interrupted; (4) doesn't require much knowledge to accomplish.

To carry out a suspension hanging, you can simply tie one end of the ligature to a fixed point (doorknob, hook, rafter, etc.) and the other end to your neck. You can and should protect the airway from unnecessary compression and pain by firmly padding the front quarter of the neck and (more important) by placing the knot high and at the front of your face.

Complete suspension is unnecessary and is generally more painful than partial suspension; however, standing on and kicking away a chair is sometimes done in the same spirit as diving, rather than wading, into icy water. Unconsciousness occurs quickly and without enough warning to count on time to change your mind: *This is a lethal method and is not suitable for a "suicidal gesture."*

You need an uninterrupted twenty minutes (half an hour to take into account last-minute vicissitudes) to be sure that you won't be cut down and "saved" with permanent brain damage. Since you may thrash around while unconscious, take into account the possibility of attracting unwanted intervention because of the noise. Because the cadaver is sometimes gruesome and always shocking, consider not hanging yourself where loved ones will find the body. If you use a hotel or motel, leave a good tip for the cleaning person.

DROP: (1) Requires a strong, low-stretch rope. Manila (sisal) or hemp works (2) requires a 5 to 15 foot drop (see drop table or calculations); (3) is quick, possibly painless—nobody knows, and none of the questionnaires have been returned—and generally cannot be interrupted once set into motion; (4) requires detailed knowledge of how and where to attach rope, how and how far to jump (down, but not out), and a place to jump from. To execute a drop hanging, the drop distance can be estimated as follows,

$$\text{drop in feet} = \frac{1260}{\text{your weight in pounds}}$$

The type of knot is not important as long as it doesn't loosen. However, its position is, unlike in suspension hanging, critical. The knot should be as near the chin as convenient, and in any case no further back than the cheekbone. Note which way the knot rotates when pulled up, and adjust it to the side of your head so that it will rotate toward the chin and snap the head backwards. If it ends up behind the ear, it will be much less likely to produce a cleanly broken neck, and may leave you to strangle unpleasantly.

The drop should be as close to straight down as possible; don't take a running jump.

The rope should be at least an inch thick and must not be one intended to stretch in order to ease a fall, for example, mountain-climbing rope. Attach the other end to something that won't break or come loose.

This method is harder to get the hang of than is suspension, and is not recommended unless you're confident that you fully understand it. Mistakes usually transpose into some unpleasant form of suspension hanging, unless the rope breaks.

SUICIDAL STRANGULATION

If, for some reason, there is no attachment point available for a ligature, strangulation is a possibility. This method consists of wrapping a cord around your neck and tightening it. The disadvantages are: (a) Depending on the amount of tension applied, it may compress your airway as well as the major blood vessels (carotid and/or jugular) unless you protect the front of the neck; (b) since there is no weight on the ligature, it may loosen when you become unconscious. Some methods to solve this latter problem are:

- use a high-friction ligature that will stay in place;
- use a double knot;
- wrap thin cord, as many times as possible in five to ten seconds, around your neck, relying on friction to maintain the tension. A slip knot is helpful, but may loosen unless wrapped;
- make a loose loop around your neck. Insert a thin, rigid item, for example, a wooden spoon or pen, between the neck and the loop, and twist the rod until it tightens the ligature; then tuck the end of the rod between the neck and the cord to keep it in place. If you use a bar that is around 8 inches (20 cm) long, there is a good chance that it will stay in place under your chin even if not tucked in.

The most reliable of these methods is to buy a racheting "tie down." These are available at auto, motorcycle, and some hardware stores for between $5 and $10 and are generally used for attaching cargo. Once tight, a spring-loaded cam release (or equivalent) must be pressed to remove tension. The main caveat is that, if you're not familiar with them, it may take a few minutes to figure out how the racheting mechanism works. A friction-actuated version is easier to use, and is also easier to release, but can't be tightened as much. In all cases, bending forward increases the diameter of the neck, and thus the constrictive effect of the ligature.

Drop hanging, suspension hanging, and ligature strangulation are effective and lethal means of suicide and are not suitable for a suicidal gesture. Drop hanging requires knowing what you're doing and is unforgiving of mistakes; its main virtue is that it is quick and, allegedly, painless. Suspension or ligature asphyxia requires about an uninterrupted half hour, does not require complete suspension, and can be carried out by people with limited physical abilities. Pain can be minimized by protecting the front of the neck. Since finding such a cadaver may be traumatic, care should be given to choosing a location.

Notes

[a]This is not the only possible explanation. For example, New York City has a large proportion of immigrants, a population which tends to use hanging as a means of suicide. In this study, 73 of 100 hanging suicides were by people born outside the United States (but 70 percent of them had lived in the States for more than ten years).

[b]However, the prison population differs from the general population in (among other things) age, sex, and race. In 1988 1.4 percent of deaths in the United States were due to suicide. For males it was 2.1 percent; among males between 20 and 29 years old it was 14.4 percent. Most studies of inmate suicide find that 20 to 30 percent of deaths are officially suicides (Frost, 1988).

[c]People who hang themselves in jail generally do so within the first month, and often, first couple of days. They are, frequently first-time offenders, and there seems to be little correlation between length of sentence and likelihood of suicide (Lanphear, 1987; Frost, 1988).

[d]Mitchell Rope, a four-hundred-pound convicted murderer in Washington State appealed his death sentence. In that enlightened state, the condemned are given the "choice" of hanging or lethal injection; hanging is the default if they refuse to choose. This man, who declined to make a choice, then claimed that hanging would be constitutionally prohibited "cruel and unusual punishment" because his head might separate from his body due to his heavy weight, which he has done everything possible to increase while in jail. And now, for the best part:

The Washington State Supreme Court, in a fit of collective idiocy, bought this preposterous notion.

[e]A few people have such a sensitive carotid sinus that they faint from a tight collar, shaving over the carotid region, or even turning their head to one side.

[f]As an aside, if someone tries to put a sleeper hold on you with their arm (from behind), turn your head to the right and down, to relieve some pressure, and either stomp hard on their instep, send an elbow to their solar plexus, or grab gonads (if available) and twist.

[g]My calculations do not support this mechanism. Normal arterial systolic blood pressure is around 120 mmHg; assume that it can go up to 250 mmHg in an emergency without blowing out the plumbing. This corresponds to a bit less than 5 pounds per square inch (760 mmHg = 14.7 pounds per square inch). However, it took 33 pounds pressure on a ligature (of unspecified thickness) to compress the trachea. [Brouardel, 1887, in Polson p386]

If the rope is half an inch thick, and it compresses a six-inch arc of the neck (arbitrary, but conservative, numbers), we have 3 square inches of neck being compressed by 33 pounds, or 11 pounds per square inch needed to block the airway. This is more than twice the pressure of 250 mmHg put out by the heart. Thus, these estimates do not support the idea that the heart can pump with enough pressure to close the airway. They also suggest that blood pressure from a beating heart is not enough to force open compressed neck arteries, let alone veins.

[h]A tube from the lower part of the airway to outside the body, intended to avoid a breathing blockage further up the neck—in this instance an inoperable throat cancer.

[i]One reason for such a high male/female ratio is that women tend not to be so obvious, since they don't generally use unusual clothes or devices. A related reason is that they are prone to be misdiagnosed: Four of nine such cases in women were initially wrongly considered to be murder (two), attempted suicide (one), and accidental death during sex with a partner (one) (Byard, 1993).

[j]I wonder if this encourages people to commit suicide by, say, "stumbling" in front of a train. It would be interesting to see the "accidental" death rate among life insurance policyholders with and without double payout for accidental deaths.

[k]Isn't this what they also give medals for?

[l]Hanging several people simultaneously, but without a drop, that is, pulling on the rope in order to lift the victim off the ground by the neck.

24
HYPOTHERMIA

●

Many are cold, but few are frozen.

—Anonymous

Hypothermia, (*hypo*, low; *thermia*, temperature) is an effective, but infrequently used suicide method. It is a poor choice for a suicidal gesture, unless one is sure of timely intervention.

FATALITY RATE: More than 30 percent
PERMANENT INJURY: Moderately likely
PROS AND CONS OF HYPOTHERMIA FOR SUICIDE

Pros: • Not severely painful
      • Often lethal in the absence of intervention
      • Requires no special equipment and minimal knowledge
      • Usually some time to change your mind, without ill effects

Cons:• Rate of hypothermia highly variable: dependent on one's physical fitness and body fat content as well as on temperature and weather conditions
      • Sometimes severe injury in survivors
      • Requires temperatures that are seasonally and geographically limited
      • May take a long time
      • Victims may be revivable even several hours after clinical "death"

- Insidious: people often don't notice signs of hypothermia in themselves

What Is Hypothermia?

The freezing point of water, under standard conditions, is 32 degrees F (0 degrees C) and its boiling point is 212 degrees F (100 degrees C). Normal human body temperature is around 98.6 degrees F (37 degrees C) and is tightly regulated by a variety of physiological mechanisms. Even a 3.6 degrees F (2 degrees C) change is significant; a 5.4 degrees F (3 degrees C) fever is a medical emergency.

Systemic hypothermia is generally defined as a body temperature below 95 degrees F (35 degrees C). Severity is rated by how low the core body temperature falls: 89.6 to 95 degrees F (32-35 degrees C) is mild hypothermia; 80.6 to 89.6 degrees F (27-32 degrees C) is moderate; below 80.6 degrees F (27 degrees C) is severe.

Hypothermia is also divided into "acute" and "chronic" categories. Acute hypothermia occurs quickly, roughly within two or three hours; chronic hypothermia takes longer. While the boundary is fuzzy, the distinction is more than academic, since both treatment and prognosis differ between the two.

What Causes Hypothermia?

Hypothermia occurs when the quantity of body heat lost to the external environment substantially exceeds the heat generated from metabolism. This can be caused by a decrease in heat production, or an increase in heat loss, or both.

Heat Production

Low heat production is usually due to insufficient food, illness, injury, or some drugs.

An average resting body gives off about 50 kilocalories (kcal) or "kitchen" calories—the same calories you see on food labels—of heat per square meter of skin per hour. Multiplied by the average person's 1.7 square meters of skin and 24 hours, you lose around 2,000 kcal per day to the outside world, which is about the amount that you generate at rest from the food that you've eaten. This is called "basal metabolism."

If your muscles are working, metabolic heat production goes way up. For example, while you're shivering, you generate roughly five time as much heat as when sitting quietly; while exercising, ten times as much.[1]

However, exercise is a two-edged sword in hypothermia. While it produces heat, which is needed to keep body and mind functioning, it also increases blood flow to your active muscles, and thus heat loss from them. In addition, it uses up energy stores quickly. The decision whether to exercise in a potentially hypothermic situation depends on the circumstances: How long the conditions are expected to last, availability of food and shelter, and need for clear thinking.

To some degree there is no choice in the matter: shivering is a form of involuntary exercise. It increases heat production by 200 to 700 percent,[2] but is accompanied by an increase in blood flow to/from the muscle, resulting in about a 25 percent increase in heat loss, too. Shivering is an effective means of generating heat, until muscles run low on energy.

The common warning against going to sleep in the cold is certainly appropriate if you're in the process of walking out of trouble, but that is not always the right thing to do. For example, someone with reasonable cold-weather clothing caught in a mountain blizzard might be better off building a snow-hole or shelter, staying as dry and warm as possible, and sleeping through the storm.

HEAT LOSS

Excessive heat loss is due to cold surroundings or to a failure in the body's temperature regulating mechanism. There are four physical mechanisms of heat loss:

1. Convection: heat loss by means of molecular transfer of energy via air or water currents.
2. Conduction: heat loss by touching something that's colder than you are. This is, fundamentally, the same process as convection, but mostly applies to solids.

3. Radiation: heat loss from invisible infrared-wavelength energy you give off.
4. Evaporation: heat loss from the cooling effect of changing a liquid into a gas.

Looking at these in more detail:

CONVECTION AND CONDUCTION

Most heat loss in hypothermia is from contact with cold air or cold water: You're always generating a micro-environment of warm air (or water, if that's where you are) around your body, but this is easily stripped away by air/water currents or your own movements. You can easily demonstrate this by putting your hands into a container of cold water, and holding them still for a few seconds. If you then move your hands, they will feel suddenly colder, as un-warmed water contacts them.

At a molecular level, what happens is that cold air/water molecules hit your skin, pick up some heat (energy) and bounce off, leaving cooler skin behind (hot air/water warms you by the same process, with the hot molecules transferring energy to your skin). This cooler skin, being in contact with the rest of the body, is in turn warmed by the body core, which is thereby cooled. The colder the air/water molecules, the faster this occurs.

The rate of convective heat loss also depends on the density of the moving substance (heat loss in water is much faster than in air of the same temperature) and the velocity of the moving substance (the faster the air/water current, the faster the heat exchange).

Another variable in heat loss is surface area. The more surface area, the more heat transfer. Curling up in the fetal position minimizes heat exchange by minimizing surface area, and thus evaporation, radiation, and convection. It may also be comforting for atavistic reasons.

With cold air, some of the variables that affect heat loss are: temperature, wind speed, insulation, and humidity. We'll look at their effects in a bit more detail.

WIND. Wind speed is the cause of the often-misunderstood "wind-chill factor." "Wind chill" is just a practical demonstration of air convection and involves nothing more complicated than wind removing the warmed (by you) air molecules from near your body and replacing them with cold ones. This results in your body being hit by more cold air molecules per minute, and so being cooled more. For example, 0 degrees F (-18 degrees C) with no wind causes heat loss at the same *rate* as 30 degrees F (-1 degrees C) and 25 mile-per-hour (40 kilometer-per-hour) breeze.[3] However, the latter case would not drop *below* 30 degrees F (-1 degrees C), in the absence of evaporative effects.

EVAPORATION. A second consideration, which is not technically part of wind-chill factor calculations but is biologically important, is that more wind will cause faster evaporation of sweat. This will remove from your body around two and a half kilocalories per teaspoon of evaporated sweat, and thus additional cooling.

Evaporation cools you because energy (heat) is always required to change a liquid into a gas. If the liquid is on or near your skin (sweat, water, or wet clothing), the heat comes from you, leaving you cooler. This is handy in the desert, but not so good if you're trying to keep from freezing. Thus, a dry body will cool faster in the presence rather than in the absence of wind ("wind chill"), but it won't get below ambient temperature. A wet body in the wind will cool both faster and further, and may drop far below ambient temperature.

RADIATION. Another way heat is lost is by radiating it away in the form of infrared (electromagnetic) energy.[a] This requires a temperature difference between you and the outside world. The greater the difference, the larger and faster the heat loss (or gain, if the environment is at a higher temperature).

Infrared wavelengths are longer than the unaided human eye can detect, but electronic enhancement permits these wavelengths to be "translated" into our visible range. One sort of night-vision goggles is sensitive to infrared wavelengths, allowing you to see things that are at a different temperature than their background.[b] (Another kind amplifies existing light.) Since about one-fifth of the heart's output of blood goes to the head (15 percent to the brain),[4] it's not surprising that in cold weather an uncovered head may be responsible for more than half the body's total heat loss.[5] Under these circumstances a bare head shows up, on an infrared detector, like a beacon.

INSULATION. External insulation consists of clothing and shelter. In cold climates both function to keep the air nearest your body, which you have spent precious calories warming, from leaving quickly and being replaced by cold air.

Sweating increases heat loss in two ways: In addition to causing heat loss from evaporation, it replaces some trapped air in clothing and blankets. Since water conducts heat about 25 times faster than does dry air, this will increase heat loss under cold conditions.[c6]

Some materials, like wool and a variety of synthetics (Fiberfill, Holofil, Capilene, Thermax, etc.), maintain their loft (and thus insulating ability) better than others (cotton, down) that mat down when they get wet. Nevertheless, *any* clothing that gets wet or even damp will allow faster heat loss than would the same item dry.

Internal insulation involves fat and bulk.[d] It is not an accident that mammals in cold climates are, as a rule, larger than closely related warmer-environment species.[e] They also have a smaller surface-to-volume ratio; they are rounder and have smaller ears, nose, and tail, and thus less heat loss. You can see these differences if you compare, say, cold- and warm-region rabbits or bears.

Fat is very useful in cold climates. Because fat tissue has relatively low blood flow, it acts as a good barrier to heat loss from important core organs. Equally important, it also is a concentrated metabolic energy (heat) source, providing about 9 kilocalories per gram, compared to some 4 kcal per gram of protein or carbohydrate.

HUMIDITY. The low humidity level of frigid air can play a role in hypothermia. On the one hand, the higher the humidity (gaseous water molecules), the more particles will be available to snatch heat from the skin (though this is offset by the lower density of warm air). On the same side of the equation, humidity will decrease the insulating properties of clothing. However, the humidity is limited by the temperature. For example, the maximum possible humidity at 32 degrees F (0 degrees C) is only one-tenth the maximum at 98 degrees F (36.6 degrees C). Thus, at temperatures below the freezing point of water there simply isn't enough gaseous water in the air for these processes to matter much.

On the other hand, low humidity increases the net evaporation of sweat, which is a major cooling mechanism (and which is why people are much less comfortable on a hot humid day than a hot dry one). Low atmospheric humidity can also contribute to dehydration for other reasons, since (1) the body sweats to keep skin from drying out (a humidity level of 70 percent nearest the skin is ideal); (2) exhaled air is close to 100 percent relative humidity. (The condensation you see from your breath on a cold day is a visual reminder of this.) I estimate the daily amount of water lost in breath at freezing temperatures to be about 1.3 pints (0.6 liters).

DEMOGRAPHICS: WHO DIES FROM HYPOTHERMIA?

In a recent study of 234 cases of hypothermia in Switzerland, 43 (18 percent) were attempted suicides, 141 were due to accidents or mountaineering-related, and the rest were attributed to a variety of causes. Three-quarters occurred in cold air; the others in cold water. Sixty-eight (29 percent) of the 234 died. The coldest survivor had a core temperature of 63.5 degrees F (17.5 degrees C) and the longest heart stoppage in a survivor was 4.75 hours.[7]

Hypothermia is not uncommon among the elderly, who often are in frail health, frequently live alone, and may not be able to afford adequate heating or food. These people are at high risk of dying of cold. In some British studies, 3 to 4 percent of elderly admissions to hospitals were hypothermic.[8] Similar circumstances apply to the homeless; in Chicago, 8 of 22 (36 percent) hypothermia deaths were among the homeless.[9] In the United States there were an average of 780 annual deaths attributed to hypothermia between 1979 and 1990;[10] however, only a handful (less than ten a year) are officially suicides.

You might be surprised—I certainly was—at the geographical distribution of the top ten hypothermic-death-rate states in the United States.[11] While Alaska and Illinois are northern states with severe winters, the others are not: Alabama, South Carolina, North Carolina, Virginia, Arizona, New Mexico, Oklahoma, and Tennessee.

What's going on here? Cold weather turns out to be only one of several relevant factors. Another is how quickly and unpredictably temperatures change, due to unstable weather patterns, as in the Carolinas and Virginia. High elevation and clear skies cause large temperature drops from day to night time; this is the situation in New Mexico and Arizona (twenty-three people died of hypothermia in New Mexico during the 1993-94 winter). It may also be that people in the south have little experience with severe cold and underestimate its danger. Two other interrelated factors are poverty (people can't afford adequate shelter and heat) and a high proportion of older residents; older folks are more susceptible to cold injury, more likely to be poor, and more likely to live alone and unnoticed. Half of hypothermia deaths in this country are among people sixty-five or older.[12]

What Are the Physiological Effects of Cold?

Temperature Regulation. Central temperature regulation in mammals is located in the anterior hypothalamus section of the brain. It is sensitive to blood temperature changes of as little as 1 degree F (0.5 degrees C) and also reacts to nerve impulses sent from nerve endings in the skin. Injury or tumors in the hypothalamus can lead to fatal loss of thermal control even at room temperatures.

Heat Conservation. In cold conditions, heat is first conserved by decreasing blood flow to the skin and skeletal muscles, and is controlled by the "sympathetic" nervous system.

Interestingly, some marine mammals, such as seals, have an additional full-time heat conservation method called "countercurrent" blood flow. Normally, warm-blooded creatures in cold water would be expected to lose a lot of heat from their flippers and fins, which have and need a large surface area for propulsion. However this heat loss is decreased because the arteries and the veins in the flippers/fins run right next to each other. This allows heat transfer between the two and means that some of the heat contained by the arterial blood warms the returning venous blood rather than being wasted in warming the seawater. Very crafty.

In humans, typical blood flow to the skin is 300-500 ml/min. Maximum physiological constriction can decrease this to around 30 ml/min. One of the consequences of this is that blood will pool in the core organs at higher-than-normal pressure. This, in turn, forces the kidneys to increase urine output ("cold diuresis"), which is only a minor heat loss, but may be a significant cause of dehydration, and increases the load on the heart because the blood is more viscous. Nothing has only one effect.

Heat Generation. Additional heat is generated by shivering. This reflex is set off by lowered temperature either in the skin or deeper in the body. The fact that it is not under voluntary nervous control is shown by its existence in paraplegics and in people temporarily paralyzed by curare.[e13] Shivering continues down to a core temperature of around 90 degrees F (32 degrees C), but falters below there, and stops altogether at around 86 degrees F (30 degrees C).[14] It also ceases, during slow hypothermia, if muscles use up their energy stores (glucose/glycogen); this occurs after a few hours. In either case, body temperature drops precipitously after the shivering reflex fails.

"Goosebumps" (piloerection), which lift hairs or feathers away from the body, increase the amount of trapped air—insulation—near the skin. Unfortunately, since humans are more-or-less hairless over most of their bodies, this process doesn't do us much good. But it was a fine idea when we were furry and is still an interesting sensation.[f]

RATE OF HEAT LOSS. As a practical matter, most hypothermia is the result of contact with either cold air or cold water. Since air has a much lower ability to remove heat than does water, hypothermia in air normally takes many hours and is usually "chronic" or "slow." "Acute" (fast) hypothermia, generally in or due to water, has some significantly different characteristics from the chronic variety.

In slow, as compared to fast, hypothermia, the body has more time to make some physiological responses: Deep veins are in a "neurovascular bundle," with arteries and veins next to each other. Cold causes a shift of blood from surface veins to deeper ones. Thus, like the marine mammals mentioned earlier, we have a way of warming the returning venous blood with outgoing arterial blood. In warm conditions, where getting rid of excess heat is necessary, the surface veins carry more blood and this "countercurrent heat exchange" is minimized. Blood flow to the limbs and skin decreases, blood pools in the core organs, and shivering continues until metabolic energy supplies are depleted. People develop the physical and mental lethargy commonly associated with hypothermia.

One of the hazards specific to fast hypothermia is a phenomenon called "afterdrop," wherein the core temperature continues to fall even after a person has been taken to a warm place. This is because blood vessels in the arms and legs get larger (dilate) as they start to be rewarmed. As a consequence:

1. Blood moves from the core into the limbs (which, despite warming, are still colder than the core), and gets chilled further. This results in more cold blood moving from the periphery into the core, further decreasing core temperature, which can be lethal;
2. Redistribution of blood from the core to the periphery decreases blood pressure, and may lead to heart failure ("shock");
3. The stagnant blood from the limbs is very acidic (from lactic acid and carbon dioxide buildup), which may cause cardiac arrhythmias and death.

Afterdrop can best be avoided by not rewarming the periphery until after warming the core. This was observed by one of Napoleon's army doctors during the retreat from Moscow, when he noticed that the hypothermic soldiers placed closest to warming fires tended to die more often than those further away.

Fatal chilling may occur before physical and mental abilities are seriously retarded: In 1980, sixteen Danish fishermen spent about one-and-a-half hours in the North Sea when their boat went down. When rescued, all could climb into the cargo net, and walk across the deck of the rescue vessel. They went below to the galley for hot drinks (good idea) and to warm up quickly (bad idea). Every one of them died of afterdrop hypothermia.[15]

SUSCEPTIBILITY TO COLD

There are age, race, and gender differences affecting susceptibility to cold. Infants and the elderly are much more likely to be injured than are young adults. Fat people are less subject to hypothermia than are thin ones. Men are more vulnerable to hypothermia than are women, even though they are larger, because women have more subcutaneous fat, which is better insulation (less blood flow) and stores more energy (more calories per gram) than muscle. Blacks seem more sensitive to cold than are Inuits or Caucasians.[16] Interestingly, Australian Aborigines apparently lower their body temperature (and, as a result, metabolism and food needs) to around 95 degrees F (35 degrees C) on cold nights.[g17]

EFFECTS OF COLD

BEHAVIOR AND REFLEXES. In slow hypothermia, by the time body temperature drops to 90 degrees F (32 degrees C) both the central and peripheral nervous systems are impaired, primarily due to decreased blood flow to the brain (6 to 7 percent per degree C[18]): People become physically and mentally clumsy, show decreased sensitivity to pain, have slowed reflexes, and may hallucinate. Thus, a medical school mnemonic for hypothermia symptoms: "stumbles, mumbles, fumbles, and grumbles," which summarizes changes in motor coordination and consciousness.

Sleepiness ("cold narcosis") occurs at around 86 degrees F (30 degrees C) core temperature. At around 81 degrees F (27 degrees C), people stop responding to verbal commands and some reflexes (such as the reaction of eye pupils to light) stop working entirely. Knee jerk is the last reflex to go,[h19] at 79 degrees F (26 degrees C). The body's temperature-regulating mechanisms also fail and there is quick cooling until the body reaches ambient temperature. However, there is the usual individual variability, with recorded reflexes as low as 68 degrees F (20 degrees C).[20]

HEART. The heart's response to hypothermia is usually the actual cause of death. Initially, the heart merely slows down and shows some electrocardiograph changes. Dehydration—blood really is thicker than water—makes it harder for the heart to pump increasingly viscous blood. Ventricular fibrillation is often—but not always—seen below 89.6 degrees F (32 degrees C), and reaches a maximum between 82.4 and 86 degrees F (28 to 30 degrees C).[21]

Ventricular fibrillation occurs when different parts of the muscle surrounding the main pumping chambers beat in a chaotic, unsynchronized fashion; as a result the heart can't send blood through the arteries—with fatal consequences unless reversed. In hypothermic conditions fibrillation may easily be set off by even minor exertion. If the heart escapes fibrillation, it slows further as the temperature drops. In one case, a woman had a pulse of four beats per minute (around 75 per minute is normal) with a body temperature of 52 degrees F (11 degrees C), and the heart stopped pumping entirely at 51 degrees F (10.5 degrees C). Her heart restarted when she was rewarmed.[22]

BRAIN. At normal body temperature, brain damage starts in about five minutes, in the absence of blood flow; at lower temperatures the length of time before brain (and other organ) injury is substantially longer. This is because cellular metabolism and oxygen needs drop sharply with lowered temperature. For example, oxygen consumption is reduced by 50 percent at 82.4 degrees F (28 degrees C); 75 percent at 71.6 F (22 degrees C); and 92 percent at 50 F (10 degrees C).[23]

However, people whose bodies cool down faster than they run out of oxygen (for example, fast hypothermia in air, drowning in icy water) can be revived longer. Those who run out of oxygen faster than their temperature drops (for example, avalanche, drowning in warmer water) will not be revivable as long. Some hypothermic people have been given CPR for up to 3.5 hours and have recovered without neurological damage.

CAUSE OF DEATH

Death is generally from circulatory failure: The heart either goes into ventricular fibrillation or slows down and stops altogether. In people who have survived the first couple of days after rescue, organ failure, particularly of the pancreas, may lead to delayed death.[24] A wide range of other organs also may show acute damage from cold, but these injuries, while sometimes severe, are not usually fatal.

SIGNS AND SYMPTOMS OF HYPOTHERMIA

Looking at signs and symptoms in relation to specific temperatures, rather than by organ systems, give a somewhat different perspective.

The following chart[25] shows the body core temperature and corresponding signs and symptoms. Not all hypothermic people exhibit all of these symptoms, which will also change as the person's core temperature changes.

Core temperature	Signs and symptoms
99 to 97 F (37 to 36C)	Normal temperature range, shivering may begin.
97 to 95F (36 to 35C)	Cold sensation, goosebumps, unable to perform complex tasks with hands, shivering mild to severe, skin numb.
95 to 93F (35 to 34C)	Shivering intense, lack of muscle coordination becomes apparent, movements slow and labored, stumbling pace, mild confusion, may appear alert, unable to walk straight.

93 to 90F (34 to 32C)	Violent shivering persists, difficulty speaking, sluggish thinking, amnesia starts to appear and may be retrograde, gross muscle movements sluggish, unable to use hands, stumbles frequently, difficulty speaking.
90 to 86F (32 to 30C)	Shivering stops in chronic hypothermia, exposed skin blue or puffy, muscle coordination very poor with inability to walk, confusion, incoherent, irrational behavior, but may be able to maintain posture and the appearance of awareness.
86 to 82F (30 to 27.7C)	Muscles severely rigid, semiconscious, stupor, loss of awareness of others, pulse and respiration slow, pupils can dilate.
82 to 78F (27 to 25.5C)	Unconsciousness, heart beat and respiration erratic, pulse and heart beat may be unobtainable, muscle tendon reflexes cease.
78 to 75F (25 to 24C)	Pulmonary edema, failure of cardiac and respiratory centers, probable death. *Death may occur before this level.*

WHAT ARE THE CLINICAL SIGNS OF HYPOTHERMIA?

In addition to the behavioral symptoms mentioned, there is often swelling, especially of the face and ears, as fluid leaks out of the circulation. This is another cause of viscous blood, which overworks the heart. Blood pressure is low and sometimes unmeasurable, as are pulse and respiration. There may be no signs of life whatsoever below temperatures of 64 to 81 degrees F (18 to 27 degrees C).[26] And with good reason: Most of these people are dead. However, there have been occasional cases of survival despite extreme temperatures. Perhaps the most astonishing was that of a man found with a body temperature of 32 degrees F (0 degrees C), who felt frozen and had no signs of life.[27] Yet, when thawed, he revived.[i] Thus, in the felicitous phrase of Dr. R. T. Gregory, "No one is dead until warm and dead."[28]

SOME RISK FACTORS: ALCOHOL, DRUGS, EXERCISE

The role of alcohol in hypothermia is controversial. On the one hand, it predisposes to hypothermia by several mechanisms:

1. It produces an increase in blood flow (and thus heat loss) near the skin ("cutaneous vasodilation"). Since the skin contains many temperature receptors, drinking alcohol generates a sensation of warmth, but this comes at the expense of internal heat;
2. Alcohol causes hypoglycemia (low blood sugar), which decreases the body's ability to produce heat;
3. As a central nervous system depressant, alcohol slows metabolism and promotes sleepiness;
4. And certainly alcohol impairs judgment, which may be critical under adverse conditions.

Many hypothermia victims have blood alcohol concentrations (BAC) ranging from 0.13 to 0.25 gm/100 ml blood.[29] "Legally impaired" in most of the United States is 0.08-0.10 gm/100 ml BAC. Since exercise also increases blood flow to the skin, the combination of alcohol with strenuous exercise would seem to cause maximum heat loss.

On the other hand, alcohol appears to protect the heart against fibrillation (and has been used for that purpose during low-temperature medical operations, at levels of 0.40 gm/100 ml blood.)[30] Perhaps this protective effect causes the observed higher survival rate in hypothermics who had been drinking, compared to those who were sober.[31]

In addition, alcohol protects limbs against frostbite (freezing) by increasing their blood flow, but again, this is at the expense of core temperature.

Some other drugs that have central nervous system depressant effects can also produce hypothermia, for example barbiturates, opiates, and the "major tranquilizer" chlorpromazine (Thorazine) and related compounds; but also some nonsedatives like acetaminophen (Tylenol) and lithium ion (used to treat manic-depressive behavior). These drugs interfere with temperature regulation at the hypothalamic regulatory center in the brain, and may cause hypothermia even at room temperatures. Of 103 consecutive

Intensive Care Unit drug overdose admissions, twenty-seven were hypothermic.[32]

SURVIVAL FACTORS

In the Swiss study of 234 cases of hypothermia,[33] some of the factors that tended to be associated with the death of the victims were, in decreasing order of importance: (1) asphyxia (as would happen in an avalanche); (2) invasive rewarming methods; (3) slow rate of cooling. Positive survival factors were (1) fast cooling rate; (2) presence of ventricular fibrillation in cardiac arrest cases; (3) presence of alcohol and/or narcotics in the body.

WHAT ARE THE MEDICAL TREATMENTS FOR HYPOTHERMIA?

Treatment depends on the severity of the hypothermia, its underlying cause, and the age and general condition of the patient. In the mildest cases, warm, nonalcoholic drinks, food, and a few blankets are enough.

If the hypothermia is moderate, or if the patient has low heat production due to exhaustion, illness, drugs, or malnutrition, more active warming is appropriate. This usually involves heating pads/blankets, hot water bottles, or other external sources of heat applied to the trunk. In wilderness situations, the best emergency rewarming may consist of sandwiching the (dried) hypothermic person in between two warm people, all inside or under a sleeping bag.

In severe or acute hypothermia "active core rewarming" (ACR) is often used. There are many varieties of ACR. For example, heated liquids may be circulated around the stomach by a tube running through the nose, or heated IV fluids may be administered. In the most critical cases, those whose hearts have stopped, blood is often withdrawn from the femoral vein[j] (the largest vein in the leg, conveniently close to the surface near the groin), heated to 104 degrees F (40 degrees C) and oxygenated, and reinjected into the femoral artery.[34]

HOW LONG DO PEOPLE SURVIVE UNDER COLD STRESS?

In one recent study, eight of eleven people with deep hypothermia and cardiac arrest were resuscitated.[35] Five of the eleven had no heartbeat and six had ventricular fibrillation. None were breathing and all were clinically dead with wide, nonreactive pupils, and were supported by external heart massage and ventilation (CPR). The average (mean) length of exposure to the cold in the survivors was 4.4 hours, and average core temperature was 72.5 degrees F (22.5 degrees C). All three of the patients who died had also been asphyxiated (one in an avalanche, two in drownings).

COLD WATER

Data from shipwrecks and accidents suggest that a well-nourished man can survive roughly two hours in water at 39 degrees F (4 degrees C).[36] At 32 degrees F (0 degrees C) survival time is only about a half an hour.[37] Since swimming, like other exercise, increases heat loss (as well as heat production) due to increasing blood flow near the skin, this may account for some accidental "drownings" in cold water among good swimmers. On the other hand, at temperatures above around 68 degrees F (20 degrees C), fit swimmers can continue for many hours. Swimmers attempting the English Channel, which has summer water temperatures in the mid- to upper 50s F (13 to 15 degrees C), coat themselves with grease (more for insulation and to decrease water absorption than for buoyancy), and take hot drinks and quick-energy carbohydrate foods provided by their support boat every half hour or so.[k]

However, if one is not exercising *and* taking in lots of calories, the same water temperature can be deadly: In March 1995, four U.S. Army Rangers died of hypothermia in Florida after spending several hours in water between 52 and 59 degrees F (11 to 15 degrees C) while training. Similarly, a man died of hypothermia after getting stuck in the mud of a 15-foot-diameter pond, which was no more than 3 feet deep.[38] Air temperature was 70 degrees F (21 degrees C) and water temperature was 52 degrees F (11.5 degrees C). Even warm (for example, 95 degrees F, or 35 degrees C) water will chill you after an hour or so unless you are actively exercising.

As always, there is substantial variability between people. For example, the lowest temperature water in which different young men and women at rest could maintain a steady body temperature ranged from below 53.6 degrees F (12 degrees C) to 89.6 degrees F (32 degrees C). This depended on both insulation (primarily thickness of the fat layer on the trunk of the body) and metabolic heat production. Each of these factors was about equally important: Fast metabolizers could maintain body temperature in water 18 degrees F (10 degrees C) colder than slow metabolizers who had the same amount of body fat.[39]

COLD AIR

Immersion in cold water seems to cause loss of body heat about twenty-five to thirty times as fast as air at the same temperature.[40] As a result, survival time in cold air is much longer than in water of the same temperature. Consequently, secondary factors, such as wind speed, precipitation, and amount and type of clothing worn, are more important in cold air than in cold water.

COLD COMFORT: HOW TO DO IT

ON LAND. Make arrangements so you won't be looked for: for example, tell people you're going away for a few days. Go to a cold, secluded spot where you won't be seen. Drink alcohol and/or take sedatives. You can speed up the process by removing clothing and/or getting wet. Obviously, the amount of time needed will also be very dependent on temperature and wind conditions, and your size, weight, and fat content. These are too many variables to make even rough time estimates.

Use of a home freezer has been recommended,[41] but the air supply in such freezers is so limited that asphyxia will occur long before hypothermia. Commercial freezers are a possibility, but the risk of untimely discovery must be considered.

IN WATER. Since heat loss in water is much faster than in air of the same temperature, the amount of time that one is subject to being saved is correspondingly diminished. The main concern will be to avoid being seen, both to avoid unwanted rescue and to prevent risk to potential rescuers. Depending on the temperature of the water and your physical condition, fatal hypothermia can occur in as little as thirty minutes or so; less after alcohol and/or sedatives. Be aware that unless the water is very shallow (and even then if you end up facedown), you are likely to actually die of drowning while insensible from cold, rather than from hypothermia.

SUMMARY

Hypothermia is an underappreciated means of suicide: It is relatively painless, though certainly uncomfortable, and generally fatal if not interrupted. The main disadvantage is that it normally takes several hours on land (but much less in water), during which time permanent injury is quite possible if rescue occurs. A second major disadvantage is that hypothermia as a means of suicide is limited by climate and season.

As a suicidal gesture, hypothermia is a bad choice, because the length of time is so dependent on both weather and individual variables. And while, in principle, you can change your mind, in practice you lose too much capacity to think and/or act rationally when hypothermic for this to be a reliable survival net.

NOTES:

[a]This seems like a bizarre notion at first; that we are continuously giving off electromagnetic waves, similar to light and radio. If we were at a (few hundred degrees) higher temperature, we would give off higher-energy waves, and might be seen to glow red-hot; at a much lower temperature, we could be our own radio transmitters.

[b]The relative (to goose down) heat conductivity of a few materials follows:

Down	1
Hollow polyester	1.6
Solid polyester	1.9
Cardboard	5.0
Water	140
Ice	570

[c]So how, then, do ducks and geese keep *their* down from getting soggy and becoming worthless as insulation? Preening transfers oily, water-repelling material from a gland on their backs to the feathers, as well as fluffing them up.

[d]It's claimed that mosquitoes also show this characteristic. The smaller tropical mosquitoes apparently have to suck blood more often, and are thus more likely to spread disease from one person to another than are temperate-climate mosquitoes (Martens, 1995).

[e]Curare is used as a muscle relaxant during surgery. As an aside, major-surgery patients who are not kep warm—that is, most of them—have been recently (Kurz, 1996) found to have a significantly higher infection rate and slower recovery than those who are covered

by blankets during surgery. The combination of chilly operating rooms (for the benefit of gowned and capped staff) and impaired temperature control in anesthetized patients thus caused hypothermia, increased susceptibility to infection, and delayed healing. On the other hand, deliberately induced hypothermia decreased brain damage in comatose patients who had suffered head injury (Marion, 1997).

[f]Another physiological reason for piloerection is that it makes us look bigger, which may deter a predator or intimidate a rival.

[g]Actually, all of us have temperatures that vary about one degree Fahrenheit over the course of a day, being lowest just before we get up and highest about twelve hours later. It's also possible to regulate your temperature (within limits) through yoga, meditation, or biofeedback techniques. These methods also can be used to gain some voluntary control over heart rate and blood pressure, and, probably autonomic functions.

[h]Liberals, note.

[i]But who would have thawed it?

[j]According to William Forgey, Inuit wear extra clothing—short pants—over the femoral area in order to decrease heat losses. He also notes that Western explorers to the Arctic survived more often when they copied the Inuit high-fat diet.

[k]Since seawater contains a greater concentration of antifreeze (mostly dissolved salts) than you do, its freezing point is around 29 degrees F (-1.9 degrees C) compared to human skin, which freezes around 31 degrees F (-0.6 degrees C). Thus it's possible to literally freeze in liquid seawater (Tedeschi, pp 767; Keating 1960).

25
JUMPING

•

I instantly realized I had made a mistake. I can't tell you how frightening that was.

—A survivor[1]

Caution: Cape does not enable user to fly.

—Batman costume warning label

LETHAL INTENT: High
FATALITIES: 40 to 60 percent
PERMANENT INJURIES: Frequent
PROS AND CONS OF JUMPING AS A SUICIDE METHOD
Pros: • Usually fatal, with a high enough jump site
• Some contemplation time on the way down
Cons:• Can't do much about it once you're in the air
• Not reliably lethal for jumps of less than 150 feet
• High incidence of permanent injury
• Risk of injuring others
• Fear of heights is common

Jumps from higher than 150 feet (ten to twelve stories high) over land and 250 feet over water are almost always fatal; however, most suicide attempts are made from considerably lower heights. The consequences of lower jumps

376

are unpredictable. Permanent injuries, including paralysis, are common. Jumping is thus a particularly bad choice for a suicidal gesture. There is about a fifty-fifty chance of surviving a one-story (12 foot) fall if you land on your head; three to four stories if you land on your side; four to five stories if you land on your feet.[2]

The word "jumper" was apparently used in the *Codebook of Federal Security Agencies* to describe someone attempting suicide by jumping from a height.[3] The term has commonly come to include accidental and homicidal high falls, which is how we'll use it.

The two major questions a potential jumper might want answered are:

- Is jumping a reliable way to kill yourself? The short answer is that it's about 95 to 98 percent lethal if you fall more than 150 feet (ten to twelve stories) over land—but sometimes a much shorter fall is fatal (2.5 feet in one case).
- What are the risks of long-term injury among those surviving a fall? Short answer: quite high; more than half the survivors in one study were either still hospitalized or permanently unable to work a year after their jump.[4]

We'll look later at the available data in order to answer these questions in greater detail.

DEMOGRAPHICS: WHO AND WHY

U.S. NATIONAL STATISTICS

There are roughly 30,000 suicides per year in the United States. About 2.2 percent are due to jumping.

In four smaller samples the percentage of suicides due to jumping were 8 percent in Leeds, England (1960),[5] 6 percent in (the American state of) Georgia (1975 through 1984)[6], approximately 5 percent in Finland,[7] and around 3 percent in Australia.[8]

U.S. sex and racial data for jumping suicides in 1994 and 1979 to 1994 are presented below.[a]

Table 25.1 Suicide by Jumping, E957			Rate/100,000	
	Deaths,1994	Population (millions)	1994	1979-94
Total	1438	260,423,572	0.28	0.30
All male	506	127,118,264	0.40	0.42
All female	213	133,305,308	0.16	0.18
White male	419	106,178,839	0.39	0.40
White female	179	110,371,063	0.16	0.18
Black male	60	15,500,047	0.38	0.46
Black female	12	17,189,697	0.06	0.15
Other male	27	5,439,378	0.49	0.50
Other female	22	5,744,548	0.38	0.26

Source: Centers for Disease Control; E-numbers are International Classification of Disease (ICD) codes.

WHAT ARE THE CHARACTERISTICS OF SUICIDAL JUMPERS?

I've found only one detailed, recent study of suicidal jumps (other sources combine accidental and unknown-cause falls, or have other limitations, for our purposes). This report is from Finland,[9] and gives us some interesting information about the jumpers, their injuries, and their situation a year later.

Between 1982 and 1984, eighty known suicidal jumpers were brought to the University Center Hospital in Helsinki, Finland. Twenty (25 percent) of these people died; 7 were dead-on-arrival (DOA) or within an hour, and 13 died while in the hospital, 12 of these within twenty-four hours. This death rate of 13 in 73 (18 percent) for those alive on reaching the hospital is similar to the 17 percent reported in the most comparable American study.[10] However, how many were dead at the scene (DAS) was not reported.

THE JUMPERS. Some of the characteristics of these Finnish jumpers follow:

- Age range was 15 to 65 years, with an average (mean) of 29.8
- 40 percent (29 of 73) were female
- The average (median) hospital stay was forty-nine days

- The patient's home was the most common place to jump from (see Table 25.2)
- A history of "mental illness" was found in 21 percent (15 of 73)
- 10 percent (7 of 73) had a physical illness
- 15 percent (11 of 73) were chronic alcoholics
- Alcohol was found in 34 percent (25 of 73); 15 percent (11 of 73) had breath levels over 0.15 percent (0.08-0.10 percent is "legally impaired" in most of the United States)
- A previous suicide attempt was known in 18 percent (13 of 73) of the jumpers

These figures are similar to U.S. data shown later in this chapter.

HEIGHT OF FALLS. Interestingly, 40 percent fell between 16 and 26 feet (5 to 8 meters), or two to three stories;[b] 38 percent between 26 and 40 feet (8 to 12 meters); 22 percent from higher than 40 feet (12 meters). I'm surprised that so many people intending suicide would jump from such low heights. This suggests impulsive, impaired, ignorant, or irrational decisions in many of these jumps.

WHERE THEY JUMPED FROM.

Table 25.2 Scene of Suicidal Jumps, Finland, 1982-1984[11]

	Male	Female
Own home in apartment house	23	14
Other private residence	5	6
Public structure (e.g., bridge)	12	4
Psychiatric hospital	4	5
Total	44	29

MONTHLY DISTRIBUTION OF JUMPS. A minor curiosity is that monthly distribution of suicidally intentioned jumps in Finland is similar to that from Seattle and New York, but different from overall suicides in Finland and elsewhere.[12] The peaks of jumping occur in the fall; overall suicides in spring and summer.[c] In Australia, the suicide peak is also in the springtime,[13] which is September through November in the southern hemisphere.

SURVIVOR'S OUTCOMES. One year later:

- 19 of 53 (36 percent) had gone back to work
- 20 of 53 (38 percent) were out of hospital, but physically unable to work ("permanently pensioned")
- 9 of 53 (17 percent) were considered mentally unable to work, mostly from preexisting conditions ("permanently pensioned")
- 12 of 53 (23 percent) were still institutionalized, of whom 8 (15 percent) were completely paraplegic (paralyzed throughout the lower half of their bodies)

In thinking about these outcomes, remember that the numbers do not include people dead at the scene or dead on arrival.

Less detailed, but more recent, data from Scotland show somewhat lower survival rates than those from Finland. This is probably because the canny Scots jumped from greater heights: 40 percent jumped from higher than four floors. Also, while about half the jumpers (28 of 58) touched down head first, all eight who jumped from higher than the thirteenth floor landed on their heads, though at such heights, it wouldn't have mattered: The highest survivor (on land) jumped from the fifth floor. About half of the jumpers (31 of 58) got to hospital alive; 35 percent (11 of 31) of these later died, giving a total fatality rate of 66 percent (38 of 58).[14]

U.S. DATA

Data on suicidal jumpers from the United States are less informative: Local surveys tend to combine suicide and accident data, and there are no detailed national data. Nevertheless, it's all we have.

In a frequently cited study from New York in 1965,[15] we get some interesting, if noncurrent, numbers. In 1963, there were 748 deaths from falls in New York City. Two hundred ninety (39 percent) were suicides, and 458 (61 percent) "accidental." Of fifty-three of these people, whose falls were three or more stories and who were brought to Harlem Hospital, twenty-two (41.5 percent) survived, despite major multiple-organ injuries. Age, sex, and circumstance distribution are shown in Table 25.3.

Table 25.3 Age, Sex, and Circumstances Distribution in 53 Jumpers, Harlem Hospital, 1963

	Number	(percent)	Lived	Died (percent)
Age				
0-5	8	(15 percent)	1	7 (88)
6-21	12	(23 percent)	9	3 (25)
22-40	24	(45 percent)	11	13 (54)
41-	9	(17 percent)	1	8 (89)
Total	53		22	31 (58)
Sex				
Female	12	(23 percent)	3	9 (75)
Male	41	(77 percent)	19	22 (54)
Circumstances				
Suicide	9	(17 percent)*	4	5 (56)
Accident	27	(51 percent)	10	17 (63)
Crime	11	(21 percent)	7	4 (36)
Undetermined	8	(15 percent)	1	7 (88)

*20 percent of known circumstances

From a larger and somewhat more recent study,[16] we get generally similar age/gender distribution (Table 25.4). However, the percentage of deaths is much higher in the earlier group because: (1) the Harlem Hospital data excluded jumps from less than three stories; and (2) included those dead on arrival and dead at the scene.

Table 25.4 Age and Sex Distribution in 200 Consecutive Jumpers, Bronx, N.Y. (Reynolds, 1970)

Sex
Female=66 (33 percent)
Male=134 (67 percent)

Circumstances
Suicide=12 (6 percent)*
Accident=148 (74 percent)
Undetermined=40 (20 percent)

Age	Number	(%)	Lived	Died	Died %
0-5	47	(23.5%)	38	9	(19)
6-10	38	(19%)	33	5	(13)
11-20	29	(14.5%)	29	0	(0)
21-30	37	(18.5%)	33	4	(11)
31-40	19	(9.5%)	17	2	(11)
41-50	8	(4%)	8	0	(0)
51-	22	(11%)	8	14	(64)
Total	200		166	34	(17)

*7.5 percent of known circumstances

In both studies these falls were more lethal to the youngest and oldest jumpers' group, and there were substantially more male than female jumpers.

Since about three-quarters of dead jumpers die before getting to the hospital,[17] and 34 of 200 (above) died after being hospitalized, we can make a rough calculation that about 45 percent of suicidal jumps are fatal. This is quite consistent with other U.S. data.[18]

An oddity in the data from the Bronx is that only 6 to 7.5 percent of the jumps were described as "suicidal," a much smaller percentage than the 20 to 45 percent generally cited elsewhere.[19] Lewis felt that more of his patients had actually attempted suicide than are reflected in his numbers, because (1) a witness or a suicide note was required for a suicide verdict when the jumper was dead, and (2) the social and religious stigma attached to suicide discouraged survivors from admitting their intent. These latter factors might be even more significant in Reynolds's Catholic hospital.

In Lewis's study, 75 percent of the female, but only 54 percent of the male jumpers died. This surprising gender distribution of lethal falls is consistent with the notion of women being the weaker sex, but is better explained by the fact that the average height of the females' falls was greater than the male ones (6.3 stories versus 5.2 stories). Racial distribution of jumpers was representative of the area's population: 46 blacks, 7 whites.

One might have expected the suicidal jumpers to have a higher death rate than those who fell by accident, since, presumably, those intending suicide would make a point of jumping from what they considered a sufficiently lethal height. The numbers don't bear this out: Suicidal jumpers died at about the same rate (56 percent), as those who fell accidentally (63 percent). As in Finland, many suicidal jumpers in the United States seem to be either unaware of how survivable their jumps are or are not rational when they jump. In Austria, on the other hand, suicidal jumpers fell from almost twice the average height as accidental jumpers.[20]

Two other possible explanation for the observed similarity in death rates are: (1) The apartment buildings in Harlem are mostly five or six floors high, making it difficult to climb higher for a deliberate fall than for an accidental one; (2) more suicidal than accidental jumpers leap from lethal heights. They would more likely be dead at the scene, and thus ineligible to take part in Lewis's study of hospitalized jumpers.

Of the 53 jumpers, six (11 percent) had a known history of treatment for mental illness, and one-third were alcoholics. On autopsy, 7 of 11 had brain alcohol levels of 0.10 percent (0.10 grams alcohol per 100 grams tissue) or more. A level of 0.08-0.10 percent is "legally intoxicated" in the United States, but such a level wouldn't much impair a chronic alcoholic, so the significance of this finding is unclear.

How Dangerous Is Jumping Compared to Other Methods of Attempted Suicide?

The data in Table 16.1 show that suicidal jumping injuries fall into the middle group in lethality, with a death rate of 42 percent. Since minor injuries tend to be underreported, the actual fatality rates are lower than the figures cited.

What Do We Know About Fatal-fall Injury?

A more recent study from London[21] looked at *dead* jumpers between 1958 and 1978. Information the author collected includes:

- heights and circumstances of fatal falls
- age and sex distribution among suicidal jumpers
- physical and mental illness among suicidal jumpers
- causes of fatal accidents
- detailed information on the nature and distribution of fatal injuries

Heights and circumstances of fatal falls. The heights of the fatal falls in this series ranged from 2.5 feet (brain injury) to 170 feet (severe multiple organ injury). One hundred eleven (76 percent) were dead at the scene or on arrival at the hospital; 35 (24 percent) lived for lengths of time ranging between 3 hours and 120 days. Twenty-five percent were suicides, 57 percent accidents, and 18 percent undetermined.

Age range and sex distribution among jumpers. The youngest fatality was eighteen months old, a child who fell from a fourth-story window; oldest was a ninety-two-year-old man who fell from a first-floor window. The ratio of males to females was 108 (74 percent) to 38 (26 percent), roughly 3:1. This is similar to male/female ratios reported elsewhere.

Physical and mental illness among suicidal jumpers. Among the suicides, the following characteristics were seen:

Table 25.5 Physical and mental illness among suicidal jumpers, London, 1958-1978

	Physical illness	Previous history of mental Illness or overdose	No mental or physical disabilities	Total
Male	8	6	5	19
Female	1	15	3	19
Total[d]	9	21	8	38

Source: Goonetilleke, 1980

The medical problems of some of the suicides with physical illnesses were quite serious: Three had probably terminal cancer, one had had a heart attack, one was a "respiratory cripple." The other four had problems that, apparently had not been fully diagnosed and may have been treatable; two had enlarged prostates and couldn't pass urine, one was coughing up blood, and one had severe abdominal pain. All of these people jumped from hospital windows, the abdominal pain patient pulling out IV lines in order to do so. Apparently, he was not given adequate pain medication.

ACCIDENTAL FALLS. The eighty-three victims of accidents included thirty-five who fell at work, typically while constructing, demolishing, repairing, or cleaning buildings. One stunt man managed to kill himself by landing on his head when he jumped from a ladder onto a mattress.

Nineteen (one woman, eighteen men) died while working on their own or on a friend's house. Eight of these men fell while cleaning windows, as did the sole woman.

The twenty-nine miscellaneous accidental falls included eleven from a window or balcony, and one each from a table and from a kitchen draining board. One person was killed by jumping from a first-floor window to escape a fire, and one from a first-floor window to escape police.

WHAT IS THE NATURE AND SITE OF THE INJURIES IN FATAL FALLS AND JUMPS?

In about 85 percent of these cases, the part of the body the victim landed on could be established by witnesses or the nature of the injuries and the position of the body.

HEAD IMPACT. Sixty-six (45 percent of total) of these people fell on their heads. In only four cases was the skull not fractured, and in three of these four there was brain damage, anyhow. The skull sustained the only fracture in thirty-one of these sixty-six deaths.

BUTTOCKS IMPACT. Eleven (7.5 percent of total) landed on their buttocks, including one who was impaled on a wooden railing. In addition to 4 skull fractures (36 percent), there were 5 spinal fractures (45 percent), and 9 pelvic fractures (82 percent). Organ damage included brain hemorrhage (6 cases), liver laceration (4 cases), heart laceration (3 cases), ruptured aorta (main artery from heart) (2 cases), and ruptured spleen (1 case).

LOWER LIMB IMPACT. Twenty-one (14 percent of total) landed on their feet or knees. Nine had skull fractures despite landing vertically, and of those without skull damage (12 or 13; the text and data numbers don't match again), 9 had brain injuries, mostly hemorrhages. Fourteen of the 21 broke both legs; 5 broke one leg; 2 broke neither. There were 4 spinal fractures.

SIDE OF BODY IMPACT. Of the 25 (17 percent of total) people in this group, 7 had skull fractures, 5 had broken backs, 2 had a ruptured heart, 1 a lacerated liver, and 1 a lacerated kidney and spleen. Most of the deaths were due to shock and blood loss from multiple fractures.

Brain injury was found in 72 percent (105 of 146) of the victims, and 97 percent (64 of 66) of those who landed on their heads. Brain hemorrhage was the most frequent finding and was generally fatal, independent of additional wounds. Brain damage, while almost certain when a jumper landed on his/her head, was also common (51 percent) when there was a different impact site.

Interestingly, the extent of brain injury was not proportional to the height of the fall: Of 23 falls between 50 and 170 feet, 13 (57 percent) had brain damage, while 30 of 38 (79 percent) falls from the first floor (less than 15 feet) showed such injury. Two fatalities from falls of less than 4 feet were due to brain injury.

The reason(s) for this lack of proportionality are not certain, but possibly

(1) in higher falls, people have enough time to orient themselves to avoid hitting head first; (2) this is a study of fatal injuries: People with short falls who did *not* land on their heads are unlikely to die; thus the data are skewed toward finding more head injuries in short falls *because* they were fatal.

There were 32 heart injuries, of which 24 were considered to be the cause of death. These included 4 fractures of the heart and 8 tears of the sac surrounding the heart, the pericardium. Unlike the case with head injuries, the incidence of other injuries was roughly proportional to the height of the fall. The liver was the most height-sensitive abdominal organ: In falls of more than 50 feet, 43 percent of the jumpers had liver lacerations; in shorter falls, this was only 4 percent.

What Is the Relationship Between Height of Fall and Severity of Injury?

The data in the previous section describe injuries from fatal falls; what about those that were survived? The severity of non-head injuries roughly corresponds to the height of the fall, but there are often exceptions and a wide range of injury is seen from similar-height jumps: the lowest (9) and highest (66) ISS scores were both found in 8 to 12 meter (26 to 39 foot) falls. Some people survive much more severe injury than do others (one survived an ISS 58; another died from ISS 28).[c]

As we might expect, there is a correlation between how far someone falls and the likelihood of their dying, but the association is not as clear as one might suppose.

Three studies from the United States provide some information on the relationship between height of the fall, survivability of urban falls/jumps, and the length of subsequent hospitalization.

In the most recent, from Brooklyn, 161 adult jumpers who lived long enough to get out of the emergency room were studied.[22] Thus those dead at the scene or on arrival, or shortly afterwards, were not included. Each had fallen between one and seven stories, which were around 12 (newer buildings) to 15 (older buildings) feet per story.

The age range was 13 to 74 years with an average (mean) of 31.7. Twenty-three percent were female and 77 percent male. In the half of the cases where the circumstances were known, roughly 40 percent were attempted suicides,

50 percent accidents and 5 percent crime-related. The length of the hospitalization ranged from 1 to 120 days, with an average (mean) of 28.5 days.

Putting this in table form and comparing it to earlier studies:

Table 25.6 Relationship of Hospitalization Time, Deaths,[f] and Height of Fall										
Height of Fall/Jump in Stories										
	1	2	3	4	5	6	7	8	9+	Unknown Total
[Scalea, 1986]										
Number of Patients	29	45	38	29	9	6	5	0	0**	161
Average hospital stay, days	13	14	28	42	42	86	106			28.5
Deaths	0	0	0	3	1	2	2			8
Percent dying*	0	0	0	10	11	33	40			5
[Reynolds, 1970]										
Number of patients	37	54	31	27	25				26*	200
Average hospital stay, days										NA
Deaths	2	6	3	6	8				9*	34
Percent dying*	5	11	10	22	32				35*	17
[Lewis, 1965]										
Number of patients	NA	NA	15	11	7	11	2	1	6**	53
Average hospital stay, days										47
Deaths	NA	NA	5	7	2	10	1	0	6**	31
Percent dying*	NA	NA	33	64	38	91	50	0	100**	58

*From the death rates, it appears that medical care improved from 1965 to 1986. However, these studies are not directly comparable because Lewis includes only third-story and above jumpers in his data, while Scalea excludes those dead at the scene, dead on arrival, or dead before getting out of the emergency room.

What I find most striking in these data is the fact that such a large number (40 of 72) of jumpers survived fifth-floor and higher falls. The authors point out that these urban falls might be different from falls into water or in a rural setting; those who jump or fall from buildings may hit fire escapes or other projections, and can land on a number of possibly yielding surfaces: car roofs, soil, awnings, garbage piles, and pedestrians, among others.

There was a wide range of severe injuries to all parts of the body (Table 25.7). The most common was fracture: 79 percent of Scalea's patients had at least one major fracture (spine, pelvis, or long bone of arm or leg). While this was almost invariably true for falls of four or more stories (48 of 49 or 98 percent), even one-story falls had a significant number of such injuries. The overall survival rate was 95 percent (154 of 161) for those who made it out of the emergency room.

Table 25.7 (Scalea, 1986) Distribution of Bone Fractures by Height of Jump

Height Stories	1	2	3	4	5	6	7	Total
Number of patients at each height:	29	45	38	29	9	6	5	161
Percentage with:								
Spinal fracture								
Major	10%	18%	8%	24%	33%	50%	20%	18%
Minor	10%	2%	8%	3%	0%	16%	20%	6%
Pelvic fracture	10%	11%	16%	35%	55%	66%	60%	23%
Limb fracture	65%	80%	84%	78%	88%	83%	100%	79%

[May be greater than 100 percent, due to multiple fractures.]

Eleven of the twenty-eight (39 percent) with major spinal fracture had "neurological deficits": One had partial paralysis of all four limbs, one partial paralysis of the lower half of the body and the others complete paralysis of the lower half of the body. This is not exactly a desirable outcome whether you're trying to kill yourself or you intend a suicidal gesture.[g]

CASE REPORTS. A few unusual case report summaries may be of interest.

1. Landing in deep snow, if you can arrange it, is probably your best bet for surviving a long fall or jump. A twenty-one-year-old man jumped from seventeen stories and hit in a snowbank. He lived, but both legs had to be amputated. Another survived a 35,000 foot (almost 6.6 mile; 10.7 km) fall from an airplane.[23]

2. In another case, an eighteen-year-old jumped or fell from a fifth-floor roof. It had been raining so heavily that he sank one and a half feet into the soil and was uninjured.[24]

3. A fifteen-year-old fell out of a silo into a pile of dried cow manure. He bounced and landed on his side, breaking his wrist in the second fall.[25]

4. A forty-year-old "committed infanticide and then attempted suicide, jumping a distance of 44'5" from the roof of a tenement. He landed, barefoot, on a granite block. . . . His only injuries were a minimal fracture of the right pubic ramus and of a cervical vertebrae. He remained conscious after impacting and wandered off. . . . Police at first refused to believe that he had jumped."[26]

A DIGRESSION

After all this hard reading you deserve a break. The following cautionary tale is quoted from John W. Watts:

> At the 1994 annual awards dinner given by the American Association for Forensic Science, AAFS President Don Harper Mills astounded his audience in San Diego with the legal complications of a bizarre death. Here is the story. On 23 March 1994, the medical examiner viewed the body of Ronald Opus and concluded that he

died from a shotgun wound to the head. The decedent [about to turn twenty-one years old] had jumped from the top of a ten-story building intending to commit suicide. (He left a note indicating his despondency.) As he fell past the ninth floor, his life was interrupted by a shotgun blast through a window, which killed him instantly. Neither the shooter nor the decedent was aware that a safety net had been erected at the eighth floor level to protect some window washers and that Opus would not have been able to complete his suicide anyway because of this.

Ordinarily, Dr. Mills continued, a person who sets out to commit suicide ultimately succeeds, even though the mechanism might not be what he intended. That Opus was shot on the way to certain death nine stories below probably would not have changed his mode of death from suicide to homicide. But the fact that his suicidal intent would not have been successful caused the medical examiner to feel that he had a homicide on his hands.

The room on the ninth floor whence the shotgun blast emanated was occupied by an elderly man and his wife. They were arguing and he was threatening her with the shotgun. He was so upset that, when he pulled the trigger, he completely missed his wife and the pellets went through a window striking Opus. When one intends to kill subject A but kills subject B in the attempt, one is guilty of the murder of subject B. When confronted with this charge, the old man and his wife were both adamant that neither knew that the shotgun was loaded. The old man said it was his long-standing habit to threaten his wife with the unloaded shotgun. He had no intention of murdering her; therefore, the killing of Opus appeared to be an accident. That is, the gun had been accidentally loaded. The continuing investigation turned up a witness who saw the old couple's son loading the shotgun approximately six weeks prior to the fatal incident. It transpired that the old lady had cut off her son's financial support and the son, knowing the propensity of his father to use the shotgun threateningly, loaded the gun with the expectation that his father would shoot his mother. The case now becomes one of murder on the part of the son for the death of Ronald Opus.

There was another twist. Further investigation revealed that the son had become increasingly despondent over the failure of his attempt to engineer his mother's murder. This led him to jump off a ten-story building on March 23, only to be killed by a shotgun blast through a ninth-story window. The medical examiner closed the case as a suicide." The son had also been something of a musician and composer. He left his final composition on the windowsill, appropriately in the key of A-flat minor and titled "Opus Posthumous."

IMPACT WITH WATER

It was the Golden Gate Bridge or nothing.[h]

—A survivor

Thus far the discussion has been limited to falling on land. Leaping from bridges or cliffs into water is a bit different and is often considered more romantic. The results are, however, similar.

The Golden Gate Bridge is to suicide what Niagara Falls is to honeymoons: The most popular site in North America.[i] Joseph Strauss, the chief engineer during the bridge's construction, predicted that his masterpiece would be "practically suicide-proof." He was a considerably better bridge builder than seer: Between the opening of the bridge in 1937 (when ten workers fell simultaneously to their deaths) and 1990, 885 people are known to have leaped from Golden Gate;[27] the actual number, including those neither seen nor recovered, is certainly higher. In addition, eighty-seven people "accidentally" fell from this bridge between 1937 and 1963.[28] This is a particularly lethal bridge as well, with only nineteen of the 885-plus (less than 2 percent) living to tell about it.[29]

One August day in 1937, H. B. Wobber, a forty-nine-year-old bargeman, took a bus to the Golden Gate Bridge, paid his way through the pedestrian turnstile, and began to walk across the mile-long span. He was accompanied by a tourist he had met on the bus, Professor Lewis Naylor of Trinity College in Connecticut. They had strolled across the bridge which stretches in a single arch from San Francisco to the hills of Marin County, and were on their way back when Wobber tossed his coat and vest to Professor Naylor. "This is where I get off," he said quietly. "I'm going to jump." As Wobber climbed over the four-foot railing. the professor managed to grab his belt, but Wobber pulled free and leaped to his death.[30]

This was the first known suicide from the bridge, and took place three months after its opening.

Golden Gate soars 250 feet (76 meters) above water at mid span.[31] This is rail-to-water distance. There is no significant barrier; most people can easily step over the four-foot-high railing. A proposal to erect a suicide-preventing fence was opposed by a two-to-one majority in San Francisco[32] and rejected by the bridge district's board of directors as unaesthetic. Instead, "crisis phones" were installed, so that potential jumpers who wanted to talk things over could do so. No report as to how often they're used.[k]

The impact velocity of an average body jumping this distance is around 74 miles per hour, and fall time is around four seconds. One might expect water to be a more forgiving surface to fall on than concrete or asphalt, and it is, but at these speeds the difference is about as important as whether a bug is squashed by a car or by a truck: The distinction is academic. A study of one hundred consecutive autopsies of Golden Gate jumpers[33] found 44 percent female, 56 percent male. Age range was 15 to 86 years, with an average (mean) of 31.5 years; 97 percent were white, 2 percent black, and 1 percent Asian (spurring claims of racial discrimination and a short-lived demand for affirmative action by the California legislature).[l34]

The San Francisco Public Library keeps a file of old newspaper clippings on Golden Gate Bridge suicides. Most people get squibs; more column-inches are devoted to the "rich or famous, the oldest (87) or youngest (5),[m] or those leaving the strangest notes. (One person left this explanation: 'Absolutely no reason, except I have a toothache'.)"[35]

The official one-hundredth fatal jump took place in 1948. Fortunato Anguiano, a fifty-three-year-old dishwasher left a note saying, "Just bury me in my own land, the one you people take away from us."

After official number 499 in 1973, ghoulish TV stations (is this redundant?) set up twenty-four-hour-a-day cameras hoping to catch the numerologically significant number 500 on film. Police patrols were increased. The first fourteen applicants for the role (one wearing a T-shirt bearing the number 500) were all stopped or talked out of jumping, but number fifteen, twenty-six-year-old Steven Houg, evaded rescuers and leaped to his death.

The cameras missed it.

In June 1995, as the official number approached one thousand, similar charming media and popular behavior reappeared; for example, a radio station offered a case of Snapple (any flavor) to the family of number one thousand.[36] Since the California Highway Patrol stopped public reporting of jumpers after 997, I don't know if they ever paid up.

TYPES OF INJURY

Golden Gate jumpers show similar injuries to people hitting land: broken bones, shattered organs, torn veins and arteries. The distribution of these injuries differs from land falls, however: There are many more fatal chest injuries and fewer head traumas and bone fractures.[37]

CHEST AREA. Bleeding into the chest cavity was found in 82 percent, and lung damage in 87 percent of Golden Gate jumpers.[38] These injuries occurred about three times as often as in fatal urban falls in London.[39] Injury to the heart area occurred in around 20 percent of these jumps, and was often associated with broken ribs.

ABDOMEN. Liver and spleen laceration were the two most frequently damaged abdominal organs. This is similar to falls from above 50 feet on dry land. Abdominal bleeding was seen in 84 percent of the bodies (abdominal or chest bleeding is often a fatal injury because some of the largest blood vessels are found in this region). There was one case of shark mutilation: A young woman was pulled in with the entire abdominal wall and gastro-intestinal tract missing, after forty-five minutes in the water.

SKELETAL. Forty-two percent of Golden Gate jumpers had broken bones (other than ribs and sternum), significantly fewer than in land falls. Nine percent had skull fractures and 3 percent spinal cord transections[40] compared to 59 percent and 7 percent respectively, on land.[41] What's happening here is that the impact velocity of around 75 miles per hour is much greater than with the typical urban fall (a drop of four stories allows you to reach around 40 mph), while deceleration is spread out over a longer time. As a result, the mechanical strength of bone is less likely to be exceeded (fewer broken bones), but that of organs/tissues more likely exceeded, causing them to be fractured or torn away from their major blood vessels.

SURVIVORS. Of 6 initial survivors, 3 had pneumothorax (air in the chest cavity, preventing inflation of lungs); 3 required removal of their spleens; 2 had fractured livers; 4 had at least one compression spinal fracture (spine compressed after entering water feet or head first).

CASE REPORTS[42]

On 27 August 1980, a thirty-four-year-old West German stuntman known as Kid Courage, dressed in wetsuit, water ski jacket, flotation vest, and boxing shoes, [and with] his wrists, and ankles, stomach and chest taped, leaped from the Golden Gate Bridge in an attempt to establish a free-fall record. One witness observed that, after jumping, "he was trying to get his feet down but never made it and hit flat on his back." Another witness, an expert diver, suggested that the 15- to 20-knot wind might have been a factor in his instability while falling. The jumper was lifeless when pulled from the water by colleagues who had watched the spectacle from below.

On autopsy he was found to have multiple spinal fractures and transection of the spinal chord. In addition, there were severe lacerations of the liver, spleen, and lungs. "Any one of these injuries would have proved fatal."[43]

Divers in Acapulco jump several times a day from 135-foot-high cliffs. This corresponds to hitting the water at about 60 miles per hour. With perfect entry into the water—arms rigidly extended and thumbs locked—they show little evidence of chronic damage even after many years of diving.[44] Perhaps they don't dive when it's windy.

Entering feet first is second-best. An "almost perfect" feet-first entry from Golden Gate Bridge still resulted in three spinal compression fractures in an otherwise uninjured seventeen-year-old jumper.[45]

OTHER BRIDGES

It seems reasonable to expect that bridges lower than Golden Gate will be less lethal, and this is the case. For example, four bridges in Denmark, which average 40 meters (130 feet) above water, have a jumper-survival rate estimated to be around 25 percent[46] and a majority of the deaths are attributed to drowning, rather than trauma.

The reason these Danish jumpers were studied is interesting. It goes back to 1974. In that year a Danish husband was accused of strangling his wife and tossing her over a 28 meter (92 foot) bridge into water. At autopsy, among other findings, there were fractures of her jaw, cheek, nose, and thyroid cartilage. The question of whether or not these injuries could be the result of a 28 meter fall into water was obviously critical, but apparently nobody knew the answer and the man was acquitted. The courts recommended the production of reference materials on this topic, which was done using undisputed suicides. In none of the ten cases autopsied, with jumps of between 35 to 51 meters (114 to 167 feet), were there any injuries of the face, jaw, or neck organs.

OTHER JUMPS

Perhaps the second-most-famous jump site in the world is the Mt. Mihara volcano in Japan. In January 1933, a girl jumped to her death there. The next month another girl from the same school did the same. A legend soon arose that they were instantly cremated and their souls went straight to heaven in a plume of smoke. On a single day in April, six people jumped and twenty-five more were forcibly prevented from doing so. By the end of 1933, there were 133 known suicides and an unknown, but large, number of others were suspected. Despite police efforts (including prohibition on sale of one-way ferry tickets to the volcano's island), there were 619 confirmed jumps in 1936 alone, but suicides here didn't stop until 1955, when a badly injured couple who had jumped were rescued from inside the crater. This destroyed the illusion of jiffy cremation and, apparently, the allure of the volcano.[47]

FALLS FROM EXTREME HEIGHTS

Due to friction with air, a human body reaches a constant (appropriately called "terminal") velocity of around 120 miles per hour (54 meters, or 60 yards, per second) after falling approximately 480 feet (35 to 40 stories).[48] Thus, if it's any consolation, you won't hit any harder from a 20,000 foot fall than from 500, though you will have a longer trip.

Terminal velocity varies, and can be significantly changed by choice of clothing and the position assumed during the fall: Vertical, with good dive form is fastest, around 185 mph; horizontal, with limbs spread is slowest, 120 mph.[49] For example, in 1885 twenty-four-year-old Sarah Henley jumped from the Clifton suspension bridge, a 250-foot-high structure in Bristol, England. According to the *Guinness Book of World Records*, her "voluminous dress and petticoat acted as a parachute," and she landed in the mud, merely "bruised and bedraggled."[50] This feat (sans dress and petticoat) was recently matched by an eighteen-year-old male.[51] He described seeing himself as a detached observer,[n] the fall as pleasurable, and time passing slowly.

Correcting for air resistance, we have impact velocities as follows:[52]

Table 25.8 Approximate Impact Velocity for Falls from Various Heights

	Height in:		Velocity at end of fall in:	
stories	feet	meters	mph	kph
3	40	13	35	56
4	53	17	41	65
5	65	21	45	71
6	78	25	49	78
16	210	70	75	119
40	520	170	120	191

However, one study found that injuries and deaths were not well-correlated with either the height of the fall or the nature of the surface landed on: "In the past two years at least ninety persons have survived falls of 100 to 900 feet, and nine have survived falls of over 1,000 feet"[53] and concludes that "some individuals survive free-falls terminating on nonyielding rigid structures at exceedingly large magnitudes of force with minor injury or, occasionally, with no apparent clinical trauma." Interesting, if true. While the author makes some speculations, the reason(s) these high falls are survived is not known.

These extreme falls are usually jumps from airplanes. One person survived for twelve hours after a seven-mile (around four-minute) fall.

Of twelve people who survived falls of more than 100 feet, ten landed on their feet.[54] Since feet have a smaller area than does the torso, the impact pressure (force per area) is greater, but this is apparently more than offset by the structural strength of the vertical bones and muscles.

However, these cases are interesting and turn up in medical journals because they are unusual; death is almost always the result of a fall of this magnitude.

SUMMARY

Suicidal jumps from higher than approximately 150 feet (10 to 12 stories) on land and 250 feet over water are about 95 to 98 percent fatal. However, a majority of jumps on land are between 20 and 50 feet. These shorter jumps are a crap shoot and often cause permanent injury, possibly paralysis and brain damage. Other than the view, there are better ways to go.

NOTES

[a]There are typically around twelve to thirteen thousand deaths from falls in the United States annually. The fraction of falls that are suicides is claimed to be between 20 to 45 percent (Goonetilleke, 1980; Lewis, 1965; Gupta, 1982). This is a lot more than the six or seven hundred cited in official U.S. statistics. Why the big discrepancy? Part of it may be because only about half of suicidal jumps are so classified (Cooper, 1995); for the rest, I have no good explanation.

[b]Finnish stories are apparently shorter than New York stories, except, perhaps, the Kalevala.

[c]The actual numbers are not dramatically different from month to month. In the United States, the 1989-1991 average number of daily suicides was: January 84.22; February 83.89; March 84.45; April 86.39; May 85.32; June 87.94; July 87.92; August 85.61; September 84.13; October 81.61; November 81.82; December 74.46 (U.S. Vital Statistics; as calculated by John L. McIntosh).

[d]It is astonishing that, in many of the journal articles I looked at, there are obvious arithmetic errors. In this instance the author claims thirty-seven suicides in the text, but the data table numbers add up to thirty-eight. Most of the discrepancies are minor, like this one, but they're not confidence-inspiring. A recent study in and of the prestigious *British Journal of Psychiatry* found that 40 percent of the articles that presented numerical data had "at least one error in [research] design, statistical analysis and/or presentation of numerical results" (McGuigan, 1995). Don't believe everything you read.

[e]The Injury Severity Score (ISS) is a widely used quantitative measure of the number and severity of injuries. An alternative explanation for the discrepancy between the ISS and jump survival is that the ISS is not a very good gauge of lethality. It has been criticized for generating higher severity scores for multiple moderately serious injuries than for a single critical one.

[f]In Scalea's patients, death was due to massive internal bleeding (three cases; one person died despite receiving 20 units of blood in an hour); head injury (two cases); infection after internal bleeding (one case); unexplained cardiac arrest (heart stopped, one case); and unrecognized tracheal stenosis (narrowing of windpipe, presumably due to injury, one case). Similarly, Lewis cited brain and chest damage, and abdominal bleeding as cause of death. In Reynolds's study, 30 of the 34 dead had skull fractures, sometimes in addition to other damage; brain trauma was the most common fatal injury.

[g]In case you haven't thought it through, complete paralysis may mean (depending on the site of the spinal damage) that you will be essentially helpless for the rest of your life: fed by someone else; reliant on someone to change your diaper (no voluntary muscle control); strapped into a wheelchair like a sack of potatoes; prey to recurrent infections; and subject to pressure sores on your back, buttocks, and legs, because you can't move around.

[h]According to the California Highway Patrol and bridge workers, about two-thirds of potential jumpers are talked out of it, and of these, apparently very few go on to kill themselves by other means (*New York Times*, July 9, 1995). In one (perhaps apocryphal) instance, a policeman is said to have shouted, "Come down or I'll shoot!" to a would-be jumper, who obediently climbed down.

[i]In the 1930s and '40s sixteen people died from jumps off the Empire State Building, but this pretty much ended with the erection of a fence around the observation tower. Golden Gate is preferred to the Bay Bridge (which connects San Francisco to the East Bay) by more than five to one despite similarities: about the same height, opened within months of each other, and near each other. Bay Bridge doesn't have pedestrian walkways; nevertheless, about three times as many car drivers jumped from Golden Gate. Indeed, as many East Bay drivers jumped from Golden Gate (fifty-eight) as from Bay Bridge (fifty-seven) (Seiden, 1983-1984).

[j]A reverse-psychology approach has also been suggested: installing a diving board, with a nearby hook for hanging one's coat and a mailbox for the convenient deposit of suicide notes.

[k]In 1977, the bridge's 40th anniversary, a rally was held by pro-barrier activists. One of the speakers said, "It is entirely fitting that on Memorial Day we are here on account of the hundreds of people who are not casualties of war, but casualties of society . . . in the final analysis, we have to bear collective responsibility for those individuals who could not find a place

to go with their burdens, who came to that place of total helplessness, total despondency, where they took their own lives here . . ." The speaker was Jim Jones, who led the mass suicide of 900 of his followers less than two years later. [Seiden 1979]

lWhile that piece of legislation is bogus, there was a presumably serious attempt to make it against the law to commit suicide by jumping from the bridge (New York Times, July 9, 1995). The effectiveness of such legislation is open to question.

mA two-year-old squeezed through a gap and fell to her death on December 22, 1997 (Washington Post, December 22, 1997), though I doubt that this was a suicide.

nOne way of responding to terror.

AFTERWORD, OR WHERE DO WE GO FROM HERE?

As of this writing, the central legal, legislative, and ethical suicide issue in the United States is physician-assisted suicide (PAS). PAS is the most reliable and least traumatic approach to suicide, and has been carried out since at least the time of the early Greeks. (Hippocrates' Oath was partly in response to this practice.) The current ethical arguments, for and against it, were laid out in the early 1870s and have changed remarkably little.[a] Meanwhile, medical ability to prolong dying has increased to the point where the public is often more afraid of dying than of death. This is the driving force for legalization of assisted suicide.

The ethical situation is not entirely clear-cut in PAS; both sides have valid points. Under the circumstances, there is really no way of knowing if opponents' fears will come to pass. Thus, the ongoing experience with PAS in Oregon will be of great importance, and should answer some of the questions of potential abuse. The three-decade-long history of PAS in the Netherlands is also generally reassuring, though the differences between Dutch and American society makes extrapolations tentative.

I do not expect many of the already decided to change their position quickly as a result of the information from Oregon starting to trickle in; people are quite capable of reaching divergent conclusions from the same data. The debate will continue, as it should; but we will at last, have some facts and evidence to guide us.

REFERENCES

INTRODUCTION

1. D. P. Phillips and A. G. Sanzone, "A Comparison of Injury Date and Death Date in 42,698 Suicides," *Am J Public Health* 78(5) (May 1988): 541–43.

2. Ted R. Miller, *Databook on Nonfatal Injury: Incidence, Costs, and Consequences* (Washington, D.C.: Urban Institute Press, 1995).

3. John Langone, *Dead End* (Boston: Little, Brown, 1986), 2.

4. Colt, 235.

CHAPTER 1: A BRIEF OVERVIEW OF SUICIDE

1. Erwin Stengel, *Suicide and Attempted Suicide* (Baltimore, Md.: Penguin, 1964), 73.

2. N. Retterstol, *Suicide: A European Perspective* (London: Cambridge University Press, 1990; trans. 1993) ix.

3. National Center for Health Statistics, 1994. Centers for Disease Control and Prevention (CDC) web site. http://wonder.cdc.gov

4. Ted R. Miller, *Databook on Nonfatal Injury: Incidence, Costs, and Consequences* (Washington, D.C.: Urban Institute Press, 1995), 166–67.

5. George Colt, *The Enigma of Suicide* (New York: Summit Books, 1991), 373.

6. Miller, 167.

7. National Center for Health Statistics, *Monthly Vital Statistics* 39 (November 28, 1990), Table 125, CDC, 1992 data.

8. D. C. Clark, " 'Rational' Suicide and People with Terminal Conditions or Disabilities," *Issues in Law and Medicine* 8(2) (Fall 1992): 147–66.

9. D. P. Phillips and T. E. Ruth, "Adequacy of Official Suicide Statistics for Scientific Research and Public Policy," *Suicide and Life-threatening Behavior* 23(4) (Winter 1993): 307–19.

10. Robert Litman, "Psycholegal Aspects of Suicide," in W. J. Curran, et al., eds. *Modern Legal Medicine Psychiatry and Forensic Science* (Philadelphia: Davis, 1980), 842.

11. Stengel, 39. E. S. Shneidman and N. L. Farberow, *Clues to Suicide* (New York: McGraw Hill, 1957) 197–215. J. Tuckman, "Emotional Content of Suicide Notes," *Am J Psychiatry* 116 (1959): 59–63. D. Lester, *The Cruelest Death: The Enigma of Adolescent Suicide* (Philadelphia: Charles Press, 1993), 35.

12. P. N. Cooper and C. M. Milroy, "The Coroner's System and Underreporting of Suicide," *Medicine Science and the Law* 35(4) (October 1995): 319–26.

13. S. E. Wallace and A. Eser, eds. *Suicide and Euthanasia* (Knoxville: University of Tennessee Press, 1981), 74–76.

14. R. F. Diekstra and W. Gulbinat, "The Epidemiology of Suicidal Behaviour: A Review of Three Continents," *World Health Statistics Quarterly* 46(1) (1993): 52–68.

15. C. L. Rich, et al., "San Diego Suicide Study: I. Young vs. Old Subjects," *Archives of General Psychiatry* 43 (1986): 577–78.

16. S. P. Baker, *The Injury Fact Book* 2nd ed. (New York: Oxford University Press, 1992) 65. M. M. Weissman, "The Epidemiology of Suicide Attempts, 1960–1971," *Archives of General Psychiatry* 30 (1974) 737–46. R. C. Bland S. C. Newman and R. I. Dyck, "The Epidemiology of Parasuicide in Edmonton," *Canadian J Psychiatry* 39(8) (October 1994): 391–6.

17. Stephen Flanders, *Suicide* (New York: Facts on File, 1991), 21.

18. C. Z. Garrison, "The Study of Suicidal Behavior in the Schools," *Suicide and Life threatening Behavior* 19(1) (Spring 1989): 120–30.

19. Colt, 96.

20. Herbert Hendin, *Suicide in America*, 1st ed., (New York: Norton, 1982), 49.

21. Karl Menninger, *Man Against Himself* (New York: Harvest/Harcourt, 1938).

22. James Carroll, *The Winter Name of God* (New York: Sheed and Ward, 1975), 87–88.

23. Tom Dunkel, "A Brief Handhold on a Dream" *Washington Post* (May 14, 1996), E1.

24. A. Alvarez, *The Savage God* (New York: Random House, 1971), 253.

25. National Center for Health Statistics. CDC (Centers for Disease Control and Prevention) web site. http: //wonder.cdc.gov

26. P. J. Meehan, et al., "Attempted Suicide Among Young Adults: Progress Toward a Meaningful Estimate of Prevalence," *Am J Psychiatry* January 1992: 41–44; comment, *Am J Psychiatry* 150 (1) (January 1993): 171. R. K. Lee, et al., "Incidence Rates of Firearm Injuries in Galveston, Texas, 1979–1981" *Am J Epidemiology* 134 (5) (September 1, 1991): 511–21. G. C. Birkhead, et al., "The Emergency Department in Surveillance of Attempted Suicide: Findings and Methodologic Considerations," *Public Health Reports* 108 (3) (May–June (1993): 323–31. P. D. Blanc, M. R. Jones, and K. R. Olson, "Surveillance of Poisoning and Drug Overdose Through Hospital Discharge Coding, Poison Control Center Reporting, and the Drug Abuse Warning Network," *Am J Emergency Med* 11 (1): (January 1993): 14–9.

27. G. H. Li and S. P. Baker, "A Comparison of Injury Death Rates in China and the United States, 1986," *Am J Public Health* 81 (1991): 605–9. C. Pritchard, "Suicide in the People's Republic of China Categorized by Age and Gender: Evidence of the Influence of Culture on Suicide," *Acta Psychiatrica Scandinavica* 93 (5) (May 1996): 362–67.

28. Ahmed Okasha and F. Lotaif, "Attempted Suicide: An Egyptian Investigation," *Acta Psychiatrica Scandinavica* 60 (1) (July 1979): 69–75. L. Headley, ed., *Suicide in Asia and the Near East* (Berkeley: University of California Press, 1993), 216.

29. Mary Holland, in *The Observer*, (1967); quoted in Alvarez, 82.

30. D. P. Phillips and T. E. Ruth, "Adequacy of Official Suicide Statistics for Scientific Research and Public Policy," *Suicide and Life-threatening Behav* 23 (4) (Winter 1993): 307–19.

31. R. Smith, "Deaths in Prison," *British Medical Journal* 288 (1984): 208–212. L. M. Hayes, "National Study of Jail Suicides," *Psychiatric Quarterly* 60 (1989): 7–29.

32. M. E. Wolfgang, "Suicide by Means of Victim-precipitated Homicide," *J Clinical and Experimental Psychopathology and Quarterly Review of Psychiatry and Neurology* 20 (1959): 335–49. See also Resnik, 90–104.

CHAPTER 2: HISTORY OF SUICIDE

1. J. H. Breasted, *Development of Religion and Thought in Ancient Egypt* (New York: Scribner's Sons, 1912), 163–69.

2. A. Alvarez, *The Savage God* (New York: Random House, 1971), 49.

3. Matthew 5:39; 43–4.

4. Tertullian, *De Corona* 11, quoted in James, Rachels *The End of Life: Euthanasia and Morality* (Oxford and New York: Oxford University Press, 1986), 10.

5. Alvarez, 49. For a more detailed (and acerbic) discussion, see D. W. Amundsen, "The Significance of Innaccurate History in Legal Considerations of Physician-assisted Suicide," in R. F. Weir, ed, *Physician-assisted Suicide* (Indianapolis: Indiana University Press, 1997), 3–32.

6. Alvarez, 50.

7. News from London newspapers around 1860, in a letter from Nicholas Ogarev to his mistress, quoted in E. H. Carr *The Romantic Exiles* (Cambridge, Mass: MIT Press, 1981; originally London: Gollancz, 1933), 389; cited in Alvarez, 43.

8. Emile Durkheim, *Suicide: A Study in Sociology* (Glencoe, Ill: Free Press, 1951), 218.

9. Alvarez, 65.

10. Ibid., 67.

11. Stephen Flanders, *Suicide* (New York: Facts on File, 1991), 10.

12. William Shakespeare, *Antony and Cleopatra*, Act IV, Scene XV, 80–82.

13. M. P. Battin, *The Least Worst Death: Essays in Bioethics on the End of Life* (New York: Oxford University Press, 1994), 190.

14. N. Clark, *The Politics of Physician Assisted Suicide* (New York: Garland Press, 1997), 35–36.

15. B. M. Barraclough, "The Bible Suicides," *Acta Psychiatrica Scandinavica* 86 (1) (July 1992): 64–69.

16. G. Rosen, "History," in S. Perlin, ed., *A Handbook for the Study of Suicide* (New York: Oxford University Press, 1975).

17. Augustine, *City of God*, book 1, chapter 21. Battin, 210–11.

18. Stengel, 69.

19. Clarke and Lester, 87.

20. Alvarez, 161.

21. S. Kovelevski, "Inmate Survives Overdose, Is Sent Back for Execution," *Washington Post* (August 12, 1995), A3.

CHAPTER 3: THREE WAYS TO STUDY SUICIDE

1. A. J. Droge and J. D. Tabor, *A Noble Death: Suicide and Martyrdom Among Christians and Jews in Antiquity* (San Francisco: HarperSanFransisco, 1992).

2. N. Retterstol, *Suicide: A European Perspective* (London: Cambridge University Press, 1990 trans. 1993), 26.

3. Retterstol, 14.

4. P. Friedman, ed., *On Suicide* (New York: International Universities Press, 1967), quoted in George Colt, *The Enigma of Suicide* (New York: Summit Books, 1991), 194.

5. Colt, 58–59.

6. K. Minkoff, A. T. Beck, and R. E. Beran, "Hopelessness, Depression, and Attempted Suicide," *Am J Psychiatry* 130: 455–59.

7. A. T. Beck, et al., "Hopelessness and Eventual Suicide: A 10-year Prospective Study of Patients Hospitalized with Suicidal Ideation," *Am J Psychiatry* 142 (1985): 559–63. See also, W. Breitbart, "Suicide Risk and Pain in Cancer and AIDS Patients," in *Current and Emerging Issues in Cancer Pain: Research and Practice*, C. R. Chapman and K. M. Foley, eds. (New York: Raven Press, 1993), 49–65.

8. J. H. Greist, et al., "A Computer Interview for Suicide Risk Prediction" *Am J Psychiatry* 130(12) (1973): 1327–32.

9. H. J. Moller, "Efficacy of Different Strategies of Aftercare for Patients Who Have Attempted Suicide," *J Royal Society of Medicine* 82(11) (November 1989): 643–647. S. A. Montgomery, et al., "Pharmacotherapy in the Prevention of Suicidal Behavior," *J Clinical Psychopharmacology* 12 (supp. 2) (April 1992): 27–31; comment: *J Clinical Psychopharmacology* 13(2) (April 1993): 159–60.

10. A. S. Hale, "Juggling Cost and Benefit in the Long-term Treatment of Depression," *Postgraduate Med J* 70 (supp. 2) (1994): 2–8.

11. W. Haberlandt, "Contributions to the Genetics of Suicide," *Folia Clinica Internacional* 17 (1967): 319–22. Brent Q. Hafen, and Kathryn J. Frandsen, *Youth Suicide, Depression and Loneliness* (Evergreen, CO: Cordillera Press, 1986), 22. K. Y. Little and D. L. Sparks, "Brain markers and suicide: can a relationship be found?" *J Forensic Science* 35(6) (November): 1393–1403.

12. S. Kety, "Genetic Features in Suicide: Family, Twins, and Adoption Studies" in S. J. Blumenthal and D. I. Kupfer, eds., *Suicide Over the Life Cycle: Risk Factors, Assessment, and Treatment of Suicidal Patients* (Washington, D.C.: American Psychiatric Press, 1990), 127–33.

13. J. Langone, *Dead End* (Boston: Little, Brown, 1986), 32.

14. M. Asberg, et al., "Biological Factors in Suicide," in Alec Roy, ed., *Suicide* (Baltimore: Williams and Wilkins, 1986). M. Asberg, in H. Meltzer, ed., *Psychopharmacology: The Third Generation of Progress* (New York: Raven Press, 1987), 655–68.

15. S. A. Montgomery, et al., "Differential Effects on Suicidal Ideation of Mianserin, Maprotiline, and Amitriptyline," *British J Clinical Pharmacology* 5 (supp. 1) (1978): 77–80. W. H. W. Inman, "Blood Disorders and Suicide in Patients Taking Mianserin or Amitriptyline," *Lancet* (July 9, 1988): 90–92.

16. Retterstol, 132.

17. David Lester, *Why People Kill Themselves: A 1990s Summary of Research Findings on Suicidal Behavior*, 3rd ed. (Springfield, Ill; Thomas, 1992).

18. N. Retterstol, "Norwegian Data on Death Due to Overdose of Antidepressants," *Acta Psychiatrica Scandinavica* 80 (supp. 354) (1989): 61–68.

19. David C. Clark, quoted in N. Angier, "Quest for Evolutionary Meaning in the Persistence of Suicide," *New York Times* (April 5, 1994): C1.

20. L. Salk, et al., "Relationship of Maternal and Perinatal Conditions to Eventual Adolescent Suicide," *Lancet* 1 (March 16, 1985): 624–27.

21. B. Jacobson, et al., "Perinatal Origin of Adult Self-destructive Behavior," *Acta Psychiatrica Scandinavica* 76 (1987): 364–71.

22. For a lucid description of the genetic basis for altruism, see Richard Dawkins, *The Selfish Gene* (New York: Oxford University Press, 1976) and E. O. Wilson, *On Human Nature* (Cambridge, MA: Harvard University Press, 1978). For its specific application to suicide there is a good *New York Times* Science article, "Quest for Evolutionary Meaning in the Persistence of Suicide," by Natalie Angier (April 5, 1994).

23. F. Rouillon, "Recurrence of Unipolar Depression and Efficacy of Maprotiline," *L'Encephale* (1989): 527–34. D. L. Gardner and R. W. Cowdry, "Alprazolam-induced Dyscontrol in Borderline Personality Disorder," *Am J Psychiatry* 142 (1) (January 1985): 98–100.

Chapter 4: Why People Attempt Suicide

1. Margaret Hyde and Elizabeth Forsyth, *Suicide: the Hidden Epidemic* (Minneapolis: Comp-Care, 1986), ch. 6.

2. Loren Coleman, *Suicide Clusters* (Boston and London: Faber and Faber, 1987), 18.

3. Coleman, 17.

4. Marvin Wolfgang, *Patterns in Criminal Homicide* (Philadelphia: University of Pennsylvania Press, 1958).

5. P. M. Marzuk, K. Tardiff and C. S. Hirsch, "The Epidemiology of Murder-suicide," *JAMA* 267(23) (June 17, 1992): 3179–83; see comment, 3194–95. Paul C. Holinger, et al., *Suicide and Homicide among Adolescents* (New York: Guilford, 1994).

6. George Colt, *The Enigma of Suicide* (New York: Summit Books, 1991), 44.

7. Brent Q. Hafen, and Kathryn J. Frandsen, *Youth Suicide, Depression and Loneliness* (Evergreen, CO: Cordillera Press, 1986), 107.

8. R. A. Goodman, et al., "Alcohol and Fatal Injuries in Oklahoma," *J Studies on Alcohol* 52(2) (1991):156–61.

9. A. S. Nielsen, et al., "Attempted Suicide, Suicidal Intent, and Alcohol," *Crisis* 14(1) (1993): 32–38.

10. H. Hendin, *Suicide in America*, 2nd ed. (New York: Norton, 1995), 42.

11. S. P. Avis and C. J. Hutton, "Dyadic Suicide. A Case Study," *Am J Forensic Med and Pathology* 15(1) (1994): 18–20.

12. D. A. Fishbain and T. E. Aldrich, "Suicide Pacts: International Comparisons," *J Clinical Psychiatryiat* 46 (1985): 11–15.

13. Loren Coleman, *Suicide Clusters*, 1987.

14. M. S. Gould, "Suicide Clusters and Media Exposure," in S. J. Blumenthal, *Suicide Over the Life Cycle*, (Washington, D.C.: Am. Psychiatric Press, 1990), 517–32.

15. Coleman, 107–9.

16. S. Fekete, et al., "The Role of Imitation in Suicidal Behavior," *Orvosi Hetilap* (*Physician's Weekly* 133(1) (January 5, 1992): 25–28.

17. C. Karlson-Stiber, and H. Persson, "Ethylene Glycol Poisoning: Experiences from an Epidemic in Sweden," *J Toxicology and Clinical Toxicology* 30(4) (1992): 565–74.

18. D. P. Phillips and L. L. Carstensen, "Clustering of Teenage Suicides after Television News Stories About Suicide," *New England J Med* 315(11) (September 11, 1986): 685–89.

19. Thomas Radecki, "Deer Hunter Deaths Climb to 43," *National Coalition on Television Violence News* 7:1–2 (January–March 1986); for a contrary view, see D. A. Phillips and D. J. Paight, "The Impact of Televised Movies About Suicide. A Replicative Study," *New England J Med* 317(13) (September 24, 1987): 809–11.

20. K. Yoshida, et al., "Clustering of Suicides Under Age 20—Seasonal Trends and the Influence of Newspaper Reports," *Nippon Koshu Eisei Zasshi* 38(5) (May 1991): 324–32.

21. D. A. Jobes, et al., "The Kurt Cobain Suicide Crisis: Perspectives from Research, Public Health, and the News Media," *Suicide and Life-threatening Behavior* 26(3) (Fall 1996): 260–69; discussion, 269–71.

22. E. W. Busse, and E. Pfeiffer, eds. *Mental Illness in Later Life* (Washington, D.C.: American Psychiatry Press, 1973).

23. Colt, 98.

24. L. Dolce, *Suicide* (New York: Chelsea House, 1992), 23.

25. A. F. Henry, and J. F. Short, Jr., *Suicide and Homicide: Some Economic Sociological, and Psychological Aspects of Aggression* (Glencoe, Ill: Free Press, 1954).

26. D. Lester, "The Association Between the Quality of Life and Suicide and Homicide Rates," *J Social Psychology* 124 (December 1984): 47–48 [1984a]. D. Lester, *Patterns of Suicide and Homicide in the World* (Commack, N.Y.: Nova Science, 1996), 45–57.

27. D. Lester, "The Quality of Life and Suicide," *J Social Psychology* 125 (1985): 279–80; more on the relationship between economics, suicide, and homicide in J. P. Gibbs, and W. T. Martin, *Status Integration and Suicide: A Sociological Study* (Eugene, Oregon: University of Oregon Press, 1964).

28. D. Lester, and B. Danto, *Suicide Behind Bars: prediction and prevention* (Philadelphia: Charles Press, 1993), 17–20.

29. K. Kwiet, *Leo Baeck Institute Yearbook* 29 (1984): 135–68.

30. Erwin Stengel, *Suicide and Attempted Suicide* (New York: J. Aronson, 1974), 28.

31. Patrick O'Carroll, "Suicide Causation; Pies, Paths and Pointless Polemics," *Suicide and Life-threatening Behavior* 23(1) (1993): 27–36.

32. E. Shneidman, in B. Bongar, ed., *Suicide: Guidelines for Assessment, Management, and Treatment* (New York: Oxford University Press, 1992), 6.

33. F. Winslow, *The Anatomy of Suicide* (London: Renshaw, 1840); quoted in A. Alvarez, *The Savage God* (New York: Random House, 1971), 212.

34. E. Stengel, and N. Cook, *Attempted Suicide: Its Social Significance and Effects* (Westport, Conn.; Greenwood Press, 1958), 19.

35. L. I. Dublin, *Suicide—A Sociological and Statistical Study* (New York: Ronald Press, 1963).

36. Robert Litman, "Psycholegal Aspects of Suicide," in W. J. Curran, et al., (eds) *Modern Legal Medicine Psychiatry and Forensic Science* (Philadelphia: Davis, 1980), 844.

37. Dublin, 10–12.

38. R. W. Ettlinger and P. Flordh, "Attempted Suicide," *Acta Psychiatrica et Neurologica Scandinavica* 103 (1955).

39. R. Plutchik, et al., "Is There a Relation Between the Seriousness of Suicidal Intent and the Lethality of the Suicide Attempt?" *Psychiatry Research* 27(1): (January 1989): 71–9. S. Greer, et al., "Subsequent Progress of Potentially Lethal Attempted Suicides," *Acta Psychiatrica Scandinavica* 43 (1967): 361. L. G. Peterson, "Self-inflicted Gunshot Wounds: Lethality of Method Versus Intent," *Am J Psychiatry* 142(2) (1985): 228–31. J. J. Card, "Lethality of Suicidal Methods and Suicide Risk: Two Distinct Concepts," *Omega* 5 (1974): 37–45.

40. J. J. Mann, et al., "Neurochemical Studies of Violent and Nonviolent Suicide," *Psychopharmacology Bulletin* 25(3) (1989): 407–13.

41. I. B. James, "Blood Alcohol Levels Following Successful Suicide," *Quarterly Journal of Studies on Alcohol* 27 (1966): 23–29.

42. D. Lester, "Personal Violence (Suicide and Homicide) in South Africa," *Acta Psychiatrica Scandinavica* 79 (1989): 235–37.

CHAPTER 5: YOUTH SUICIDE

1. M. Cimons, "Study shows a million teen suicide attempts" *Los Angeles Times,* (September 20, 1991), P A-1.

2. C. Z. Garrison, "The Study of Suicidal Behavior in the Schools," *Suicide and Life-threatening Behavior* 19(1) (Spring 1989): 120–30.

3. The Centers for Disease Control and Prevention (CDC), "Fatal and Nonfatal Suicide Attempts Among Adolescents—Oregon, 1988–1993," *MMWR: Morbidity and Mortality Weekly Report* 44(16), (April 28, 1995): 312–15, 321–23.

4. M. J. Marttunen, et al., "Suicide Among Female Adolescents: Characteristics and Comparison with Males in the Age Group 13 to 22 Years," *J Am Academy of Child and Adolescent Psychiatry* 34(10) (October 1995): 1297–307.

5. C. G. Wilber, "Some Thoughts on Suicide," *Am J Forensic Med and Pathology* 8(4) (1987): 302–8.

6. The Centers for Disease Control and Prevention (CDC), "Fatal and Nonfatal Suicide Attempts Among Adolescents—Oregon, 1988–1993," *MMWR: Morbidity and Mortality Weekly Report* 44(16), (April 28, 1995): 312–15, 321–23.

7. C. Runyan, and E. A. Gerken, "Epidemiology and Prevention of Adolescent Injury: A Review and Research Agenda," *Journal of the American Medical Association* 262 (1989): 2273–79.

8. M. Males, "Teen Suicide and Changing Cause-of-death Certification, 1953–1987," *Suicide and Life-threatening Behavior* 21(3) (1991): 245–59. M. Males, "Reply to Kim Smith, Ph.D., on *Teen Suicide and Changing Cause-of-death Certification, 1953–1987,*" *Suicide and Life-threatening Behavior* 21(4) (1991): 402–5.

9. W. Leary, "Young People Who Try Suicide May Be Succeeding More Often," *New York Times* (April 21, 1995), A15.

10. D. Lester, "Youth Suicide: A Cross-Cultural Perspective," *Adolescence* 23 (1988): 955–58.

11. D. Lester, "Changes in the Methods Used for Suicide in 16 Countries from 1960 to 1980," *Acta Psychiatrica Scandinavica* 81(3): (March 1990): 260–1.

12. George Colt, *The Enigma of Suicide* (New York: Summit Books, 1991), 48.

13. E. Shneidman, *Definition of Suicide* (New York: Wiley, 1985), 229; in Colt, 312.

14. Colt, 47.

15. Ibid., 47.

16. M. Pinguet, *Voluntary Death in Japan,* (Cambridge, UK and MA, Polity Press, 1993), 35.

17. C. H. Cantor, et al., "Suicide Trends in Eight Predominantly English-speaking Countries, 1960–1989," *Social Psychiatry and Psychiatric Epidemiology* 31 (6) (November 1996): 364–73.

CHAPTER 6: SUICIDE IN THE ELDERLY AND OTHER GROUPS

1. E. Busse, and E. Pfeiffer, *Mental Illness in Later Life* (Washington, D.C.: American Psychiatry Press, 1973), 123–26.

2. R. W. Maris, "The Developmental Perspective of Suicide," in A. A. Leenaars, (ed) *Life Span Perspective of Suicide* (New York: Plenum, 1991) 35.

3. J. L. McIntosh, "Suicide Among the Elderly: Levels and Trends," *American Journal of Orthopsychiatry* 55(2) (1985): 288–93.

4. Herbert Hendin, *Suicide in America*, 2nd ed. (New York: Norton, 1995), 81.

5. Y. Conwell, and E. D. Caine, "Rational Suicide and the Right to Die: Reality and Myth," *New England J Med* 325 (1991): 1100–3.

6. P. J. Meehan, et al., "Suicide Among Older United States Residents: Epidemiologic Characteristics and Trends," *Am J Public Health* 81 (1991): 1198–1200. National Center for Health Statistics, CDC (Centers for Disease Control and Prevention) web site. http://wonder.cdc.gov. Nat Center for Health Statistics, 39 *Monthly Vital Statistics* Nov 28, 1990.

7. Nancy J. Osgood, *Suicide in Later Life: Recognizing the Warning Signs* (New York: Lexington Books, 1992), 15.

8. P. N. Cooper and C. M. Milroy, "The Coroner's System and Underreporting of Suicide," *Medicine Science and the Law* 35(4) (October 1995): 319–26.

9. Y. Conwell, E. D. Caine, and K. Olsen, "Suicide and Cancer in Late Life," *Hospital Community Psychiatry* 41(12) (December 1990): 1334–39.

10. N. S. Patel, "A Study on Suicide," *Medicine Science and the Law* 14(2) (1973): 129–36.

11. J. W. Eisele, et al., "Teenage Suicide in King County, Washington. II. Comparison with Adult Suicides," *Am J Forensic Med and Pathology* 8(3) September: 210–6. C. L. Rich, et al., "San Diego Suicide Study: I. Young vs. Old Subjects," *Archives of General Psychiatry* 43 (1986): 577–78.

12. T. L. Dorpat, W. F. Anderson, and N. S. Ripley. "The Relationship of Physical Illness to Suicide," in H. L. P. Resnik, ed., *Suicidal Behaviors: Diagnosis and Management* (1968), 209–19. T. L. Dorpat, and N. S. Ripley, "A Study of Suicide in the Seattle Area," *Comprehensive Psychiatry* I (1960): 349–59. M. Miller, *Suicide After Sixty: The Final Alternative* (New York: Springer, 1979).

13. Brian Barraclough, *Suicide: Clinical and Epidemiological Studies* (London: Routledge Chapman & Hall, 1987).

14. M. A. Lee and L. Ganzini, "Depression in the Elderly: Effects on Patient Attitudes Toward Life-sustaining Therapy," *J Am Geriatric Society* 40(10) (October 1992): 983–88; comment, *J Am Geriatric Society* 41(3): (March 1993): 345–46.

15. V. G. Cicirelli, "Relationship of Psychosocial and Background Variables to Older Adults' End-of-life Decisions," *Psychology and Aging* 12 (1) (March 1997): 72–83.

16. L. Ganzini, et al., "The Effect of Depression Treatment on Elderly Patients' Preferences for Life-sustaining Medical Therapy," *Am J Psychiatry* 151(11) (November 1994): 1631–36.

17. David Lester, and Margot Tallmer, *Now I Lay Me Down: Suicide in the Elderly* (Philadelphia: Charles Press, 1994), 9.

18. E. S. Shneidman, and N. L. Farberow, eds., *Clues to Suicide* (New York: McGraw-Hill, 1957). A. A. Leenaars, "Suicide Across the Adult Life-span: An Archival Study," *Crisis* 10(2) (October 1989): 132–51.

19. *Trends in Indian Health* www.tucson.ihs.gov. (Indian Health Service, General Mortality Statistics, Table 4.19)

20. D. P. Phillips, and T. E. Ruth, "Adequacy of Official Suicide Statistics for Scientific Research and Public Policy," *Suicide and Life-threatening Behavior* 23(4) (Winter 1993): 307–19.

21. E. Stengel, *Suicide and Attempted Suicide* 1974, 23.

22. N. Kreitman, and S. Platt, "Suicide, Unemployment, and Domestic Gas Detoxification in Britain," *Journal of Epidemiology and Community Health* 38 (1984): 1–6.

CHAPTER 7: SOME FREQUENTLY ASKED QUESTIONS ABOUT SUICIDE

1. R. E. Drake, et al., "Suicide Among Schizophrenics," *Journal of Nervous and Mental Disease* (1984): 613–17.

2. S. B. Guze and E. Robins, "Suicide and Primary Affective Disorders," *British Journal of Psychiatry* 117 (1970): 437–48.

3. D. C. Clark, *Issues in Law and Medicine* 1992, 147–66. Higher Alcohol figure from F. Lemere, "What Happens to Alcoholics," *Am. J. Psychiatry* 109 (1953): 674–76. G. E. Murphy, and R. Wetzel, "The Lifetime Risk of Suicide in Alcoholism," *Archives of General Psychiatry* 47 (April 1990): 383–92.

4. S. J. Blumenthal, and D. J. Kupfer, eds. *Suicide Over the Life Cycle: risk factors, assessment, and treatment of suicidal patients* (Washington DC: Am. Psychiatric Press, 1990).

Alec Roy, (ed.) *Suicide* (Baltimore: Williams and Wilkins, 1986)

Bruce Danto, "Suicide Among Cancer Patients" in S. E. Wallace, and A., Eser, eds. *Suicide and Euthanasia*, 1981, 26–35.

5. T. E. Quill, "Physician-assisted Death: Progress or Peril?" *Suicide and Life-threatening Behavior* 24(4) (1994): 317.

6. Frederick Ellis, Letter to Editor *New York Times* (September 23, 1995) 22.

7. David Eddy, "A piece of my mind. A conversation with my mother." *JAMA* 272(3) (July 20, 1994): 179–81.

8. R. W. Maris, "The Developmental Perspective of Suicide" in A. A. Leenaars, (ed) *Life Span Perspective of Suicide* 1991 (New York, Plenum) 35. R. W. Maris, in A. Leenaars, (ed) *Pathways to Suicide: A survey of Self-Destructive Behaviors*, 1991, 35.

9. B. M. Barraclough, et al., "A Hundred Cases of Suicide: Clinical Aspects," *British Journal of Psychiatry* 125 (1974): 355–73.

10. E. Robins, *The Final Months: A Study of the Lives of 134 Persons Who Committed Suicide* (New York: Oxford University Press, 1981).

11. C. V. Leonard, *Understanding and Preventing Suicide* (Springfield, Ill.: Thomas, 1967).

12. A. Temoche, et al., "Suicide Rates Among Current and Former Mental Institution Patients," *J Nervous and Mental Disease* 138 (1964): 124–30.

13. George Colt, *The Enigma of Suicide* (New York: Summit Books, 1991), 343. Herbert Hendin, *Suicide in America* (New York: Norton, 1982), 189–90.

14. I. S. Lann, et al., eds., "Strategies for Studying Suicide and Suicidal Behavior," *Suicide and Life-threatening Behavior* 19 (1989): 1–146.

15. B. R. Green, and D. P. Irish, eds., *Death Education: Preparation for Living* (Cambridge, Mass.: Schenkman, 1971), 120; quoted in Colt, 343.

16. E. Robins, et al., "Some Clinical Considerations in the Prevention of Suicide Based on a Study of 134 Successful Suicides," *Am J Public Health* 49 (1959): 888–99.

17. T. Szasz, "The Ethics of Suicide," *The Antioch Review* 31 (Spring 1971): 7–17.

18. E. Slater, "Choosing the Time to Die," in M. Battin and D. Mayo, eds., *Suicide: The Philosophical Issues* (New York: St. Martin's Press, 1980), 202–3.

19. Hendin, 224–25.

20. John Langone, *Dead End* (Boston: Little, Brown, 1986), 146.

21. K. Michel, L. Valach, and V. Waeber, "Understanding Deliberate Self-harm: The Patients' Views," *Crisis* 15(4) (1994): 172–78.

22. Erwin Stengel, *Suicide and Attempted Suicide* (Baltimore, Md.: Penguin, 113, n. 4.

23. Hendin, 211.

24. D. H. Rosen, "Suicide Survivors. A Follow-up Study of Persons Who Survived Jumping from the Golden Gate Bridge and the San Francisco–Oakland Bay Bridge," *Western Journal of Medicine* 122 (1975): 289–94. D. H. Rosen, "The Serious Suicide Attempt: Five-Year Follow-up Study of 886 Patients," *JAMA* 235(19) (1976a): 2105–09.

25. K. G. Dahlgren, "Attempted Suicides 35 Years Afterward," *Suicide and Life-threatening Behavior* 7(2) (1977): 75–79.

26. Brent Hafen and Kathryn J. Frandsen, *Youth Suicide, Depression, and Loneliness* (Evergreen, CO, Cordillera Press, 1986), 20.

27. J. A. van Aalst, et al., "Long-term Follow-up of Unsuccessful Violent Suicide Attempts: Risk Factors for Subsequent Attempts," *J Trauma* 33(3) (September 1992): 457–64.

28. 80 percent figure in B. Hafen, *Youth Suicide*, 20, 1986. 40 percent in G. M. Asnis, et al., "Suicidal Behaviors in Adult Psychiatric Outpatients, I: Description and Prevalence," *Am J Psychiatry* 150 (1993): 108–12. Other data in Colt, 98; C. L. Rich, et al., "San Diego Suicide Study: I. Young vs. Old Subjects," *Archives of General Psychiatry* 43 (1986): 577–78; Roy, 129.

29. Colt, 238.

30. Hendin, 219.

31. Anne-Grace Scheinin, "The Burden of Suicide," *Newsweek* (February 7, 1983), 13.

32. Colt, 229.

33. D. J. Shaffer, "The Epidemiology of Teen Suicide: An Examination of Risk Factors," *Journal of Clinical Psychiatry* 49 (supp.) (September 1988): 36–41.

34. J. A. Motto, D. C. Heilbron, and R. P. Juster. "Development of a Clinical Instrument to Estimate Suicide Risk," *Am J Psychiatry* 142(6) (1985): 680–85.

35. A. D. Pokorny, "Prediction of Suicide in Psychiatric Patients. Report of a Prospective Study" *Archives of General Psychiatry* 40(3) (March 1983): 249–57.

36. J. H. Greist, et al., "A Computer Interview for Suicide Risk Prediction," *Am J Psychiatry* 130 (12) (1973): 1327–32; also in Colt, 311.

37. J. E. Mack and H. Hickler, *Vivienne—The Life and Suicide of an Adolescent Girl* (Boston: Little, Brown, 1981).

38. Colt, 39.

39. G. Stoney, "Frequently Asked Questions about Suicide," at greyham;@research.canon.com.au or www.grohol.com/helpme.htm.

40. Hendin, 210.

41. R. H. Seiden, "Where Are They Now? A Follow-up Study of Suicide Attempters from the Golden Gate Bridge," *Suicide and Life-threatening Behavior* 8(1978): 203–16; quoted in Colt, 333; R. Seiden, "Suicide Prevention: A Public Health/Public Policy Approach," *Omega* 8 (1977): 267–76.

42. D. H. Rosen, "Suicide Survivors: Psychotherapeutic Implications of Egocide," *Suicide and Life-threatening Behavior* 6(4) (1976): 209–15; quoted in Colt, 333; J. Boudreau, "Death Watch at the Golden Gate," *Washington Post* (July 7, 1995), A3; Rosen (1975); Rosen (1976a).

D. H. Rosen, "Suicide survivors. A Follow-Up study of Persons Who Survived Jumping from the Golden Gate Bridge and the San Francisco-Oakland Bay Bridge," *Western Journal of Medicine* 122 (1975) 289–94.//D. H. Rosen, "The Serious Suicide Attempt: Five Year Follow-Up Study of 886 Patients by Choron" *Journal of the American Medical Association*, 1976-a, v235(19) 2105–09.

43. W. Heimerzheim, "On Suicide Among Non-psychotic Individuals)," 1933; cited by Choron as a 1933 German "medical dissertation, Cologne." Choron, *Suicide* (New York: Scribner's Sons, 1972), 50.

44. N. Retterstol, *Suicide: A European Perspective* (London: Cambridge University Press, 1990), 188–89.

45. N. L. Farberow, "Personality Patterns of Suicidal Mental Hospital Patients" *Genetic Psychology Monographs*, (Provincetown: Journal Press, 1950) 42, 3–79.

H. Hendin, "Suicide" in "Psychiatric Emergencies" in A. M. Freedman, et al, (eds) *A Comprehensive Textbook of Psychiatry*, 1967, (Baltimore: Williams & Wilkins) 1173.

E. Shneidman, "Some essentials of suicide and some applications for response" in Alec Roy, (ed.) *Suicide* (Baltimore, Williams and Wilkins 1986), 1–16.

46. Hendin, 198.

47. Colt, 311.

48. B. B. Doyle, "Crisis Management of the Suicidal Patient," in S. J. Blumenthal and D. I. Kupfer eds., *Suicide Over the Life Cycle* (Washington, D.C.: American Psychiatric Press, 1990), 382.

49. D. H. Rosen, "View from the Bridge," *JAMA* 254 (1985): 3314; quoted in Blumenthal, 382.

50. Robins, 888–98.

51. Barraclough, 355–73. J. O. Obafunwa and A. Busuttil, "Clinical Contact Preceding Suicide," *Postgraduate Med J* 70(824) (June 1994): 428–32.

52. K. Michel, "Suicide and Suicide Prevention. Could the Physician Do More? Results of a Questionnaire of Relatives of Suicide Attempters and Suicide Victims," *Schweiz Med Wochenschrift* 116(23) (June 7, 1986): 770–74.

53. Obafunwa, 428–32.

54. D. W. Black, et al., "Suicide in Subtypes of Major Affective Disorder," *Archives of General Psychiatry* 44 (1987): 898–99. A. J. Martin, V. M. Tebbs, and J. J. Ashford, "Affective Disorders in General Practice. Treatment of 6000 Patients with Fluvoxamine," *Pharmatherapeutica* 5(1) (1987): 40–49.

55. R. F. Prien and D. J. Kupfer, "Continuation Drug Therapy for Major Depressive Episodes: How Long Should It Be Maintained?" *Am J Psychiatry* 143(1) (January 1986): 18–23.

56. Andrew Edmund Slaby, and Lili Garfinkel, *No One Saw My Pain: Why Teens Kill Themselves* (New York: Norton, 1994), 11.

57. P. M. Marzuk, et al., "Use of Prescription Psychotropic Drugs Among Suicide Victims in New York City," *Am J Psychiatry* 152(10) (October 1995): 1520–22.

58. G. Isacsson, et al., "Use of Antidepressants Among People Committing Suicide in Sweden)," *British Med J* 308 (February 19, 1994): 506–9.

59. F. Rouillon, "Recurrence of Unipolar Depression and Efficacy of Maprotiline," *L'Encephale* 15 (1989): 527–34. J. Mann, et al., "The Emergence of Suicidal Ideation and Behavior During Antidepressant Pharmacotherapy," *Archives of General Psychiatry* 48(11) (November 1991): 1027–33.

60. J. Mann, "The Emergence of Suicidal Ideation and Behavior During Antidepressant Pharmacotherapy," *Archives of General Psychiatry* 48 (1991): 1027–33. S. A. Montgomery, "Suicide and Antidepressants," *Drugs* 43 (supp. 2) (1992): 24–31. A. J. Rothschild, and C. A. Locke, "Reexposure to Fluoxetine After Serious Suicide Attempts by Three Patients: The Role of Akathisia," *J Clinical Psychiatry* 52(12) (December 1991): 491–93.

61. T. P. Bridge, et al., "Suicide Prevention Centers. Ecological Study of Effectiveness," *J Nervous and Mental Disease* 164 (1977):18–24. D. Lester, "Effect of Suicide Prevention Centers on Suicide Rates in the United States," *Health Services Reports* 89(1) (January–February 1974): 37–39.

62. C. J. Van Dongen, "Experiences of Family Members After a Suicide," *J Family Practice* 33(4) (October 1991): 375–80.

63. Ibid.

64. G. C. Graber, "The Rationality of Suicide," in Wallace and Eser, 51–65.

65. B. M. Barraclough, et al., "A Hundred Cases of Suicide: Clinical Aspects," *British J Psychiatry* (October 1974): 355–73. Leonard, 273.

66. Battin, 6. Farberow, 231–80.

67. B. Muller-Oerlinghausen, et al., "The Effect of Long-term Lithium Treatment on the Mortality of Patients with Manic-depressive and Schizoaffective Illness," *Acta Psychiatrica Scandinavica* (September 1992) 86 (3): 218–22. A. Coppen, et al., "Does Lithium Reduce the Mortality of Recurrent Mood Disorders?" *J Affective Disorders* 23 (1): (September 1991): 1–7. P. Vestergaard and J. Aagaard, "Five-year Mortality in Lithium-treated Manic-depressive Patients," *J Affective Disorders* 21 (1) (January 1991): 33–38. G. N. Schrauzer and K. P. Shrestha, "Lithium in Drinking Water and the Incidences of Crimes, Suicides, and Arrests Related to Drug Addictions," *Biological Trace Element Research* 25 (2) (May 1990): 105–13.

68. A. Rosen, "Detection of Suicidal Patients: An Example of Some Limitations in the Prediction of Infrequent Events," *Consulting Psychology* 18 (1954): 397–403.

69. S. A. Montgomery and S. Kasper, "Comparison of Compliance Between Serotonin Reuptake Inhibitors and Tricyclic Antidepressants: A Meta-analysis," *International Clinical Psychopharmacology* 9 (supp. 4) (January 1995): 33–40. M. S. Kramer, et al., "Distinct Mechanism for Antidepressant Activity by Blockade of Central Substance P Receptors," *Science* 281: (September 11, 1998): 1640–45.

70. Rubenstein and Federman, 9.

71. C. J. Van Dongen, "Experiences of Family Members After a Suicide," *J Family Practice* 33 (4) (October 1991): 375–80.

CHAPTER 8: IS SUICIDE APPROPRIATE? IS INTERVENTION APPROPRIATE? WHO DECIDES?

1. A. Roy, ed., *Suicide* (Baltimore: Williams and Wilkins, 1986).

2. Sherwin B. Nuland, *How We Die: Reflections on Life's Final Chapter* (New York: Knopf, 1994), 156.

3. R. Kastenbaum, "Suicide as the Preferred Way of Death," in E. Shneidman, ed. *Suicidology: Contemporary Developments* (New York Grune and Stratton, 1976), 425–41. M. R. Barrington, "Apologia for Suicide," in A. B. Downing, ed., *Euthanasia and the Right to Death* (Los Angeles: Nash, 1969), 152–70.

4. Michael Biskup, ed., *Suicide: Opposing Viewpoints* (San Diego: Greenhaven Press, 1992).

See also, S. E. Wallace, and A. Eser, eds., *Suicide and Euthanasia* (1981); Shneidman, *Suicidology* 1976; M. P. Battin and David J. Mayo, eds., *Suicide: the Philosophical Issues* (New York: St. Martin's Press, 1980), M. P. Battin, *Ethical Issues in Suicide* (Englewood Cliffs, N.J.: Prentice-Hall, 1995).

5. Nuland, 151.

6. Biskup, 20; quoted from R. W. Momeyer, *Confronting Death* (Bloomington: Indiana University Press, 1988).

7. Barbara Logue, *Last rights: Death Control and the Elderly in America* (New York: Lexington Books, 1993), 81–83.

8. A. Brandt, *Reality Police: The Experience of Insanity in America* (New York: Morrow, 1975), 146; quoted in George Colt, *The Enigma of Suicide* (New York: Summit Books, 1991), 342.

9. Herbert Hendin, *Suicide in America* (New York: Norton, 1995), 231.

10. J. P. Gibbs, "Rates of Mental Hospitalization: A Study of Societal Reaction to Deviant Behavior," *Am Sociological Review* 27 (1962): 782–92.

11. D. L. Wenger and R. Fletcher, "The Effect of Legal Counsel on Admissions to a State Mental Hospital: A Confrontation of Professions," *J Health and Social Behavior* 10(1) (1969): 66–72.

12. B. Ennis and T. Litwack, "Psychiatry and the Presumption of Expertise"; D. Greenberg, "Involuntary Psychiatric Commitments"; and G. Dix, " 'Civil' Commitment of the Mentally Ill and the Need for Data in Prediction of Dangerousness," as in *American Behavioral Scientist* 19 (1976): 318–34.

13. Hendin, 210.

14. F. Ellis, Letter to Editor, *New York Times* (September 23, 1995).

15. Hendin, 217.

16. T. Taiminen, et al., "A Suicide Epidemic in a Psychiatric Hospital," *Suicide and Life-threatening Behavior* 22(3) (1992): 350–63.

17. L. M. Moss and D. M. Hamilton, "The Psychotherapy of the Suicidal Patient," *Am. J Psychiatry* 112 (1956): 814–20.

18. R. Litman, and N. Farberow, "The Hospital's Obligation Toward Suicide-Prone Patients," *Hospitals* 40 (December 16, 1966): 64–68.

19. Hendin, 217–18.

20. R. H. Seiden, "Suicide Among Youth, a Review of Literature, 1900–1967," *Bulletin of Suicidology* (supp.) (December 1969), 415.

21. Jose Ortega y Gasset, *Revolt of the Masses* (New York: Norton, 1993).

22. Choron, *Suicide* (New York: Scribner's Sons, 1972), 4.

23. Ibid., 105.

24. V. F. Holmes, "Suicide Among Physicians," in S. J. Blumenthal and D. J. Kupfer, eds., *Suicide Over the Life Cycle* (Washington, D.C.: American Psychiatric Press, 1990), 599.

25. C. B. Thomas, "What Becomes of Medical Students: The Dark Side," *Johns Hopkins Med J* 138 (1976): 185–95; in Blumenthal, 599.

26. E. Rubenstein and D. Federman, eds., *Scientific American Medicine* 13(2) (1995): 7.

27. C. L. Rich, "Suicide by Psychiatrists," *J Clinical Psychiatry* 41(8) (1980): 261–63; also in Blumenthal, 601.

28. S. M. Schlicht, et al., "Suicide and Related Deaths in Victorian Doctors," *Med J Australia* 153(9) (November 5, 1990): 518–21.

29. E. Heim, "Job Stressors and Coping in Health Professions," *Psychotherapy and Psychomatics* 55(2–4) (1991): 90–99.

30. W. Breitbart, "Cancer Pain and Suicide," in Foley, 399–412. C. Bolund, "Suicide and Can-

cer: II. Medical and Care Factors in Suicides by Cancer Patients in Sweden, 1973–1976," *Psychosocial Oncology* 3(1) (1985): 31–52. *Principles of Analgesic Use in the Treatment of Acute Pain and Cancer Pain*, 3d ed. (Skokie, Ill.: American Pain Society, 1992). J. H. Von Roenn, et al., "Physician Attitudes and Practice in Cancer Pain Management: A Survey from the Eastern Cooperative Oncology Group," *Annals of Internal Medicine* 119 (1993): 121–26.

31. Tedeschi, 759.

Chapter 9: Assisted Suicide and Terminal Illness

1. Neal Bernards, *Euthanasia: Opposing Viewpoints* (San Diego: Greenhaven Press, 1989), 21.

2. M. P. Battin, *The Least Worst Death* (New York: Oxford, University Press, 1994), 13.

3. The President's Commission for the Study of Ethical Problems in Medicine and Biomedical and Behavioral Research, *Deciding to Forego Life-sustaining Treatment* (Washington, D.C.: Government Printing Office, 1983), 102.

4. Barbara Logue, *Last Rights: Death Control and the Elderly in America* (New York: Lexington Books, 1993), 68.

5. Philippe Aries, *Western Attitudes Toward Death from the Middle Ages to the Present* (Baltimore, Md.: Johns Hopkins University Press, 1974).

6. J. Pridonoff, in C. Wekesser, ed., "Legal Safeguards Can Prevent Euthanasia from Harming Society" *Euthanasia: Opposing Viewpoints*, 2nd ed. (San Diego: Greenhaven Press, 1995), 74.

7. C. Bolund, "Suicide and Cancer: I. Demographic and Social Characteristics of Cancer Patients Who Committed Suicide in Sweden, 1973–1976," *Journal of Psychosocial Oncology* 3(1) 1985): 17–30. C. Bolund "Suicide and Cancer: II. Medical and Care Factors in Suicides by Cancer Patients in Sweden, 1973–1976," *Journal of Psychosocial Oncology* 3(1) (1985): 31–52. B. H. Fox, F. J. Stanek, and S. C. Boyd et al., "Suicide Rates Among Cancer Patients in Connecticut," *Journal of Chronic Disease* 35 (1982): 89–100.

8. G. A Kasting, in J. M. Humber, et al., eds., "The Nonnecessity of Euthanasia," in J.M. Humber, et al., (eds.) *Physician-assisted Death* in *Biomedical Ethics Reviews* (Totowa, N.J.: Humana Press, 1993), 25–45.

9. Y. Kamisar, "Some Non-religious Views Against Proposed 'Mercy-killing' Legislation," *Minnesota Law Review* 42, (1958): 969–1042.

10. Lonny Shavelson, *A Chosen Death: The Dying Confront Assisted Suicide* (New York: Simon & Schuster, 1995), 221.

11. Russell Ogden, *Euthanasia and Assisted Suicide in Persons with Acquired Immunodeficiency Syndrome (AIDS) or Human Immunodeficiency Virus (HIV)* (New Wesminster, B.C.: Peroglyphics Publishers, 1994), 10.

12. Battin, 107.

13. T. E. Quill, "Death and Dignity: A Case of Individualized Decision Making," *New England J Med* 324 (10) (March 7, 1991): 691–94; see also his August 18, 1993 *JAMA* article entitled "Doctor, I Want to Die. Will You Help Me?" 270(7): 870–73.

14. D. W. Cox, *Hemlock's Cup* (Buffalo, N.Y.: Prometheus Books, 1993), 234–37.

15. Anthony Flew, "The Principle of Euthanasia," in J. P. Carse, and A. B. Dallery, eds., *Death and Society: A Book of Readings and Sources* (New York: Harcourt Brace Jovanovich, 1977), 101–2.

16. K. Bajwa, E. Szabo, and C. M. Kjellstrand, "A Prospective Study of Risk Factors and Deci-

sion Making in Discontinuation of Dialysis," *Archives of Internal Med* 156(22) (December 23, 1996): 2571–77. J. C. Roberts, C. M. Kjellstrand, "Choosing Death. Withdrawal from Chronic Dialysis without Medical Reason," *Acta Medica Scandinavica* 223 (1988), 181–86.

17. C. Catalano et al., "Withdrawal of Renal Replacement Therapy in Newcastle upon Tyne: 1964–1993," *Nephrology, Dialysis, Transplantation* 11(1) (January 1996): 133–39.

18. *Schloendorf v. Society of New York Hospital*, 211 N.Y. 125 (1914); quoted in M. P. Battin, *Ethical Issues in Suicide* (Englewood Cliffs: Prentice-Hall, 1982), 18.

19. *In re Quinlan*, 355 A. 2d 647, 1976; quoted in Battin, 15.

20. David Hume, *Essays Moral, Political and Literary*, vol. 2 (London, 1898), 410–12; quoted in A. Alvarez, *The Savage God* (New York: Random House, 1971), 165–66.

21. C. Barnard, *Good Life/Good Death* (Englewood Cliffs, N.J.: Prentice-Hall, 1980), 88; also in Colt, 359.

22. R. Momeyer, *Confronting Death* (1988); quoted in M. Biskup, (Bloomington: Indiana University Press) ed., *Suicide: Opposing Viewpoints*, (San Diego: Greenhaven Press, 1992), 22.

23. Executive Committee of Exit, *Exit: A Guide to Self-Deliverance* (London, 1981), 3; quoted in Colt, 373.

24. M. P. Battin, *Ethical Issues in Suicide* (1982), 191 (Englewood Cliffs, N.J.: Prentice-Hall, 1995; more detail in Sherwin B. Nuland, *How We Die* (New York: Knopf, 1994).

25. Gina Kolata, "AIDS Patients Seek Solace in Suicide but Many Risk Added Pain in Failure," *New York Times* (June 14, 1994), C1.

26. Battin. *The Least Worst Death*, 1994. 112–13.

27. M. Battin "Suicide," in W. Reich, *Encyclopedia of Bioethics* (New York: MacMillan, 1995), 2444–49.

28. Kolata. See C1.

29. P. J. Bindels et al., "Euthanasia and Physician-assisted Suicide in Homosexual Men with AIDS," *Lancet* 347(9000) (February 24, 1996): 499–504.

30. H. Kuhse and P. Singer, "Doctors' Practices and Attitudes Regarding Voluntary Euthanasia," *Medical J Australia* 148(12) (June 20, 1988): 623–27.

31. P. Baume, et al., "Euthanasia: Attitudes and Practices of Medical Practitioners)," *Medical J Australia* 161(2) (July 18, 1994): 137, 140, 142–44.

32. National Hemlock Society, *Survey of California Physicians Regarding Voluntary Euthanasia for the Terminally Ill* (1988); cited in Peter Singer, *Rethinking Life and Death: The Collapse of Our Traditional Ethics* (Melbourne, Australia: Text Publishing Co., 1994), 155.

33. Lee R. Slome, et al., "Physician-assisted Suicide and Patients with Human Immunodeficiency Virus Disease," *New England Med* 336(6) (February 6, 1997): 417–21.

34. D. E. Meier, et al., "A National Survey of Physician-assisted Suicide and Euthanasia in the United States," *New England J Med* 338(17) (April 23, 1998): 1193–1201. S. D. Goold, "Physician-assisted Suicide and Euthanasia in the United States," *New England J Med* 339(11) (September 10, 1998): 776. H. Hendin, "Physician-assisted Suicide and Euthanasia in the United States," *New England J Med* 339(11) (September 10, 1998): 775–76.

35. D. A. Asch, "The Role of Critical Care Nurses in Euthanasia and Assisted Suicide," *New England J Med* 334(21) (May 23, 1996):1374–79.

36. T. D. Kinsella and M. J. Verhoef, "Alberta Euthanasia Survey: 1. Physicians' Opinions About the Morality and Legalization of Active Euthanasia," *Canadian Med Association J* 148(11) (June 1, 1993): 1921–26; Part 2: 1929–33.

37. B. D. Onwuteake-Philipsen, et al., "Attitudes of Dutch General Practitioners and Nursing Home Physicians to Active Voluntary Euthanasia and Physician-assisted Suicide," *Archives of Family Med* 4(11) (November 1995): 951–55.

38. J. S. Cohen, et al., "Attitudes Toward Assisted Suicide and Euthanasia Among Physicians in Washington State," *New England J Med* 331(2) (July 14, 1994): 89–94.

39. R. M. Arnold, et al., "Taking Care of Patients—Does It Matter Whether the Physician Is a Woman?" *Western Med J* 149(6) (December 1988): 729–33.

40. M. A. Lee, et al., "Legalizing Assisted Suicide—Views of Physicians in Oregon," *New England J Med* 334(5) (February 1, 1996): 310–5; comment: *New England J Med* 335(7) (August 15, 1996): 518; discussion, 519–20.

41. J. G. Bachman, et al., "Attitudes of Michigan Physicians and the Public Toward Legalizing Physician-assisted Suicide and Voluntary Euthanasia," *New England J Med* 334(5) (February 1, 1996): 303–9.

42. D. J. Doukas, et al., "Attitudes and Behaviors on Physician-assisted Death: A Study of Michigan Oncologists," *J Clinical Oncology* 13(5) (May 1995): 1055–61.

43. B. McCormick, "Continued Opposition," *American Medical News* (December 20, 1993); "AMA Delegates Assail Assistance in Suicides," *Washington Post* (June 26, 1996), A3.

44. Council on Scientific Affairs and Council on Ethical and Judicial Affairs, "Persistent Vegetative State and the Decision to Withdraw or Withhold Life Support," *JAMA* 263(3) (January 19, 1990): 426–30.

45. L. Richardson, Letter to Editor, *Washington Post* (March 1, 1994), Z4.

46. M. R. Gillick, et al., "Medical Technology at the End of Life. What Would Physicians and Nurses Want for Themselves?" *Archives of Internal Med* 153(22) (November 22, 1993): 2542–47.

47. P. Darzins, et al., "Treatment for Life-threatening Illness," *New England J Med* 329(10) (September 2, 1993): 736.

48. E. J. Emanuel, et al., "Euthanasia and Physician-assisted Suicide: Attitudes and Experiences of Oncology Patients, Oncologists, and the Public," *Lancet* 347(9018) (June 29, 1996): 1805–10.

49. Logue, 81–83.

50. Ibid., 81.

51. R. L. Leinbach, "Euthanasia Attitudes of Older Persons," *Research on Aging* 15 (1993): 433–48.

52. J. A. Devereux, et al., "Can Children Withhold Consent to Treatment?" *British Med. J* 306(6890) (May 29, 1993): 1459–61.

Chapter 10: The Medical System in Terminal Illness

1. G. J. Annas, "Physician-assisted Suicide—Michigan's Temporary Solution," *New England J Med* 328(21) (May 27, 1993): 1573–76.

2. D. Colburn, "Debate on Assisted Suicide Gains Steam," *Washington Post* (May 10 1994), Z8.

3. S. Cahill, "Prescriptions for Dying; Life Support's Grim Lessons for the Kervorkian Era," *Washington Post* (February 20, 1994), C1.

4. Don Colburn, "Earl's Way," *Washington Post* (January 9, 1996), Z12.

5. G. Pettinger, M. B. Duggan, and A. R. Forrest, "Black Stuff and Babies. Accidental Ingestion of Cannabis Resin," *Medicine Science and the Law* 28 (4) (October 1988): 310–11. R. Doblin and

M. A. Kleiman, "Marijuana as Antiemetic Medicine: A Survey of Oncologists' Experiences and Attitudes," *J Clinical Oncology* 9 (1991): 1275–90.

CHAPTER 11: PAIN CONTROL AND HOSPICE CARE

1. D. Cundiff, *Euthanasia Is Not the Answer: A Hospice Physician's View* (Totowa, N.J.: Humana Press, 1992); quoted in Lonny Shavelson, *A Chosen Death* (New York: Simon & Schuster, 1995), 214.

2. C. S. Cleeland, et al., "Pain and Its Treatment in Outpatients with Metastatic Cancer," *New England J Med* 330(9) (March 3, 1994): 592–96.

3. M. Z. Solomon, et al., "Decisions Near the End of Life: Professional Views on Life-sustaining Treatments," *Am J Public Health* 83(1) (January 1993): 14–23.

4. M. Zenz, et al., "Severe Undertreatment of Cancer Pain: A 3-year Survey of the German Situation," *J Pain Symptom Management* 10(3) (April 1995): 187–91.

5. F. Larue, et al., "Multicentre Study of Cancer Pain and Its Treatment in France," *British Med J* 310(6986) (April 22, 1995): 1034–737.

6. A. Chan and R. K. Woodruff, "Palliative Care in a General Teaching Hospital. 1. Assessment of Needs," *Med J Australia* 155(9) (November 4, 1991): 597–99.

7. N. Rawal, et al., "Management of Terminal Cancer Pain in Sweden: A Nationwide Survey," *Pain* 54(2) (August 1993): 169–79.

8. C. S. Cleeland, et al., "Pain and Its Treatment in Outpatients with Metastatic Cancer," *New England J Med* 330(9) (March 3, 1994): 592–96.

9. A. Chan. L. R. Bressler, M. C. Geraci, and B. S. Schatz, "Misperceptions and Inadequate Pain Management in Cancer Patients," *Drugs in Clinical Practice* 25(11) (November 1991): 1225–30; Rawal 169–79; Cleeland 592–96, 1994; B. J. Hammes and J. M. Cain, "The Ethics of Pain Management for Cancer Patients: Case Studies and Analysis," *J Pain Symptom Management* 9(3) (April 1994): 166–70; Larue, 1034–37; Zenz; C. S. Hill, Jr., "The Barriers to Adequate Pain Management with Opioid Analgesics," *Seminars in Oncology* 20(2 supp. 1) (April 1993): 1–5.

10. Shavelson, 215.

11. Abigail Trafford, "Ends and Means," *Washington Post* (January 7, 1997), Z6.

12. D. E. Weissman, "Doctors, Opioids, and the Law: The Effect of Controlled Substances Regulations on Cancer Pain Management," *Seminars in Oncology*, 20(1) (supp. A) (1993): 53–58.

13. Weissman; D. F. Musto, *The American Disease: Origin of Narcotic Control*, (New York: Oxford University Press, 1987); C. S. Hill, "Government Regulatory Influences on Opioid Prescribing and Their Impact on the Treatment of Pain of Nonmalignant Origin," *J Pain Symptom Management* 11(5) (May 1996): 287–98.

14. J. Porter, "Addiction Rare in Patients Treated with Narcotics," *New England J Med* 302 (1980): 23; S. Perry and G. Heidrich, "Management of Pain During Debridement: A Survey of U.S. Burn Units," *Pain* 13(3) (July 1982): 267–280.

15. Hill. 1–5

16. Ibid. 287–98.

17. S. Ottesen, et al., "Is Cancer Pain Therapy Insufficient?" *Tidsskr-Nor-Laegeforen* 112(14) (May 30, 1992): 1814–16.

18. Shavelson, 215.

19. Ibid., 209.

20. Ibid., 205.

21. Renee Sahm, quoted in Shavelson, 211.

22. Timothy E. Quill, *Death and Dignity: Making Choices and Taking Charge* (New York: W. W. Norton, 1993), 166.

23. Timothy E. Quill, "The Care of Last Resort," *New York Times* (July 23, 1994), 19.

24. New York State Task Force on Life and the Law, *When Death Is Sought: Assisted Suicide and Euthanasia in the Medical Context*, 1994.

25. Timothy E. Quill, "Doctor, I Want to Die. Will You Help Me?" *Journal of the American Medical Association* 270(7) (August 18, 1993): 870–73.

26. Quill, *Death and Dignity*, 23–24.

27. D. Colburn, "Debate on Assisted Suicide Gains Steam," *Washington Post* (May 10, 1994), Z8.

28. Shavelson, 218.

29. Theresa Stephany, "Assisted Suicide: How Hospice Fails," *Journal of Hospice and Palliative Care* 11 (4) (July-August 1994): 4–5.

30. Stephen Jamison, *Final Acts of Love: Families, Friends, and Assisted Dying* (New York: Jeremy Tarcher/Putnam, 1995), 186.

31. Nicholas A. Christakis and J. J. Escarce, "Survival of Medicare Patients After Enrollment in Hospice Programs," *New England J Med* 335(3) (July 18, 1996): 172–78.

32. M. P. Battin, *The Least Worst Death* (New York: Oxford University Press, 1994), 104.

33. Timothy E. Quill, "Physician-assisted Death: Progress or Peril?" *Suicide and Life-threatening Behavior* 24(4) (Winter 1994): 316.

34. T. A. Preston and R. Mero, "Observations Concerning Terminally Ill Patients Who Choose Suicide," in *Drug Use in Assisted Suicide*, M. P. Battin and A. Lipman (eds.), (New York: Pharmaceutical Products Press, 1996), 183–92.

35. Catherine Marco, et al., "Ethical Issues of Cardiopulmonary Resuscitation: Current Practice Among Emergency Physicians," *Academic Emergency Medicine* (September 1997), 898–904.

CHAPTER 12: ADVANCE DIRECTIVES

1. Barbara Logue, *Last Rights: Death Control and the Elderly in America* (New York: Lexington Books, 1993).

2. Timothy E. Quill, *Death and Dignity: Making Choices and Taking Charge* (New York: W. W. Norton, 1993), 196.

3. Abigail Trafford, "The Subject of Dying," *Washington Post* (October 21, 1997), Z6.

4. M. Tousignant, "Often Limited, Living Wills Rarely Ensure a Simple Solution," *Washington Post* (May 8, 1994), B1.

5. Quill, 192.

6. Gerald Larue, in D. Humphry, *Let Me Die Before I Wake: Hemlock's Book of Self-deliverance for the Dying* (Los Angeles: Grove Press, 1984), 87.

7. Stephen Flanders, *Suicide* (New York: Facts on File, 1991), 78.

8. L. O. Gostin, and R. F. Weir, "Life and Death Choices after Cruzan: Case Law and Standards of Professional Conduct," *Milbank Quarterly* 69 (1991): 143–73, 147.

9. Peter Singer, *Rethinking Life and Death: The Collapse of Our Traditional Ethics* (Melbourne, Australia: Text Publishing Co., 1994), 62.

10. Lonny Shavelson, *A Chosen Death* (New York: Simon & Schuster, 1995), 220.

11. *Airedale N.H.S. Trust v. Bland (C.A.) Weekly Law Reports* 2 (February 19, 1993): quoted in Peter Singer, *Rethinking Life and Death* (Melbourne, Australia: Text Publishing Co., 1994), 66.

12. Singer, 68.

13. Ibid., 78–79.

14. See also, A. Samuels, "The Patient Is in a Very Poor State: Is it Lawful to Refuse Treatment or to Discontinue Treatment?" *Medicine Science and the Law* 34(3) (July 1994): 227–32; and J. Rachels, *The End of Life: Euthanasia and Morality* (Oxford and New York: Oxford University Press, 1986). For a contrary view, R. Campbell and D. Collinson, *Ending Lives* (Oxford UK: Basil Blackwell 1988).

15. G. Annas "Into the Hands of Strangers," *Law, Medicine and Health Care* 13 (1985): 271; David Sudnow "Dead on Arrival," in A. L. Strauss, ed., *Where Medicine Fails*, 4th ed., (New Brunswick, N.J.: Transaction Books, 1984), 399–417; (New York: Garland Publishers, 1996), 215; Kathlyn Gay, *The Right to Die*, (Brookfield, Conn: Millbrook Press, 1993), 83–84.

16. Thomas E. Finucane, "Limitations of Living Wills," Letter to Editor, *Washington Post* (November 17, 1995), A16.

17. E. L. Schucking, "Death at a New York Hospital," *Law, Med, and Health Care* 13 (1985): 261–68; quoted in Logue, 160–61.

18. G. Annas, "Into the Hands of Strangers," *Law, Med and Health Care* 13 (1985): 271.

19. Norman Paradis, "Making a Living off the Dying," *New York Times* (April 25, 1992), 23.

20. Ibid.

21. C. W. Hall, "In Va., Having a Say in Dying; Passive Euthanasia a Growing Option in U.S.," *Washington Post* (December 20, 1994), A1.

22. S. J. Regan, Letter to the Editor, *New York Times* (October 13, 1993).

23. S. D. Cohn "The Living Will from the Nurse's Perspective," *Law, Med and Health Care* 11 (1983): 122; quoted in Logue, 96.

24. M. P. Battin, *The Least Worst Death* (New York: Oxford University Press, 1994), 33.

25. Sam Brody, "We Have Lost Our Humanity," *Newsweek* (September 7, 1992).

26. Daniel Callahan, *Hastings Center Magazine* (supp) (November–December 1995), 33.

27. A. Malcolm, "Many See Mercy in Ending Empty Lives," *New York Times* (September 23, 1984); quoted in Logue, 67.

28. R. S. Morrison et al., "The Inaccessibility of Advance Directives on Transfer from Ambulatory to Acute Care Settings," *JAMA* 274(6) (August 9, 1995): 478–82; comment, 501–3.

29. J. Virmani, L. J. Schneiderman, and R. M. Kaplan, "Relationship of Advance Directives to Physician-patient Communication," *Archives of Internal Medicine* 154(8) (April 25, 1994): 909–13.

30. J. M. Teno, et al., "Preferences for Cardiopulmonary Resuscitation: Physician-patient Agreement and Hospital Resource Use. The SUPPORT Investigators," *Journal of General Internal Medicine* 10(4) (April 1995): 179–86.

31. William A. Knaus and J. Lynn, "A Controlled Trial to Improve Care for Seriously Ill Hospitalized Patients: The Study to Understand Prognoses and Preferences for Outcomes and Risks of Treatments (SUPPORT)," *JAMA* 274 (1995): 1591–98.

32. D. Colburn, "The Grace of a 'Good Death' Escapes Many," *Washington Post* (December 5, 1995).

33. Y. Kamisar, *ABA Journal* (April 1993). J. Lynn, et al., "Prognoses of Seriously Ill Hospitalized Patients on the Days Before Death: Implications for Patient Care and Public Policy," *New Horizons* 5 (1) (February 1997): 56–61.

34. D. Colburn, "The Grace of a 'Good Death' Escapes Man," *Washington Post* (December 5, 1995), Z7.

CHAPTER 13: SOME PRACTICAL ISSUES IN ASSISTED SUICIDE

1. Arthur Koestler, in *Exit: A Guide to Self-Deliverance*, Executive Committee of Exit (London, 1981), 3; quoted in George Colt *The Enigma of Suicide* (New York: Summit Books, 1991), 373.

2. J. Rachels, *End of Life* (New York: Oxford Univ Press, 1986), 86.

3. M. T. CeloCruz, "Aid-in-dying: Should We Decriminalize Physician-assisted Suicide and Physician-committed Euthanasia?" *Am J Law and Med* 18(4) (1992): 369–94.

4. D. Humphry, "Why I Believe in Voluntary Euthanasia: The Case for Rational Suicide," summarized by the Euthanasia Research and Guidance Organization (ERGO!), at http://www.islandnet.com/=Vdeathnet.

5. Esther B. Fein, "Granting Father's Wish, or Manslaughter?" *New York Times* (October 28, 1994), A1.

6. *ERGO* website at http://www.islandnet.com/=Vdeathnet.

7. Stephen Jamison, *Final Acts of Love: Families, Friends, and Assisted Dying* (Putnam, NY: Jeremy Tarcher, 1995), 5–6.

8. Stephen Jamison, "When Drugs Fail: Assisted Deaths and Not-so-lethal Drugs," *Pharmaceutical Care in Pain and Symptom Control* 4(1–2) (1996): 223–43.

9. "No Trial in Aided Suicide," *New York Times* (May 23, 1994), A13.

10. Barbara Logue, *Last Rights* (New York: Lexington Books, 1993), 99.

11. Jamison, 1996, 223–243.

12. C. Farnsworth, "Vancouver AIDS Suicide Botched," *New York Times*, Science (June 14, 1994), 12.

13. S. Jamison, in M. P. Battin, and A. G. Lipman, eds., *Drug Use in Assisted Suicide and Euthanasia* (New York: Pharmaceutical Products Press, 1996), 223–43.

14. Farnsworth, 12.

15. Ibid.

16. P. J. Bindels, et al., "Euthanasia and Physician-assisted Suicide in Homosexual Men with AIDS," *Lancet* 347(9000) (February 24, 1996): 499–504.

17. J. R. Moehringer, "Mother's Wish to Die Leaves Man in Legal Limbo," *Los Angeles Times* (April 30, 1995), A-3.

18. R. T. White, et al., "Jumping from a General Hospital," *General Hospital Psychiatry* 17(3) (May 1995): 208–15.

19. C. K. Smith, in Battin and Lipman, 139–49.

20. Battin, 257–58, 267–68. D. Daube, "The Linguistics of Suicide," *Suicide and Life-threatening Behavior* 7 (3) (1977): 132–82.

21. Battin, 19–46.

22. Singer, 135.

23. Battin, 272–75.

24. D. T. Watts, et al. "Geriatricians' Attitudes Toward Assisting Suicide of Dementia Patients," *J Am Geriatric Society* 40 (9) (September 1992):878–85.

CHAPTER 14: EUTHANASIA IN THE NETHERLANDS

1. H. Hendin, et al., "Physician-assisted Suicide and Euthanasia in the Netherlands. Lessons from the Dutch." *Journal of the American Medical Association* 277(21) (June 4, 1997): 1720–22.

2. M. Angell, "Euthanasia in the Netherlands—Good News or Bad?" *New England J Med* 335(22) (November 28, 1996): 1676–78. P. I. van der Maas et al., "Euthanasia, Physician-assisted Suicide, and Other Medical Practices Involving the End of Life in the Netherlands, 1990–1995," *New England J Med* 335(22) (November 28, 1996): 1699–1705.

3. S. Waxman, "The Dutch Way of Death; Euthanasia Is Accepted but It's Not Easy," *Washington Post* (January 31, 1995), B1. B. D. Onwuteaka-Philipsen, et al., "Active Voluntary Euthanasia or Physician-assisted Suicide?" *J Am Geriatric Society* 45(10) (October 1997): 1208–13.

4. M. Simons, "Dutch Doctors to Tighten Rules on Mercy Killings," *New York Times* (September 11, 1995), A3.

5. Simons, 3.

6. P. J. van der Maas, et al., "Euthanasia and Other Medical Decisions Concerning the End of Life," *Lancet* 338(8768) (September 14, 1991): 669–74.

7. G. van der Wal, "Euthanasia and Assisted Suicide. I. How Often Is It Practised by Family Doctors in The Netherlands?" *Family Practice* 9(2) (June 1992): 130–34.

8. Waxman.

9. L. Pijnenborg, et al., "Nationwide Study of Decisions Concerning the End of Life in General Practice in The Netherlands," *British Med J* 309(6963) (November 5, 1994): 1209–12.

10. P. J. van der Maas, et al., *Euthanasia and Other Medical Decisions Concerning the End of Life: An Investigation* (Amsterdam and New York: Elsevier, 1992).

11. L. Pijnenborg, et al., "Life-terminating Acts Without Explicit Request of Patient," *Lancet* 341(8854) (May 8, 1993): 1196–99.

12. L. Pijnenborg, et al., "Nationwide Study of Decisions Concerning the End of Life in General Practice in The Netherlands," *British Med J* 309(6963) (November 5, 1994):1209–12.

13. L. Pijnenborg, et al., "Withdrawal or Withholding of Treatment at the End of Life. Results of a Nationwide Study," *Archives of Intern Med* 155(3) (February 13, 1995): 286–92.

14. M. P. Battin, *The Least Worst Death* (New York: Oxford University Press, 1994), 94.

15. Ibid., 136.

16. M. P. Battin, *J Pain Symptom Management* 6 (5) (July 1991): 298–305. Serge F. Kovaleski, "Colombia Debates Court Ruling that Legalizes Mercy Killing," *Washington Post* (August 18, 1997), A15.

17. L. Pijnenborg, et al., "Nationwide Study of Decisions Concerning the End of Life in General Practice in The Netherlands," *British Med J* 309 (November 5, 1994): 1209–12.

CHAPTER 15: EUTHANASIA AND ASSISTED SUICIDE IN THE UNITED STATES

1. J. Persels, "Forcing the Issue of Physician-assisted Suicide. Impact of the Kevorkian Case on the Euthanasia Debate," *Legal Med* 14(1) (1993): 93–124; cited in G. K. Kimsma, "Euthanasia and Euthanizing Drugs in the Netherlands," *Pharmaceutical Care in Pain and Symptom Control* 4(1–2) (1996): 193–210.

2. William Claiborne, "In Oregon, Suicide Option Brings a Kinder Care," *Washington Post* (April 29, 1998), A1.

3. J. Sullivan, "The Immorality of Euthanasia," in M. Kohl, ed., *Beneficent Euthanasia* (Buffalo, N.Y.: Prometheus Books, 1975), 24.

4. H. K. Beecher, "Medical Research and the Individual," in Edward Shils, ed., *Life or Death: Ethics and Options* (Portland, Ore.: Reed College Press, 1968), 114–51.

5. Ibid., 146–47.

6. Ibid., 143.

7. G. Aly, et al., *Cleansing the Fatherland: Nazi Medicine and Racial Hygiene*, (Baltimore, Md.: Johns Hopkins University Press, 1994), x.

8. Ibid.

9. S. Waxman, "The Dutch Way of Death: Euthanasia Is Accepted but It's Not Easy," *Washington Post* (January 31, 1995) B1; there is a good description of the case in Herbert Hendin, *Suicide in America* (New York: Norton, 1995), 258–69.

10. M. P. Battin, *The Least Worst Death* (New York: Oxford University Press, 1994); 117–19.

11. A. P. Glascock, et al., "Social Asset or Social Burden," in C. L. Fry, et al., *Dimensions: Aging, Culture and Health* (New York: Praeger, 1981), 51. R. Gillon, "Suicide and Voluntary Euthanasia: Historical Perspective," in A. B. Downing, ed., *Euthanasia and the Right to Death: The Case for Voluntary Euthanasia* (New York: Humanities Press, 1969).

12. James. Rachels, *The End of Life: Euthanasia and Morality* (New York: Oxford University Press, 1986).

13. P. Singer, *Rethinking Life and Death* (Melbourne, Australia: Text Publishing Co., 1994), 129.

14. C. Wekesser, ed., *Euthanasia: Opposing Viewpoints* (Greenhaven Press, 1995), 50.

15. D. Callahan, "Vital Distinctions, Moral Questions," *Commonweal* (July 15, 1988), 397–404; cited in Rachels, 175–8.

16. "Sterilized: Why?" *Time* (July 23, 1973).

17. Waxman, B1.

18. R. Dworkin, "When Is It Right to Die?" *New York Times* (May 17, 1994), A19.

19. R. F. Weir, ed., *Physician-assisted Suicide* (Bloomington: Indiana University, 1997), 155–201.

20. H. W. A. Hilhorst, *Euthanasie ni het Ziekenhuis* (Lochem: De Tijdstroom, 1983); cited in Herbert Hendin, *Suicide in America* (New York: Norton, 1995), 256–57.

21. Stephen Jamison, *Final Acts of Love* (Putnam, NY: Jeremy Tarcher, 1995), 139.

22. Lonny Shavelson, *A Chosen Death* (New York: Simon & Schuster, 1995), 136–37.

23. Table 2 from I. J. Schneiderman, et al., "Attitude of Seriously Ill Patients Toward Treatment that Involves High Costs and Burdens on Others," *J Clinical Ethics* 5(2) (1994):109–12.

24. Shavelson, 103.

25. M. P. Battin, "Euthanasia: The Way We Do It; The Way They Do It," *J Pain Symptom Management* 6 (1991):298–305.

26. Modified from M. P. Battin, "Commentaries," in M. P. Battin and A. G. Lipman, eds.,

Drug Use in Assisted Suicide and Euthanasia (New York: Pharmaceutical Products Press, 1996), 285.

27. Maguire, 77–83.

28. T. de Quincy, *Murder Considered as One of the Fine Arts*, 1827; in *Bartlett's Familiar Quotations* (Boston: Little Brown, 1980), 454.

29. Clarke and Lester, 71–73.

Chapter 16: How Dangerous Are Various Methods of Suicide?

1. J. J. Card, "Lethality of Suicidal (1974): Methods and Suicide Risk: Two Distinct Concepts," *Omega* 5 (1974):37–45. N. L. Farberow, and E. S. Shneidman, *The Cry for Help* (New York: McGraw-Hill, 1961), 35.

2. J. D. Langley and S. E. Johnston, "Purposely Self-inflicted Injury Resulting in Death and Hospitalisation in New Zealand," *Community Health Studies* 14(2) (1990): 190–99. Hawaii State Dept of Health, 1989–1990 data.

3. Card.

4. C. E. Rhyne, et al., "Dimensions of Suicide: Perceptions of Lethality, Time, and Agony," *Suicide and Life-threatening Behavior* 25(3) (1995): 373–80.

5. S. Greer, et al., "Subsequent Progress of Potentially Lethal Attempted Suicides," *Acta Psychiatrica Scandinavica* 43 (1967): 361.

6. M. M. Linehan, "Suicidal People: One Population or Two?" in J. J. Mann and M. Stanley, eds., *Psychobiology of Suicidal Behavior* (New York: New York Academy of Science, 1986), 16–33.

7. M. Nordentoft and P. Rubin, "Mental Illness and Social Integration Among Suicide Attempters in Copenhagen. Comparison with the General Population and a Four-year Follow-up Study of 100 Patients," *Acta Psychiatrica Scandinavica* 88(4) (October 1993): 278–85.

8. R. Plutchik, et al., "Is There a Relation Between the Seriousness of Suicidal Intent and the Lethality of the Suicide Attempt?" *Psychiatry Research* 27(1) (January 1989): 71–79.

9. van Aalst, et al., "Long-term Follow-up of Unsuccessful Violent Suicide Attempts: Risk Factors for Subsequent Attempts," *J Trauma* 33(3) (1992): 457–64.

10. I. O'Donnell et al., "The Epidemiology of Suicide on the London Underground," *Social Science Med* 38(3) (1994): 409–18.

11. D. H. Rosen, "The Serious Suicide Attempt: Five-year Follow-up Study of 886 Patients," 235(19) (1976): 2105.

12. J. Suokas and J. Lonnqvist, "Outcome of Attempted Suicide and Psychiatric Consultation: Risk Factors and Suicide Mortality During a Five-year Follow-up," *Acta Psychiatrica Scandinavica* 84(6) (December 1991): 545–49.

13. N. J. Fisker, et al., "Death After Earlier Deliberate Self-poisoning. A 10-year Material from an Intensive Care Unit," *Ugeskr-Laeger* 155(24) (June 14, 1993): 1857–61. O. Ekeberg, et al., "Suicide and Other Causes of Death in a Five-year Follow-up of Patients Treated for Self-poisoning in Oslo," *Acta Psychiatrica Scandinavica* 83(6) (June 1991): 432–37.

14. T. F. Aufderheide, et al., "Emergency Airway Management in Hanging Victims," *Annals of Emergency Med* 24 (5) (November 1994): 879–84.

15. W. U. Spitz and R. S. Fisher, *Medicolegal Investigation of Death* 3rd ed, (Springfield Ill.: Thomas, 1993), 182.

16. M. Precker, "Stopping Soda Jerks" *Washington Post* (January 2, 1996).

17. T. D. Hornett and A. P. Haynes, "Comparison of Carbon Dioxide/Air Mixture and Nitrogen/Air Mixture for the Euthanasia of Rodents. Design of a System for Inhalation Euthanasia," *Animal Technology* 35 (1984): 93–99. J. P. Quine, W. Buckingham, and L. Strunin, "Euthanasia of Small Animals with Nitrogen: Comparison with Intravenous Pentobarbital," *Canadian Veterinary J* 29 (1988): 724–26.

18. *Handbook of Chemistry and Physics*, 37th ed. Press, (Cleveland: CRC Press, 1955), 2141–47.

19. Alvarez, 33–36.

CHAPTER 17: ASPHYXIA

1. National Center for Heath Statistics, 1994. Centers for Disease Control and Prevention (CDC) web site. http://wonder.cdc.gov

2. Bernard Knight, *Forensic Pathology*, 2nd ed. (New York: Oxford University Press, 1996), 51.

3. Arthur Guyton, *Medical Physiology*, 3rd ed. (Philadelphia: Saunders, 1966), 397.

4. Cyril J. Polson, D. J. Gee, and Bernard Knight, *The Essentials of Forensic Medicine*, 4th ed. (New York: Pergamon, 1985) 397.

5. Ibid., 389.

6. Ibid., 396 *R. v. Franklin*, York, 1971.

7. Ibid., p399.

8. W. A. Guy, and D. Ferrier, *Principles of Forensic Medicine* 7th ed. (London: W. R. Smith, 1895); cited in Polson, 399.

9. M. Frazer, and S. Rosenberg, "A Case of Suicidal Ligature Strangulation," *Am J Forensic Med and Pathology* 4(4) (December 1983): 351–54.

10. W. Roughead, *Burke and Hare* 3rd ed. (Edinburgh: Hodge, 1948) quoted in Polson, 474.

11. V. O. McCarty, R. A. Cox and B. Haglund, "Death Caused by a Constricting Snake—An Infant Death," *J Forensic Science* 34 (1) (January 1989): 239–43.

12. A. S. Taylor, *Principles and Practice of Medical Jurisprudence*, 11th ed., vol. 1 (London: Churchill, 1956), 468; Polson, 450.

13. H. Sankey, *British Medical Journal*, vol. 1 (1883), 88; cited in Polson, (New York: Pengamon), 450.

14. Knight, 354, 447–55.

15. M. S. Kearney, L. B. Dahl, and H. Stalsberg H "Can a Cat Smother and Kill a Baby?" *British Med J* 285 (September 18, 1982), 777; Polson, 451.

16. Knight, 354.

17. Ibid.

18. TOMES Medical Management, "Carbon Monoxide" (Micromedex, Inc., 1994).

19. N. I. Sax, *Dangerous Properties of Industrial Materials* (New York: Van Nostrand, 1984).

20. W. U. Spitz, R. S. Fisher, *Medicolegal Investigation of Death* 2nd ed. (Springfield Ill.: Thomas, 1980), 339.

21. E. Andrews, et al., "Report of the AVMA Panel on Euthanasia," *J Am Veterinary Med Association* 202(2), (January 15, 1993): 229–49.

22. J. B. Hudnall, A. Suruda, and D. L. Campbell DL "Deaths Involving Airline Respirators Connected to Inert Gas Sources," *Am Industrial Hygiene Association* 54(1) (January 1993):32–35.

23. "Report of the the AVMA Panel on Euthanasia" *J Am Veterinary Med Association* 173 (1978):

59–72. R. A. Herin, P. Hall, J. W. Fitch, "Nitrogen Inhalation as a method of Euthanasia in Dogs," *Am J Veterinary Research* 39 (1978): 989–91. J. P. Quine, "Euthanasia by Hypoxia Using Nitrogen. A Review After Four Years of Operations Involving 20,500 Animals," *Canadian Veterinary J* 21 (1980): 320.

24. H. G. Glass, F. F. Snyder, and E. Webster, "The Rate of Decline in Resistance to Anoxia of Rabbits, Dogs, and Guinea Pigs from the Onset of Viability to Adult Life," *Am J Physiology* 140 (1944): 609–15. Herin, 989–91.

25. Spitz, 486.

26. R. V. Clarke, and D. Lester, *Suicide: Closing the Exits* (New York: Springer Verlag, 1989), 34.

27. George Colt, *The Enigma of Suicide* (New York: Summit, Books, 1991), 335.

28. A. Wiedenmann and S. Weyerer, "The Impact of Availability, Attraction and Lethality of Suicide Methods on Suicide Rates in Germany," *Acta Psychiatrica Scandinavica* 88(5) (November 1993): 364–68.

29. Robert Litman, "Psychological Aspects of Suicide," in W. J. Curran, et al., *Modern Legal Medicine Psychiatry and Forensic Science* (Davis, 1980), 844.

30. R. Hoenderken, "Electrical and Carbon Dioxide Stunning of Pigs for Slaughter," in G. Eikelenboom, ed., *Stunning of Animals for Slaughter* (Boston: Martinus Nijhoff Publishers, 1982), 59–63. N. G. Gregory, B. W. Moss, R. H. Leeson, "An Assessment of Carbon Dioxide Stunning in Pigs," *Veterinary Record* 121 (1987): 517–18.

31. R. E. Gosselin, et al., *Clinical Toxicology of Commercial Products* 5th ed. (Baltimore, Md.: Williams and Wilkins, 1984), 95.

32. Robert H. Dreisbach, *Handbook of Poisoning: Prevention, Diagnosis, and Treatment*, 12th ed. (Los Altos, Calif.: Lange, 1987), 259.

33. Ibid. 261.

34. G. L. Nelson, "Low Levels of Carbon Monoxide and Their Effects," in M. M. Hirschler, et al., eds., *Carbon Monoxide and Human Lethality* (London: Elsevier, 1993), 5.

35. TOMES Medical Management.

36. K. B. Van Hoesen, et al., "Should Hyperbaric Oxygen Be Used to Treat the Pregnant Patient for Acute Carbon Monoxide Poisoning? A Case Report and Literature Review" *JAMA* 261 (7) (February 17, 1989): 1039–43.

37. Matthew Ellenhorn, *Medical Toxicology: Diagnosis and Treatment of Human Poisoning* (London: Elsevier, 1988), 70.

38. Spitz, 488.

39. Spitz, 489.

40. L. S. King, "Effect of Ethanol in Fatal Carbon Monoxide Poisonings," *Human Toxicology* 2 (1983) 155–57. Nelson, 9, 47–52.

41. J. Haldane, "The Action of Carbonic Oxide in Man," *J Physiology* 18 (1895): 430–62.

42. Dreisbach, 262.

43. J. D. Bloom, "Some Considerations in Establishing Divers' Breathing Gas Purity Standards for Carbon Monoxide," *Aerospace Medicine* 43 (1972):633–36.

44. T. L. Ramsey and J. H Eilmann, "Carbon Monoxide: Acute and Chronic Poisoning and Experimental Studies," *J Laboratory and Clinical Med* 17 (1932): 415–27. Hansen N. Enggaard, A. Creutzberg, and H. B. Simonsen, "Euthanasia of Mink (Mustela vison) by Means of Carbon Dioxide (CO_2), Carbon Monoxide (CO) and Nitrogen (N_2)," *British-Veterinary J* 147(2) (March 1991): 140–46.

45. S. Tsunenari, et al., "Suicidal Carbon Monoxide Inhalation of Exhaust Fumes. Investigation of Cases," *Am J Forensic Med and Pathology* 6(3) (September 1985): 233–39.

46. Dreisbach, 253.

47. Poisindex, "Cyanide," (Micromedex, Inc., 1994).

CHAPTER 18: CUTTING AND STABBING

1. George Colt, *The Enigma of Suicide* (New York: Summit Books, 1991), 95.

2. Colt, 96. S. P. Baker, *Injury Fact Book* (1992), 65;// M. M. Weissman, "The Epidemiology of Suicide Attempts, 1960 to 1971," *Archives of General Psychiatry* 30 (1974): 737–46. R. C. Bland, S. C. Newman, R. J. Dyck, "The Epidemiology of Parasuicide in Edmonton," *Canadian J Psychiatry* 39(8) (October 1994): 391–96.

3. To Karlsson, K. Ormstad, and J. Rajs "Patterns in Sharp Force Fatalities—A Comprehensive Forensic Medical Study: Part 2. Suicidal Sharp Force Injury in the Stockholm Area, 1972–1984," *J Forensic Science* 33(2) (March 1988): 448–61.

4. G. Beaumont, "Suicide and Antidepressant Overdosage in General Practice," *British J Psychiatry* 155 (supp. 6) (1989): 27–31.

5. T. Watanabe, Y. Kobayashi, and S. Hata, "Harakiri and Suicide by Sharp Instruments in Japan," *Forensic Science* 2 (2) (May 1973):191–99.

6. Karlsson, 448–61.

7. Watanabe, 191-99.

8. Karlsson, 448–61.

9. A. Cugino, et al., "Searching for a Pattern: Repeat Suicide Attempts," *J Psychosocial Nursing and Mental Health Services* 30(3) (March 1992): 23–26.

10. R. J. Rosenthal, et al., "Wrist-cutting Syndrome: The Meaning of a Gesture," *Am J Psychiatry* 128(11) (May 1972): 1363–68. M. A. Simpson, "The Phenomenology of Self-mutilation in a General Hospital Setting," *Canadian Psychiatric Association J* 20(6) (October 1975): 429–34. K. Hawton, and J. Catalan, *Attempted Suicide: A Practical Guide to Its Nature and Management* (London: UK, Oxford Medical Publications), 1987), 150–59.

11. R. H. Schwartz, et al., "Self-harm Behaviors (Carving) in Female Adolescent Drug Abusers," *Clinical Pediatrics* 28(8) (August 1989): 340–46.

12. D. Tantam and J. Whittaker, "Personality Disorder and Self-wounding," *British J Psychiatry* 161 (October 1992): 451–64.

13. Karlsson.

14. Cyril J. Polson, D. J. Gee, and Bernard Knight, *The Essentials of Forensic Medicine*, 4th ed. (New York: Pergamona, 1985), 117.

15. Ibid. 114.

16. T. Sigrist and K. Dirnhofer, "Suicide by Cutting the Radial Artery of the Wrist. Report of 2 Cases," *Zeitschrift fur Rechtsmedizin* 91(2) (1983):159–64; cited in Karlsson, 460.

17. W. Rabl and T. Sigrist, "Fatal Exsanguination from a Small Venous Injury," *Archiv Kriminol* 190(5–6) (November 1992): 171–75.

18. Karlsson, 453.

19. Polson, 132.

20. D. Rogers, "Autoamputation of the Left Arm—A Bizarre Suicide," *Am J Forensic Med and Pathology* 9 (1) (1988): 64–65.

21. M. Segerberg-Kontinnen, "Suicide by the Use of a Chain Saw," *J Forensic Science* 29 (4) (October 1984): 1249–52.

22. Polson, 125.

23. Ibid., 130.

24. Karlsson, 456.

25. J. M., Webster, 1960, confirming *Birmingham Mail* (June 4, 1948); cited in Polson, 122.

26. Polson, 122.

27. Ibid., 127.

28. R. Crompton, "Georgi Markov—Death in a Pellet," *Medical Legal J* 48(2) (1980): 51–62.

29. Polson, 123.

30. G. Zimmer, E. Miltner, and R. Mattern, "Capacity to Act After Stab and Cutting Injury," *Archiv Kriminol* 194(3–4) (September 1994): 95–104.

31. H. Shiono, and Y. Takaesu, "Suicide by Self-inflicted Stab Wound of The Chest," *Am J Forensic Med Pathology* 7 (1) (1986): 72–73.

32. Watanabe, 448-61.

33. Lester James, 1961; cited in Polson, 126.

34. Werner U. Spitz, and R.S. Fisher, *Medicolegal Investigation of Death*, 3rd ed. (Springfield, Ill: Thomas, 1993), 271.

35. Karlsson, 457.

36. Spitz, 274.

37. T. C. Welu, "Psychological Reactions of Emergency Room Staff to Suicide Attempters," *Omega* 3(2) (1972): 103–9.

38. J. A. van Aalst, "Long-term Follow-up of Unsuccessful Violent Attempts," *J Trauma* 33(3) (September 1992): 457–64.

39. Internet newsgroup, *Alt.Suicide.Holiday*, "Methods" file.

40. M. B. Collin Corby, "Chiasma—Shooting or Stabbing," *Medical Legal J* 33 (1965): 12–28. 1965.

41. D. C. Clark, " 'Rational' Suicide and People with Terminal Conditions or Disabilities," *Issues in Law and Medicine* 8(2) (fall 1992): 147–66. T. B. Mackenzie, "Medical Illnes and Suicide," in S. J. Blumenthal and D. J. Kupfer, eds., *Suicide Over the Life Cycle* (Washington, D.C.: American Psychiatric Press, 1990), 205–32.

CHAPTER 19: DROWNING

1. K. C. Wong, "Physiology and Pharmacology of Hypothermia," *Western J Med* 138 (1983): 227–232.

2. T. D. Kvittengen and A. Naess, "Recovery from Drowning in Fresh Water," *British Med J* 5341 (1963): 1315–7. R. T. Payne, "Treatment of Drowning and Electrocution," *British Med J* 1 (1940): 819–22.

3. R. G. Bolte, P. G. Black, and R. S. Bowers, et al., "The Use of Extracorporeal Rewarming in a Child Submerged for 66 Minutes," *JAMA* 1988; 260 (1988): 377–79.

4. R. S. K. Young, E. L. Zalneraitis, and E. C. Dooling, "Neurological Outcome in Cold Water Drowning," *JAMA Medical Association 1980*; 244 (1980): 1233–35.

5. J. H. Modell, S. A. Graves, and A. Ketover, "Clinical Course of 91 Consecutive Near-drowning Victims," *Chest* 70 (1976): 231–38.

6. J. H. Modell, S. A. Graves, and E. J. Kuck, "Near-drowning: Correlation of Level of Consciousness and Survival," Canadian Anaesthetists Society J 27 (3) (May 1980): 211–15. S. Cavalier, "Drownings," National Pool and Spa Safety Conference (Washington, D.C.: US Consumer Product Safety Commission, 1985), 9–12.

7. Spitz, 504; Tedeschi, 1324; Polson, 428.

8. C. Simonin, Medicine Legale Judiciare, 3rd ed. (Paris: Maloine); cited in Tedeschi, Forensic Medicine, 1323.

9. Cyril J. Polson, D. J. Gee, and Bernard Knight, The Essentials of Forensic Medicine, 4th ed. (New York: Pergamon, 1985) 432

10. Spitz, 502.

11. P. Brouardel, La Pendaison, la Strangulation, la Suffocation, La Submersion (Paris: Bailliere, 1897), 425, 453.; cited in Polson, p 425.

12. B. Mueller, Gerichtliche Medizin (Berlin: Springer-Verlag, 1953); cited in Tedeschi, 1322.

13. J. H. Modell, "Biology of Drowning," Annual Review of Med 29 (1978): 1–8.

14. J.H. Arthur Modell. Guyton, Medical Physiology, 3rd ed., (Philadelphia: Saunders, 1966) 646. Rubenstein, Scientific American Medicine (1995) 1.

15. Spitz, 503.

16. E. Gardner, "Mechanism of Certain Forms of Sudden Death in Medico-legal Practice," Medico-legal and Criminology Review 10 (1942): 120–33; quoted in Polson, 438.

17. Arthur Guyton, Medical Physiology, 3rd ed. (Philadelphia: Saunders, 1966), 646.

18. Sherwin B. Nuland, How We Die (New York: Knopf, 1994) 161.

19. J. K. Bloom, "Waterways Give Up Grim Telltale Signs of Spring," New York Times (April 30, 1995), 38.

20. Polson, 425.

21. Spitz, 499.

22. Tedeschi, 1322.

23. H. G. Swann, et al., "Body Salt and Water Changes During Fresh and Sea Water Drowning," Texas Reports on Biology and Medicine 9 (1951): 356; also in Tedeschi, 1322.

24. K. W. Donald and W. D. Paton, "Gases Administered in Artificial Respiration; with Particular Reference to the Use of Carbon Dioxide," British Med J II (1955): 155–60.

25. Spitz, 498.

26. Ibid., 499; Tedeschi, 1323.

27. Polson, 425.

28. Nuland, 161.

29. Polson, 437.

30. Herbert Hendin, Suicide in America 2nd ed. (New York: Norton 1995), 168.

31. S. P. Avis, "Suicidal Drowning," J Forensic Science 38: 6 (November 1993): 1422–26.

32. I. R. Rockett and G. S. Smith, "Covert Suicide Among Elderly Japanese Females: Questioning Unintentional Drownings," Social Science and Medicine 36 (11) (June 1993): 1467–72.

33. Hendin, 168.

34. A. R. Copeland, "Suicide by Drowning," Am J Forensic Med and Pathology 8 (1) (March 1987): 18–22.

35. P. N. Cooper and C. M. Milroy, "The Coroner's System and Underreporting of Suicide," Med Science and the Law 35 (4) (October 1995): 319–26.

36. V. D. Plueckhahn, "Alcohol and Accidental Submersion from Watercraft and Surrounds," *Med Science and the Law* (1977) 246–50.

37. Garcia, 1994, personal communication.

38. "Warning on Infant Hazard)," *New York Times* (May 24, 1992), 28.

39. A. B. Craig, "Underwater Swimming and Loss of Consciousness," *JAMA* 176 (April, 29 1961): 255–58.

40. W. R. Keatinge, "Immediate Respiratory Response to Sudden Cooling of the Skin," *J Applied Physiology* 20 (1965): 65.

41. W. R. Keatinge and R. A. McCance, "Increase in Venous and Arterial Pressures During Sudden Exposure to Cold," *Lancet* II (1957): 208.

42. "What Drowning Feels Like" *British Med J* (October 13, 1894), 823.

43. Ibid., 824.

44. W. L. Cullen, "What Drowning Feels Like; by One Who Narrowly Escaped" *British Med J* II (1894): 941–42.

45. Spitz, 500.

46. P. Geertinger and J. Voigt, "Death in the Bath. A Survey of Bathtub Deaths in Copenhagen, Denmark, and Gothenburg, Sweden, from 1961 to 1969," *J Forensic Med* 17 (4) (October 1970): 136–47.

47. Tedeschi, 1330; Copeland, 18-22.

48. Polson, 422.

49. Ibid.

50. Tedeschi, 1330.

51. K. Simpson, ed., *Taylor's Principles and Practice of Medical Jurisprudence*, 12th ed. (London: Churchill, 1965).

52. V. J. Birkinshaw, et al., "Investigations in a Case of Murder by Insulin Poisoning," *British Med J* 2; (1958): 463.

53. Guyton.

54. Raymond Chang, *Chemistry*, 3rd ed. (New York: McGraw-Hill, 1988), 848.

55. A. Auer, "Suicide by Drowning in Uusimaa Province in Southern Finland," *Medicine, Science and the Law* 30 (2) (April 1990): 175–79.

56. B. Meier, "A Public Safety Campaign Falls Short of Its Mark," *New York Times, (January 11, 1992)* 48.

57. E. R. Watson, *Trial of G. J. Smith, Notable British Trials Series*, (Edinburgh: Hodge, 1992); cited in Polson, 444.

CHAPTER 20: DRUGS, CHEMICALS, AND POISONS

1. K. Hawton et al., "Motivational Aspects of Deliberate Self-poisoning in Adolescents," *British J Psychiatry* 141 (September 1982): 286–91.

2. R. M. Cooper and C. M. Milory, "The Coroner's System and Underreporting of Suicide," *Med Science and the Law* 1995 35 (4) (October 1995): 319–26.

3. Centers for Disease Control and Prevention (CDC) web site, http://wonder/cdc.gov; U.S. National Center for Health Statistics, *Vital Statistics of the United States* annual.

4. P. D. Dukes, et al., "Wellington Coroner Autopsy Cases 1970–89: Acute Deaths Due

to Drugs, Alcohol and Poisons," *New Zealand Med J* 105 (927) (February 12, 1992): 25–27.

5. S. P. Baker, *The Injury Fact Book*, (New York: Oxford University Press, 1984) 186.

6. Drug Awareness Warning Network (DAWN) Statistical Series, *Annual Emergency Room Data*, Series 1, Number 11-A (Rockville, Md.: Dept of Health and Human Services 1991).

7. Centers for Disease Control and Prevention (CDC) web site, http://wonder/cdc.gov. U.S. National Center for Health Statistics, *Vital Statistics of the United States*, annual. Drug Awareness Warning Network (DAWN) Statistical Series *Annual Emergency Room Data* Series 1, Numbers 11-A, B (Rockville, Md.: Dept of Health and Human Services 1991).

8. *Vital Statistics of the United States* (Washington, D.C.: Government Printing Office, 1990).

9. Ellenhorn, *Medical Toxicology* (London, NY: Elsevier 1988), 8. N. A. Buckley, et al., "Self-poisoning in Newcastle, 1987–1992," *Med J Australia* 162 (4) (February 20, 1995): 190–93.

10. Y. Leykin, et al., "Acute Poisoning Treated in the Intensive Care Unit: A Case Series," *Israel J Med Science* 25 (2) (February 1989): 98–102. J. Strom et al., "Self-poisoning Treated in an ICU: Drug Pattern, Acute Mortality and Short-term Survival," Acta Anaesthesiology Scandinavica. 30 (2) (February 1986): 148–53. S. P. Lockhart, and J. H. Baron, "Changing Ethnic and Social Characteristics of Patients Admitted for Self-poisoning in West London During 1971/2 and 1983/4," *J Royal Society Med* 80 (3) (March 1987): 145–48. R. R. Bouknight, et al., "Self-poisoning: Outcome and Complications in the Community Hospital," *J Family Practice* 23 (3) (September 1986): 223–25. N. J. Fisker, "Death After Earlier Deliberate Self-poisoning. A 10-year Material from an Intensive Care Unit," *Ugeskr-Laeger* 155 (24) (June 14, 1993): 1857–61.

11. T. L. Litovitz, et al., "1991 Annual Report of the American Association of Poison Control Centers National Data Collection System," *Am J Emergency Med* 10 (5) (September 1992) (5): 452–505.

12. J. J. Card, "Lethality of Suicidal Methods and Suicide Risk: Two Distinct Concepts," *Omega* 5 (1974): 37–45.

13. K. Hawton, et al., "Motivational Aspects of Deliberate Self-poisoning in Adolescents," *British J Psychiatry* 141 (1982): 286–91.

14. B. P. McNicholl, "Toxicity Awareness and Unintended Suicide in Drug Overdoses," *Archives of Emergency Med* 9 (2) (June 1992): 214–19.

15. K. Hawton, *British J Psychiatry* 141 (1982): 286–91.

16. R. V. Clarke and D. Lester, *Suicide: Closing the Exits*, (New York: Springer-Verlag, 1989), 12.

17. W. C. Myers, et al., "Acetaminophen Overdose as a Suicidal Gesture: A Survey of Adolescents' Knowledge of Its Potential for Toxicity," *J Am Academy of Child and Adolescent Psychiatry* 31 (4) (July 1992): 686–90.

18. Ellenhorn, 74–85.

19. L. E. Fazen, III, F. H. Lovejoy, Jr., and R. K. Crone, "Acute Poisoning in a Children's Hospital: A 2-year Experience," *Pediatrics* 77 (2) (February 1986): 144–51.

20. Leykin.

21. T. L. Litovitz, et al., "1992 Annual Report of the American Association of Poison Control Centers Toxic Exposure Surveillance System," *Am J Emergency Med* 11 (5) (September 1993): 494–555.

22. T. L. Litovitz, "1993 Annual Report of the American Association of Poison Control Centers National Data Collection System," *Am J Emergency Med* 12 (1994): 546–84.

23. Leykin, 98–102.

24. L. Borgia, *Un Veleno per Ogni Occasione* (1519). Reprinted 1996, Cosa Pres, Palermo, Italy.

25. A. Heath and D. Selander, "Self-poisoning Treated in the ICU," *Acta Medica Scandinavica* 206(1–2) (1979): 51–54.

26. Ellenhorn, 402. C. M. Steel, et al., "Clinical Effects and Treatment of Imipramine and Amitriptyline Poisoning in Children," *British Med J* 3 (566) (September 9, 1967):663–67. M. Callaham and D. Kassel, "Epidemiology of Fatal Tricyclic Antidepressant Ingestion: Implications for Management," *Annals of Emergency Med* 14 (1) (January 1985): 1–9.

27. Leykin, 98.

28. B. P. McNicholl, "Toxicity Awareness and Unintended Suicide in Drug Overdoses," *Archives of Emergency Med* 9 (2) (June 1992): 214–19. S. Hagen, et al., "Admissions Due to Over-doses of Aromatic Analgesics Have Increased in Scotland," *British Med J* 312 (June 15, 1996): 1538.

29. C. H. Cantor, "Substances Involved in Fatal Drug Overdoses in Brisbane, 1979–1987," *Acta Psychiatrica Scandinavica* 354 (supp.) (1989): 69–71.

30. C. T. Tan, "Suicidal Poisoning Deaths in Singapore 1975–1984," *Annals of the Academy of Med of Singapore* 16 (2), (1987): 300–2. K. Chirasirisap, et al., "A study of Major Causes and Types of Poisoning in Khonkaen, Thailand," *Veterinary and Human Toxicology* 34 (6) (December 1992): 489–92.

31. L. R. Berger, "Suicides and Pesticides in Sri Lanka," *A J Public Health* 78, (1988): 826–28.

32. Litovitz. 1992, 452–505 Drug Awareness Warning Network (DAWN) Statistical Series, *Annual Emergency Room Data*, Series 1, Numbers 11-A, 21–32 B16–48. (1991).

33. Ibid.

34. Ellenhorn, 782.

35. A. J. McBay and P. Hudson, "Drug Deaths in North Carolina: A Brief Survey of Deaths Attributed to Drugs in North Carolina, 1973," *North Carolina Med J* 35 (9) (September, 1974): 542–24. Y. H. Caplan, et al., "Drug and Chemical Related Deaths: Incidence in the State of Mary-land—1975 to 1980," *J Forensic Science* 30 (4) (October 1985): 1012–21. S. M. Froede, et al., "An Analysis of Toxic Deaths, 1982 to 1985, Pima County, Arizona," *J Forensic Science* 32 (6) (November 1987): 1676–93.

36. Litovitz (1991), 452–505.

37. C. Lamanna, "The Most Poisonous Poison," *Science* 130 (September 25, 1959): 763–72.

38. Anthony, Tu, ed., "Reptile Venoms and Toxins," *Handbook of Natural Toxins*, vol. 5 (New York: Dekker, 1991), 435. J. Meier, et al., eds., *Clinical Toxicology of Animal Venoms and Poisons* (Cleveland: CRC Press, 1995), 162.

39. J. T. Biggs, "Clinical Pharmacology and Toxicology of Antidepressants," *Hospital Practice* 13 (2) (1978): 80.

40. T. M. Ludden, "Sex-related Differences in the Pharmacokinetics and Dynamics of Drugs," *Am Society of Hospital Pharmacy Midyear-Clinical-Meeting*, 30 (December 1995):1–11.

41. L. M. Haddad, et al., *Clinical Management of Poisoning and Drug Overdose* (Philadelphia: Saunders, 1990).

42. N. Wright, "An Assessment of the Unreaibility of the History Given by the Self-poi-soned Patient," *Clinical Toxicology* 16 (1980) 381–84.

43. Poisindex, "Barbiturates" (Denver, CO: Micromedex, Inc., 1994)

44. R. H. Cravey, et al., "Toxicology Data from Documented Drug-induced or Drug-related Fatal Cases," *J Toxicology and Clinical Toxicology* 10 (1977): 327–39.

45. Robert H. Dreisbach, *Handbook of Poisoning* 12th ed. (Los Altos: Lange, 1987), 310.

46. W. J. Fremouw, et al., *Suicide Risk: Assessment and Response Guidelines* (New York: Pergamon, 1990).

47. F. L. Glauser and W. R. Smith, "Physiologic and Biochemical Abnormalities in Self-induced Drug Overdosage," *Archives of Intern Med* 135 (11) (November 1975): 1468–73. Ellenhorn, 575.

48. Tedeschi, 1204.

49. S. Jamison, "When Drugs Fail: Assisted Deaths and Not-so-lethal Drugs," *J Pharmaceutical Care in Pain and Symptom Control* 4 (1–2) (1996): 223–43.

50. R. Ogden, *Euthanasia, Assisted Suicide and AIDS* (New Wesminster, B.C.: Peroglyphics Pub., 1994).

51. L. Adelson, "Homicidal Poisoning. A Dying Modality of Lethal Violence?" *Am J Forensic Med and Pathology* 8 (3) (September 1987): 245–51.

52. D. Humphry, "Lethal Drugs for Assisted Suicide: How the Public Sees It," *J Pharmaceutical Care in Pain and Symptom Control* 4 (1–2) (1996): 177–82.

53. Personal communication, C. Casteneda, 1986.

54. Derek Humphrey, *Final Exit*, (Eugene, OR: Hemlock Society), 91.

55. C. Docker, and C. Smith, *Departing Drugs* (Victoria, B.C.: Right to Die Society of Canada, 1993), 30.

56. H. C. Mofenson, "Ingestions Considered Nontoxic," *Clinical Laboratory Med* 4 (1984): 587–602.

57. Gina Kolata, "AIDS Patients Seek Solace in Suicide but Many Risk Added Pain in Failure," *New York Times* (June 14, 1994), C1.

58. T. Preston and R. Mero, in M. P. Battin and A. G. Lipman, eds., *Drug Use in Assisted Suicide and Euthanasia* (New York: Pharmaceutical Products Press, 1996), 183–96.

59. L. Binder and L. Fredrickson, "Poisonings in Laboratory Personnel and Health-care Professionals," *Am J Emergency Med* 9 (1) (January 1991): 11–15.

60. J. Setter, et al., "Barbiturate Intoxication. Evaluation of Therapy Including Dialysis in a Large Series Selectively Referred Because of Severity," *Archives of Internal Med* 117 (February 1966): 224–36.

61. T. Preston and R. Mero, in Battin and Lipman, (New York: Pharmaceutical Products Press, 1996), 183–96.

62. D. Humphrey, in Battin and Lipman, 181.

63. B. B. Lystbaek and P. Norregaard, "A Case of Sustained-release Paracetamol Poisoning with Fatal Outcome," *Ugeskr-Laeger* 157 (7) (February 13, 1995): 899–900.

64. R. D. Farmer and R. M. Pinder, "Why Do Fatal Overdose Rates Vary Between Antidepressants?" *Acta Psychiatrica Scandinavica* 354 (supp.) (1989): 25–35.

65. J. B. Marshall and A. D. Forker, "Cardiovascular Effects of Tricyclic Antidepressant Drugs: Therapeutic Usage, Overdose, and Management of Complications," *Am Heart J* 103 (1982): 401–14.

66. M. Callaham and D. Kassel, "Epidemiology of Fatal Tricyclic Antidepressant Ingestion: Implications for Management," *Annals of Emergency Med* 14 (1) (1985). 1.5 to 3.2 hours according to *The Art and Science of Suicide* Cheryl Smith, Ch 5, p5.

67. Poisindex, "Potassium" (Micromedex, Inc., 1994).

68. Humphrey, 123.

69. J. Jones, Personal communication, 1976.

70. C. Docker, *Departing Drugs*, (Victoria, B.C.: Right to Die Society of Canada, 1993), 53.

71. R. E. Gosselin, et al., *Clinical Toxicology of Commercial Products* III, 127 (Baltimore: Williams and Wilkins, 1984).

72. J. A. Schofferman, "A Clinical Comparison of Syrup of Ipecac and Apomorphine Use in Adults," *JACEP* 5 (1976): 22–25.

73. G. C. Rodgers, et al., "Use of Liquid Dishwashing Detergent as an Emetic," *Veterinary and Human Toxicology* 28 (1985): 321.

74. W. D. Meesler, "Emesis and Lavage," *Veterinary and Human Toxicology* 28 (1985): 225–34.

75. D. C. Corby, et al., "The Efficacy of Methods Used to Evacuate the Stomach After Acute Ingestions," *Pediatrics* 40 (1967): 871–74.

76. Ellenhorn, 60.

77. K. Kulig, et al., "Management of Acutely Poisoned Patients Without Gastric Emptying," *Annals of Emergency Medicine* 14 (1985): 562–67.

78. P. Ott, et al., "Consumption, Overdose and Death from analgesics During a Period of Over-the-counter Availability of Paracetamol in Denmark," *J Internal Med* 227 (6) (June 1990): 423–28.

79. Ellenhorn, 8.

80. B. S. Finkle, et al., "Diazepam and Drug-Associated Deaths," *J Am Med Assn* 242, (1979): 429–33.

81. P. D. Dukes, et al., "Wellington Coroner Autopsy Cases 1970–89: Acute Deaths Due to Drugs, Alcohol and Poisons," *New Zealand Med J* 105 (February 12, 1992): 25–27.

82. M. J. Kelleher, "The Influence of Antidepressants in Overdose on the Increased Suicide Rate in Ireland Between 1971 and 1988," *Brit J Psychiatry* 161 (1992): 625–28.

83. R. D. T. Farmer and Ram. Pinder, "Why Do Fatal Overdose Rates Vary Between Antidepressants?" *Acta Psychiatrica Scandinavica* 80 (supp. 354 (1989): 25–35. D. Baldwin, et al., "5-HT Reuptake Inhibitors, Tricyclic Antidepressants and Suicidal Behaviour" *International Clinical Psychopharmacology* 6 (supp. 3) (December 1991): 49–55; discussion 55–56. D. L. Frankenfield, et al., "Fluoxetine and Violent Death in Maryland," *Forensic Science International* 64 (2–3) (February 1994): 107–17. A. Molcho and M. Stanley, "Antidepressants and Suicide Risk: Issues of Chemical and Behavioral toxicity," *J Clinical Psychopharmicology* 12 (supp. 2) (1992): 13–18.

84. L. T. Sigell and H. C. Flessa, "Drug Interactions with Anticoagulants," *J Am Med Assn* 214 (11) (December 14, 1970): 2035–38.

85. G. K. Kimsma, "Euthanasia and Euthanizing Drugs in the Netherlands," *J Pharmaceutical Care in Pain and Symptom Control* 4 (1–2), (1996): 193–210.

CHAPTER 21: ELECTROCUTION

1. Cyril J. Polson, D. J. Gee, and Bernard Knight, (New York: Pergamon, 1985), *The Essentials of Forensic Medicine*, 4th ed. 279.

2. J. S. Hammond and C. G. Ward, "High-voltage Electrical Injuries: Management and Outcome of 60 Cases," *Southern Med J* 81 (1988): 1351–52.

3. J. C. Holder, "An unusual Method of Attempted Suicide," *Med Legal J* 28 (1960): 41. F. P. Bornstein, "Homicide by Electrocution," *J Forensic Science* 7 (1962): 516.

4. B. Klun, et al., "Stunning Device as a Suicide Weapon," *Acta Neurochir Wien* 97 (3–4) (1989): 111–3.

5. Polson, 271.

6. I. B. Cohen, *Benjamin Franklin's Experiments* (Cambridge, Mass.; Harvard University Press, 1941), 271.

7. R. K. Wright and J. H. Davis, "The Investigation of Electrical Deaths: A Report of 220 Fatalities," *J Forensic Science* 25 (3) (July 1980): 514–21.

8. CDC, "Fatal Occupational Injuries—Texas 1982," *MMWR: Morbidity and Mortality Weekly Report* 34 (10) (1985): 130–34, 139.

9. CDC, "Deaths Associated with Hurricane Hugo—Puerto Rico" *MMWR* 38 (39) (1989): 680–82.

10. N. Wright, 514–21.

11. *Statistical Abstract of the United States* (Department of Commerce, 1994), 848.

12. Hammond, 1351–52.

13. H. Bissig, *Electromedizin* 5 (1960): 154; cited in Tedeschi, 655.

14. National Center for Health Statistics, CDC web site, http://wonder.cdc.gov.

15. Tedeschi, 669 S. Steinbaum, et al., "Lightning Strike to the Head: Case Report," *J Trauma* 36(1) (January 1994): 113–5.

16. W. R. Lee, "The Mechanisms of Death from Electric Shock," *Med Science and the Law* 5 (1965) 23–28; quoted in Polson, 277.

17. Polson, 277.

18. E. Leygraf, "Suicidal Electric Fatalities Outside the Bathtub (with 3 Case Reports")" *Beitrage zur Gerichtlichen Medizen* 48 (1990): 551–59.

19. Arthur Guyton, *Medical Physiology*, 3rd ed. (Philadelphia: Saunders, 1966), 193.

20. R. Fish, "Electric Shock, Part II: Nature and Mechanisms of Injury," *J Emergency Med* 11(4) (July–August 1993): 457–62.

21. O. Lobl, *ETZ-A80* (1959): 97; cited in Tedeschi, 647.

22. Fish, 458.

23. Lobl; cited in Tedeschi, 647.

24. M. E. Goodson, "Electrically Induced Deaths Involving Water Immersion," *Am J Forensic Med and Pathology* 14(4) (December 1993): 330–33.

25. J. Cabanes, in R. C. Lee, ed., *Electrical Trauma* (London: Cambridge 1992) University Press, 15–32.

26. R. Fish, "Electric Shock, Part I: Physics and Pathophysiology, *J Emergency Med* 11(3) (May–June 1993): 309–12.

27. Tedeschi, 649.

28. T. Bernstein, "Effects of Electricity and Lightning on Man and Animals," *J Forensic Science* 18(1) (January 1973): 3–11.

29. A. Sances, S. J. Larson, and J. Myklebust, et al., "Electrical Injuries," *Surgery, Gynecology and Obstetrics* 149 (1979): 97–108.

30. W. R. Lee, "A Clinical Study of Electrical Accidents," *British J Industrial Med* 18 (1961): 260–69.

31. Wright, 515.

32. Polson, 301.

33. Tedeschi, 656.

34. Ibid., 666.

35. Werner U. Spitz, R.S. Fisher, *Mediolegal Investigation of Death* 3rd ed. (Springield, Ill.: Thomas, (1993), 524.

36. Tedeschi, 667.

37. Wright, 518.

38. M. A. Cooper, "Lightning Injuries: Prognostic Signs for Death," *Annals of Emergency Med* 9(3) (March 1980): 134–38.

39. Whichello, *Lancet* i (1899), 1490; quoted in Polson, 309.

40. S. Koeppen, *Electromedizin* 6 (1961): 215; cited in Tedeschi, 647.

41. Fish, 460.

42. C. D. Hodgman (ed.) *Handbook of Chem and Physics*, 37th ed., (Cleveland: CRC Press), 2322.

43. Polson, 301. J. E. Ennis, "Electrocution on a Haystack," *Med Science and the Law* 7(3) (July 1967): 142–44.

44. "Electric Arc Hazards," *CEE*, [formerly, *Construction Electrical Equipment*] *News* (May 1995), 11.

45. Polson, 292.

46. Fish, 461.

47. Polson, 293.

48. Hammond.

49. R. H. Jaffe, "Electropathology: Review of Pathologic Changes Produced by Electric Currents," *Archives of Pathology* 5 (1928): 837–70.

50. A. Patel and R. Lo, "Electric Injury with Cerebral Venous Thrombosis. Case Report and Review of the Literature," *Stroke* 24(6) (June 1993): 903–5.

51. Polson, 313.

52. Fish, 457.

53. Fish, 457. B. J. Grube, et al., "Neurologic Consequences of Electrical Burns," *J Trauma* 30(3) (March 1990): 254–58.

54. A. R. Grossman, et al., "Auditory and Neuropsychiatric Behavior Patterns After Electrical Injury," *J Burn Care and Rehabilitation* 14(2, pt. 1) (March–April 1993): 169–75.

55. *CEE News*, 11. T. J. Janus and J. Barrash, "Neurologic and Neurobehavioral Effects of Electric and Lightning Injuries," *J Burn Care and Rehabilitation* 17(5) (September 1996): 409–15.

56. J. Cabanes, in R. C. Lee, ed., *Electrical Trauma* (London: Cambridge University Press, 1992), 15–32.

57. Tedeschi, 650.

58. E. A. Spitzka and H. E. Radasch, "The Brain Lesions Produced by Electricity as Observed After Legal Execution," *Am J Med Science* 144 (1912): 341–47; *New York Times* (August 7, 1890).

59. A. H. Werner, "Death by Electricity," *New York Med J* 118 (1923): 498.

60. S. Jellinek, *Der Electrische Unfall* (1927); cited in Polson, 277, 301.

61. Polson, 304.

62. W. Bonte, R. Sprung, and W. Huckenbeck, "Problems in the Evaluation of Electrocution Fatalities in the Bathtub," *Z Rechtsmed* 97 (1) (1986): 7–19.

63. W. MacLachlan, "Electric Shock: Interpretation of Field Notes," *J Industrial Hygiene* 12 (1930): 291–19; cited in Polson, 80.

64. Polson, 312. T. H. Strong, Jr., et al., "Electrical Shock in Pregnancy: A Case Report," *J Emergency Med* 5 (1987): 381–83.

65. M. A. Logan, "Electrical Burns Caused by Fishing Rod Contact with Overhead Electric Cables: A Potential Hazard to Fishermen," *Burns* 19 (6) (December 1993): 535–37.

66. G. W. Grumet, "Attempted Suicide by Electrocution. Review and Case Report," *Bulletin of the Menninger Clinic* 53 (6) (November 1989): 512–21.

67. F. E. Camps, ed., *Gradwohl's Legal Medicine*, 3rd ed. (1976), 62. P. Benmeir, et al., "Very Deep Burns of the Hand Due to Low Voltage Electrical Laboratory Equipment: A Potential Hazard for Scientists," *Burns* 19 (5) (October 1993): 450–51.

68. W. C. Sellar and R. J. Yeatman, *1066 and All That* (New York: Dutton, 1931).

69. John Laurence, *A History of Capital Punishment* (Port Washington, N.Y.: Kennikat Press, 1971). T. S. Reynolds and T. Bernstein, "Edison and the Chair," *Institute of Electrical and Electronics Engineers (IEEE) Technology Society Magazine* 8 (1) (1989): 19–28.

70. "Hazardous Hair Dryers," *Washington Post* (May 14, 1997), C5.

CHAPTER 22: GUNSHOT WOUNDS

1. Ted Miller, et al., "Costs of Penetrating Injury" in Rao Ivatury, et al., *Textbook of Penetrating Trauma* (Baltimore: Williams and Wilkins, 1995), 49–59. N. L. Farberow, and E. S. Shneidman, *The Cry for Help* (New York: McGraw-Hill, 1961). R. K. Lee et al., "Incidence Rates of Firearm Injuries in Galveston, Texas, 1979–1981," *Am J Epidemiology* 134(5) (September 1, 1991): 511–21. L. Riddick, et al., "Gunshot Injuries in Mobile County, Alabama: 1985–1987," *Am J Forensic Med and Pathology* 14 (3) (1993): 215–25. J. J. Card, "Lethality of Suicidal Methods and Suicide Risk: Two Distinct Concepts" *Omega* 5 (1974): 37–45. O. Bostman, et al., "Firearm Injuries in Finland, 1985–1989," *Annals of Chir Gynaecol* 82(1) (1993): 47–49. P. Cummings, M. LeMier, and D. B. Keck, "Trends in Firearm-related Injuries in Washington State, 1989–1995," *Annals of Emergency Med* 32(1) (July 1998): 37–43.

2. H. H. Kaufman, et al., "Gunshot Wounds to the Head: A Perspective," *Neurosurgery* 18 (6) (June 1986): 689–95.

3. Kaufman. 689–95. Cummings, 37–43

4. Cummings, 37–43.

5. Bostman, 47–49

6. Miller, 49–59.

7. T. R. Miller, "Costs Associated with Gunshot Wounds in Canada in 1991," *Canadian Med Association J* 153 (9) (November 1, 1995) 1261–68.

8. L. G. Peterson, et al., "Self-inflicted Gunshot Wounds: Lethality of Method Versus Intent" *Am J Psychiatry* 142 (2) (1985): 228–31. National Center for Health Statistics, CDC web site, http://wonder.cdc.gov.

9. J. D. Wright, P. H. Rossi, and K. Daly, *Under the Gun* (New York: Aldine, 1983). L. M. Conn, B. F. Rudnick, and J. R. Lion, "Psychiatric Care for Patients with Self-inflicted Gunshot Wounds," *Am J Psychiatry* 141(2) (February 1984): 261–63. J. Boyd, "The Increasing Rate of Suicide by Firearms," *New England J Med* 308 (1983): 872–98. L. G. Peterson, et al., "Self-inflicted Gunshot Wounds: Lethality of Method Versus Intent," *Am J Psychiatry* 142 (2) (February 1985): 228–31.

10. D. Lester, "The Availability of Firearms and the Use of Firearms for Suicide: A Study of 20 Countries," *Acta Psychiatrica Scandinavica* 81 (2) (February 1990) 146–47. R. V. Clarke and D. Lester, *Suicide: Closing the Exits* (1989), 49–83.

11. J. Chapman and C. M. Milroy, "Firearm Deaths in Yorkshire and Humberside," *Forensic Science International* 57 (2) (December 1992): 181–91. 1992 Dec.

12. I. D. Anderson, M. Woodford, and M. H. Irving, "Preventability of Death from Penetrating Injury in England and Wales," *Injury* 20 (2) (March 1989): 69–71.

13. C. H. Cantor, J. Brodie, and J. McMillen, "Firearm Victims—Who Were They?" *Med J Australia* 155 (7) (October 7, 1991): 442–6.

14. Cantor. R. D. T. Farmer and J. R. Rohde, "Effect of Availability and Acceptability of Lethal Instruments on Suicide Mortality," *Acta Psychiatrica Scandinavia* 62 (1980): 436–46.

15. *Causes of Death 1972–1984, Official Statistics of Sweden* National Central Bureau of Statistics, Stockholm; cited in Karlsson, 1988.

16. I. C. Stone, "Characteristics of Firearms and Gunshot Wounds as Markers of Suicide," *Am J Forensic Med and Pathology* 13(4) (December 1992): 275–80.

17. National Center for Heath Statistics, CDC web site. http://wonder.cdc.gov

18. A. L. Kellermann, et al., "Suicide in the Home in Relation to Gun Ownership," *New England J Med* 327 (7) (August 13, 1992): 467–72. A. L. Kellermann, et al., "The Epidemiologic Basis for the Prevention of Firearm Injuries," *Annual Revue of Public Health* 12 (1991): 17–40. Lester, 146–47. M. Killias, "International Correlations Between Gun Ownership and Rates of Homicide and Suicide," *Canadian Med Association J* 148 (10) (May 15, 1993): 1721–25. J. H. Sloan, et al., "Firearm Regulations and Rates of Suicide. A Comparison of Two Metropolitan Areas," *New England J Med* 322 (6) (February 8, 1990): 369–73. Clarke and Lester, 49–83. C. L. Rich, et al., "Guns and Suicide: Possible Effects of Some Specific Legislation," *Am J Psychiatry* 147 (3) (March 1990): 342–46.

19. J. H. Sloan, et al., "Firearm Regulations and Rates of Suicide. A Comparison of Two Metropolitan Areas," *New England J Med* 322 (6) (February 8, 1990): 369–73.

20. 1980 World Health Organization data.

21. Herbert Hendin, *Suicide in America* (New York: Norton, 1995), 28.

22. C. E Koop and G. B. Lundberg, "Violence in America: A Public Health Emergency. Time to Bite the Bullet," *Journal of the American Medical Association* 267 (22) (June 10, 1992): 3075–76.

23. Kellermann, 470–71.

24. Clarke and Lester, 52–61.

25. D. A. Brent and J. A. Perper, "The Presence and Accessibility of Firearms in the Homes of Adolescent Suicides. A Case-control Study," *JAMA* 266 (21) (December 4, 1991): 2989–95.

26. R. L. Frierson and S. B. Lippmann, "Psychiatric Consultation for Patients with Self-inflicted Gunshot Wounds," *Psychosomatics* 31 (1) (winter 1990): 67–74.

27. R. E. Markush and A. A. Bartolucci, "Firearms and Suicide in the United States," *Am J Public Health* 74 (2) (February 1984): 123–27. F. E. Zimring, and G. Hawkins, *The Citizen's Guide to Gun Control* (New York: Macmillan, 1987).

28. Wright, 25–63, 81–149.

29. G. J. Wintemute, et al., "The Choice of Weapons in Firearm Suicides," *Am J Public Health* 78 (7) (July 1988): 824–26.

30. George Colt, *The Enigma of Suicide* (New York: Summit Books, 1991) 53.

31. Boyd, 872–98.

32. R. L. Frierson, "Women Who Shoot Themselves," *Hospital Community Psychiatry* 40 (8) (August 1989): 841–43.

33. Ibid. D. Lester and M. Murrell, "The Influence of Gun Control Laws on Suicidal Behaviour," *Am J Psychiatry* 137 (1980): 121–22. C. Loftin, et al., "Effects of Restrictive Licensing of Handguns on Homicide and Suicide in the District of Columbia," *New England J Med* 325 (23) (December 5, 1991): 1615–20.

34. Rich, 342–46. Sloan, 369–73.

35. D. Lester, and B. Danto, *Suicide Behind Bars: Prediction and Prevention* (Philadelphia: Charles

Press, 1993). R. Frost and P. Hanzlick. "Deaths in Custody," *Forensic Medicine and Pathology* 9 (1988): 207–11; Hendin, 214–35.

36. Miller, in Ivatury, 49–59.

37. Spitz, *Medicolegal Investigation of Death*, 3rd ed. (1993), 363.

38. Cyril J. Polson, D. J. Gee, and Bernard Knight, *The Essentials of Forensic Medicine*, 3rd ed. (New York: Permagon, 1977), 63.

39. Stone, 275–80.

40. W. Roughead, *Trial of John Donald Merrett* (Edinburgh: Hodge, 1929); in Polson, 261.

41. G. K. Murphy, "Murders for Profit. The Case of John Donald Merrett," *Am J Forensic Med and Pathology* 6 (4) (1985): 325–28.

42. P. Hudson, "Multishot Firearm Suicide," *Am J Forensic Med and Pathology* 2 (3) (1981): 39–42.

43. Ibid.

44. Tedeschi, 1004.

45. B. Jacob, et al., "Multiple Suicidal Gunshots to the Head," *Am J Forensic Med and Pathology* 10 (4) (December 1989): 289–294. E. Introna, "Suicide from Multiple Gunshot Wounds," *Am J Forensic Med and Pathology* 10 (4) (December 1989): 275–84.

46. Ibid.

47. Cyril J. Polson, D. J. Gee, and Bernard Knight, *The Essentials of Forensic Medicine* 4th ed. (New York: Pergamon, 1985), 212.

48. D. H. Collins, "Bullet Embolism: Case of Pulmonary Embolism Following Entry of Bullet into Right Ventricle of Heart," *J Pathology and Bacteriology* 60 (1948): 205.

49. V. J. DiMaio, et al., "A Fatal Case of Lead Poisoning Due to a Retained Bullet," *Am J Forensic Med and Pathology* 1983 4 (2) (June 1983): 165–69.

50. W. Machle, "Lead Absorption from Bullets Lodged in Tissues: Report of 2 Cases," *JAMA* 115 (ii) (1940): 1536–41.

51. G. C. Johnson, "Unusual Shotgun Injury," *Am J Forensic Med and Pathology* 6 (3) (1985): 244–47.

52. Polson, 4th ed., 241.

53. Spitz, 476.

54. B. S. Selden, et al., "Outcome of Self-inflicted Gunshot Wounds of the Brain," *Annals of Emergency Med* 17 (3) (March 1988): 247–53.

55. W. U. Spitz, et al., "Physical Activity Until Collapse Following Fatal Injury by Firearms and Sharp Pointed Weapons," *J Forensic Science* 6 (1961): 290–96. S. O. Thoresen and T. O. Rognum, "Survival Time and Acting Capability After Fatal Injury by Sharp Weapons," *Forensic Science International* 31 (3) (July 14, 1986): 181–87.

56. S. Smith, *Police J* 16 (1943) 108–10; quoted in Polson, 267.

57. B. Karger, "Penetrating Gunshots to the Head and Lack of Immediate Incapacitation. II. Review of Case Reports," *International J Legal Med* 108 (3) (1995): 117–26.

58. A. R. Copeland, "Concepts in Survival from Lethal Handgun Wounds," *Am J Forensic Med and Pathology* 6 (2) (June 1985): 175–79.

59. J. W. Eisele, D. T. Reay, and A. Cook A "Sites of Suicidal Gunshot Wounds," *J Forensic Science* 26 (3) (July 1981): 480–85.

60. Stone, 275–80.

61. T. Suwanjutha, "Direction, Site and the Muzzle Target Distance of Bullet in the Head and Neck at Close Range as an Indication of Suicide or Homicide," *Forensic Science International* 37 (3) (May 1988): 223–29.

62. Eisele, 480–85.

63. S. Cohle, "Handgun Suicides," *Forensic Science Gazette* 8 (2) (1977): 2. J. S. Mitchell, "Shotgun Suicides," *Forensic Science Gazette* 8 (2) (1977): 3.

64. I. C. Stone, "Observations and Statistics Relating to Suicide Weapons," *J Forensic Science* 35 (1) (January 1990): 10–12.

65. Frierson and Lippmann, 67–74.

66. J. A. van Aalst, et al., "Long-term Follow-up of Unsuccessful Violent Suicide Attempts: Risk Factors for Subsequent Attempts," *J Trauma* 33 (3) (September 1992): 457–64.

67. L. W. Shuck, M. G. Orgel, and A. V. Vogel, "Self-inflicted Gunshot Wounds to the Face: A Review of 18 Cases," *J Trauma* 20 (5) (May 1980) 370–77. R. H. Mathog, et al., "Self-inflicted Shotgun Wounds of the Face: Surgical and Psychiatric Considerations," *Otolaryngology—Head and Neck Surgery* 98 (6) (June 1988): 568–74.

68. Frierson and Lippmann, 67–74.

69. R. C. Harruff, "Comparison of Contact Shotgun Wounds of the Head Produced by Different Gauge Shotguns," *J Forensic Science* 40 (5) (1995): 801–04.

70. Mathog, 569.

71. Kaufman, 689–95.

72. A. Platz, M. Heinzelmann, and H. G. Imhof, "Outcome After Craniocerebral Gunshot Injury," *Swiss Surgery* 2 (1985): 118–21.

73. T. W. Grahm, et al., "Civilian Gunshot Wounds to the Head: A Prospective Study," *Neurosurgery* 27 (5) (November 1990): 696–700.

74. M. G. Nagib, et al., "Civilian Gunshot Wounds to the Brain: Prognosis and Management," *Neurosurgery* 18 (5) (May 1986): 533–37. Selden, 247–53. Kaufman, 689–95.

75. Ted Miller, et al., "Costs of Penetrating Injury," in Ivatury, 49–59.

76. Selden, 247–53.

77. L. Solyom, "A Case of Self-inflicted Leucotomy," *British J Psychiatry* 151 (December 1987): 855–57.

78. Frierson, 67–74.

79. Polson, 3rd ed., 262.

80. D. V. Feliciano, et al., "Abdominal Gunshot Wounds. An Urban Trauma Center's Experience with 300 Consecutive Patients," *Annals of Surg* 208 (3) (September 1988): 362–70.

81. S. M. Hoekstra, J. S. Bender, and M. A. Levison, "The Management of Large Soft-tissue Defects Following Close-range Shotgun Injury," *J Trauma* 30 (12) (December 1990): 1489–93.

82. Polson, 4th ed., 212.

83. M. S. Owen-Smith, *High Velocity Missile Wounds* (London: Arnold, 1981).

84. Frierson, 67–74.

85. L. Riddick, "Gunshot Injuries in Mobile, Ala.," *Am J Forensic Med and Pathology* 14 (3) (1993): 215–25.

86. P. L. Lillard, "Five Years Experience with Penetrating Craniocerebral Gunshot Wounds," *Surgical Neurology* 9 (2) (February 1978): 79–83. J. B. Kirkpatrick V. Di Maio, "Civilian Gunshot Wounds of the Brain," *J Neurosurgery* 49 (2) (August 1978): 185–198. M. G. Nagib, et al., "Civilian Gunshot Wounds to the Brain: Prognosis and Management," *Neurosurgery* 18 (5) (May 1986): 533–37.

87. Grahm, 696–700.

88. P. Cummings, M. LeMier, and D. B. Keck, "Trends in Firearm-related Injuries in Washington State, 1989–1995," *Annals of Emergency Med* 32 (1) (July 1998): 37–43.

89. E. E. Jones, "The Rocky Road from Acts to Dispositions," *American Psychologist* 34 (1979):

107–17. G. J. S. Wilde, "Beyond the Concept of Risk Homeostasis," *Accident Analysis and Prevention* 18 (1986): 377–401.

90. K. A. Smith, C. G. Fairburn and P. J. Cowen, "Relapse of Depression After Rapid Depletion of Tryptophan," *Lancet* 349 (March 29, 1997): 915–19. David Lester, *Patterns of Suicide and Homicide in the World* (Commack, N.Y.: Nova Science Publishers, 1996).

91. Alvarez, 104.

92. T. C. Grey, "The Incredible Bouncing Bullet: Projectile Exit Through the Entrance Wound," *J Forensic Science* 38 (5) (September 1993): 1222–26.

93. P. J. Knudsen, and P. Theilade, "Terminal Ballistics of the 7.62 mm NATO Bullet. Autopsy Findings," *International J Legal Med* 106 (2) (1993): 61–67.

94. L. Riddick, "Gunshot Injuries in Mobile, Ala.," *Am J Forensic Med and Pathology* 14 (3) (1993): 215–25.

95. P. Betz, O. Peschel, and W. Eisenmenger, "Suicidal Gunshot Wounds—Site and Characteristics," *Archiv fur Kriminologie* 193 (3–4) (March–April 1994): 65–71.

96. V. di Maio, *Gunshot Wounds* (London: Elsevier, 1985), 298–99.

Chapter 23: Hanging and Strangulation

1. A. A. Medalia, A. E. Merriam, and J. H. Ehrenreich, "The Neuropsychological Sequelae of Attempted Hanging," *J Neurology Neurosurgery and Psychiatry* 54 (6) (June 1991): 546–48.

2. D. R. Chambers and J. G. Harvey, "Inner Urban and National Suicide Rates, a Simple Comparative Study," *Med Science and the Law* 29(3) (July 1989): 182–85.

3. D. A. Bowen, "Hanging—A Review," *Forensic Science International* 20(3) (November 1982): 247–49.

4. J. Simonsen, "Patho-anatomic Findings in Neck Structures in Asphyxiation Due to Hanging: A Survey of 80 Cases," *Forensic Science International* 38(1–2) (July–August 1988): 83–91.

5. J. L. Luke, "Asphyxial Deaths by Hanging in New York City, 1964–1965," *J Forensic Science* 12(3) (July 1967): 359–69.

6. J. Guarner, and R. Hanzlick, "Suicide by Hanging. A Review of 56 Cases," *Am J Forensic Med and Pathology* 8(1) (March 1987): 23–26.

7. A. R. Copeland, "Fatal Suicidal Hangings Among Prisoners in Jail," *Med Science and the Law* 29(4) (October 1989): 341–45: see comments in, *Med Sci Law* 30(3) (July 1990): 273. R. Frost and P. Hanzlick, "Deaths in Custody," *Am J Forensic Medicine and Pathology* 9: (1988) 207–11. B. P. Lanphear, "Deaths in Custody in Shelby County, Tennessee, January 1970–July 1985," *Am J Forensic Med and Pathology* 8(4) (December 1987): 299–301.

8. Bowen, 247–49

9. J. L. Luke, et al., "Correlation of Circumstances with Pathological Findings in Deaths by Hanging," *J Forensic Science* 30 (1985): 1140–47.

10. Guarner, 23–26.

11. T. P. Aufderheide, et al., "Emergency Airway Management in Hanging Victims," *Annals of Emergency Med* 24(5) (November 1994): 879–84.

12. Arthur Guyton, *Medical Physiology*, 3rd ed. (Philadelphia : Saunders, 1966) 322.

13. R. James and R. Nasmyth-Jones, "The Occurrence of Cervical Fractures in Victims of Judicial Hanging," *Forensic Science International* 54(1) (April 1992): 81–91.

14. Cyril Polson, D. J. Gee, and Bernard Knight, *The Essentials of Forensic Medicine*, 4th ed. (New York: Pergamon, 1985) 369.

15. E. Kalle, abstract, in *Med Leg Rev* 2 (1934): 119; cited in Polson, 369–70.

16. H. G. Swann, et al., "The Cardiorespiratory and Biochemical Events During Rapid Anoxic Death," *Texas Reports on Biology and Medicine* 7 (1949): 593–603.

17. D. T. Reay and G. A. Holloway, Jr., "Changes in Carotid Blood Flow Produced by Neck Compression," *Am J Forensic Med and Pathology* 3(3) (September 1982a): 199–202.

18. S. A. Schreck, "Cerebral Anoxia," in A. B. Baker, R. J. Joynt, eds., *Clinical Neurology*, 2nd ed. (Hagerstown, Md.: 1988), 7.

19. D. T. Reay and J. W. Eisele, "Death from Law Enforcement Neck Holds," *Am J Forensic Med and Pathology* 3(3) (September 1982b): 253–58.

20. Reay (1982b), 254.

21. Polson, 369.

22. Brouardel (1897); cited in Polson, 368–69.

23. Ibid., 368.

24. Sherwin Nuland, *How We Die* (New York: Knopf, 1994), 159.

25. A. Davison and T. K. Marshall, "Hanging in Northern Ireland—A Survey," *Med Science and the Law* 26(1) (January 1986): 23–28.

26. Polson, 370.

27. Simonsen, 83–91.

28. B. J. Ficarra, "Death by Hanging," *Legal Med* (1987): 44–60.

29. A. H. Boyarsky, L. Flancbaum, and S. Z. Trooskin, "The Suicidal Jailhouse Hanging," *Annals of Emergency Med* 17(5) (May 1988): 537–39.

30. H. E. Emson, "Accidental Hanging in Autoeroticism. An Unusual Case Occurring Outdoors," *Am J Forensic Med and Pathology* 4(4) (December 1983b): 337–40.

31. F. E. Camps, "The Case of Emmett-Dunne," *Medical Legal J* 27 (1959): 156–61. H. E. Emson, "The Case of Emmett-Dunne. A Personal Reminiscence," *Am J Forensic Med and Pathology* 4(3) (September 1983a): 255–58.

32. Luke (1967), 359–69. Bowen, 247–49. Simonsen, 83–91. Luke, 1140–47 (1985).

33. Ficarra, 44–60.

34. J. Sterna, "Cases of Probable Suicide in Young Persons Without Obvious Motivations," *Maine Med Association Journal* 44(5) (1958): 16. cited in Ficarra, 55. B. Henry, "Death During Deviant Sexual Activity," paper delivered at annual meeting of the American Association Forensic Science, 1968; cited in Ficarra, 55. Luke 359–69 (1967).

35. Polson, 366, 379.

36. J. Hiss, et al., "Swinging in the Park," *Am J Forensic Med and Pathology* 6(3) (1985): 250–5.

37. F. Walsh, et al., "Autoerotic Asphyxial Deaths: A Medicolegal Analysis of Forty-three Cases," in E. H. Wecht, ed., *Legal Medicine Annual* (New York; Appleton, 1977), 157–82.

38. Peter Freuchen, *Book of the Eskimos* (New York: World Publications, 1961), 212.

39. Ficarra, 56.

40. A. Pierrepoint, *Executioner: Pierrepoint* (London: Harrap, 1974).

41. Similar scene described in Daniel Maguire, *Death by Choice* (Garden City, NY: Image Books, 1984), 172.

42. Charles Duff, *Handbook of Hanging* (Boston: Hale, Cushman & Flint, 1929).

43. Pierrepoint, quoted in Ficarra, 47.

44. "M. P.s Say No to New Gallows by Wide Margin," *New York Times* (July 17, 1983); cited in Ficarra, 49.

45. Just guessing.[?? 104]

46. Polson, 358.

47. Luke (1985).

48. Luke (1967, 359–69.

49. Polson, 358.

50. Luke (1985), 1140–47.

51. Polson, 359.

52. Ibid., 358.

53. Ibid., 366.

54. Ibid., 367.

55. H. Soderman and J. O'Connell, *Modern Criminal Investigation* (New York: Funk & Wagnalls, 1947), 128.

56. Simonsen, 83–91.

57. A. Tardieu, *Etude medico-legale sur la pendaison, la stranglation et la suffocation*, 2nd ed. (Paris, 1879); cited in Polson, 367.

58. Luke (1965).

59. E. Szekely, *Beitrage zur Gerichtlichen Medizen* 6 (1924): 133–364; cited in Polson, 368.

60. Polson, 386.

61. A. Riembault, *Annals of Hyg. publ. Paris* 2nd series, 27 (1867): 164–74; cited in Polson, 386.

62. H. Littlejohn, *Forensic Medicine* (London: Churchill, 1925); cited in Polson, 387.

63. J. C. Rupp, "Suicidal Garrotting and Manual Self-strangulation," *J Forensic Science* 15(1) (January 1970): 71–77.

64. M. Frazer and S. Rosenberg, "A Case of Suicidal Ligature Strangulation," *Am J Forensic Med and Pathology* 4(4) (December 1983): 351–54.

65. Tardieu, 1879; cited in Polson, 400.

66. Marc, *Annals of Hyg. publ. Paris* 5 (1851) 156–224; cited in Polson, 370.

67. C. Tidy, *Legal Medicine*, vol. II (London: Smith Elder, 1883), 409–45; cited in Polson, 371.

68. *Medical Times and Gazette*, 1882; cited in Polson, 371.

69. E. Martin, *Precis de Med. Leg.*, 3rd ed. (Paris: Doin, 1950); cited in Polson, 371.

70. *Yorkshire Post* (May 1, 1948); quoted in Polson, 372.

71. F. Ogston, ed., *Lectures on Medical Jurisprudence* (London: Churchill, 1878); cited in Polson, 374.

72. Ibid.

73. Ibid.

74. B. K. Gupta, "Studies on 101 Cases of Death Due to Hanging," *J Indian Med Association* 45 (1965) 135–40. J. Simonsen, *Forensic Science International*, July–August; 38 1–2(1988): 83–91.

75. Reay (1982b). S. A. Schreck, in Joynt, 5.

76. Boyarsky, 537–39.

77. I. Vande Krol, et al., "The Emergency Department Management of Near-hanging Victims," *J Emergency Med* 12(3) (May–June 1994): 285–92.

78. M. J. Calache and N. S. Achamallah, "Spontaneous Remission of Depression After Attempted Suicide by Hanging: A Case Report and Literature Review," *International J Psychosomatics* 38(1–4) (1991): 89–91.

79. E. N. McQuillen and J. B. McQuillen, "Pain and Suffering . . . and Unconsciousness," *Am J Forensic Med and Pathology* 15(2) (June 1994): 174–79.

80. James and Nasmyth-Jones, 81–91.

81. D. T. Reay, W. Cohen, and S. Ames, "Injuries Produced by Judicial Hanging. A Case Report," *Am J Forensic Med and Pathology* 15(3) (September 1994): 183–86.

82. G. Sternbach and M. J. Bresler, "Near-fatal Suicidal Hanging," *J Emergency Med* 7(5) (September–October 1989): 513–6.

83. Boyarsky, 537–39.

84. Ibid.

85. Sternbach, 513–16.

86. J. T. Hughes, "Miraculous Deliverance of Anne Green: An Oxford Case of Resuscitation in the Seventeenth Century," *British Med J* 285(6357) (December 18, 1982): 1792–93. For the full contemporary account; see, " 'Newes from the Dead or A True and Exact Narration of the miraculous deliverance of Anne Green.' Written by a Scholler in Oxford: Printed by Leonard Lichfield for Tho Robinson, 1651."

87. R. Frost and P. Hanzlick, "Death in Custody," *Forensic Medicine and Pathology* 9 (1988): 207–11.

88. B. P. Lanphear, "Deaths in Custody in Shelby County, Tennessee, January 1970–July 1985," *Forensic Medicine and Pathology* 8 (4) (December 1987).: 299–301. Ibid.

89. P. Brouardel, (1897); cited in Polson, 386.

90. R. W. Byard, S. J. Hucker, and R. R. Hazelwood, "Fatal and Near-fatal Autoerotic Asphyxial Episodes in Women. Characteristic Features Based on a Review of Nine Cases," *Forensic Medicine and Pathology* 14 (1) (March 1993): 70–73.

CHAPTER 24: HYPOTHERMIA

1. Warren Bowman quoted in R. Weiss, "The Cold Facts; How the Body Responds to Winter Weather," *Washington Post* (February 7, 1995), Z7.

2. W. Forgey, *Hypothermia: Death by Exposure* (Merrillville, Ind.: ICS Press, 1985), 21.

3. Ibid., 15.

4. Arthur Guyton, *Medical Physiology*, 3rd ed. (Philadelphia: Saunders, 1966), 322.

5. Forgey, 10.

6. C. D. Hodgman *Handbook of Chemistry and Physics*, 37th ed. CRC Press, (Cleveland: 1955), 2253.

7. T. Locher, et al., "Accidental Hypothermia in Switzerland (1980–1987)—Case Reports and Prognostic Factors," *Schweiz Med Wochenschr* 121 (27–18) (July 9, 1991): 1020–28.

8. W. R. Keatinge, "Seasonal Mortality Among Elderly People with Unrestricted Home Heating," *British Med J* 293 (1986): 732–33.

9. CDC, "Hypothermia-related Deaths—Cook County, Illinois, November 1992–March 1993," *MMWR: Morbidity and Mortality Weekly Report* 42 (1993): 917–19.

10. Ibid.

11. CDC, "Hypothermia-related Deaths—New Mexico, October 1993–March 1994)," *MMWR: Morbidity and Mortality Weekly Report* 44 (50) (December 22, 1995): 933–35.

12. CDC, *MMWR Morbidity and Mortality Weekly Report* "Hypothermia—United States,"

34(50) December 20, 1985): 753–54, and 44(50) (December 22, 1995). D. Colburn, "Hypothermia's Top 10 May Include your State," *Washington Post* (January 2, 1996), Z5.

13. J. A. Downey, et al., "The Response of Tetraplegia Patients to Cold," *Archives of Physical Medicine and Rehabilitation* 48(12) December 1967): 645–49. R. H. Johnson, "Oxygen Consumption of Paralysed Men Exposed to Cold," *J Physiology* 169 (1963): 584, 1963.

14. A. C. Burton, and O. Edholm, *Man in a Cold Environment; Physiological and Pathological Effects of Exposure to Low Temperatures* (New York: Hafner, 1969).

15. Forgey, 8.

16. C. H. Wyndham, et al., "Physiological Response to Cold by Bushmen, Bantu, and Caucasian Males," *J Applied Physiology* 19 (1964):868–76. W. R. Keatinge, *Survival in Cold Water: The Physiology and Treatment of Immersion Hypothermia and of Drowning* (Oxford and Edinburgh: Blackwell Scientific, 1969). H. T. Hammel "Effect of Race on Responses to Cold," *Federation Proceedings* 22: (1963): 795.

17. C. G. Tedeschi, et al., *Forensic Medicine*, (3 volumes), (Philadelphia: Saunders, 1977). 759.

18. W. R. Ehrmantraut H. E. Ticktin, and J. F. Fazekras J F: "Cerebral Hemodynamics and Metabolism in Accidental Hypothermia," *Archives of Internal Med* 99 (1957): 57–59.

19. D. MacLean and D. Emslie-Smith, *Accidental Hypothermia* (Philadelphia: Lippincott, 1977).

20. K. H. Fischbeck and R. P. Simon R P, "Neurological Manifestations of Accidental Hypothermia," *Annals of Neurology* 10 (1981):384–87.

21. TOMES Medical Management, "Hypothermia" (Denver, CO: Micromedex, Inc., 1994).

22. S. A. Niazi, and F. J. Lewis, "Profound Hypothermia in Man: Report of a Case" *Annals of Surgery* 147(1) (1958): 264–660.

23. K. C. Wong, "Physiology and Pharmacology of Hypothermia," *Western J Med* 138 (1983): 227–32. Paul S. Auerbach, ed., *Wilderness Medicine* (St. Louis, MO: Mosby, 1995).

24. Cyril J. Polson, D. J. Gee, and Bernard Knight, *The Essentials of Forensic Medicine*, 4th ed. (New York: Pergamon, 1985), 342.

25. Forgey, 12.

26. H. A. Edwars, et al., "Apparent Death with Accidental Hypothermia: A Case Report," *British J Anaesthesia* 42 (1970): 906.

27. P. Grinsted, "Combined Accidental Hypothermia and Barbiturate Poisoning," *Ugeskr. Laeger* 132(20) (May 14, 1970): 933–36; cited in Tedeschi, 762.

28. R. T. Gregory and J. R. Patton, "Treatment After Exposure to Cold," *Lancet* 1 (1972): 377.

29. Tedeschi, 762.

30. D. C. White and N. W. Nowell, "The Effects of Alcohol on the Cardiac Arrest Temperature in Hypothermic Rats," *Clinical Science* 28 (1965) 395. D. C. MacGregor et al., "The Effects of Ether, Ethanol, Propanol and Butanol on Tolerance to Deep Hypothermia. Experimental and Clinical Observations," *Diseases of the Chest* 50(5) (November 1966): 523–29.

31. Locher, 1020–28.

32. J. Kallenbach, P. Bogg, and C. Feldman et al., "Experience with Acute Poisoning in an Intensive-Care Unit," *South African Med J* 59 (1981): 587–89.

33. Locher, 1020–28.

34. B. Walpoth, et al., "Accidental Deep Hypothermia with Cardiopulmonary Arrest: Extracorporeal Blood Rewarming in 11 Patients," *European J Cardiothoracic Surgery* 4 (7) (1990): 390–93.

35. Ibid.

36. G. W. Molnar, "Survival of Hypothermia by Men Immersed in Ocean," 131 (1946): 1046–50, 1946; G. Horn, "Death from Hypothermia," *Artzl. Wochenschr* 6 (1951): 376; cited in Tedeschi, 762.

37. K. E. Cooper, et al., "Accidental Hypothermia," *International Anesthesiology Clinics* (1964): 999.

38. M. B. McGee, "An Unusual Case of Accidental Hypothermia Due to Cold Water Immersion," *Am J Forensic Med and Pathology* 10(2) (June 1989): 152–55.

39. M. G. Hayward and W. R. Keatinge, "Roles of Subcutaneous Fat and Thermoregulatory Reflexes in Determining Ability to Stabilize Body Temperature in Water," *J Physiology* 320 (November 1981): 229–51.

40. TOMES Medical Management. *Handbook of Chemistry and Physics*, 37th ed. C. D. Hodgman, ed. (Cleveland: CRC Press, 1955).

41. Internet newsgroup Alt.Suicide.Holiday, "Methods" file, (March 1995).

42. W. J. Martens, "Climate Change and Malaria: Exploring the Risks," *Medicine in War* 11(4), (October 1995): 202–13.

43. A. Kurz, D. L., Sessler, and R. Lenhardt, "Perioperative Normothermia to Reduce the Incidence of Surgical-Wound Infection and Shorten Hospitalization," *New England J Med* 334 (19) (May 9, 1994): 1209–15. D. W. Marion, et al., "Treatment of Traumatic Brain Injury with Moderate Hypothermia," *New England J Med* 336 (8) (February 20, 1997): 540–46.

44. W. Forgey, *Hypothermia: Death by Exposure* (Merrillville, Ind.: ICS Press, 1985).

45. Tedeschi, 767. W. R. Keatinge, P. Cannon, "Freezing Point of Human Skin," *Lancet* i (January 2, 1960): 11–4.

CHAPTER 25: JUMPING

1. George Colt, *The Enigma of Suicide* (New York: Summit Books, 1991) 341.

2. E. S. Isbister and J. A. Roberts, "Autokabalesis: A Study of International Vertical Deceleration Injuries," *Injury* 23(2) (1992): 119–22.

3. W. S. ˜20Lewis, A. B. Lee, Jr., and S. A. Grantham, "Jumpers Syndrome: The Trauma of High Free Fall as Seen at Harlem Hospital," *J Trauma* 5(6) (November 1965): 812–18.

4. O. M. Bostman, "Suicidal Attempts by Jumping from Heights. A Three-year Prospective Study of Patients Admitted to an Urban University Accident Department," *Scandinavian J Social Med* 15(3) (1987): 199–203.

5. D. Parkin and E. Stengel, "Incidence of Suicidal Attempts in an Urban Community," *British Med J* 2 (July 17, 1965): 133–38.

6. G. T. Gowitt and R. L. Hanzlick, "Suicide in Fulton County, Georgia (1975–1984)," *J Forensic Science* 31(3) (July 1986): 1029–38.

7. Bostman, 199–203.

8. C. H. Cantor, M. A. Hill, and E. K. McLachlan, "Suicide and Related Behaviour from River Bridges. A Clinical Perspective," *British J Psychiatry* 155 (December 1989b): 829–35. R. G. Snyder, "Human Tolerance Limits in Water Impact," *Aerospace Med* 36 (10) (October 1965): 40–47. B. M. Reynolds, N. A. and Balsano, F. X. Reynolds, "Falls from Heights: A Surgical Experience of 200 Consecutive Cases," *Annals of Surg* 174(2) (August 1971): 304–8.

9. Bostman, 199–203.

10. Reynolds, 304–08.

11. Bostman, 199–203.

12. Bostman. G. S. Fortner, et al., "The Effects of Prehospital Trauma Care on Survival from a 50-meter Fall," *J Trauma* 23(11) (November 1983): 976–81. S. Nayha, "The Bi-seasonal Incidence of Some Suicides. Experience from Finland by Marital Status, 1961–1976," *Acta Psychiatrica Scandinavica* 67 (1) (January 1983): 32–42. Y. Yamamoto, et al., "Statistical Studies on Suicides in Shiga Prefecture During the 15-year Period, 1974 to 1988)," *Nippon-Hoigaku-Zasshi* 44(2) (April 1990): 190–98.

13. N. Retterstol, *Suicide: A European Perspective* (London: Cambridge University Press, 1990).

14. Isbister.

15. Lewis, 812–18.

16. Reynolds.

17. U. K. Goonetilleke, "Injuries Caused by Falls from Heights," *Med Science and the Law* 20(4) (October 1980): 262–75.

18. J. J. Card, "Lethality of Suicidal Methods and Suicide Risk: Two Distinct Concepts," *Omega* 5 (1974): 37–45. N. Farberow and E. S. Shneidman, *Clues to Suicide,* (New York: McGraw-Hill, 1959).

19. T. M. Scalea, et al., "An Analysis of 161 Falls from a Height: the 'Jumper Syndrome' " *J Trauma* 26–8 (1986): 706–12. S. M. Gupta, J. Chandra, and T. D. Dogra, "Blunt Force Lesions Related to the Heights of a Fall," *Am J Forensic Med and Pathology* 3(1) (March 1982): 5–43. Lewis, 812–18, Goonetilleke, 262–75.

20. D. Risser, et al., "Risk of Dying After a Free Fall from Height," *Forensic-Science-International* 78(3) (April 23, 1996): 187–91.

21. Goonetilleke, 262–75.

22. Scalea.

23. R. A. White, et al., "Peripheral Vascular Injuries Associated with Falls from Heights," *J Trauma* 27(4) (April 1987): 411–14. R. G. Snyder: "Terminal Velocity Impacts into Snow," *Military Medicine* 131(10), (1966): 1290–98.

24. R. G. Snyder, "Human Tolerance to Extreme Impacts in Free Fall," *Aerospace Medicine* 8(1963): 695–709.

25. Snyder, 695–709.

26. Ibid.

27. Colt, 334.

28. Snyderr, 695–709.

29. Colt, 332. G. M. Lukas, et al., "Injuries Sustained from High Velocity Impact with Water: An Experience from the Golden Gate Bridge," *J Trauma* 21(8), (August 1981): 612–18.

30. A. Brown, *Golden Gate: Biography of a Bridge* (New York: Doubleday, 1965); quotation from Colt, 329.

31. Lukas, 612–18.

32. Colt, 332.

33. Lukas, 612–18.

34. Smile, 1.

35. Jeff Stryker, "An Awful Milestone for the Golden Gate Bridge," *New York Times* (July 9, 1995), sec. 4, 3.

36. John. Boudreau, "Death Watch at the Golden Gate," *Washington Post* (July 7, 1995), A3.

37. R. G. and C. C. Snyder Snow, "Fatal Injuries Resulting from Extreme Water Impact," *Aerospace Med* 38(8) (1967): 779–83.

38. Lukas, 612–18.

39. Goonetilleke, 262–75.

40. Lukas, 612–18.

41. Goonetilleke, 262–75.

42. Lukas, 612–18.

43. Ibid.

44. R. C. Schneider, et al., "The Efects of Recurrent Spinal Trauma in High-diving," *J Bone and Joint Surgery* 44-A(1962): 648–56.

45. Lukas, 612–18.

46. J. Simonsen, "Injuries Sustained from High-velocity Impact with Water after Jumps from High Bridges," *Am J Forensic Med and Pathology* 4(2) (June 1983): 139–42.

47. E. R. Ellis and G. N. Allen, *Traitor Within: Our Suicide Problem* (New York: Doubleday, 1961); cited in R. V. Clarke and D. Lester, *Suicide: Closing the Exits* (1989), 87.

48. Snyder, 940–47.

49. *Guinness Book of World Records* (1977).

50. Ibid.

51. G. Roberts and D. Ellison, "Jumping from a Great Height," *British J Psychiatry* 145 (December 1984) 670–71.

52. Lewis, 812–18

53. Snyder, 659–709.

54. Ibid.

55. U. K. Goonetilleke, "Injuries Caused by Falls from Heights," *Medicine, Science and the Law* 20 (4) (October 1980): 262–75. W. S. Lewis, A. B. Lee, Jr, and S. A. Grantham, "Jumpers Syndrome. The Trauma of High Free Fall as Seen at Harlem Hospital," *J Trauma* 5 (6) (November 1965): 812–18. S. M. Gupta, J. Chandra, and T. D. Dogra, "Blunt Force Lesions Related to the Heights S. M. of a Fall," *Am J Forensic Med Pathology* 3 (1) (March 1982): 35–43. P. M. Cooper and C. M. Milroy, "The Coroner's System and Under reporting of Suicide," *Medicine, Science and the Law* 35 (4) (October 1995): 319–26.

56. S. M. McGuigan, "The Use of Statistics in the British Journal of Psychiatry," *Brit J Psychiatry* 167 (5) (November 1995): 683–88.

57. Jeff Stryker, "An Awful Milestone for the Golden Gate Bridge," *New York Times* (July 9, 1995), sec. 4, 3.

58. R. H. Seiden, and M. Spence, "A Tale of Two Bridges" *Omega* 14 (3) (1983–1984) 201–29.

59. R. H. Seiden, "Reverend Jones on Suicide," *Suicide and Life-threatening Behavior* 9 (2)(1979): 116–9.

60. Stryker.

61. *Washington Post* (December 22, 1997), A7.

AFTERWORD AND NOTES

[a] W. B. Fye, "Active Euthanasia: An Historical Survey of its Conceptual Origins and Introduction int Medical Though," *Bulletin of the History of Medicine* 52 (1979):492–502.

1. H. V. Vanderpool, "Doctors and the Dying of Patients in American History," R. F. Weir. (ed) *Physician-assisted Suicide* (Bloomington: Indiana University Press, 1997) 33–66.

TABLES

1. Poisindex, "Carbon Monoxide" (Denver, CO: Micromedex, Inc.); M. Ellenhorn, *Medical Toxicology* (1988).

2. TOMES Medical Management, "Hypothermia" (Denver, CO: Micromedex, Inc.).

3. T. Karlsson, K. Ormstad, J. Rajs, *J Forensic Science* 33(2) (March 1988): 448–61. U.S. National Center for Health Statistics web site, http://wonder.cdc.gov.

4. Karlsson, 448–61.

5. National Center for Health Statistics web site, http://wonder.cdc.gov.

6. *World Health Statistics Annual* (Geneva, Switzerland: World Health Organization, 1980); cited by D. Lester, "Changes in the Methods Used for Suicide in 16 Countries from 1960 to 1980," *Acta Psychiatrica Scandinavica* 81(3) (March 1990): 260–61.

7. National Center for Health Statistics web site, http://wonder.cdc.gov.

8. T. L. Litovitz, et al. *Am J Emergency Med* 10(5) (September 1992): 452–505.

9. Y. Leykin, et al. *Israel et al J Med Science* 25(2) (February 1989): 98–102.

10. Ibid.

11. L. A. King and A. C. Moffat, "A Possible Index of Fatal Drug Toxicity in Humans," *Medicine, Science and the Law* 23(3): (1983) 193–98.

12. J. A. Henry, "Fatal Toxicity Index for Antidepressants," *Acta Psychiatrica Scandinavica* 80 (supp. 354) (1989): 37–54.

13. S. A. Montgomery, et al., "Pharmacotherapy in the Prevention of Suicidal Behavior," *J. Clinical Psychopharmacology* 12(2 supp.) (April 1992): 7.

14. H. C. Mofenson H, "Ingestions Considered Nontoxic," *Clinical Laboratory Med* 4 (1984): 587–602.

15. H. H. Kaufman, et al., "Gunshot Wounds to the Head: A Perspective." *Neurosurgery* 18(6) (June 1986): 689–95. T. W. Grahm, et al., "Civilian Gunshot Wounds to the Head: A Prospective Study" *Neurosurgery* 27(5) (November 1990): 696–700.

16. J. W. Eisele, D. T. Reay, and A. Cook, "Sites of Suicidal Gunshot Wounds," *J Forensic Science* 26(3) (July 1981): 480–85.

17. B. S. Selden, et al., "Outcome of Self-inflicted Gunshot Wounds of the Brain," *Annals of Emergency Med* 17(3) (March 1988): 247–53. Grahm, 696–700.

18. P. Hudson, "Multishot Firearm Suicide," *Am J Forensic Med and Pathology* 2(3) (1981): 239–42.

19. T. Karlsson K. Ormstad, J. Rajs, (1988); National Center for Health Statistics web site, http://wonder.cdc.gov.

20. J. Guarner and R. Hanzlick, "Suicide by Hanging. A Review of 56 Cases," *Am J Forensic Med and Pathology* 8(1) (March 1987): 23–26.

21. J. L. Luke, "Asphyxial Deaths by Hanging in New York City, 1964–1965," *J Forensic Science* 12(3) (July 1967): 359–69. D. A. Bowen, "Hanging—A Review," *Forensic Science International* 20(3) (November 1982): 247–49. J. Simonsen, "Patho-anatomic Findings in Neck Structures in Asphyxiation Due to Hanging: A Survey of 80 Cases," *Forensic Science International* 38(1–2) (July–August 1788): 83–91. J. L. Luke, et al., "Correlation of Circumstances with Pathological Findings in Deaths by Hanging," *J Forensic Science* 30 (1985): 1140–47.

22. V. K. Goonetilleke, "Injuries Caused by Falls from Heights," *Med Science and the Law* 20(4) (October 1980): 262–75.

23. P. Sainsbury, "Differences Between Suicide Rates" *Science* 220 (1968): 1252. L.I. Dublin (New York: Ronald Press, 1963). *World Health Statistics Annual* (1965); cited in D. Lester, *Patterns of Suicide and Homicide in the World* (Commack, NY: Nova Science, 1996), 15.

24. N. Retterstol, *Suicide: A European Perspective* (New York: Knopf, 1993), 64. R. A. Kalish, "Suicide," *Bulletin of Suicidology* (December 1968): 37–43.

25. *World Health Statistics Annual*; cited in D. Lester, *The Cruelest Death: The Enigma of Adolescent Suicide* (1993), 27–32.

26. *World Health Statistics Annual*; cited in Lester, *The Cruelest Death*, 24.

27. *World Health Statistics Annual* (1992). For U.S.: National Center for Health Statistics web site, http://wonder.cdc.gov.

28. A. R. Copeland, "Suicide Among the Elderly—the Metro-Dade County Experience, 1981–83." *Med Science and the Law* 1987 27(1) (1987): 35.

29. L. J. Schneiderman, et al., Table 2, in *Euthanasia: Opposing Viewpoints*, 84–89, from L. J. Schneiderman, et al. *J Clinical Ethics* 5(2) (1994): 109–12.

30. C. E. Rhyne, et al., "Dimensions of Suicide: Perceptions of Lethality, Time, and Agony," *Suicide and Life-threatening Behavior* 25(3) (1995): 373–80.

SOME SUICIDE RESOURCES: HOTLINES AND THE INTERNET

Because of space limitations I have posted the drug appendix on my web site. The following are other sources for similar information, both paper and electronic (Web):

A widely available toxicology handbook is Robert H. Dreisbach, *Handbook of Poisoning: Prevention, Diagnosis, and Treatment* 12th ed. (Lange, Los Altos). 1987. It's laid out for quick and clear reference and provides toxicity data, but is written for people who already have a reasonable knowledge of drugs and poisons.

Consumer Reports annually publishes *Drug Information for the Consumer* which provides understandable information on over 5,000 drugs: uses for particular drugs; generic and trade names; related drugs; drug interactions. What it does not provide is numerical toxicity data.

Online resources tend to be overwhelming in quantity and underwhelming in organization and usability. An example is *Martindale's* (www.sci.lib.uci.edu.HSG/Pharmacy/html), which has loads of wonderful information . . . somewhere. Other magasites that may also be worth a visit are:

www.emory.edu/MEDWEB (*MEDWEB*)

www.medlib.iupui.edu/hw/tox (*Health-WEB*)

www.igm.nlm.nih.gov/index (*Medline, Toxline* databases, and National Library of Medicine, among other things)

More modest sites are sometimes more useful. Three that are good sources of drug/chemical data are:

www.rxlist.com

www.newcastle.edu.au/department/md/htas/tox0001/htm (more technical than the other two sites)

www.merck.com (*Merck Manual; Merck Manual of Geriatrics*)

BIBLIOGRAPHY

The literature on suicide is immense. I mention here only a few of the books available that I found particularly valuable.

GENERAL

Alvarez, A. *The Savage God*. Random House, 1972. A brilliantly written study of suicide, somewhat schizophrenically divided into an opening essay about Sylvia Plath and material about everything else.

Colt, George Howe. *The Enigma of Suicide*. Summit Books, 1991. Readable and erudite. Much of the book is in the form of stories of the suicides of young people, interspersed with interviews and research findings. The historical material is especially well done.

Hendin, Herbert. *Suicide in America*. W.W. Norton, 1982, 1995. One of the best general works on American suicide. More medically and psychiatrically oriented (and less anecdotal) than Colt. I prefer the 1982 edition, because I feel it's more evenhanded than the 1995 revision. They are interesting to read side-by-side.

FORENSIC MEDICINE

Polson, Cyril J., D. J. Gee, Bernard Knight. *The Essentials of Forensic Medicine*, 4th ed. Pergamon, 1985. The best single book on the subject.

Knight, Bernard. *Forensic and Pathology*, 2nd ed. Oxford University Press, 1996, and Spitz and R. S. Fisher. *Medicolegal Investigation of Death*, 3rd. ed. Thomas, 1993, are more up-to-date and have better printing (useful for photographs), but can't match the breadth of Polson.

MEDICINE

Blumenthal, S. J., and D. J., Kupfer eds. *Suicide Over the Life Cycle*. American Psychiatric Press, 1990. Excellent academic study of risk factors, assessment, and treatment. Articles written by some of the leading researchers in the field.

SOCIOLOGY

Lester, David. *Why People Kill Themselves: A 1990s Summary of Research Findings on Suicidal Behavior*, 3rd ed. Thomas, 1992. You want numbers, correlations, associations? Look no further.

PHILOSOPHY/ETHICS

Opposing Viewpoints Series, Greenhaven Press. Consists of several books on bioethics (*Suicide, Medical Ethics, Euthanasia, Death and Dying*), all in the same format: one- to ten-page experts or articles (and an occasional cartoon), paired up as "opposing viewpoints." They treat the topics fairly and understandably, if not in great depth. Perhaps the best place to get an overview of the issues, as presented by their advocates.

Smith, D. L., and R. M. Veatch, eds. *Medical Ethics Series*. Indiana University Press, covers the same material as the proceeding series, but in much greater depth and academic focus. About twenty volumes as of 1998.

Humber, J. M., R. F. Almeder, and G. A. Kasting, eds. *Physician-assisted Death* in *Biomedical Ethics Reviews (series)*. Humana Press, 1993. Intermediate in depth and range compared to the two proceeding titles.

Hastings Center Reports/Magazine. Hastings-on-Hudson, New York looks at topics in biomedical ethics through a quarterly magazine. Timely coverage and thoughtful articles.

Maguire, Daniel C. *Death by Choice*. Schocken Books, 1984. A thoughtful, wide-ranging set of essays, examining the concept of "death by choice" as it applies to suicide, abortion, capital punishment, and war.

Rachels, James. *The End of Life*. Oxford University Press, 1986. This is a straight-up philosophy book, tightly reasoned and clearly laid out. It examines the question of why killing is wrong, and under what circumstances it might not be.

Battin, M. Pabst, and A. G. Lipman, eds. *Drug Use in Assisted Suicide and Euthanasia*. Pharmaceutical Products Press, 1996. The title is a bit misleading; the book is a good collection of essays covering a wide range of issues related to physician-assisted suicide: legal, ethical, and medical.

———. *The Least Worst Death: Essays in Bioethics on the End of Life*. Oxford University Press, 1994. This book provides a timely and cross-cultural perspective on end-of-life issues.

Index